BRITAIN AND EUROPE
SINCE 1945

Published in our
centenary year
≈ **2004** ≈
MANCHESTER
UNIVERSITY
PRESS

Britain and Europe since 1945

Historiographical perspectives on integration

OLIVER J. DADDOW

Manchester University Press

Manchester and New York

distributed exclusively in the USA by Palgrave

Published by Manchester University Press
Oxford Road, Manchester M13 9NR, UK
and Room 400, 175 Fifth Avenue, New York, NY 10010, USA
www.manchesteruniversitypress.co.uk

Distributed exclusively in the USA by
Palgrave, 175 Fifth Avenue, New York NY 10010, USA

Distributed exclusively in Canada by
UBC Press, University of British Columbia, 2029 West Mall,
Vancouver, BC, Canada V6T 1Z2

British Library Cataloguing-in-Publication Data
A catalogue record for this book is available from the British Library

Library of Congress Cataloging-in-Publication Data
A catalog record for this book is available from the Library of Congress

ISBN 13: 978 0 7190 8216 0 paperback

This paperback edition published 2011

Printed by Lightning Source

Contents

List of figures

For mum and nan

Acknowledgements

I have spoken about Britain's relations with Europe with a number of people over the years. First and foremost I am indebted to my doctoral supervisors, Richard Aldrich and Anthony Forster. They have unhesitatingly provided an ideal blend of friendship, support and constructive criticism of my work and I can safely say that without their efforts this book would never have been written.

As the project progressed I have benefited from conversations with Anthony Adamthwaite, Philip Alexander, David Allen, Alex Bellamy, Katharina Böhmer, Peter Boyle, John Campbell, Peter Catterall, Geoffrey Edwards, Harriet Jones, Michael Kandiah, Piers Ludlow, Alun Munslow, Helen Parr, Michael Smith and Gillian Staerck. I am especially grateful to those who have kindly given me their time in interviews: the late Lord Beloff, Peter Hennessy, John Kent, Anthony Seldon, Geoffrey Warner and John Young. James Ellison and George Wilkes read some of my early work on the subject and I would like to record my appreciation of the perceptive comments that they were able to give me. Any errors or omissions below are, of course, my responsibility.

Alison Welsby and Jonathan Bevan at Manchester University Press have been a constant source of help and encouragement throughout this project, and I would like to recognise their efforts on my behalf, as I also would the anonymous readers of earlier drafts of the manuscript. The bulk of the research was carried out while I was at the University of Nottingham, and I am grateful to both the University and the School of Politics for their financial support during my time there. It was also a great help to be able to bounce my ideas off students in the School of Continuing Education at the University of Nottingham and in the Department of Engineering at Nottingham Trent University. More recently it has been beneficial to try out my ideas on colleagues in the Defence Studies Department, King's College London and Advanced Course students at the Joint Services Command and Staff College.

For their permission to reproduce the cartoons and pictures that appear below I am grateful to David Simonds, Ranan Lurie, Atlantic Syndication Partners, Cartoonews, Conservative Central Office, the Observer and the Centre for the Study of Cartoons and Caricature at the University of Kent. I would like to express my thanks to Rebecca Barnard, Jane Newton, Sonja Singleton, and Marja Winkel, who provided crucial help and advice in this process. Liz Craft and Jerome Freeman at the QCA kindly helped me get to grips with educational developments relating to the EU in Chapter 1, and John Walker of the Labour History

Archive and Study Centre kindly found me the biographic details of John Edwards used in Chapter 2. Thanks also to Hugh Wilford for alerting me to the whereabouts of the primary sources used in Chapter 2 and to Idelle Nissila-Stone at the Ford Foundation for getting them copied and posted to me.

The analysis, opinions and conclusions expressed or implied in this book are those of the author and do not necessarily represent the views of the JSCSC, the UK MOD or any other government agency.

List of abbreviations

ACUE	American Committee on a United Europe
ACUSE	Action Committee for a United States of Europe
AGM	Annual General Meeting
CBI	Confederation of British Industry
CIA	Central Intelligence Agency
DC	Italian Christian Democratic Party
DFES	Department for Education and Skills
EC	European Community
ECA	Economic Cooperation Administration
ECSC	European Coal and Steel Community
EDC	European Defence Community
EEC	European Economic Community
EFTA	European Free Trade Association
EIU	Economist Intelligence Unit
ERM	Exchange Rate Mechanism
ERP	European Recovery Programme
ESRC	Economic and Social Research Council
EU	European Union
FFA	Ford Foundation Archives
FTA	Free Trade Area
GCSE	General Certificate of Secondary Education
HESA	Higher Education Statistics Agency
ICBH	Institute of Contemporary British History
IRD	Information Research Department
JSCSC	Joint Services Command and Staff College
MOD	Ministry of Defence
MP	Member of Parliament
NAFTA	North American Free Trade Agreement
NAT	North Atlantic Treaty
NATO	North Atlantic Treaty Organisation
OEEC	Organisation for European Economic Cooperation
OSS	Office of Strategic Services
PCF	French Communist Party
PCI	Italian Communist Party
PEP	Political and Economic Planning
PIR	Public Information Research
PRO	Public Record Office
QCA	Qualifications and Curriculum Authority
RAE	Research Assessment Exercise

RIIA	Royal Institute of International Affairs
RPI	Italian Republican Party
SEA	Single European Act
TEPSA	Trans-European Policy Studies Association
UACES	University Association for Contemporary European Studies
UN	United Nations
WEU	Western European Union

Introduction: using history, making policy

Lying as it does at the heart of the country's tortuous attempts to define for itself a role in the post-war and now the post-Cold War worlds, European integration has been one of the most hotly debated issues in British politics since the Second World War. The Europe question has, says Hugo Young, been 'long-drenched in opinionated emotion' and generated heated discussion well before the formal structures of the European Economic Community (EEC) and the European Union (EU) were put in place to bring about 'ever closer union' among the countries of western Europe.[1] It has dominated, some would say dogged, the foreign policy agendas of all Prime Ministers since 1945.[2] Clement Attlee, Winston Churchill, Anthony Eden, Harold Macmillan, Alec Douglas-Home, Harold Wilson, Edward Heath, James Callaghan, Margaret Thatcher, John Major and now Tony Blair have all found themselves in the unenviable position of trying to construct European policy against the backdrop of a divided Cabinet, significant parliamentary opposition, and fluctuating business, pressure-group, public and media opinion.

On 1 January 2002 the single currency, the euro, became legal tender in the twelve EU member states that chose to be part of the 'eurozone'.[3] This reinvigorated discussion in Britain about the rights and wrongs of New Labour's European policy, centring on the timing of its promised referendum on whether or not the country should join the single currency. One newspaper found that the launch of the euro and the concurrent disputes about Britain's opt-out generated more

---

1 H. Young, *This Blessed Plot: Britain and Europe from Churchill to Blair* (Basingstoke, Macmillan, 1998), p. 3. It is important at the outset to establish the terminology employed in this book. The term 'European Communities' incorporates the European Coal and Steel Community, founded in 1951, the European Economic Community, founded in 1957, and the European Atomic Energy Authority, also founded in 1957. In 1965 a merger Treaty made each a legally distinct organisation sharing common institutions, and in 1993 the Maastricht Treaty on European Union renamed the European Economic Community the European Community (EC) and created the European Union. Following general usage of the terms in Britain, this book makes use of the shorthand 'EEC' or 'Community' to refer to all the institutions created by the 1951 Treaty of Paris and 'European Union' (EU) for the period since 1993.

2 One historian points out that it first became a high-profile political issue in 1929; but even before that, since the end of the nineteenth century, Britain had 'been under pressure to interest itself in more closely in events on the Continent': J. W. Young, *Britain and European Unity 1945–1999*, 2nd edn (Basingstoke, Macmillan, 2000), p. 2. It has been the norm, however, for commentators to focus on developments in the aftermath of the Second World War.

3 Belgium, Germany, Greece, Spain, France, Ireland, Italy, Luxembourg, the Netherlands, Austria, Portugal and Finland.

column inches in the main British papers in the week of 6 to 12 January 2002 than any other, beating the 'war on terrorism' in Afghanistan by 55 inches and domestic rail problems by over 150 inches.[4]

Despite what the government might say, or wish the country to believe, the outcome of the referendum will be dependent on more than dispassionate economic cost-benefit analysis alone. The euro debate is laced with politics and burdened by history and the current press outpouring on the subject is witnessing arguments raging along familiar lines. Amidst an array of rhetorical strategies designed to sway the public and government one way or the other, propagandists on the 'sceptic' and the 'enthusiast' side regularly make emotional appeals to history in support of their position.[5]

British eurosceptic discourse

The sceptics seek to arouse the British against a European future by appealing to the nation's sense of pride in its imperial past and military history. Take as an example the following headline and first paragraph of an article by Robert Shrimsley, which appeared in the *Daily Telegraph* in August 1998:

> **Blair orders big push on joining Euro**
> Tony Blair has privately entrusted Peter Mandelson with master-minding the campaign to take Britain into the single European currency. The new Trade and Industry Secretary has been told to work behind the scenes to galvanise support for abolishing the pound by the Prime Minister.[6]

There are three ways in which the author infuses his article with scepticism about the euro. The first and most obvious is that he uses the emotive phrase 'abolish the pound', a popular rallying cry of sceptics throughout British politics, business and the media. The word 'abolish' is freighted with negative connotations and presumably will not be appearing in the referendum question when the government devises it; it might opt instead for something less sensitive, such as 'Should Britain replace the pound with the euro?' or 'Should Britain join the euro?'.

---

4 *Guardian*, 12 January 2002, p. 3.
5 The reason terms such as 'sceptic' and 'enthusiast' have initially been placed in quotation marks is that defining these terms remains highly problematical. In one of the first academic books to address the phenomenon of scepticism, Anthony Forster says that sceptics can oppose either the political or the economic aspects of integration (so that one might be 'pro-EU' but 'anti-euro'), but that a broad definition encompasses those who doubt 'the value of Britain's involvement with moves towards supranational European integration. ... [T]hey share many of the same core concerns, above all a focus on sovereignty, national identity, and the need for economic and political independence': A. Forster, *Euroscepticism in British Politics: Opposition to Europe in the Conservative and Labour Parties since 1945* (London, Routledge, 2002), pp. 1–9, these quotes from p. 2.
6 *Daily Telegraph*, 24 August 1998, p. 1.

The second indicator of Shrimsley's scepticism is that the article is liber-ally sprinkled with military metaphors such as 'big push' and 'masterminding the campaign', evoking memories of Britain standing alone against all the odds after the fall of France to Nazi Germany in 1940. They serve to sustain the impression that Britain's relationship with the Continent is conflictual rather than co-operative, one exaggerated by a succession of Prime Ministers who have returned triumphantly from European summits claiming how hard they have fought for British interests. Appealing to the glories of Britain's military past also summons memory of an age when the country possessed a global empire and when, soon after the Second World War, it was a proud member of the so-called 'Big Three', along with the United States and Russia. Britain, the argument goes, should not, cannot, join the single currency, because its wartime record represents an insuperable psychological barrier to the country ever being or feeling 'European'.

The final way in which Shrimsley infuses the article with a sceptical tone is by using the terms 'privately entrusted' and working 'behind the scenes', which communicate his assumption that the conduct of British European policy is a secretive exercise undertaken 'behind closed doors' by a 'pro-European' diplo-matic elite acting against the wishes of the public but at the behest of their coun-terparts on the Continent. To show the pervasiveness of these ways of framing British European policy, it is interesting to note that the use of military terminol-ogy and the idea that European policy is made on an un-democratic basis recurred in a piece by Philip Johnston that appeared in the *Daily Telegraph* almost four years after Shrimsley's, on 14 May 2002.[7] According to a report he obtained from the Prime Minister's personal polling consultancy, he wrote, 'A secret "war plan" has been drawn up by senior Labour Party strategists for a referendum on joining the euro.'

Now that the euro has become legal tender across the eurozone, the scep-tics' fear is that the government will endeavour to 'sneak' the euro into Britain.[8] In the *Daily Mail* in December 2001, Simon Walters wrote of more 'secret docu-ments' obtained from the Treasury disclosing a series of 'secret meetings of the Treasury's Euro Preparations and Information and Phasing Group', which discussed ways of 'persuading people to accept and use the new currency'. These subversive methods allegedly include new laws to change the school curriculum to 'force' children to learn about the euro, 'secretly' using televi-sion shows such as Channel 4's 'Big Brother' and ITV's 'Who Wants To Be A Millionaire?' to 'promote pro-euro propaganda' and making millions of euro

---

7 www.telegraph.co.uk/news/main.jhtml?xml=/news/2002/05/13/neur13.xml.
8 For a lively overview of the major threads of the sceptic position on the euro at the turn of 2002 see *Observer*, 6 January 2002, p. 13.

starter packs so visually unattractive that people who buy them will throw away the packaging and spend the euros instead.[9] The paper's Comment on the same day warned that the Treasury is working 'to bamboozle and seduce us into using this funny money from Frankfurt and abandoning the pound without a vote'.[10]

Hostility to the European project appears to flow from the assumption that Britain, in terms of its identity, economic orientation and political traditions, is not a European country. Indeed, some writers advocate that Britain should withdraw from the EU because it does not serve the country's 'interests' (left undefined, but presumably some combination of the above) and because the British do not share the continentals' desire for political union. This position was evident in a feverish article by Andrew Alexander, published in the *Daily Mail* in December 2000, in which he judged that '[T]he Nice summit is merely serving to underline our incompatibility with the structure and the aims of the Union, with the certainty of more differences to come.' He went on to claim that Britain does not depend on the EU economically, politically or strategically. 'As a genuinely independent nation we would be entirely at liberty to make our own rules.'[11] Lady Thatcher took the same line in a speech to promote her book, Statecraft. Calling the EU 'fundamentally unreformable' and blaming Europe for most of the world's problems (Nazism and Marxism, for example) she urged Britain to begin the process of withdrawal and to join the North American Free Trade Agreement (NAFTA) instead.[12] At the very least, she advocated, Britain should seek to renegotiate its terms of membership, and far more radically than Harold Wilson did in 1974–75. An ironic twist has been put on Thatcher's remarks by Timothy Garton Ash, who suggests leaving the Union for quite different reasons, to stop Britain holding back the integration process through its laggardly attitude to integration.[13]

The sceptics' focus on the incompatibility between Britain and the EU, and the loss of identity resulting from deeper integration, is nicely captured in a Conservative Party election poster, used only in Scotland during the 2001 general election.

Featuring a map of Europe with the south-east of England joined to France's north-west coast and the slogan 'Lose the pound. Lose our independence', this image underscores the notion that Britain is and should remain separate from the Continent. Europe is implicitly being identified as a danger in this poster, most obviously to Britain's economic and political 'independence', but also to Britain's

9 *Daily Mail*, 30 December 2001, p. 2.
10 *Ibid.*, p. 22.
11 *Daily Mail*, 9 December 2000, pp. 12–13.
12 See the 'Britain and the EU' section of the *Guardian Unlimited*, http//politics.guardian.co.uk/eu /story/0,9061,669387,00.html.
13 *Guardian*, 31 October 2002, p. 21.

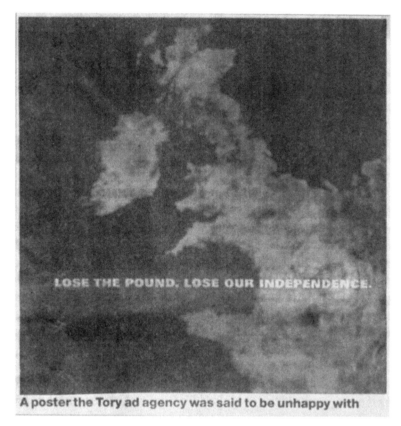

1 'Lose the pound. Lose our independence' (Conservative general election poster 2001)

ties with the United States and its status as a global actor. Joining the single currency, it suggests, would be a further step on the road to Britain's being subsumed in a United States of Europe. What the poster does, in sum, is appeal to British sensitivities about being part of a supranational European organisation. As such, it demonstrates the multidimensional nature of the sceptics' case on the euro and the EU in Britain. They draw upon economics, politics and, above all, history to advance their argument that the British public should reject a European future.

British euroenthusiast discourse

The euroenthusiasts in Britain also call on history, but in support of the converse argument that the British should embrace the single currency. None other than Prime Minister Tony Blair presented the most blatant expression of this viewpoint on 23 November 2001. In a speech to mark the opening of the European Research

Institute at the University of Birmingham, he drew on post-war developments in European integration to argue that '[T]he history of our engagement with Europe is one of opportunities missed in the name of illusions – and Britain suffering as a result.' He went on to chart the succession of integrative schemes Britain refused to involve itself with in the 1950s and London's gradual but reluctant admission in the 1960s that it needed to be part of the integration process, rather than margin-alised from it. He ended with the clarion call that 'Britain's future is in Europe.'[14] He thus remains committed to his 2001 election manifesto pledge that New Labour will seek the 'consent of the British people in a referendum' on whether or not to join the single currency.[15]

His bold words go against the government's tendency since the 2001 general election to dampen rather than stoke the European debate, for two main reasons. To begin, there is an apparent split on the timing of the referendum between the Prime Minister and the Chancellor of the Exchequer, Gordon Brown. For example, at the Labour Party annual conference in Brighton in October 2001, Blair paid lip-service to the need for the British economy to meet the five economic tests set down by the Treasury, but was adamant that 'we should have the courage of our argument, to ask the British people for their consent in this Parliament'.[16] The tests come in the form of five questions that the Treasury will have to answer. Are business cycles and economic structures compatible, so that Britain and others could live comfortably with euro interest rates on a permanent basis? If problems emerge, is there sufficient flexibility to deal with them? Would joining the euro create better conditions for firms making long-term decisions to invest in Britain? What impact would entry have on the competitive position of Britain's financial services, especially the City's wholesale markets? And will joining the euro promote higher growth, stability, and a lasting increase in jobs?[17] Only when these tests have been met, the government says, will it put the refer-endum to the British people.

---

14 *The Times*, 24 November 2001, p. 6. For a full transcript of the speech see www.phoenix-tv.net/ubirmingham/eriscript.htm. See also his interview on BBC 2's 'Newsnight', 15 May 2002, an edited transcript of which is on the Foreign Office's website, www.fco.gov.uk/new/newstext.asp?6225. His words would appear to contradict the Conservative Member of Parliament Michael Portillo's claim that 'Mr Blair has little interest in history' in *Daily Mail*, 31 December 2001, p. 22, in an article containing much of the sceptical discourse explored in this chapter. Some press commentators claim that the significance lay in the 'timing and tone', not in the substance of his speech, (*The Times*, 24 November 2001, p. 27), while others were more enthusiastic, (*Guardian*, 24 November 2001, p. 6).

15 *Ambitions for Britain: Labour's Manifesto 2001*, p. 36.

16 Tony Blair's speech to the Labour Party Conference, quoted in *Guardian Archive*, www.guardian.co.uk/Archive/Article/0,4723,4268838,00.html.

17 A. Gamble and G. Kelly, 'Britain and EMU', in K. Dyson (ed.), *European States and the Euro: Europeanization, Variation and Convergence* (Oxford, Oxford University Press, 2002), pp. 97–119 (p. 104).

Speaking a month later to the Confederation of British Industry (CBI) in Birmingham, Brown was hesitant, reiterating his support for the euro 'in principle', but concentrating instead on the significance of passing the tests and the serious impact the British economy's failure to do so would have on the timing of the referendum. In short, it was reported, he was attempting 'to counter the impression left by Mr Blair's address ... that an early plebiscite would be held by spring 2003'.[18] The same pattern was repeated at the 2002 conference in Blackpool. Brown and Blair both highlighted the key role that will be played by the economic tests in determining when the subject goes to referendum, but the Prime Minister went considerably further than the Chancellor's statement that if they are met 'we will recommend joining the euro', by saying that 'if the tests are passed, we go for it'.[19]

Even if one were to judge the apparent divide between the two men to be a cynical ploy to appease all elements of Labour Party opinion on the euro, and perhaps all the more so because of it, the balancing out of the rhetoric on Labour's policy towards the single currency bears witness to the caution with which British Prime Ministers have tended to tread on the question of European integration. As the Conservative Party discovered during the Maastricht negotiations, the effects of which are still being felt, the issue of Europe has the potential to create as many tensions within Britain's two leading parties as between them. Intra-party debates can be as fierce and destructive as inter-party ones.[20]

Allied to the argument that it is in Labour's interests to avoid fanning the flames of the Europe debate for fear of splitting the Cabinet and party, the second consideration is that, since the terrorist attacks on New York and Washington on 11 September 2001, the 'war on terrorism' and now a second Gulf War with Iraq, British European policy has dropped down the domestic political agenda. Foreign policy did not inspire a particularly heated battle of words during the 2001 general election, although the Conservatives played the 'keep the pound' card to some visual if not obvious electoral success.[21] The mechanics and broader implications of the referendum on joining the single currency were glossed over rather than discussed in detail. But what Blair has done now is to turn the tables on the sceptics

18 *Guardian*, 5 November 2001, p. 2.
19 Brown's speech, www.labour.org.uk/gbconfspeech/; Blair's speech, www.labour.org.uk/tbconfspeech/. My italics.
20 Steve Ludlam notes that the Conservative Party 'has been convulsed by divisions over European integration' since the middle of the 1980s, in 'The Cauldron: Conservative Parliamentarians and European Integration', in D. Baker and D. Seawright (eds), *Britain For and Against Europe: British Politics and the Question of European Integration* (Oxford, Clarendon Press, 1998), pp. 31–56 (p. 31).
21 Sceptics have praised the smooth introduction of the single currency, though they are at pains to point out that it has not quelled their opposition to it. See for instance *Daily Telegraph*, 3 January 2002, pp. 10 and 23 respectively.

by suggesting that Britain's approach to the single currency should be rooted in a broader strategy aimed at consolidating a 'rock solid' alliance with the United States in the defence arena.[22]

Hence, for the enthusiasts as for the sceptics, the Europe question is a multi-faceted one that relies very much on history as the starting-point for their judgements on why Britain should or should not move closer to the EU, supporting Young's verdict that writing the history of British European policy entails writing 'the history of an attitude to history itself'.[23] What his quotation unintentionally obscures is that the two sets of protagonists formulate their arguments on the back of competing perceptions of history. It is this degree of 'incommensurability' between them that limits the scope for constructive engagement, because they problematise a different past.[24] 'Political debate in Britain', notes John Pinder, 'by demonising the word federal, has made it difficult for British people to consider the development of the Union and its relationship with the federal idea in an objective way',[25] a comment that illuminates 'the role of intersubjective meanings vested in particular words by political actors' in different nation-states and by different actors within those states.[26]

On the one hand, the sceptics play upon Britain's imperial past and wartime record to suggest Britain should remain outside the euro. Implicit in their discourse is the idea that the workings of the international system are such that states such as Britain can retain a measure of 'independence' within it.[27] On the other hand, the enthusiasts highlight the history of European integration as the reason why Britain should be part of it, drawing out the essential

22 Blair's speech, www.guardian.co.uk/Archive/Article/0,4723,4268838,00.html.
23 Young, *This Blessed Plot*, p. 1.
24 The word 'incommensurability' is taken from Thomas S. Kuhn's seminal text on the philosophy of science, *The Structure of Scientific Revolutions* (London, The University of Chicago Press, 1970), and refers to the way in which different communities of like-minded researchers hold contrasting perceptions of the phenomenon in need of explanation or measurement. It does not, points out Alexander Bird, mean *non*-comparability: 'The thesis of incommensurability is the claim that there is no common measure for theories from distinct paradigms', a major part of the cause being that 'key terms change their meaning as a result of scientific revolutions': A. Bird, *Thomas Kuhn* (Chesham, Acumen, 2000), p. 204. For more on incommensurability see T. S. Kuhn, 'The Road since *Structure*', in A. I. Tauber (ed.), *Science and the Quest for Reality* (Basingstoke, Macmillan, 1997), pp. 231–45 (pp. 231–5) and on Kuhn's model on the growth of scientific knowledge see R. Richards, 'Theories of Scientific Change', in Tauber (ed.), *Science and the Quest for Reality*, pp. 203–30 (pp. 210–13).
25 J. Pinder, 'Introduction', in J. Pinder (ed.), *Altiero Spinelli and the British Federalists: Writings by Beveridge, Robbins and Spinelli 1937–43* (London, Federal Trust, 1998), pp. 1–18 (p. 1).
26 R. Koslowski, 'Understanding the European Union as a Federal Polity', in Thomas Christiansen, Knud Erik Jørgensen and Antje Wiener (eds), *The Social Construction of Europe* (London, Sage, 2001), pp. 32–49 (p. 40).
27 See for example Conservative Party leader Iain Duncan Smith's address to the party conference at Bournemouth, 10 October 2002, printed in full at www.conservatives.com/conference/2002news.cfm?obj_id=41258&class_id=Speeches.

interconnectedness and interdependence of states within the international system. They are not operating from the same set of initial assumptions about what 'Europe' is, about what Britain's vital European interests are. They do not see the same international system, nor, consequently, do they agree on the definition and ramifications for the debate of key terms such as 'sovereignty' (in all its forms: political, economic and legal), 'federation' and 'independence'.

Lost history

In *War and Peace*, Leo Tolstoy has the tragic hero, Count Pierre Bezúkhov, alluding to the intellectual problems resulting from incommensurability: 'I am afraid my way of looking at the world is so opposed to yours that we shall not understand one another.'[28] As it is played out in Britain, the Europe debate is a good example of networks of individuals talking past each other. Protagonists on all sides of the debate possess distinctive points of reference, rhetorical conventions, linguistic codes and ways of seeing the world, which severely narrows the scope for the mutually advantageous exchange of opinions. It is also indicative of the constructed nature of political debate, reminding us that politics, economics and history have pasts that need interrogating if one is to understand the origins and development of competing ideologies and modes of accessing and perceiving world affairs.[29]

It would be unsatisfactory to try to incorporate analysis of the construction of both enthusiast and sceptic discourses on Europe in a book of this length, mainly because of the amount of detail that would have to be skimmed over or omitted altogether.[30] It is the aim of this study, therefore, to examine not the sceptic line on Britain and Europe, but instead the enthusiast interpretation of British European policy, which has come to dominate mainstream academic historiography in Britain and to which Blair made reference in his Birmingham speech, when he referred to Britain's post-war 'missed opportunities' with respect to the Continent.

---

28 L. Tolstoy, *War and Peace* (Ware, Wordsworth Editions, 1993), Book 5, Chapter 2, p. 464.

29 It should be noted that there are different strains of 'constructivism', and many implications that flow from saying that something is 'constructed'. However, John Ruggie's general definition suffices to convey how this book uses the terms: 'Constructivists hold the view that the building blocks of international reality are ideational as well as material; that the ideational factors have normative as well as instrumental dimensions; that they express not only individual but also collective intentionality; and that the meaning and significance of ideational factors are not independent of time and place', quoted in Thomas Christiansen, Knud Erik Jørgensen and Antje Wiener, 'Introduction', in Christiansen, Jørgensen and Wiener (eds), *The Social Construction of Europe*, pp. 1–19 (p. 3).

30 There are research projects waiting to be done on the origins and development of the debate on Europe in the British press, on the interchange of ideas between journalists, sceptics and enthusiasts and on the changing meaning over time of key words and phrases used in the Europe debate.

There are two main reasons for eschewing examination of the sceptic case. Given that the British people have been largely exempt from the feeling of what one newspaper termed the 'Europhoria' of exchanging sterling for the euro,[31] the first reason is that now is a most propitious moment to pause and reassess the history of British European policy, in order that one might come to a better understanding of how the current point in the relationship has been reached. The second is that the thrust of the enthusiasts' case, concentrating on the history of Britain's policy towards European integration, is not nearly so widely known in Britain as the sceptic case. It has received a lot of attention in news magazines such as the *Economist* and has developed into a sub-field of contemporary history at university level in Britain. But for all intents and purposes it could be called a 'lost history' in the sense that, until Blair's speech, major events in the history of British European policy have rarely received more then peripheral attention in the British media. A worrying manifestation of this dearth of understanding in Britain about the origins and development of the EEC and EU is an eighteen-page pamphlet, 'EU Cannot be Serious: the Truth about Europe', distributed by the anti-European pressure group the Democracy Movement, which opens with the line 'There are so few good arguments for being in the European Union today that it is hard to remember why it started.'[32]

There are a number of methods one might use to go in search of the history of British European policy. One temptation is to write this period of contemporary international history again, analysing events through the remnants of them left to us in the presently available primary sources. Even setting aside the epistemological and methodological concerns about this form of 'reconstructionist' history raised by philosophers of history since the 1970s,[33] the weaknesses in this approach are obvious. The primary one is that to write a diplomatic history based on primary sources, enriched by secondary material, oral history and the other paraphernalia generally said to go into writing 'good' history for the entire postwar period, is too vast an undertaking for a single individual in terms of time, cost and resources. This is especially so at a time when the Research Assessment Exercise (RAE) and academic departments place heavy demands on scholars to publish a constant flow of written material.[34]

The second weakness is that it is hard to justify in intellectual terms, because there is such a rich seam of history on British European policy since the Second

---

31 *Observer*, 6 January 2002, p. 13.

32 For more information see www.democracy-movement.org.uk.

33 Cogently presented in A. Munslow, *Deconstructing History* (London, Routledge, 1997), especially pp. 36–56, and critiqued on pp. 99–119.

34 On the impact of the RAE see T. Becher and P. R. Trowler, *Academic Tribes and Territories*, 2nd edn (Buckingham, The Society for Research into Higher Education and Open University Press, 2001), pp. 77–8, 119.

World War that the chances of making an original contribution based on anything other than the latest releases to the Public Record Office (PRO) under the Thirty Year Rule are slim. The third weakness, highly pertinent in the context of the current debate about the nature of history as a scholarly pursuit, is that the primary source documentation in the PRO, the sources on which the academic historiography has been based, currently runs out in the early 1970s, making a primary source history from 1945 to the present day an impossibility. And all this before deciding which actors, government departments, organisations and pressure groups made the history.

Rather than attempting another history of British European policy, then, this study enlightens our understanding of British European policy through historiographical dissection of existing texts on the subject. The next chapter develops in greater detail the historiographic method of research and the rationale of applying it to this body of literature; but it is useful here briefly to define the term as it is used below. It is conventionally employed in the titles of books that analyse how history has been conceived and written, so historiography is, according to W. Roger Louis, 'the art of explaining why historians wrote as they did at certain times' and to Robin Winks 'an examination of why a body of writing has taken the shape it has'.[35] To Peter Burke it is the same, the 'history of history-writing'. He continued, 'This awakening of interest in history's own past goes with an increased self-consciousness on the part of historians, and a rejection of the idea that they can produce an "objective" description, uncontaminated by their own attitudes and values, of what actually happened.'[36] It involves, writes Patrick Finney, quoting Hans Kellner to make his case, the scrutiny of the purveyors of historical knowledge, of the processes by which one comes to understand historical events, rather than the events themselves:

> exploring the manner in which history writing has been shaped by the contexts of its production, and reading it against the grain to decipher the ideological forces and tensions at work within it, unfocusing it 'in order to put into the foreground the constructed, rhetorical nature of our knowledge about the past, and to bring out the purposes, often hidden and unrecognised, of our retrospective creations'.[37]

---

35 W. Roger Louis, 'Foreword' and R. W. Winks, 'Preface', in R. W. Winks (ed.), *The Oxford History of the British Empire, Volume 5: Historiography* (Oxford, Oxford University Press, 2001), pp. 7–11 (p. 8) and pp. 13–15 (p. 13) respectively.

36 Peter Burke's definition in A. Bullock and O. Stallybrass (eds), *The Fontana Dictionary of Modern Thought* (London, Collins, 1977), p. 286. On the origins and development of historiography see M. Bentley, *Modern Historiography: An Introduction* (London, Routledge, 1999) and G. G. Iggers, *Historiography in the Twentieth Century: From Scientific Objectivity to the Postmodern Challenge* (Hanover, NH, Wesleyan University Press, 1997).

37 P. Finney, 'Still "Marking Time"? Text, Discourse and Truth in International History', *Review of International Studies*, 27:2 (2001), 291–308 (305).

This effort to map the extent of our historical knowledge about a given subject requires an exploration of how the history of British European policy has been constructed: how it has been written about, who the key players in the field are and what this reveals about the philosophical underpinnings and goals of the various commentators who narrate the past. In essence it seeks to explain 'how the different perspectives of historians enter into their books'.[38] In this sense, the book might be seen as a microcosm of Tony Becher and Paul Trowler's *Academic Tribes and Territories*, in which they undertake a survey of academic disciplines and draw conclusions about the nature of knowledge produced by academics and the infrastructure, culture and values held by members of those disciplines.

The need for research into how knowledge accumulates is, they say, acute, and nowhere more so than in history: 'Historians … offer a fairly prolific choice of historiographical works, and of quasi-philosophical or methodological disquisitions on the nature of "the historian's craft", but have little to say about themselves as an academic community.'[39] Their judgement echoes an oft-made observation that historians 'are not given at length to reflecting on the nature of their discipline'.[40] This is where historiographers step in, because they are crucially concerned with the drive behind narrating the past, how historical texts are put together and how interpretations are born and perpetuated across time. 'It is not only a question of understanding the past, but more specifically of how the past is perceived and interpreted by the communities involved.'[41]

The study of the art of history-writing thus proceeds from the assumption, made starkly clear in the work of postmodernists, poststructuralists and social constructivists, that the idea of 'the truth' is up for grabs, meaning different things to different individuals and communities of like-minded individuals. History, according to this perspective, is just one more discipline in which claims about uncovering an untainted, objective body of knowledge are severely flawed. Lustick summarises this position with his observation that there is no 'transparently true and theoretically neutral historical record'.[42] Alex Callinicos also reminds us that history is not just about the analysis of untainted sources, and that scepticism about history flows from the very way in which the distinction between primary and secondary sources has been collapsed through interrogation of the concepts of 'author' and 'text'. It is not, for him, a surprise 'that contemporary scepticism about historical knowledge should focus on the fact that historians work

38 J. Appleby, L. Hunt, and M. Jacob, *Telling the Truth about History* (London, W. W. Norton, 1994), p. 246.

39 Becher and Trowler, *Academic Tribes and Territories*, p. 53.

40 J. Tosh, *The Pursuit of History*, 3rd edn (London, Longman, 2000), p. 215.

41 W. Thompson, *What Happened to History?* (London, Pluto, 2000), p. 1.

42 I. Lustick, 'History, Historiography, and Political Science: Multiple Historical Records and the Problem of Selection Bias', *American Political Science Review*, 90:3 (1996), 605–18 (613).

on texts to produce other texts'.[43] Hayden White would agree: 'It is because real events do not offer themselves as stories that their narrativisation is so difficult. ... Historiography is especially good ground on which to consider that nature of narration and narrativity because it is here that our desire for the imaginary, the possible must contest with imperatives of the real, the actual.'[44]

The historiographical approach will not appeal to all who read this book, for there are some who claim that primary-source history written by scholars is the only 'reliable' history available and that 'without work in the archives ... the supply of new history would simply terminate'.[45] Should all historians switch from studying history to studying historiography then, yes, new archive-based history would stop being produced. But the argument that one can only find new things to say about the past by looking in archives is profoundly open to question. Investigating the construction of historical topics through analysis of the intellectual development of the field through historiography is one way of inspiring our interest in the study of the past, and of highlighting gaps in our knowledge that might fruitfully be filled in the years ahead; so in a very real way historiography can help archive historians and, therefore, the production of 'new' history to which Marwick alludes.

Moreover, if one defines history, like Marwick, as 'bodies of knowledge about the past and all that is involved in producing this knowledge, communicating it, and teaching about it,'[46] historiography is being put at centre stage, rather than in the wings. Thus, at the same time as denouncing the 'metaphysical nonsense of postmodernists', who, he says, are attempting to 'wipe out all existing historical knowledge',[47] he loads history with a definition that extends the possible contributors to history far beyond professional or scholarly historians burrowing into the archives, raising huge methodological, epistemological and ontological questions about history as a pursuit and its broader societal functions.[48]

---

43 A. Callinicos, *Theories and Narratives: Reflections on the Philosophy of History* (Cambridge, Polity Press, 1995), p. 65.

44 H. White, *The Content of the Form: Narrative Discourse and Historical Representation* (London, The Johns Hopkins University Press, 1992), p. 4.

45 A. Marwick, *The New Nature of History: Knowledge, Evidence, Language* (Basingstoke, Palgrave, 2001), p. 268 and preface, p. 13. It should also be pointed out that there are varying shades of this position: not all in the reconstructionist/constructionist camp are as stridently opposed to historiography and 'postmodern' concerns about history as he, a point well made in Finney, 'Still "Marking Time"?', 294–5.

46 Marwick, *The New Nature of History*, p. 269.

47 *Ibid.*, preface, p. 16 and p. 19. H. Kozicki (ed.), *Developments in Modern Historiography* (Basingstoke, Palgrave, 1998) has put together a collection of articles on the study of history in the 1980s, asserting on p. 8 of the preface that 'despite current theoretical distractions the historical discipline is soundly based on traditional practices properly understood'.

48 Thompson's judgement is that Marwick's views on history are 'unsustainable and proceed simply by ignoring or distorting the arguments of the new style', in Thompson, *What Happened to History?*, preface, p. 9.

This broader definition of history brings historiography to the fore as a source of new knowledge because of its intrinsic concern with history as a scholarly and a social practice. History is the pursuit of scholars, but drives and is in turn driven by ideas, evidence and interpretation from a gamut of other forms of writing, for example biography, autobiography, memoir and news reporting, and from policies and events as they unfold in the present. If history is to perform useful social and cultural functions, greater attention needs to be paid to the very 'postmodern' concerns Marwick identifies in his definition of history, about who produces history, how it is used and abused publicly, and how it is communicated and taught.

The hard reconstructionist position is, to be fair, in the minority among historians today, although many of them recoil from what they see as the overly provocative claims of the 'post-ists'. Most would be inclined to agree with John Lewis Gaddis, who writes:

> I assume the contingent nature of all historical interpretation. Historians are products and prisoners of their own time and place. They can no more escape their preconceptions that they can levitate benignly above their word processors or their students. I have tried to approach this new evidence with an open mind; but I will not claim ... to have allowed the chips to fall where they may. I have arranged them, as most scholars do, in patterns that seem to me to make sense.[49]

Taking a historiographical approach to British European policy gives this book a wide appeal. It is aimed at five principal audiences. The first, obviously, consists of international historians and doctoral research students working on post-war British European policy. The book is, at root, an analysis of what historians have been writing but, more importantly, of why they have been adopting particular interpretations. It thus significantly extends the historiographic elements contained in the work of scholars such as John Young and George Wilkes, because it is more comprehensive both horizontally, in terms of citing who gives a particular interpretation, and vertically, in terms of why writers arrive at a particular interpretation.[50]

It is hoped that the delineation below of distinct schools of writing on Britain and Europe will provide the stimulus for a sustained debate among British historians about the microfoundations of their craft. It is historians, after all, who are in the best position to explain what they do, why they do it and where they see themselves fitting into the academic and wider worlds of politics and policy-making:

---

49 J. L. Gaddis, *Now We Know: Rethinking Cold War History* (Oxford, Oxford University Press, 1998), preface p. 8.

50 Young, *Britain and European Unity, 1945–1999* and G. Wilkes, 'The First Failure to Steer Britain into the European Communities: An Introduction', in G. Wilkes (ed.), *Britain's Failure to Enter the European Community 1961–63: The Enlargement Negotiations and Crises in European, Atlantic and Commonwealth Relations* (London, Frank Cass, 1997), pp. 1–32.

'Why a given work or author becomes famous, how fame is perpetuated over periods of time, what factors increase or diminish a reputation – all these questions involve the historian as much as the sociologist or psychologist.'[51] The responses this study engenders from historians will inform future historiographical accounts of British European policy and future writing on the art of history in Britain.

That is the main audience for this book, but not the only one. It should, secondly, appeal to historiographers and students of historiography. In the same way that Gaddis identified competing bodies of writing (equated to the 'schools' here) about the origins and development of the Cold War in the United States,[52] and thus provoked scholarly reassessment of the origins of the Cold War on both the empirical and theoretical levels, this study seeks to stimulate work on historiography in Britain. In particular, it seeks to provoke discussion about what it means to belong to a school of writing. Is it a conscious or an unconscious decision, and why is it important? Can the schools model be applied to other areas of post-war British foreign policy, such as imperial and Commonwealth history and the 'special relationship'? And if so, what does this reveal about the nature of historiography in post-war Britain? What are the intellectual ideas that underpin the discipline and what input, if any, have historians made to shaping government policy, and is their capacity to do so now increasing or diminishing?

It is because historiography explores who writes what, who is published where, the relationships among writers and wider issues associated with the nature of history, that this book will appeal, thirdly, to philosophers of history. Sadly, a gap has opened between the communities of philosophy and history, as Marwick's latest offering makes plain. Highlighting in particular the work of the American philosopher Hayden White and Britain's Keith Jenkins,[53] historians in Britain have tended either to leap like Richard Evans to the 'defence of history',[54] or to dismiss the philosophy of history as a passing distraction from the scholarly process of writing about 'what really happened' in times gone by.[55] Marwick's parting shot in *The New Nature of History* makes this

---

51 R. Holub, *Reception Theory: A Critical Introduction* (London, Methuen, 1984), p. 47.

52 J. L. Gaddis, 'The Emerging Post-Revisionist Synthesis on the Origins of the Cold War', *Diplomatic History*, 7:3 (1983), 171–90. See also R. A. Melanson, *Writing History and Making Policy: The Cold War, Vietnam and Revisionism, Volume 6* (London, Lanham, 1983). For a historiographical assessment of earlier themes in American foreign policy, see B. McKercher, 'Reaching for the Brass Ring: The Recent Historiography of Interwar American Foreign Relations', *Diplomatic History*, 15:4 (1991), pp. 565–98.

53 H. White, *Metahistory: The Historical Imagination in Nineteenth-Century Europe* (London, The Johns Hopkins University Press, 1975); White, *The Content of the Form*; K. Jenkins, *On 'What is History?' From Carr and Elton to Rorty and White* (London, Routledge, 1995) and K. Jenkins, *Why History? Ethics and Postmodernity* (London, Routledge, 1999).

54 R. J. Evans, *In Defence of History* (London, Granta, 1997).

55 For Finney, 'Still "Marking Time"?', 292, the common response to theoretical challenges 'has been one of ambivalence if not hostility'.

sentiment all too apparent. 'I now eagerly return to serious research and, I hope, the production of history, rather than mere historiography and historical epistemology.'[56] The short shrift he gives philosophical thinking on history shows him as the latest in a long line of historians in Britain who are quick to shelter behind Geoffrey Elton's judgement that 'a philosophic concern with such problems as the reality of historical knowledge or the nature of thought only hinders the practice of history'.[57]

The problems reconstructionists have with the postmodern turn in philosophy seem to flow from two assumptions: that 'post-ist' thinkers are Marxists who want to undermine or even 'wipe out all existing historical knowledge',[58] or that, in its attitude to the 'facts' of history, this line of inquiry can be equated with relativism and/or Holocaust 'revisionism' such as that espoused by David Irving.[59] Key 'post-ist' writers such as White might be of left-wing persuasion, but is that any reason to dismiss their analysis of the dynamics of history and historiography? And to conflate the broad epistemological tenets of postmodern thought with the extreme single-issue agenda of such right-wing groups, who have pressed relativism to its limits, is to confuse propaganda with scholarship.[60]

This book works at the collision point between philosophy and history by highlighting the oft-misunderstood point that postmodernism, history and historiography are locked in a symbiotic relationship. To see the organic link between them, one need only to compare the definition of history given above by Marwick, which centres on how knowledge is accumulated and the mechanisms by which belief systems are generated and sustained, with a summary of the

---

56 Marwick, *The New Nature of History*, p. 273.

57 G. Elton, *The Practice of History* (London, Methuen, 1967), preface, p. 7. On p. 57 he was less kind, calling the concern with interpretation 'pernicious nonsense'. The 'practice of history' to which he refers is the positivist approach that assumes 'there is ... a truth to be discovered if only we can find it' (see p. 54). See also G. Elton, *Return to Essentials* (Cambridge, Cambridge University Press, 1991).

58 Marwick, *The New Nature of History*, p. 19. See also pp. 5–9, 16.

59 Their approach is summarised in Evans, *In Defence of History*, pp. 238–40. David Howarth is also alert to the 'relativistic nihilism' which, he argues, makes the label 'postmodernism' 'something of a misnomer': see his 'Discourse Theory', in D. Marsh and G. Stoker (eds), *Theory and Methods in Political Science* (Basingstoke, Macmillan, 1995), pp. 115–33 (p. 116). Alex Callinicos discusses the Holocaust-related dimension of postmodernism in *Theories and Narratives*, pp. 66–75. See also Iggers, *Historiography*, p. 13.

60 Further indication of the misunderstanding surrounding White's work is to be found in C. Wight, 'Meta Campbell: The Epistemological Problematics of Perspectivism', *Review of International Studies*, 25:2 (1999), 311–16. Selectively quoting throughout, he erroneously assumes that White sees no value at all in using historical facts as the basis of narrative reconstruction. David Campbell responds in 'Contra Wight: The Errors of Premature Writing', *Review of International Studies*, 25:2 (1999), 317–21 (319). 'Wight is greatly confused about White on the status of the historical record', he remarks.

aims of another bête noire of historians, the French philosopher Michel Foucault. By emphasising 'the constitutive role of discourse in the production of subject identities',[61] Foucault sought, Paul Rabinow argues, to explore 'how and around what concepts [disciplines of inquiry] formed, how they were used and where they developed'.[62]

The two disciplines overlap considerably in terms of their recognition of history's cultural functions; but where historians generally ignore them or put them on the fringes of the discipline, postmodernists make the study of the interests and power-relations involved in producing history central to their broader study of the politics of knowledge accumulation. Munslow thus suggests that the reason why Foucault's ideas are so contentious among historians is that he dismisses 'crude myths' about 'brute factualism, disinterested historians, objectivity, progress, stability, continuity, roots, and the demarcation between history, ideology, fiction and perspective.'[63] The very identity of historians as authoritative purveyors of credible narratives about the past is challenged by the philosophy of history (and, because it is part of that project, historiography conceived as the study of history-writing); but that should not make historians defensive about philosophising about their subject. As White puts it, 'proper history and speculative philosophy of history are distinguishable only in emphasis, not in their respective contents'.[64]

The fourth audience to which this book is geared is that group of undergraduate and postgraduate students new to the fields of Britain and Europe, European integration history and historiography. The growth of interest in this subject as an area of research and teaching in higher education institutions has been matched by a significant rise in the volume of literature on Britain and Europe published in the last fifteen to twenty years. Treating the literature historiographically helps bring order to what might seem a dauntingly complex debate (and for students a long reading-list). It also provides a set of bibliographic references to supplement those lists. I would direct newcomers to the field to Chapters two, three and four should they not wish, or not have time, to engage with the philosophical debates about historiography as a method and the relationship between postmodernism and history. It is those chapters that set out the interpretations placed upon events by writers in each school, and where the underpinnings of the schools are analysed.

---

61 T. Diez, 'Speaking "Europe": The Politics of Integration Discourse', in Christiansen, Jørgensen and Wiener (eds), *The Social Construction of Europe*, pp. 85–100 (p. 90).

62 P. Rabinow, introduction to *The Foucault Reader: An Introduction to Foucault's Thought* (London, Penguin, 1991), p. 12. See also G. Danaher, T. Schirato and J. Webb, *Understanding Foucault* (London, Sage, 2000), pp. 97–105.

63 Munslow, *Deconstructing History*, pp. 120–39, this from p. 124.

64 White, *Metahistory*, p. 427.

It might seem over-ambitious to aim an academic text at policy-makers and the general public,[65] but, in light of the current debate about the euro referendum, it can be argued that now is the ideal time for informed general readers to learn more about the history of Britain's relationship with the Continent as a way of informing their choice at the ballot box. These two groups of people make the fifth audience for this book. 'For all of us, as for Mr Blair, it is make your mind up time.'[66]

All ministers, officials and diplomats involved in devising and implementing British foreign policy should find this book of interest, as it deals with how history has been used to construct policy and how it might be deployed more convincingly in the future, particularly over the issue of Europe. The Europe debate is a particularly stark example of the way in which people are swayed not by the 'facts' put before them (however they are defined) but by how those facts are collated together to make an argument that relates history to current events and current events to future choices. In short, the facts are used and abused as a means of shaping perceptions, those hard-to-measure yet vital elements of people's educational and psychological make-up. The referendum campaign will thus be fought out at the level of rhetoric, propaganda and discourse, and it is here that educating people about the 'lost history' of British European policy will take on significance.

Overview of the book

This book enriches our understanding of the evolution of the enthusiasts' interpretation of British European policy through analysis of how that interpretation emerged and has come to assume the position it has in political and academic discourse and among those who have moulded the debate in Britain about European unity. The remainder of the study is divided into four main chapters and a conclusion. The first is a lengthy but warranted digression into the epistemological foundations of the critical historiographic method that informs my reading of British European policy. It attempts to answer three main questions. The first is: Why choose to study the writing of British European policy? The second is: Why take the historiographic approach to this literature? The third is: How does one define and construct schools of writing? Delving into the intellectual underpinnings of the book is more than an introspective exercise in navel-gazing; it introduces a methodology that has rarely been used in this way in Britain, and explains the rationale behind the use of the heuristic device of schools to explain historiographic change.

---

65 The relative paucity of historians, and academics in general, who have managed to bridge the divide between the world of academe and the worlds of the media and the public is a pressing one, and taken up in *The Times Higher Education Supplement*, 9 November 2001, pp. 16–17.

66 Leader, *Guardian*, 24 November 2001, p. 21.

The opening chapter goes on to state the core argument pursued through the book, that there are three schools of writing on Britain and Europe. Each school is the product of a complex intermixture of sociological factors, methods of research, the questions its members ask of the past, their implicit conceptual and theoretical assumptions, the type of study they write and the way they go about presenting their evidence. The distinct lack of attention hitherto paid to studying these elements of the historiographical process is a poor reflection of the important role they play in the spinning of historical stories.

The body of the book details the interpretations and workings of the three schools. The second chapter concentrates on the orthodox school, which is broadly critical of the course Britain has taken in Europe and the world since 1945. It identifies this interpretation with an influential transnational body of politicians in Europe, the United States and Britain, all hoping to change the course of British foreign policy, if not for the same reasons. On the enthusiast side the most vocal critics of British European policy have been the founding fathers and those associated with inspiring the integration process on the Continent and in Washington. Their criticisms have been used as a way of persuading governments in London to consent to a greater degree of supranational, Commission-led integration.

They have been joined in Britain by a host of political and media critics, reacting to perceptions of British decline through the 1950s and 1960s, who saw entering Europe as a panacea for the political and economic ills bedevilling the country at that time. The nationalistic idea of Britain leading the process of integration is most common among these writers, providing an interesting contrast with the Europeanist critics, who wanted, ideally, British participation in their schemes, but, if not, at least London's blessing. What also comes through in the writing of this school is the diverse array of opinions housed under the label 'orthodox', though that is of secondary importance to the fact that the 'missed opportunities' interpretation has become a standard reference point for a plethora of people disaffected with post-war British foreign policy in general and British European policy in particular. The very vagueness and ambiguity of the terminology employed might even be said to be its greatest virtue, giving it a wide appeal as a political discourse that can be repeated time after time in a number of contexts.

The third chapter examines the reaction among academic historians against what they saw as an over-simplification of the history by orthodox writers, which resulted in the emergence through the 1980s of the revisionist school of writing about Britain and European unity. Looking at the history through new conceptual lenses, academics have been providing a new interpretation based on scrutiny of official government documentation released to the Public Record Office. The argument they advance is that the British have been neither as myopic nor as negative when it comes to European policy as orthodox writers have suggested, providing a picture that is altogether more complicated.

Furthermore, revisionists assert that, even if it had had the will to do so, London would have found it extremely difficult to lead the integration process, as the orthodox seem to have hoped it might. The Europeans, with the backing of the Americans, were engaged in a project to create a supranational organisation capable in the first instance of eliminating enmity between France and Germany and, hopefully, of standing up to Russia in the event of 'hot war' between the superpower blocs. While they wanted London on board their bus, they did not want it to crash because of British hesitancy. They would certainly not have wanted to water down the supranational elements of the various organisations to suit Britain – a finding that casts light on the numerous obstacles in the way of closer British involvement with the Continent at this time. Analysis of the revisionist school shows the way in which changing interpretations of history are intrinsically related to changes in the social fabric of the sub-field under scrutiny. Academics have approached the field of British European policy with the task, not of explaining failure, but of understanding what happened and how: a quite different goal has been instrumental in determining how they have reconfigured and re-imagined the past.

The fourth chapter argues that the historiography is now entering a third stage, with the development of a post-revisionist school of writing. The rewriting of the history on the back of the consultation of new sources has brought with it a more subtle, nuanced view of British policy and policy-making in this era. A second wave of revisionists have, in essence, injected a sense of messiness into our understanding of the British foreign policy-making process, by suggesting that key individuals and departments of government held views on Europe that shifted rapidly over time. Away from the neat stories espoused by orthodox and revisionist writers, post-revisionism is either evidence that narrative modes of telling histories have passed their sell-by date or, simply, that a younger generation of historians cannot make up its mind on what was happening in the Whitehall machine as more and more sources are brought to bear on the reconstruction of the past. This school, and the mode of analysis its members present, does not yet have the widespread appeal in terms of its ability to explain broader trends in British European policy that the orthodox and revisionist schools do. However, by stressing that British European policy was the product of incoherence, disorganisation and an inability to decide on key issues, it may in time come to be seen as a new way of representing other themes in British European and foreign policy, which have been put in logical, ordered form where perhaps none existed.

Either way, it serves to support the argument of philosophers and intellectual historians that history is conceived in the mind of the historian, and that both its form and content are always positioned. It is the historian who is responsible for designing the research project and choosing which sources to consult; it is the historian who colligates the evidence, picks patterns in the past, refracts the evidence through his or her mind to produce an interpretation, and who elects how to narrate the history. The concluding chapter picks up on this and related themes in a discussion that explores both the theoretical and policy-relevant themes that emerge from the book, as well as offering two areas up for further research. One is the need for deeper exploration of the workings of the schools of writing, concentrating on what continental scholars and politicians have been writing about British European policy. The other is the requirement for a comparison of the writing in this area with that about other sub-fields of contemporary history.

Before looking to the future, however, it is necessary to establish the means by which this study has been constructed and the argument it seeks to develop, and that is the subject of the next chapter.

1   Method and argument

The last chapter showed how, in their attempts to sway the British public and political establishment on the issue of whether or not Britain should adopt the euro as its currency, the sceptics and the enthusiasts regularly evoke memories of the past. But they do not talk about the *same* past. By stressing what the then Labour Party leader Hugh Gaitskell called in 1962 the 'thousand years' of history that would be lost if Britain attempted to involve itself with a European federation,[1] the sceptics conveniently sidestep the political, economic and strategic factors used by the enthusiasts to expose what they see as the weaknesses in Britain's policy after the Second World War. It is difficult to say why populist representations of Britain's policy towards Europe are oriented in such a way, but it may have something to do with the fact that we know less about the post-1945 era than we do any other period in British history. The teaching of history in Britain has been slow to extend into the post-war years and, traditionally, curricula in schools and at universities have concentrated on 'great events', 'great personalities' and wars and conquest rather than on events since the Second World War, leading to a situation in which 'Britain's perception of herself internationally is shaped by a martial history in which a small group of islands imposed Pax Britannica on the world.'[2]

Such a thesis is easier to assert than to defend, not least because anomalies in the statistics make it difficult to measure precisely the take-up of courses on European integration history, especially at the level of higher education. Statistics from the Higher Education Statistics Agency (HESA) on numbers of students pursuing degrees in European studies are inconclusive. Not only are there numerous courses that offer students the chance of taking European studies modules (languages, area studies, history, politics and economics), but European studies is included under the catch-all headings 'History' and 'Other European languages, literature and culture'.[3] For the record, the number of students taking

1   Gaitskell's views on Europe feature prominently in the biography by G. McDermott, *Leader Lost: A Biography of Hugh Gaitskell* (London, Leslie Frewin, 1972), pp. 235–56 (his conference speech is examined on pp. 248–54) and get a chapter of their own in B. Brivati, *Hugh Gaitskell* (London, Richard Cohen, 1997), pp. 404–31. Willy Brandt remarked wryly that the speech 'disappointed some of his friends on the Continent', in 'The Division of Europe', in W. T. Rodgers (ed.), *Hugh Gaitskell 1906–1963* (London, Thames and Hudson, 1964), pp. 133–9 (p. 139), a view echoed in Roy Jenkins's preceding chapter, 'Leader of the Opposition', pp. 115–31 (p. 130).

2   J. Paxman, *Friends in High Places: Who Runs Britain?* (London, Penguin, 1991), p. 243.

3   See HESA's website, www.hesa.ac.uk/holisdocs/pubinfo/student/subject78.htm.

History rose between 1997–98 and 2000–1 (only helped by a sharp jump in the final year, however), while the number taking Other European languages fell consistently from 4,885 in 1997–98 to 3,575 in 2000–1, rendering it massively problematic to judge the number of students exposed to contemporary British and European history.

Lower down the educational spectrum one finds an equally patchy picture. Through the 1990s, A-Level boards incorporated more and more post-1945 history but, sadly for the Euroenthusiasts, the teaching of contemporary history does not hold a high place in school curricula in Britain. It does not feature in the English national history curriculum at all until Key Stage Three (children ages eleven to fourteen), and only then as a non-statutory part of the programme of study, where schools can choose to study it as part of the history of the twentieth century. This perceived failing in the education system was one of the reasons why Anthony Seldon and Peter Hennessy founded the Institute of Contemporary British History (ICBH) in 1986, together with *Contemporary Record*, the first journal of the ICBH, about which more in the concluding chapter.[4] Despite the impediments in the way of drawing firm conclusions about the time spent teaching European integration history in schools and at universities, all the signs are that it is not a well-known theme in terms of how the British view the history of the nation and the country's place in the contemporary international system.

In a jointly written article on development of nation-state identities in the era of supranational integration in Europe, Martin Marcussen, Thomas Risse, Daniela Engelman-Martin, Hans Joachim Knopf and Klaus Roscher illustrate the impact this perception of the past has had on the Europe debate in Britain:

> British attitudes towards the European project reflect collectively held beliefs about British, particularly *Anglo-Saxon* identity which, as William Wallace put it, 'is as old as Shakespeare, matured through the experiences of the English Civil War and the struggles against the threat of Catholic absolutism, first from Spain and then from France: a free England defying an unfree continent'.[5]

The consequences, they say, have been far-reaching:

> The collective identification with *national* symbols, history and institutions is far greater in the British political discourse than a potential identification with *European* symbols, history and institutions ... 'Europe' simply does not resonate well with identity constructions deeply embedded in national political institutions and in political culture.[6]

---

4 Telephone interview with Seldon, 23 April 2002.
5 Martin Marcussen Thomas Risse, Daniela Engelman-Martin, Hans Joachim Knopf and Klaus Roscher, 'Constructing Europe? The Evolution of Nation-State Identities', in Christiansen, Jørgensen and Wiener (eds), *The Social Construction of Europe*, pp. 101–20 (p. 112). Italics in original.
6 *Ibid.*, p. 113. Emphasis in original.

An American commentator, writing in the 1960s, also insinuated that the idea of Britain's not being a truly 'European' country is deeply rooted in a particular sense of the past that comes to the British from an early age and persists in public discourses about the country's place in the world.

> From the Elizabethan Age to the twentieth century, England turned primarily to the world beyond the seas for trade and expansion. Historically, the interest in the building of an overseas empire, together with the isolation from European neighbours provided by the Channel, molded to a large extent contemporary British thought about Europe. As a result, even in the mid-twentieth century, the British found it difficult to consider themselves fully 'European'.[7]

Two developments in the field of education may bring about future change in Britain's attitudes to Europe. One is the EU's own publicity efforts, an example of which is *Euroquest: A Trail of Questions and Answers about the European Union*.[8] This activity book, for use at Key Stage Two level (children ages seven to eleven), is 'intended to provide teachers and children in primary schools with information about the European Union', in which the learning of facts goes hand in hand with learning 'about how the EU affects their own lives'.[9] The other is that the new programme of study for citizenship at Key Stages Three and Four (children ages fourteen to sixteen) becomes statutory in August 2002 and includes a requirement for pupils to be taught about the role of the EU and Britain's relations with it.[10]

Further guidelines have been produced for this new National Curriculum subject in the Qualifications and Curriculum Authority (QCA) scheme of work for citizenship. Unit Eleven, entitled 'Europe: Who Decides?', is intended to provide 'a framework within which to explore and debate issues that affect the United Kingdom's relations with Europe and relate to decision-making at different levels of government. The single European currency is used here as a focus, but this could be changed to another issue that is topical at the time of teaching.' The background information continues:

> The unit contains opportunities for pupils to explore and engage in discussion about issues relating to membership of the European Union and about the single currency. Pupils find out the facts about Europe through their own research, and exchange views with pupils in other European countries through school linking and internet discussion forums. They explore the advantages and disadvantages of the single currency both for individuals and for organisations. A debate is held in which a

---

7 R. L. Pfaltzgraff, Jr., *Britain Faces Europe* (Philadelphia, University of Pennsylvania Press, 1969), p. 2.

8 First published by the Representation of the European Commission in the United Kingdom in 1998.

9 Geoffrey Martin's opening remarks, p. 2.

10 Thus realising the *Daily Mail*'s fears, noted in the previous chapter, that children are going to be forced to learn about the euro through curriculum change.

range of points of view are presented and discussed, and this is followed by a vote/referendum on the issue.[11]

Teaching about Europe and European issues also forms part of General Certificate of Secondary Education (GCSE) courses, notably modern world history, geography, economics and modern foreign languages.[12]

There is invariably a void between teaching children about the EU and changing deeply established national attitudes, especially discourses about Europe in the popular media, and these initiatives will take time to work into the collective British psyche about Europe. But on the back of the work by the ICBH higher up the spectrum they can nonetheless be seen as recognition on the part of the government and the European Commission that they need to be more proactive in selling the idea of Europe to the British people. Of immediate concern to the Prime Minister, however, is that while he publicly laments Britain's missed opportunities in Europe he runs a country that, for the most part, seems blissfully unaware of the significance of the past events he uses in support of his enthusiasm for Britain joining the eurozone.

The focus of this book *is* about Britain's relations with Europe after 1945; but before analysing the historiography it is necessary in this chapter to discuss the method by which I have set about developing it. The first section considers the rationale for historiographical treatment of the literature; the second section introduces the taxonomy and labelling used below to trace the evolution of the literature; the third section concentrates on the major points of division between the schools of writing identified on Britain and European integration, as a way of framing the core argument of the book that history, conceived in its broadest sense, is a socially constructed phenomenon.

The case study

This is not a historical account of Britain's policy towards European integration since 1945, but a historiographical one. It seeks not to narrate events nor to delve into the webs of interaction in Downing Street and Whitehall that produced British European policy, but to explore how that morass of historical evidence has been manipulated by politicians, journalists and historians into competing interpretations of the past. This critical distinction between the two

---

11 The unit builds on builds on Key Stage Three unit fourteen, 'Developing skills of democratic participation' in the Key Stage Three scheme of work, and links with unit ten, 'Rights and responsibilities in the world of work', unit one, 'Human rights', unit five, 'How the economy functions' and unit 6, 'Business and enterprise'. For more information see www.standards.dfes.gov.uk/schemes2/ks4citizenship/cit11/.

12 I am grateful to Liz Craft and Jerome Freeman of the QCA for pointing this out to me and for giving me details of the new guidelines.

methods is well described by Robert Holub: historiography, he notes, substitutes 'for the objective depiction of events and individuals the history of their becoming events and individuals for us.'[13]

The book was inspired by the observation that the number of publications making reference to Britain's troubled relationship with the Continent has increased dramatically since European integration became a hot political issue in the 1950s, bringing with it growing disagreement over the intentions behind that policy and the underlying aspirations of the key policy-makers concerned in its formulation. Why do writers disagree with some in a given field but not others? Is it a function of their methodology, the sources they use or their political affiliation? What is it that shapes these factors in the first place? Huge questions admittedly, but ones that historiography can begin to answer and, where gaps are left, for which it can suggest avenues down which future researchers might travel to provide answers. That the study concentrates on historiography and not history means that it is founded almost entirely on secondary as opposed to primary sources: monographs, edited collections, journal articles, memoirs, biographies, autobiographies, newspaper stories and book reviews, supplemented by interviews with historians working, and who have worked, in this area.

The field to date

Like the historian, the historiographer does not start with a blank sheet of paper. Just as historians have to make choices about what to study, how to study it, which periods to analyse and how to emplot their evidence into narrative form, historiographers also have to make choices about what subject, period of study and writers to analyse. Both are critically influenced in the first instance by the nature of the published material available and, on top of that, by what parts they study and what they ignore. Both have to assemble the published material into a story about how events unfolded across time.

In terms of this project, the result is a book that concentrates mainly on the literature on British European policy in the later 1940s, 1950s and early 1960s. Favouring the first three post-war decades is a reflection of the material available, because it is here, and especially over policy in the 1940s and 1950s, that the major debates about Britain and Europe have been raging. Indeed, there is a general consensus among writers that there has been a series of turning-points in Britain's relationship with the Continent over the years since 1945 that needs investigating and which constitutes the 'history' of that relationship. First, in June 1950, Clement Attlee's Labour government refused to join the

13 Holub, *Reception Theory*, p. 49.

European Coal and Steel Community (ECSC).[14] Then, between October 1950 and August 1954, Britain stood aloof from efforts to found the European Defence Community (EDC).[15] Finally, in November 1955, Britain withdrew its representative from the Messina process that led to the creation of the EEC. Following the release of documents to the PRO under the Thirty Year Rule, Britain's response to the creation of the EEC by the signing of the Treaty of Rome in 1957 and its part in founding the European Free Trade Area (EFTA) in 1959 now receive more detailed attention from historians.[16] Britain's first application to join the EEC in the period 1961–63 has always had a relatively large body of literature associated with it, and that too is expanding.[17] Britain's second bid to enter the EEC, made under Harold Wilson in 1967, receives less attention, as does the country's accession under Heath in 1973, though that situation is changing.[18]

One way of portraying the implicit agreement among writers on what events constitute the history of British European policy is to examine how three of the key textbooks carve up the subject. Stephen George, now Professor of Politics at the University of Sheffield, first published *An Awkward Partner: Britain in the European Community* in 1990. In what has become one of the seminal texts on the subject, he explored how Britain had gained its reputation for being at odds with the process of European integration. He organised his material chronologically, examining 'the background', 1945–73, then the governments of Edward Heath, Wilson, James Callaghan, Margaret Thatcher and John Major, Prime Minister when the 1994 edition of the book was published.[19] In the background chapter that most interests us here he analyses the attempts to build a European

---

14 Based on the May 1950 proposal of the French Foreign Minister, Robert Schuman, to pool the coal and steel resources of France and Germany under the control of a supranational 'High Authority'

15 Based on – but significantly extending – the October 1950 proposal of the French Prime Minister, René Pleven, for a supranational European Army in which 'there would be no independent German Army or General Staff for the forces of nationalism to rally around, just small German units operating alongside similar units from other member states under the direction of a European Command:' K. Ruane, *The Rise and Fall of the European Defence Community: Anglo-American Relations and the Crisis of European Defence, 1950–55* (Basingstoke, Macmillan, 2000), p. 4 and p. 15.

16 For instance J. Ellison, *Threatening Europe: Britain and the Creation of the European Community 1955–58* (Basingstoke, Macmillan, 2000).

17 P. Winand, *Eisenhower, Kennedy, and the United States of Europe* (Basingstoke, Macmillan, 1993); N. P. Ludlow, *Dealing With Britain: The Six and the First UK Application to the EEC* (Cambridge, Cambridge University Press, 1997) and Wilkes (ed.), *Britain's Failure to Enter the European Community*.

18 A. May (ed.), *Britain, the Commonwealth and Europe: The Commonwealth and Britain's Applications to Join the European Communities* (Basingstoke, Palgrave, 2001); O. J. Daddow (ed.), *Harold Wilson and European Integration: Britain's Second Application to Join the EEC* (London, Frank Cass, 2003).

19 S. George, *An Awkward Partner: Britain in the European Community*, 2nd edn (New York, Oxford University Press, 1994).

'third force' in the late 1940s and follows it up with analysis of British policy towards the Schuman Plan, the EDC, the Messina negotiations and their outcome, the founding of the EEC. He continues the chapter with a survey of the reasons behind Britain's applications to join the EEC in 1961 and 1967 and concludes with Britain's accession to the Community.

There is a noticeable difference in the number and type of sources he uses in the background compared to the rest of the book. In the former he relies mainly on secondary sources, supplemented by politicians' diaries and memoirs, and although it is in the main a textbook history of events, in places it reads as a historiographical overview, and he is able at one point to allude to the dispute among writers over the origins of Macmillan's EEC application.[20] As the book reaches nearer and nearer the present day, however, one notices greater recourse to *Hansard*, the record of parliamentary debate, and to newspaper articles and academic books and articles written at the time events were unfolding, signifying that the historiographical debate is less well defined the nearer one approaches the present.

Two authors who published shortly after George weight their narratives differently, but concentrate on the same major themes and points of controversy, reflecting their aim of understanding the sequence of events in British European policy as much as explaining how Britain has accrued its 'awkward' label in Europe.[21] Sean Greenwood, currently Professor of Modern History at Canterbury Christ Church College, University of Kent, published *Britain and European Cooperation Since 1945* in 1991, as part of Blackwell's 'Historical Association Studies' series.[22] Where George dealt with the material in fewer than forty pages, Greenwood devoted over ninety, almost his entire book, to the period 1945–73. After a brief overview of trends in European unity prior to 1945, Greenwood's chapters include British policy in 1945–47 and 1947–49, the Schuman Plan, the Conservative Governments 1951–55, the founding of the EEC, the applications in the 1960s and entry to the EEC in the 1970s. As had George, Greenwood relied on secondary texts for much of his information.

Now Professor of International History at the University of Nottingham, John Young organised *Britain and European Unity 1945–1999*, the second edition of a book originally published as *Britain and European Unity 1945–1992*,[23] in a similar fashion to Greenwood. After a chapter entitled 'The Birth of European Unity, 1929–49', which includes analysis of the efforts to

20 *Ibid.*, p. 31.
21 For an account of the methodological distinction between 'understanding' and 'explaining' see M. Hollis and S. Smith, *Explaining and Understanding International Relations* (Oxford, Clarendon Press, 1991).
22 S. Greenwood, *Britain and European Cooperation Since 1945* (Oxford, Blackwell, 1992).
23 Young's *Britain and European Unity* books are part of the 'British History in Perspective' series.

create a 'third force' in Europe after the Second World War, Young goes on to cover the Schuman Plan, the European Defence Community and the Treaties of Rome in Chapter 2, Macmillan and the first application in Chapter 3, Wilson's application in Chapter 4 and Britain's EEC membership and beyond in Chapters 5 and 6. The key distinction between Young's and the other textbooks is in the extra volume of primary sources he uses to narrate the period until the Wilson governments of 1964, drawing on his single and co-authored works on Britain and European unity dating back to the early 1980s. He also spends more time than previous writers on unravelling the historiographical debates among writers. But despite the inevitable variations in scope, outlook and time spent by each historian on each of the core themes in British European policy, the significant observation here is that Young's book both identified and reinforced the existing tendency among writers to examine British European policy in the context of the key steps in European integration after 1945.

Accounts published since George, Greenwood and Young have tended to conform to the pattern they set down. One is David Gowland and Arthur Turner's *Reluctant Europeans: Britain and European Integration, 1945–1998*.[24] With the odd variation, notably chapters specifically on the 'special relationship' and European unity and the Commonwealth dimension, this text follows the chronological pattern of its predecessors, and is especially reminiscent of George's *Awkward Partner*. The other is Roger Broad and Virginia Preston's edited collection, *Moored to the Continent? Britain and European Integration* (London: Institute of Historical Research, 2001).[25] The product of a conference organised to mark the fortieth anniversary of the signing of the Treaty of Rome, it is more diverse in nature, and brings together academics and practitioners to discuss different aspects of the British approach to Europe. It thus combines the historical with the current *à la* George and to a lesser extent Greenwood and Young, and branches out into areas such as the constitutional implications of membership.[26] But on the whole the contents page includes analysis of the historical themes one has come to expect: the 1940s and the Schuman Plan, the Treaties of Rome, the applications and the entry and the referendum form four of the ten main chapters on offer.

The historiography presented in this book is an effort to reflect the historians' agenda and to deconstruct it with a view to discovering what has been driving forward the competing interpretations that spring from it. Having established that agenda, it is now necessary to explore two questions that flow immediately

---

24 D. Gowland and A. Turner, *Reluctant Europeans: Britain and European Integration, 1945–1998* (London, Pearson, 2000).

25 R. Broad and V. Preston (eds), *Moored to the Continent? Britain and European Integration* (London, Institute of Historical Research, 2001).

26 See Colin Turpin's chapter, pp. 127–44.

from it: why is it important to study British policy towards European integration at all, and why take a historiographical approach to the subject?

The first question can be tackled on an empirical level, where the main reason is that Britain has carved out for itself a significant role for itself on the international stage since 1945; indeed, Britain's role in creating and sustaining international organisations such as the United Nations (UN) has often been used as a stick with which to beat policy-makers over its European policy. In spite, or perhaps because of, its perceived political and economic decline,[27] London took the lead in organising Western Europe's response to the offer of Marshall Aid from America in 1947, culminating in the establishment of the European Recovery Programme (ERP) and, in 1948, the Organisation for European Economic Cooperation (OEEC), which oversaw the recovery of post-war Europe.[28] Outside the EEC, Britain was in 1959 a founder member of EFTA. In the security arena, meanwhile, London played a significant role at Washington's side in the Cold War. It was a prime mover in bringing to fruition the Dunkirk Treaty with France in 1947, which was transformed a year later into the Brussels Treaty with the additional signatures of Belgium, Luxembourg and the Netherlands; in 1949 Britain was a signatory of the Washington Treaty and a founder member of the North Atlantic Treaty Organisation (NATO). Five years later, in 1954, it was Prime Minister Anthony Eden who provided the security dimension for Western Europe through an expanded Brussels Treaty establishing the Western European Union (WEU), following the collapse of the EDC at the hands of the French National Assembly.

On the negative side, Britain has consistently acted as an impediment to supranationalism in Western Europe. In the words of Pierre-Henri Laurent, London has acted as an 'internal inhibitor' to the process of integration, as is shown in its watering down of the powers of the Council of Europe, its rejection of the Schuman Plan and a supranational European Army as part of the EDC and its acrimonious withdrawal from the Messina process that led to the founding of the EEC.[29] For these reasons, Britain is still seen as a reluctant or just plain naughty member of the EU, an approach that seems to be at odds with trends and developments in other sectors of its foreign policy, which possess more of an internationalist flavour.

---

27 A view most vigorously held by C. Barnett, *The Audit of War: The Illusion and Reality of Britain as a Great Nation* (London, Papermac, 1987). The purpose of the book, he says on p. 11 of the Author's Preface, is 'to uncover the causes of Britain's protracted decline as an industrial country since the Second World War'. See also C. Barnett, *The Lost Victory: British Dreams, British Realities 1945–1950* (Basingstoke, Macmillan, 1995).

28 It was renamed the Organisation for Economic Co-operation and Development in 1961, and its mandate and membership were simultaneously expanded.

29 P. Laurent, 'Reappraising the Origins of European Integration', in H. J. Michelmann and P. Soldatos (eds), *European Integration: Theories and Approaches* (Lanham, MD, University Press of America, 1994), pp. 99–112 (p. 104).

Recognition is growing, however, that labelling Britain the awkward partner is a convenient ploy to deflect criticism from fellow member states who share some of its concerns about the pace and direction of European integration. London is, according to this perspective, merely the spokesman for an informal coalition of member states 'content to shelter behind British objections rather than take up the argument themselves'.[30] The case of Britain is also interesting, therefore, in that only now are scholars beginning to devote serious research time to the idea of, and dynamics behind, Euroscepticism as a phenomenon. This, one scholar remarks, reflects the agenda of a generally 'pre-integration' academic community, 'which for a variety of reasons has treated Euroscepticism in an asymmetrical way [compared] to pro-integration groups such as the European Movement. The academic community has therefore routinely overlooked Eurosceptics and Euroscepticism and by design or default has often failed to treat it as a serious phenomenon or object of study.'[31] Consistently low and falling turnouts at European elections have brought into doubt the public's affinity for the idea of 'ever closer union' enshrined in the Treaty of Rome, making Britain an important test-case in our attempts to grapple with the factors that account for Euroscepticism in member states. Britain's approach to European unity is, finally, revealing about the problems applicant states and the EEC have had in coming to terms with the economic and political ramifications of enlargement.[32]

With member states agreeing at the EU Copenhagen summit of December 2002 to enlarge the Union to ten new countries (Cyprus, the Czech Republic, Estonia, Hungary, Latvia, Lithuania, Malta, Poland, Slovakia and Slovenia), the history of Britain's attitude towards European integration may yield important lessons about how to proceed to make the process as smooth as possible both to applicant states and to the EU.[33] As one commentator warns, however, while conclusions about present problems and barriers to EU expansion based upon Britain's experience *could* be drawn, it is dangerous to transpose them

---

30 S. George, *Politics and Policy in the European Community*, 2nd edn (Oxford, Oxford University Press, 1991), p. 204.

31 Forster, *Euroscepticism in British Politics*, p. 3. See in addition A. Alexandre-Collier, *La Grande-Bretagne Eurosceptique? L'enjeu Européen dans le Débat Politique Britannique* (Nantes, Editions du Temps, 2002).

32 The phenomenon of 'scepticism' now receives devoted academic attention from the Economic and Social Research Council-funded 'Opposing Europe Research Network', based at the University of Sussex European Institute. This brings together scholars and research students from across the Continent to explore all aspects of scepticism towards the EU, the euro and Europeanisation, publishing in the form of working papers, briefing papers and election briefings; details are at www.sussex.ac.uk/Units/SEI/oern/index.html.

33 For further information on the enlargement of the EU see http://europa.eu.int/scadplus/leg/en/lvb/e4001.htm and related pages.

simplistically on to current events: 'a far more nuanced set of conclusions needs to be drawn concerning the more recent process of enlargement'.[34]

The uses of historiography

Sidney Monas's playful assessment is that 'Deconstructive criticism can be applied to anything; it is rather fun to practice, lends itself adoptably to the support or demolition of almost any ideology and requires the mastery of a methodology and a vocabulary rather than the command of a great deal of erudition.'[35] Suffice to say, the present author believes there is more to the historiographic enterprise than Monas suggests, though the question 'Why adopt a historiographical methodology?' undoubtedly demands a response, given the paucity of existing literature on the subject. There are four principal reasons why it is useful to write the historiography: the first is to fill a large gap in the literature on Britain and Europe; the second operates on the philosophical level and is that it sheds much-needed light on the practice of contemporary history; the third is that it should help refine political science work on British foreign policy-making; and the fourth is that it should help sharpen the use of history by policy-makers.

Turning first of all to the gap in the literature, it can be argued that students have been poorly served by existing studies of British European policy. Despite the subject-matter being of vital importance to understanding British and international political history since 1945, no full historiographical account of British European policy has yet been published. The subject was deemed important enough to warrant its own chapter in *The Contemporary History Handbook*, but in a relatively short chapter and, as the title suggests, Young only had the space to give the 'shape' of the debate as opposed to detailing the underlying forces that had combined to produce that shape.[36] He had already made considerably greater advances in *Britain and European Unity* as, to a lesser extent, did Sean Greenwood in *Britain and European Co-operation*. Before them, in 1987, Jan Melissen and Bert Zeeman published a historiographical article in *International Affairs* that introduced in highly readable fashion many of the same themes, although it only covered the years 1945–51.[37]

---

34 A. Forster, 'No Entry: Britain and the EEC in the 1960s', *Contemporary British History*, 12:2 (1998), 139–46 (144).

35 S. Monas, 'Introduction: Contemporary Historiography', in Kozicki (ed.), *Developments in Modern Historiography*, pp. 1–16 (p. 4).

36 J. W. Young, 'Britain and "Europe", The Shape of the Historiographical Debate', in B. Brivati, J. Buxton, and A. Seldon (eds), *The Contemporary History Handbook* (Manchester, Manchester University Press, 1996), pp. 207–14, especially pp. 207–8.

37 J. Melissen and B. Zeeman, 'Britain and Western Europe, 1945–51: Opportunities Lost?', *International Affairs*, 63:1 (1987), 81–95.

Furthermore, the histories on this subject rarely contain methodological sections explaining why and how the research was conceived and put into practice in the way that it was, and which theories and/or concepts were used to inform the decision made about which sources to consult. The exception is David Sanders's *Losing an Empire, Finding a Role*, which devotes a whole chapter, unusually located at the end of the book, to an exposition of the theoretical lenses through which he views British foreign policy.[38] What marks out Sanders's book from the majority examined below is first of all that it is written by a political scientist who treats the material in an explicitly theoretical fashion, and secondly that it is devoted to the broad sweep of events rather than developments in European policy *per se*. It would not be considered a mainstream text on Britain and Europe, as would those referred to above, and therefore does not cast much light on the philosophical concerns about history to which this book speaks. The collective failing of the earlier historiographical contributions is, in sum, the limited time they are able to devote to the range of factors at work on historical interpretation and to the implications these have for the 'nature of history' debate.

This is the second reason for treating British European policy historiographically: what it can expose about current trends in the nature and practice of contemporary history in Britain, which either historians are reluctant to analyse in their own texts or get accidentally overlooked owing to lack of time or space. As Alun Munslow has remarked, 'Every history contains ideas or theories about the nature of change and continuity as held by historians – some are overt, others deeply buried, and some just poorly formulated.'[39] This is a sub-field of history about which the epistemological concerns associated with the 'objectivity' or 'certainty' of knowledge raised by social constructivists, postmodernists and poststructuralists are highly pertinent. Contemporary historical events, usually taken to be those within living memory, are most acutely open to interpretation and reinterpretation, firstly because their ramifications impact upon events happening in the present, and secondly because so many different sorts of writer evoke memories of the immediate past in support of their ideas about the present and the future.

Anthony Seldon confirmed in the middle of the 1990s that

> contemporary history as studied in Britain has become a pluralistic, almost chaotic pursuit, not just produced by conventional academics in universities, but with some of the best products coming from television and radio producers and writers, from journalists, schoolteachers and professional authors, and indeed from the general public.[40]

---

38 D. Sanders, *Losing an Empire, Finding a Role: British Foreign Policy Since 1945* (Basingstoke, Macmillan, 1990), Chapter 9.

39 Munslow, *Deconstructing History*, p. 5.

40 A. Seldon, 'Preface' in Brivati, Buxton and Seldon (eds), *The Contemporary History Handbook*, pp. 11–14 (p. 13).

It is within these webs of influence, intricately woven by academics, journalists and policy-makers, that implicit agreements emerge about how rapidly developing events and the machinations of individuals are to be interpreted and recorded, and from which accepted historical wisdoms, or orthodoxies, emerge.

But historiography does more than help us locate and assess the impact on historical interpretation of changing currents in world affairs; it seeks to uncover how historians as a community define their craft: their shared norms and expectations about what constitutes 'proper' history and the means of writing it. Because of the pre-eminence within British historical research of PRO documentation, this study pays particular attention to the methodological and epistemological aspects of history by centring on the impact on historical scholarship of the Thirty Year Rule on the release of government documentation, with a view to discovering if one can identify a collective mindset about contemporary history and the process of historical research on the part of British historians through analysis of their sources and modes of narrative reconstruction. Access to the papers commonly scrutinised by diplomatic historians is governed by this rule that means records are opened 'in the January 30 years after the date of the last paper or entry in a record, plus 1 extra year, to ensure that all papers on the file are thirty years old'.[41] Hence, at the beginning of 2003, records with a last date of 1972 were released into the public domain. Here one is also compelled to ask supplementary questions, such as: Why are some sources chosen and not others? What does the clamour to get to the newly released files say about the infrastructure of the history industry?

A third reason for employing the historiographic method is that it should help political scientists modelling British foreign policy. There is a debate, principally conducted today in academic circles in the United States,[42] but with its origins in the nineteenth-century disputes between the Neo-Kantians and the Neo-Hegelians,[43] about the relationship between the disciplines of history and political science. The conventional wisdom is that they are divided along a nomothetic–ideographic faultline, the former of these adjectives referring to political science and the latter to history. 'Nomothetic methodologies are deductive and objective, characterised by systematic protocol and technique; ideographic methodologies are inductive and subjective, characterised by "getting

---

41 See the PRO website, 'Access to the Public records' section at www.pro.gov.uk/about/access/access.htm.

42 The year 1997 saw the publication of an *International Security* symposium that contained articles by writers on both sides of the history–political science divide in the United States. Nothing comparable has yet been published in Britain.

43 White, *Metahistory*, pp. 381–8.

inside" situations.'[44] Put another way, the distinction is held to be that historians understand the particular, while political scientists explain the general.

This alleged contrast between 'richness and rigour'[45] has, writes Anthony Forster, fostered a major source of inter-disciplinary tension:

> This is more than a matter of semantics with the major controversy over how political science and history study international relations. The key differences concern the aspiration to prediction, policy relevance, complexity versus simplicity, and whether scholars should seek to understand single events rather than generalise about classes of events.[46]

The debate is not without its precedent in Britain, as this quotation shows, but it has not kindled as large a volume of literature as across the Atlantic. But where it is in evidence, the exchanges have been fairly heated, and have tended to reinforce the mutual suspicion that exists between the two communities of academics.

In 1975, Alan Bullock and Ritchie Ovendale crossed swords following a reference Ovendale made in a book review of Joseph Frankel's *British Foreign Policy* that, he said, as a 'social science' text would be of 'more limited' value to historical scholars than to social scientists concerned with 'paradigms', 'parameters of action' and 'saliences'.[47] The correspondence that ensued between the two was published in a later edition of *International Affairs*. Bullock replied that Ovendale's review was 'disparaging' and 'supercilious' and suggested that Frankel's book *did* say something valuable to the historian working on post-war British foreign policy. For his part, Ovendale said that Bullock had intentionally misrepresented his opinion through a misquotation of his review. The original, he argued, stated that Frankel's text was of more limited value to historical scholars, whereas Bullock in his letter claims Ovendale's review said the book was of limited value to scholars full stop, an altogether stronger claim.

In 1992, Colin Seymour-Ure took a similar, albeit stronger, line to Ovendale by remarking that political scientists have a 'preoccupation with the contemporary' that obscures the relevance of their work to historians; and, in 1995, John

---

44 C. Condon, 'A Semiotic Approach to the Use of Metaphor in Human–Computer Interfaces', Brunel University Ph.D., 2000, electronic version p. 5.1.2.3. The thesis is downloadable from the internet at www.redwines.btinternet.co.uk/chris/phd.html.

45 J. S. Levy, 'Too Important to Leave to the Other: History and Political Science in the Study of International Relations', *International Security*, 22:1 (1997), 22–33 (24). See also C. Elman and M. F. Elman, 'Diplomatic History and International Relations Theory: Respecting Differences and Crossing Boundaries', *International Security*, 22:1 (1997), 5–21 (11); R. H. Immerman, 'In Search of History – and Relevancy: Breaking Through the Encrustations of "Interpretation"', *Diplomatic History*, 12:2 (1988), 341–56 (342) and A. S. Elms, *Uncovering Lives: The Uneasy Alliance of Biography and Psychology* (Oxford, Oxford University Press, 1994), pp. 15–16.

46 Forster, 'No Entry', pp. 139–40.

47 R. Ovendale, review, 'British Foreign Policy 1945–1973. By Joseph Frankel', *International Affairs*, 51:4 (1975), 574–5 (575).

Kent was disparaging about the 'crude theorising' of historical events by political scientists.[48] The heated dialogue now under way between philosophers and historians is thus reminiscent of the territorial disputes that have long been going on between political scientists and historians, and supports Becher and Trowler's contention that, despite fairly radical external and internal changes over the last decade or so, the academic world will continue to be characterised by arguments between the 'academic tribes' and 'disciplinary territories' of which it is constituted.[49]

Perhaps the antagonism aroused by this debate has obscured the close connection between the disciplines. As the majority of the American contributors to the 1997 *International Security* symposium agreed, as Bullock also pointed out in his correspondence with Ovendale, and as Dennis Kavanagh pointed out to British audiences (apparently without much success) in 1991,[50] cross-fertilisation between political scientists and historians has always occurred, if only unwittingly. The boundaries are not as watertight as the construction of the debate in zero-sum terms might lead us to suggest. For example, to home in on the 'specific versus general' distinction: how does one know what is specific or unique about a past event if one does not have *a priori* knowledge of the wider historical context of that event, together with knowledge of events from other historical epochs? To quote the sociologist Max Weber's words to the historian George von Below in 1914: 'We are absolutely in accord that history should establish what is specific, say, to the medieval city; but this is possible only if we first find what is missing in other cities (ancient, Chinese, Islamic).'

Historians may not self-consciously use *theory*, but they do employ *models* and *concepts* culled from neighbouring disciplines, even if they do not recognise that they do so.[51] Thus, wrote E. H. Carr, 'The very use of language commits the historian, like the scientists, to generalisation ... The historian is not really interested in the unique, but in what is general in the unique.'[52] He cites historians' use of terms such as 'war' and 'revolution' to describe events that were clearly very different, such as the French, Chinese and Russian Revolutions. These signifiers, he contends, contain implicit generalisations about the causes

---

48 C. Seymour-Ure, review, 'Cabinet Decisions on Foreign Policy: The British Experience October 1938–June 1941. By Christopher Hill', *International Affairs*, 68:1 (1992), 170; J. Kent, review, 'The End of Superpower: British Foreign Office Conceptions of a Changing World. By Stuart Croft', *Contemporary Record*, 9:2 (1995), 477–9 (478). Another British writer to take up the debate is A. Deighton, 'The Cold War in Europe, 1945–1947: Three Approaches', in N. Woods (ed.), *Explaining International Relations Since 1945* (Oxford, Oxford University Press, 1997), pp. 81–97 (p. 89).

49 Becher and Trowler, *Academic Tribes and Territories*.

50 D. Kavanagh, 'Why Political Science Needs History', *Political Studies*, 39 (1991), pp. 479–95.

51 P. Burke, *History and Social Theory* (Cambridge, Polity Press, 2001), p. 23; see also pp. 28–9.

52 E. H. Carr, *What is History?* (Harmondsworth, Penguin, 1990), p. 63.

of wars and revolutions, from which flows more historical literature by scholars presumably subscribing to that particular understanding of the term.
'History', he concluded, 'is concerned with the relation between the unique and
the general. As a historian, you can no more separate them, or give precedence
to one over the other, than you can separate fact and interpretation.'[53] Thus,
wrote Frankel, 'Both the historical and the theoretical approaches are important. Only improved theory can lead to better historical monographs employing similar frameworks which would make comparisons possible; *only such
monographs can serve as a sound basis for checking, refining and improving
theory.*'[54]

According to this line of argument, history for all intents and purposes *is* a
form of social theory. We may not be aware, we may not want to be aware and
we may not care what the theory is that underpins historical work, but it is significant that writing history involves choices: choices about what to study, choices
about how to study it, choices about where to publish, choices about what type of
study to write, and choices about where to start and stop stories about the past.
All of these intimately affect what interpretations are placed on events and which
stories are told about the past. Historical interpretation is, therefore, implicated
with the theory historians possess about how to appropriate the past.

By the same token, political scientists frequently rely on history in their
efforts to construct models or theories about how the world works. Three examples will serve to support this contention. First, the literature on British foreign
policy-making. There is a long record of scholars and decision-makers attempting to explain the workings of foreign policy machinery in Britain, from David
Vital's 1971 *The Making of British Foreign Policy,*[55] to Anthony Forster and
Alasdair Blair's *The Making of Britain's European Foreign Policy*, published
in 2002.[56] The supporting evidence used in the construction of these texts highlights the interconnectedness between history and political science that Frankel
had earlier referred to in a comparative analysis of foreign policy-making
machines. Forster and Blair state that although of a political science orientation, their book is a contribution to the debates among historians about 'the

---

53 *Ibid.*, p. 65.
54 J. Frankel, *The Making of Foreign Policy: An Analysis of Decision Making* (Oxford, Oxford
    University Press, 1968), preface p. 7. My emphasis.
55 D. Vital, *The Making of British Foreign Policy* (London, George Allen and Unwin, 1971).
56 A. Forster and A. Blair, *The Making of Britain's European Foreign Policy* (London, Pearson,
    2002). See also R. E. Jones, *The Changing Structure of British Foreign Policy* (London, Longman,
    1974); J. Barber, *Who Makes British Foreign Policy?* (Milton Keynes, The Open University Press,
    1976); W. Wallace, *The Foreign Policy Process in Britain*, 2nd edn (London, Royal Institute of
    International Affairs, 1977); Sanders, *Losing an Empire, Finding a Role*; Sir J. Cable, 'Foreign
    Policy Making, Planning or Reflex?', *Diplomacy and Statecraft*, 3:3 (1992), 357–81 and J. Coles,
    The Making of Foreign Policy: A Certain Idea of Britain (London, John Murray, 2000), pp. 83–106.

reluctance of successive British governments to commit to Europe'. In return, they contextualise their study by opening with a chapter entitled 'British European policy in historical perspective'.[57]

The second example comes from another field of political science, civil–military relations. There, one of the core texts still used by writers is Samuel Huntington's *The Soldier and the State*.[58] Writing shortly after the Second World War, he aimed to develop 'a theory of civil–military relations' based on a reading of the experiences of Germany and Japan from the nineteenth century. His theory that the governance of states should entail careful separation between the political and military spheres of influence is a function of his interpretation that these countries shared unhappy experiences as a result of too much military input to political decision-making in the years he studied. There is little antagonism here between political science and history; instead they are locked in a mutually reinforcing relationship. For this reason, surmises Jeffry Checkel, 'solid empirical work is often a prerequisite for theory building'.[59]

The use by political scientists of a broader historical base may, indeed, help prevent him or her from falling victim to the problem of 'selection bias' when it comes to explaining how individuals, governments and states act in the international system. David Collier states that 'selection bias' occurs when 'the *non*random selection of cases results in inferences, based on the resulting sample, that are not statistically representative'.[60] Using Collier's definition, Ian Lustick explains the pitfalls of using history uncritically:

> On most periods and themes of interest available accounts differ, not only substantively but also with respect to the implicit theories and conceptual frameworks used to establish salience or produce commonsensical explanations. Un-selfconscious use of historical monographs thus easily results in selection bias ... [R]esponsible techniques for using historical sources are available, but they require understanding of the extent to which patterns within historiography, rather than 'History', must be the direct focus of investigation and explanation.[61]

Theories and models are constructed, refined, challenged and resurrected over time in response to many factors. Developments in historical interpretation have a key role to play in this process, first of all because they form the basis for our view of what has happened in the past, and therefore about how we view the world in which we live today, and secondly because of the transmission of ideas

---

57 Forster and Blair, *The Making of Britain's European Foreign Policy*, p. 1 and Chapter 1.
58 S. P. Huntington, *The Soldier and the State: The Theory and Politics of Civil–Military Relations* (London, The Belknap Press of Harvard University Press, 1998).
59 J. T. Checkel, 'Social Construction and European Integration', in Christiansen, Jørgensen and Wiener (eds), *The Social Construction of Europe*, pp. 50–64, (p. 61).
60 Quoted in Lustick, 'History, Historiography, and Political Science', p. 606. Emphasis in original.
61 *Ibid.*, p. 605.

around academic disciplines: 'increasingly we accept as reasonable that historians are always active in the creation of the past through model-building'.[62]
Lustick's observation that political scientists need to be aware of competing
historical accounts when they construct their theories taps into the idea that the
explanatory and predictive powers of models will surely be increased the bigger
sample of data they use, because they will be more representative.
Historiographic studies can thus be of use to political scientists because they offer
them a ready source of data on the major forces at work in the construction of
texts about the past that can be used to test and refine existing models.

Modelling the workings of Whitehall's foreign policy-making machinery
necessarily relies on the history of British foreign policy, and the writing of
British European policy is just one of the areas that political scientists will need
to explore in their efforts to explain the intricate web of relations between ministers, civil servants, committees, departments, interest and pressure groups and
non-governmental organisations, which all attempt to influence British foreign
policy in one direction or another. At the very least, political scientists need to be
aware that historians grapple with more than the problem of source deficiencies
alone. In writing history, they project their own personalities, politics and social
theories on to the past. That this is often unacknowledged is a severe problem,
but something historiographic studies should be able to bring to the fore.

The third example of the symbiosis between the two disciplines is to be
found in the work of Jacqueline Tratt, whose study of the Macmillan government's turn to Europe in 1960 is based on the archival record, but attempts
throughout to transgress the divide to political science. The opening to Chapter
2, for instance, contains analysis of the ramifications for policy of the relationship between 'the different perceptions and responses of government ministers
and officials to the European issue'. Later, at the start of the fifth chapter, she
argues that the government seems to have suffered from 'groupthink', a syndrome
'which impairs the ability of decision-makers to arrive, through the process of
rational debate, at the optimum solution'.[63] Here, political science theories are
being used to inform analysis of the historical material, and political scientists
could usefully refer to Tratt's account to inform their modelling of the British
foreign – and especially European – policy process.

The fourth reason why it is valuable to write historiography takes further
the need to avoid selection bias, and concerns policy-makers' use of history to
inform their decisions. Richard Melanson has observed that the relationship
between historians and policy-makers is not necessarily a happy one, where it is

---

62 Munslow, *Deconstructing History*, p. 172.
63 J. Tratt, *The Macmillan Government and Europe: A Study in the Process of Policy Development*
(Basingstoke, Macmillan, 1996), pp. 30 and 71–2.

possible to discover one at all. 'Those who write history and those who make
policy will probably remain locked in their reciprocal, but frustrating relationship'.[64] On the one hand, it has been argued that policy-makers should not use
history to inform their decisions because, as Harold Macmillan put it, 'history
does not repeat itself'.[65] Max Beloff concurred that 'the "lessons of history"
cannot be applied in any simple or mechanical fashion ... All one can hope to
have are suggestions and intimations that set the imagination working.'[66] Evans
likewise judges that 'Time and again history has proved a very bad predictor of
future events. This is because history never repeats itself; nothing in human society, the main concern of the historian, ever happens twice under exactly the same
conditions or in exactly the same way.'[67]

On the other hand, as we saw in the introduction, the extent to which policy-
makers, like the rest of society, regularly use history in support of their ideologies should not be overlooked. This can be illustrated by referring to the work of
Dan Reiter and to the co-authored work of Richard Neustadt and Ernest May.
Examining quantitative data on the alliance politics of what he labels 'minor
powers' in the twentieth century, and without wishing to go into too much detail,
the central claim of Reiter's piece is that 'states make alliance policy in accordance with lessons drawn from formative historical experiences'.[68] Neustadt
and May, both of whom have informed American foreign policy-making
in the post-war era,[69] found that a host of American Presidents and their
senior policy advisers have regularly used history systematically, if inappropri-
ately, to draw 'fuzzy analogies' about current problems. A way round this,
they argue, is for policy-makers to be 'taught' to use history as an analytical
framework within which to develop more appropriate responses to foreign and
domestic problems.[70] These are two of the most striking examples drawn from a
corpus of literature on American foreign relations that is littered with references
to the bearing that different interpretations of history have had on Washington

---

64 Melanson, *Writing History*, p. 226.
65 Quoted in R. Lamb, *The Macmillan Years 1957–1963: The Emerging Truth* (London, John Murray,
    1995), p. 65.
66 M. Beloff, *An Historian in the Twentieth Century: Chapters in Intellectual Autobiography*
    (London, Yale University Press, 1992), p. 129.
67 Evans, *In Defence of History*, p. 59. The Italian philosopher of history, Benedetto Croce, was of
    the same mind, see White, *Metahistory*, pp. 398–404.
68 D. Reiter, 'Learning, Realism and Alliances: The Weight of the Shadow of the Past', *World
    Politics*, 46:4 (1994), 490–526 (490).
69 Neustadt was a junior aide to President Truman at the start of the Korean War, later becoming a
    consultant to Presidents Kennedy and Johnson. A decade younger than Neustadt, May was a histo-
    rian for the Joint Chiefs of Staff during the Korean War. He later worked for the Pentagon in
    Johnson's time and oversaw a review of the strategic arms race between the superpowers.
70 R. C. Neustadt and E. R. May, *Thinking in Time: The Uses of History for Decision-Makers* (New
    York, The Free Press, 1986), pp. 32–3.

policy-makers.[71] For these writers, the direct historical experiences of policy-makers and the prevailing wisdom about events within the particular administration they head combine to create a simple yet potent historical model that they turn to when they want to find precedents to inform contemporary policy choices.

There have been few British studies to replicate Neustadt and May's.[72] Then again, there is considerable evidence to suggest that British policy-makers have used crude models of history to inform foreign policy decision-making. Christopher Lord argues that 'Decision-makers will tend to appraise new situations in the light of lessons drawn from previous experiences'.[73] Sanders remarks that since the 1930s they have often turned to a 'simplified' structural-realist model to inform their understanding of international affairs.[74] He notes as an example the lesson learnt by Anthony Eden's generation about the need after 1945 'to avoid repeating the errors of "appeasement"' which has manifested itself in the tendency, persistent to the present day, to compare troublesome heads of state with dictators.[75]

Sanders's observation about the psychological impact of the Second World War on the British attitude to 'dictators' brings to mind other examples. Ernest Bevin, Labour Foreign Secretary 1945–51, memorably likened the Soviet Foreign Minister (Vyacheslav Molotov) to Adolf Hitler during the London Council of Foreign Ministers in September 1945.[76] The long shadow cast by Hitler over British politics in the twentieth century, particularly prominent in the country's 'anti-German' sentiment, is also evident in the unfortunate comment made about the EU by the then Conservative government minister Nicholas Ridley in July 1990: 'I'm not against giving up sovereignty in principle, but not to this lot. You might just as well give it up to Adolf Hitler.'[77] Times of crisis in

---

71 Bruce Kuklick drew conclusions about policy-makers' uses of history in *American Policy and the Division of Germany: The Clash with Russia over Reparations* (London, Cornell University Press, 1972). See also Melanson, *Writing History*, pp. 4–6.

72 The nearest in terms of weight of evidence and conclusions are to be found in M. Smith, S. Smith and B. White (eds), *British Foreign Policy: Tradition, Change and Transformation* (London, Hyman, 1988), especially the chapters by C. Hill, 'The Historical Background: Past and Present in British Foreign Policy', pp. 24–49 and R. Little, 'The Study of British Foreign Policy', pp. 245–59. See also C. Lord, *British Entry to the European Community under the Heath Government of 1970–4* (Aldershot, Gower, 1985), pp. 3–8 and Z. Steiner, 'The Historian and the Foreign Office', in C. Hill, and P. Beshoff (eds), *Two Worlds of International Relations: Academics, Practitioners and the Trade in Ideas* (London, Routledge, 1994), pp. 45–9.

73 Lord, *British Entry to the European Community*, p. 7.

74 Sanders, *Losing an Empire, Finding a Role* p. 265.

75 *Ibid.*, p. 276. See also Steiner, 'The Historian and the Foreign Office', pp. 48–9.

76 A. Bullock, *Ernest Bevin: Foreign Secretary* (London, Heinemann, 1983), pp. 132–4. Bevin said Molotov's actions in refusing to admit France to the Council made him 'the nearest thing to the Hitler theory I have ever heard', cited in F. Williams, *Ernest Bevin: Portrait of a Great Englishman* (London, Hutchinson, 1952), p. 253.

77 Quoted in C. Pilkington, *Britain in the European Union Today*, 2nd edn (Manchester, Manchester University Press, 2001), p. 80.

the international system seem to sharpen the propensity for leaders to seek simplified historical analogies, not least for propaganda reasons and to swing public opinion behind the cause they are pushing.

For another example of the weight of history bearing on the present, one might note British politicians' paranoia about the psychological ramifications of devaluation. Possession of a relatively strong currency, especially an international reserve currency such as the dollar or, formerly, the pound sterling, has tended to be equated with a country's standing in the international hierarchy of states. Add this to the perception, expressed by one of Harold Wilson's economic advisers shortly before the 1967 devaluation, that determining the value of one's currency is one of the prime expressions of 'complete self-government',[78] and it can be seen how devaluation has commonly been associated with political and economic weakness or a fall from grace within the system.

Wilson's resistance to devaluation, eventually forced upon him by economic troubles in 1967, was, one biographer observed, an 'article of faith' traceable back to his traumatic days as President of the Board of Trade during the 1947–49 sterling crisis.[79] Note also the furore surrounding 'Black Wednesday' in September 1992, when sterling was forced out of the Exchange Rate Mechanism (ERM) and Chancellor Norman Lamont out of his job. Finally, in the wake of the launch of the euro, the eurosceptics who implied that a weak euro was a sign that the longer-term integration project was in jeopardy leapt on every shift downward it made against the pound as evidence that it was not a credible currency.

The historiography of Britain's approach to Europe in the 1950s also suggests that the immediate past, particularly Britain's wartime experience, significantly influenced London's decision to remain aloof from the efforts to found the ECSC and the EEC, so soon after the failure of the EDC. In discussions about whether or not to join in Monnet's schemes for uniting Europe, it has been found that key policy-makers in London were hesitant about joining supranational integration not just for dogmatic or ideological reasons; they were concerned about the troubled past of potential partners, especially the French. In short, memories of wartime events loomed large in their thinking: why throw in Britain's lot with countries that had so recently been overrun in the Second World War? 'The legacy of 1940', Geoffrey Warner has written, 'certainly died hard.'[80]

An equally prominent doubt in Whitehall, about whether there was sufficient political will on the Continent to succeed, turned on whether the Six could

78 Lord Kaldor, quoted in R. Dahrendorf, *On Britain* (London, British Broadcasting Corporation, 1982), p. 129.
79 A. Morgan, *Harold Wilson* (London, Pluto, 1992), p. 266.
80 G. Warner, 'The Reconstruction and Defence of Western Europe after 1945', in N. Waites (ed.), *Troubled Neighbours: Franco-British Relations in the Twentieth Century* (London, Weidenfeld and Nicolson, 1971), pp. 259–92 (p. 276).

unite on economic grounds given the historical protectionism of the French.[81] Examination of the official record has reinforced the idea that British policy-makers are no different from their American counterparts in mentally moulding historical events into a model of how the world works and how states and individuals work within it.[82]

Yet the world policy-makers perceive is not the same as the world as it actually exists. Foreign policy is developed and projected in a complex domestic and international environment in which 'perception matters as much as reality'.[83] 'Images', remarked Avi Shlaim, 'are a crucial component of the belief system and, therefore, have a decisive effect on foreign policy since decision-makers act in accordance with their perception of reality, not reality itself.'[84] The problems of uncovering the 'objective reality' of foreign policy are as insurmountable for the policy-maker as they are for the scholar.[85] The former's reaction to events will, John Mearsheimer explains, always be 'shaped by [his or her] implicit preference for one theory of international relations over another'.[86] Here he refers to international relations theory, rather than history, but the implications are the same. To corrupt a phrase from Alexander Wendt, the world is

81 E. Barker, *Britain in a Divided Europe 1945–1970* (London, Weidenfeld and Nicolson, 1971), p. 151; M. Charlton, *The Price of Victory* (London, BBC, 1983), p. 165; R. Denman, *Missed Chances: Britain and Europe in the Twentieth Century* (London, Cassell, 1996), p. 194; George, *An Awkward Partner*, p. 26; I. Gilmour and M. Garnett, *Whatever Happened to the Tories: The Conservative Party Since 1945* (London, Fourth Estate, 1997), p. 99; F. S. Northedge, *British Foreign Policy: The Process of Readjustment 1945–1961* (London, George Allen and Unwin, 1961), p. 166; A. Sked and C. Cook, *Post-War Britain: A Political History*, 4th edn (London, Penguin, 1993), p. 148.

82 See for example S. Burgess and G. Edwards, 'The Six Plus One: British Policy-Making and the Question of European Economic Integration, 1955', *International Affairs*, 64:3 (1988), 393–413 (396–7); W. Kaiser, *Using Europe, Abusing the Europeans: Britain and European Integration 1945–63* (Basingstoke, Macmillan, 1996), p. 42; R. Lamb, *The Failure of the Eden Government* (London, Sidgwick and Jackson, 1987), p. 68; Ludlow, *Dealing with Britain*, p. 19; J. Turner, *Macmillan* (London, Longman, 1994), p. 97; J. W. Young, '"The Parting of Ways"? Britain, the Messina Conference and the Spaak Committee, June–December 1955', in M. Dockrill and J. W. Young (eds), *British Foreign Policy, 1945–56* (Basingstoke, Macmillan, 1989), pp. 197–224 (p. 199).

83 D. Reynolds, *Britannia Overruled: British Policy and World Power in the Twentieth Century* (London, Longman, 1991), p. 253.

84 A. Shlaim, 'The Foreign Secretary and the Making of Foreign Policy', in A. Shlaim, P. Jones and K. Sainsbury (eds), *British Foreign Secretaries Since 1945* (London, David & Charles, 1977), pp. 13–26 (p. 16).

85 J. E. Dougherty and R. L. Pfaltzgraff, *Decision Making Theories: Contending Theories on International Relations* (New York, Harper and Row, 1990), p. 458. For a British focus on the problems of what Michael Smith calls the 'control of policy in complex settings' see S. Smith and M. Smith, 'The Analytical Background, Approaches to the Study of Foreign Policy', in Smith, Smith and White (eds), *British Foreign Policy*, pp. 3–23.

86 J. J. Mearsheimer, 'Back to the Future: Instability in Europe after the Cold War', *International Security*, 15:1 (1990), 5–56 (9).

what states and, by association, policy-makers make of it, and history too is what they make of it.[87]

What are the chances, then, that policy-makers can be taught to use history more effectively, as Neustadt and May suggest they might? The pessimistic answer is 'not great'. Hill argues that '[T]he relationship between academics and policy practitioners has become steadily more significant over the course of this century.'[88] Unlike what happens in America, however, where academics regularly contribute to the policy debate, the British system of government is less porous in terms of academics coming and going from Whitehall. Or at least that is how it looks.

Washington's policy-making machinery may be more obviously infiltrated by scholars than Whitehall's, but there is a growing band of academics called on by the government to advise on all sorts of issues, from foreign and defence policy (as in the Strategic Defence Review 1997–98), to agriculture, transport and economics. That many of the academics are drawn from the nexus of universities in London and from Oxford and Cambridge is significant, because it highlights the fact that ease of access to the capital can be important in terms of selecting who advises policy-makers when. It may also play a part in determining who the capital's broadcast media contact to act as specialists on news programmes dealing with breaking stories of national and international significance. Although travel concerns and speed of response are surely not the only or the most important factors in determining which academics populate our radio waves and television pictures, being London-based surely helps one get noticed by politicians and the media. The British system of government may not, then, be quite as open to influence as the American, but there is an establishment tradition whereby academics do make themselves heard in Whitehall, both formally through policy advice and informally through the media.

Offering policy advice is one thing, however, using written academic tracts is quite another, and it appears unlikely that policy-makers will develop the habit of regularly using academic studies to frame policy choices. Politicians are chronically constrained by time and resources, often preferring official histories written hastily in response to particular problems, rather than dense academic tracts which would develop their thinking along the lines suggested by Neustadt and May; hence the widespread scepticism that academic perspectives will ever feature highly in political thinking.[89] Foreign policy-makers are particularly

87 A. Wendt, 'Anarchy is What States Make of It: The Social Construction of Power Politics', *International Organization*, 46:2 (1992), 391–425. See also N. Onuf, *World of our Making* (Columbia, University of South Carolina Press, 1989).

88 Christopher Hill, 'Academic International Relations: The Siren Song of Policy Relevance', in Hill and Beshoff (eds), *Two Worlds of International Relations*, pp. 3–25, p. 3.

89 For an expression of this view see Steiner, 'The Historian and the Foreign Office', pp. 45–8.

overloaded in terms of paperwork, travel and meetings, and it appears increasingly likely that, if current trends continue, Douglas Hurd's assessment of new
Foreign Secretaries only being able to 'alter the compass [of British foreign
policy] by 'a few degrees' will hold in the future.[90]

Until further research is carried out into British policy-makers' uses of
history, and unless academics wish to compromise the intellectual content of their
studies to appeal to policy-makers (which is unlikely), there are only limited
possibilities for developing closer links between the historical and political
communities in Britain. However, as Blair's reference in November 2001 to the
'missed opportunities' in British European policy shows, the history of British
European policy is beginning to arouse attention in elite circles and among the
British population at large.

It can therefore be argued that for these four reasons, which operate on
both the theoretical and the empirical levels, historiography is a useful way of
accessing the past, because it helps us to refine our understanding of what it
means to write and use history. Having examined the rationale for writing the
historiography of Britain's relations with Europe, it is now appropriate to
explore in greater depth the 'schools' approach to explaining historiographical
evolution.

Constructing schools of writing

Cold War historiography provides a useful reference point for those wishing to
understand what is being attempted in this book, which explores the writing of
British European policy through the taxonomy of historiographic evolution set
out by writers such as John Lewis Gaddis in books and in journals such as
Diplomatic History. Gaddis found that Cold War historiography had been driven
by successive waves of writing, the interpretations of which have been guided by
a combination of factors: changes in the international system, changes in the
prevailing political climate of opinion within America and, not least, the examination of newly declassified sources.

It is not appropriate to explain the dynamics of Gaddis's explanation for the
key trends in Cold War historiography in their entirety; it is his central claim and
the way he presented it that interests us here. Against an 'orthodox' body of writing that was generally supportive of American foreign policy, and disparaging
about Soviet foreign policy, after 1945, there emerged a 'revisionist' body of writing that, Bullock noted, highlighted the 'tendency in American historiography in
the 1960s and early 1970s to rewrite the history of the Cold War and shift blame

---

90 Quoted in K. Theakston, 'The Changing Role of the Foreign Secretary', in K. Theakston (ed.),
British Foreign Secretaries Since 1974 (London, Frank Cass, forthcoming).

for it onto the USA'.[91] In large measure this reappraisal of American policy was a reaction to the Vietnam War, which shocked a generation out of its post-war centre-right apathy and led to the re-emergence of left-wing opinion. This 'New Left' group of writers then looked back on earlier American foreign policy and reinterpreted it more critically than had their predecessors, arguing that Russia was not the only country responsible for the rise of Cold War tensions after the Second World War. The United States, they asserted, had been pursuing its own brand of 'imperialism'.[92]

In the 1980s, Gaddis proposed a synthesis of the two interpretations, 'post-revisionism', which balanced out the apportionment of blame for the origins of the Cold War between American and Russia. His account has since been challenged by what he labels 'corporatist', 'international', 'cultural' and 'post-modernist' historians.[93] This, albeit simplified, overview of Gaddis's model of Cold War historiography serves as a useful tool for explaining historiographical evolution. That is why it has been adopted in this study and amended to take account of current directions in the philosophy of history.

Schools as knowledge communities

Of the many issues that arise from the historiography of the origins and development of the Cold War, two are significant in the context of this study: the grouping of writers into schools and the labels attached to these schools. Turning first to the grouping of writers in schools, this is not universally recognised as a device for explaining historiographical progression. The major dissenting voice in America has been that of Warren Kimball, who argues that for Gaddis to 'lump' writers together in schools 'suggests that he sees a high degree of unity' among them, a unity unwarranted judging by the degree to which writers in the schools he identifies, especially the revisionists, disagree with each other on certain key points.[94] Is the oversimplification that modelling entails not *too* artificial, he asks,

91 A. Bullock, definition of 'revisionism' in Bullock and Stallybrass (eds), *The Fontana Dictionary of Modern Thought*, p. 542.

92 Gaddis, 'The Emerging Post-Revisionist Synthesis'. For more on the politics of revisionism see G. Smith, '"Harry, We Hardly Know You": Revisionism, Politics and Diplomacy, 1945–54', *American Political Science Review*, 70 (1976), 560–82 and Thompson, *What Happened to History?*, pp. 44–7.

93 Gaddis, *Now We Know*, pp. 281–95; J. L. Gaddis, 'Corporatism: A Skeptical View', *Diplomatic History*, 10:4 (1986), 356–62; M. J. Hogan, 'Corporatism: A Positive Appraisal', *Diplomatic History*, 10:4 (1986), 363–72. See also M. J. Hogan, *A Cross of Iron: Harry S. Truman and the Origins of the National Security State, 1945–1954* (Cambridge, Cambridge University Press, 1998) and D. S. Painter, *Private Power and Public Policy: Multinational Oil Corporations and US Foreign Policy 1941–1954* (London, I. B. Tauris, 1986).

94 L. C. Gardner, L. S. Kaplan, W. F. Kimball, and B. R. Kuniholm, 'Responses to John Lewis Gaddis', *Diplomatic History*, 7:3 (1983), 191–204 (198).

when it means putting writers who quite plainly disagree with each other on vital issues in the same school? Are not historical works so personal to the writer in terms of evidence, organisation, nuance and subtlety of interpretation that to group them together is to bring unwarranted cleanness to this field of inquiry?

Many more writers on Cold War historiography would argue not. Consequently, the term 'school' is generally accepted in Cold War historiography to denote a body of writers that, allowing for variations on specifics, adhere to the same or similar interpretation of American foreign policy and the origins of the Cold War.[95]

Part of the confusion about whether or not it is appropriate to attach the term 'school' to the various waves of writing on a given subject stems from the fact that there is no clearly articulated definition of what it means to belong to a 'school'. The term is used synonymously with words such as 'approach' and 'understanding' to convey the idea that writers come from the same or similar intellectual tradition in terms of their field of study, methods and/or interpretations.[96] Outside the realms of Cold War historiography, Hayden White uses the label to distinguish between different strands of historical writing in the nineteenth century and competing approaches to psychology in the post-war era;[97] Ernst Haas applies the term to the three sub-divisions that co-exist within the constructivist approach to the study of international relations;[98] and Jeffrey Checkel contrasts the rationalist and social constructivist 'schools' of research into European integration.[99]

Martin Hollis and Steve Smith have described the contending theories within international relations as 'schools', remarking that 'International Relations at the start of the 1990s is ... a subject in dispute. There is no dominant theory. Instead, there are several schools, each with its own set of assumptions and theories.'[100] Derek Urwin has used the term to describe the competing theoretical approaches to European integration.[101] Looking back to ancient history, Moses

95 See Gaddis, 'The Emerging Post-Revisionist Synthesis', p. 171; J. S. Walker, 'Historians and Cold War Origins, The New Consensus', in G. K. Haines and J. S. Walker (eds), *American Foreign Relations: A Historiographical Review* (London, Francis Pinter, 1981), pp. 207–36; R. U. Gramer, 'On Poststructuralisms, Revisionisms, and Cold Wars', *Diplomatic History*, 19:3 (1995), 515–24; Melanson, *Writing History and Making Policy*.

96 Even in the same text these terms can be interchanged. See for instance Gramer, 'On Poststructuralisms', pp. 517–19; Melanson, *Writing History*, p. 7; J. A. Combs, 'Review Essay: Norman Graebner and the Realist View of American Diplomatic History', *Diplomatic History*, 11:3 (1987), 251–64 (253).

97 White, *Metahistory*, pp. 427 and 431.

98 E. B. Haas, 'Does Constructivism Subsume Neo-Functionalism?', in Christiansen, Jørgensen and Wiener (eds), *The Social Construction of Europe*, pp. 22–31 (p. 26).

99 Checkel, 'Social Construction and European Integration', p. 61.

100 Hollis and Smith, *Explaining and Understanding International Relations*, p. 38.

101 D. Urwin, review, 'The Origins and Development of the European Union 1945–95: A History of European Integration. By M. J. Dedman', *Journal of Common Market Studies*, 35:1 (1997), 170.

Finley separated the different sides of the scholarly debate over Thucydides' method into 'schools'.[102] R. G. Collingwood saw the competing views of the Stoics and the Epicureans on ethics as competing 'schools' and the Enlightenment as encompassing a 'school' aiming 'to secularise every department of human life and thought'.[103] In his work on the philosophy of the natural sciences, Thomas Kuhn employs the term in a slightly different way, referring to 'schools' as precursors to the emergence of a dominant 'paradigm' that grips a field of study.[104]

To arrive at its definition of what constitutes a school, I have drawn in this book on Willie Thompson's opinion that schools are built around their own 'apparatus of academic personnel, textbooks, journals and conferences' and that they are founded on 'the kind of evidence taken account of and the methodological application preferred by their adherents'.[105] This fits nicely alongside the argument that members of schools 'see' the world in the same way, even if in terms of interpreting it they do not necessarily agree with their colleagues in a given school on everything. Furthermore, scholars regularly say who they do not agree with on fundamentals, making the elucidation of schools a function of what members say they are *not* as much as a function of what they *are*.

The apparatus to which Thompson refers has rarely before been the subject of scrutiny on its own,[106] but historiography is an ideal forum to begin this process. As Karl Popper notes, historiography is theory about theory, in other words theory about the way in which theories about the past grow and evolve.[107] What also comes through in the above quotations is that, especially in history, placing writers in schools tends to be a retrospective process. It tends to be historiographers such as Gaddis, looking back, who identify the boundaries between schools. Historians at the time might have been aware that they wrote in opposition to one or another writer, but more often than not historians see methodological and epistemological self-criticism as an unpalatable or even pointless distraction from writing history. It is necessary to undertake a historiography of British European policy in the hope that it will enable a deeper understanding of what it means to practise and write international history, for, as Georg Iggers puts

102 See his introductory remarks to Thucydides, *History of the Peloponnesian War*, 2nd edn (London, Guild, 1993), p. 12.

103 R. G. Collingwood, *The Idea of History* (Oxford, Oxford University Press, 1961), pp. 36 and 76.

104 Kuhn, *The Structure of Scientific Revolutions*, p. 163.

105 Thompson, *What Happened to History?*, p. 2.

106 P. J. Marshall, 'The First British Empire', in Winks (ed.), *Historiography*, pp. 43–53 (pp. 44 and 48) identifies an 'Imperial School' within American historiography of the British Empire but does not have the room in a short article to dwell at length on its construction. This task is left to S. Foster, 'British North America in the Seventeenth and Eighteenth Centuries', in Winks (ed.), *Historiography*, pp. 73–92 (pp. 74–5).

107 K. R. Popper, *Objective Knowledge: An Evolutionary Approach* (Oxford, Oxford University Press, 1972), p. 286.

it: 'every historical account is a construct, but a construct arising from a dialogue between the historian and the past, one that does not occur in a vacuum but within a community of inquiring minds who share criteria of plausibility'.[108]

The significance of labels

The second issue that needs further analysis here is that of the terminology employed in this book. Following the lexicon, the vocabulary, of Cold War historiography, the schools of writing on Britain and Europe identified below are labelled 'orthodox', 'revisionist' and 'post-revisionist'. It is important to note now that the labels denote chronological progression and do not carry the heavy political or ideological connotations that they do in Cold War scholarship.

'Revisionism' is a term that carries a peculiarly wide array of meanings. The first is 'a critical reinterpretation of Marxist theories and/or doctrinal deviation from the official ideological position among Communist factions, parties and states'. The second operates in the context of the inter-war years, when it was applied to 'the claims of countries such as Germany, Hungary and Bulgaria to the territories which they had lost in World War One'.[109] And in the wake of the much-publicised courtroom battle between Deborah Lipstadt and David Irving, 'revisionism' has now also come to be associated with the 'Holocaust revisionists' of the far right, who deny Hitler's role in the 'Final Solution', as well as the scale of that solution.[110]

In Cold War historiography the term carries left-wing connotations that, as far as one can establish, are not held to the same degree or as obviously by the writers explored in the revisionist chapter below. There, 'revisionist' refers to historians who, in the words of Chris Cook, 'overturn a generally accepted view of historical events in the light of new evidence and modified interpretation',[111] tapping into the oft-made observation that 'historians are constantly engaged in revision'.[112] Political persuasion seems to be far less of a factor than methodological persuasion in determining the timing and nature of the academic revision that has been occurring on the subject of Britain and Europe.

Having examined the methodology and terminology employed below, this is a convenient point at which to pause and reflect on the core argument that runs throughout this book, as a way into the detailed analysis that follows.

---

108 Iggers, *Historiography*, p. 145.
109 Bullock, definition in Bullock and Stallybrass (eds), *The Fontana Dictionary*, pp. 541–2. See also I. McLean, *The Oxford Concise Dictionary of Politics* (Oxford, Oxford University Press, 1996), p. 430.
110 For a discussion and critique of their views see Evans, *In Defence of History*, pp. 238–43 and for an account of the Lipstadt case see R. J. Evans, *Telling Lies About Hitler: The Holocaust, Hitler and the David Irving Trial* (London, Verso, 2002).
111 C. Cook, *A Dictionary of Historical Terms*, 3rd edn (Basingstoke, Macmillan, 1998), p. 310.
112 The words of Deborah Lipstadt, quoted in Evans, *In Defence of History*, p. 240.

Core argument

The central claim advanced in this book is that the historiography of British European policy can be grouped into three schools, identifiable by the sharply conflicting interpretations they place upon developments in European integration history: an orthodox school, a revisionist school and an emerging post-revisionist school. These schools, it is suggested, are socially constructed, that is, driven by different communities of individuals who look at the world in different ways, who have opposing agendas and who cite different sources in support of their respective cases.

It is significant that the various waves of writing identified below are termed 'schools', because this takes the study further than all previous historiographical treatment of this literature, and it is therefore important to probe here why that choice has been made. Just as Warren Kimball argued in relation to Cold War historiography that it was misguided to identify schools because they necessarily overlook or play down the differences between writers in the same school, it has also been argued that historians in Britain cannot be grouped into schools. Of the three responses to a draft article that attempted something similar to what has now been moulded into this book, one stood out because it was so sceptical of the idea of building the schools along the lines suggested below. The reader said that 'Miriam Camps alone proves the article's own methodology wrong: proper historical research on British European policy cannot be classified into schools, at least not in the categories the author suggests.'[113] An anonymous reader on an early draft of this manuscript concurred: 'treatments of postwar British approaches to European integration do not lend themselves to being ordered into "schools" in the same way that has happened on US works on the Cold War'; to do so is an exercise in 'creating order out of what is essentially haphazard'.[114]

It would have been convenient had it not been possible to delineate any schools. In that situation, one could have drawn conclusions about the conflicting drivers of historiography processes in Britain and America and trumpeted the interpretative eclecticism of British historians, their methodological experimentalism and their ability to represent the past in a bewildering number of ways. One could go on to explain the differing historiographical trends between the countries in the context of sharply differing political and cultural experiences since 1945. First, one might have pointed to the absence in Britain of an equivalent trauma to the Vietnam War, which so influenced the social, political and historical outlook of an entire generation that nothing less than a 'new version of the

---

113 Anonymous referee's report on draft article, received 11 October 1999.
114 Anonymous reader's report on draft manuscript, received 16 July 2002.

American past was created'.[115] The relationship between Britain and Europe might be contentious, but it generates far less antagonism and passion than does the Vietnam War in America. Scholarly debates over Britain's relationship with the Continent have not to date impelled 'normally placid professors to behave like gladiators at scholarly meetings', as Gaddis reports Vietnam regularly did across the Atlantic.[116]

The absence of polarisation between left and right on the question of Europe might have been the second explanation for why there are no distinct schools of writing on Britain and Europe. What Stephen George describes as a 'degree of continuity across changes in office'[117] is reflected in the writing on British foreign policy that draws attention to the notion of consensus between the main parties in government since 1945. 'Consensus', Dennis Kavanagh and Peter Morris note, 'does not mean absence of conflict' between parties. 'It is more appropriate to think of it as *a set of parameters which bounded the set of policy options regarded by senior politicians and civil servants*'.[118]

Leonard Tivey is of the same mind. Despite the consensus, he says, 'party rivalry and bitter argument flourished', yet from 1945–74 the main parties of government in Britain shared 'a set of attitudes' towards seven key issues, amongst them foreign policy and defence.[119] Others who share this opinion include Shlaim, who writes that 'disagreement on foreign policy issues has tended to be on emphasis, timing and detail, and has not extended to the main principles')[120] and John Saville, who argues 'Tradition and continuity have been the remarkable characteristics of British political life in general throughout the

115 Thompson, *What Happened to History?*, p. 45.
116 Gaddis, 'The Emerging Post-Revisionist Synthesis', p. 171. For more examples see Becher and Trowler, *Academic Tribes and Territories*, pp. 126–7.
117 George, *Politics and Policy*, p. 112. See also George, *An Awkward Partner*, pp. 5–41; C. Lord, 'Sovereign or Confused? The "Great Debate" About British Entry to the European Community 20 Years On', *Journal of Common Market Studies*, 30:4 (1992), 419–36 and A. J. Nicholls, 'Britain and the EC: The Historical Background', in S. Bulmer, S. George and A. Scott (eds), *The UK and EC Membership Evaluated* (London, Pinter, 1992), pp. 3–9.
118 D. Kavanagh and P. Morris, *Consensus Politics From Attlee to Major*, 2nd edn (Oxford, Blackwell, 1994), p. 13. Emphasis in original. See also B. Pimlott, *Frustrate Their Knavish Tricks: Writings on Biography, History and Politics* (London, HarperCollins, 1994), p. 232; R. H. Ullman, 'America, Britain, and the Soviet Threat in Historical and Present Perspective', in W. R. Louis and H. Bull (eds), *The Special Relationship: Anglo-American Relations Since 1945* (Oxford, Clarendon Press, 1989), pp. 103–14 (pp. 104–5).
119 Those issues were firstly, support for foreign and defence policies that put Britain at the heart of NATO; second, support in the 1950s and 1960s for independence for most colonies; third, support for Keynesian economic management; fourth, support for a mixed economy; fifth, the maintenance of a range of social welfare services; sixth, the development of systems of town planning and regional economic subsidies; and finally, the continuation of agricultural subsidies: L. Tivey, *Interpretations of British Politics: The Image and the System* (Hemel Hempstead, Harvester-Wheatsheaf, 1988), p. 118.
120 Shlaim, 'The Foreign Secretary', p. 26.

twentieth century ... No department of State has illustrated the process of continuity in more impressive fashion than the Foreign Office after 1945.'[121]

Paul Kennedy puts this cross-party agreement down to economic decline. Britain's economic troubles have, he said, 'overshadowed, ominously, continuously, restrictively, almost every consideration of the country's external role and have thus been the greatest influence of all in its decline as a major power'.[122] Michael Clarke, meanwhile, argues that foreign policy is 'above' the comings and goings of electoral politicking and party political machinations. 'Ideology is always difficult to translate into action, and foreign policy is an area which time and again blunts ideological fervour in favour of a more cautious pragmatism.'[123] At least until 1961, concludes Guy de Carmoy, 'foreign policy was to a large extent bipartisan, whether it was a question of relations with the super powers, the Commonwealth or western Europe.'[124]

A further explanation might be found in the policy process itself:

> It is a paradox of the job that the very tools Foreign Secretaries rely on – their civil servants and Whitehall's planning machinery – to help them navigate Britain's path through a forever changing, fluid and uncertain international environment, generate almost insuperable constraints upon their ability to impose themselves in anything other than an ephemeral, short-term way.[125]

Jeremy Paxman adds that the narrow social and educational backgrounds of those who have run the country ('the Great and the Good'), which has been heavily biased towards Eton and Oxbridge, can be held responsible for 'the succession of consensus administrations which ruled Britain for thirty years after the war'.[126] The absence of an equivalent to Vietnam and the broad consensus in British foreign policy could, therefore, explain why there were no readily identifiable schools of writing on British European policy.

But schools of writing that place sharply contrasting interpretations on the key stages in British European policy *have* been found to exist – and some historians have even begun employing the terminology of orthodoxy and revisionism

121 J. Saville, *The Politics of Continuity: British Foreign Policy and the Labour Government 1945–46* (London, Verso, 1993), p. 12.

122 P. Kennedy, *The Realities Behind Diplomacy: Background Influences on British External Policy 1865–1980* (London, Fontana, 1985), p. 320.

123 M. Clarke, 'The Policy-Making Process', in Smith, Smith and White (eds), *British Foreign Policy*, pp. 71–95 (p. 84). Consensus has also been observed in the arena of British defence policy, see T. McGrew, 'Security and Order, The Military Dimension', in Smith, Smith and White (eds), *British Foreign Policy*, pp. 99–123 (p. 114). See also Little, 'The Study of British Foreign Policy', p. 245.

124 G. de Carmoy, 'Defence and Unity of Western Europe since 1958', in N. Waites (ed.), *Troubled Neighbours: Franco-British Relations in the Twentieth Century* (London, Weidenfeld and Nicolson, 1971), pp. 344–74 (p. 345). See also Pfaltzgraff, *Britain Faces Europe*, pp. 5–6 and 8.

125 O. J. Daddow, 'Does a Change of Foreign Secretary Make a Difference?', British Foreign Policy Network newsletter, http://foreign-policy.dsd.kcl.ac.uk/daddow.htm.

126 Paxman, *Friends in High Places*, preface, p. 11.

to set their works into historiographical context.[127] So it is worth dwelling briefly on why, in blatant contradiction to the opinion of the anonymous readers cited above, this should be the case.

The comments of the second reader can be dismissed fairly quickly. It is a matter of personal choice whether or not one believes that works of history can be worked into schools; some historians see the validity in this approach, some do not, and no doubt the arguments will continue in the future. The first reader makes more telling points, but predicates his or her judgement on too narrow a conception of history; hence the revealing choice of words. Camps's interpretation, he or she states, has not been based up on 'proper historical research', and so lies outside the field of professional or academic history. Presumably 'proper' historical research is Marwickian in nature and incorporates writing founded on the careful scrutiny of primary sources, as opposed to the 'instant history' penned by Camps. Schools of writing on Britain and Europe would, according to this opinion, revolve around the clashes between historians working in the field since the 1980s, those with access to the government documentation in the PRO, to the Conservative and Labour Party archives, to private papers and so on.

The question of what should be classed 'proper' history is, however, a highly subjective one. Camps's work would not live up to the professional standards that govern the production of history in academic history departments, for the very reason that her interpretation was not predicated upon primary sources (or not openly so),[128] and therefore would not live up to the high standards of technical proficiency and academic rigour that are demanded of professional historians in Britain. So if one believes that only academic historians count, the next chapter on Camps and the other orthodox school writers will be of little or no interest.

But from my perspective, it is important to include writers such as Camps alongside academic writers of contemporary history for two main reasons. First of all, if one excludes Camps one seems compelled by extension to write out of the historiography all sorts of other writers on Britain and Europe, from politicians and civil servants to diplomats and journalists. Yet, it is argued below, they have been crucial to the development of the historiography of Britain's relations with Europe. Without them the field would not have developed in the way that it has. Furthermore, judging by the number of times academics cite these writers in their footnotes and bibliographies, professional historians certainly count as history the books by Camps and her peers Elisabeth Barker and Nora Beloff and oral testimony from politicians and diplomats developing

---

127 For example Ruane, *The Rise and Fall of the European Defence Community*, p. 8.

128 As the next chapter demonstrates, her ideas were formed on the back of systematic research into the economics of European integration in the 1950s and 1960s.

policy at the time.[129] Blair's use of Camps's interpretation and terminology in his Birmingham speech would seem to suggest that policy-makers also view her work as historical. And if it is not history, what is it? Autobiography? Political propaganda?

The blurring of the boundaries between professional history and other forms of history forms the backdrop to the second reason why it is inappropriate to exclude Camps and her contemporaries from the historiography of Britain's relationship with Europe: all works of history can be seen as positioned. The widely held assumption among diplomatic historians is that 'the Thirty Year Rule governing the release of archival material ... has meant that historians are now able to piece together systematically the events ... more accurately than ever before.'[130] Writers such as Hayden White and Keith Jenkins would ask: who are we to prioritise one form of history over another? For the former, all historical writing 'must be understood primarily as a form of ideology'.[131] For the latter, 'upper case history' ('History'), the grand metanarratives of writers such as Marx, has now all but been eschewed in favour of 'lower case history' of the type written by professional historians, which has more limited objectives but, apparently, greater rigour.

But is lower-case history any less positioned or innocent than upper-case history? Not according to Jenkins. He argues that elevating primary-source history to the level of 'ideal type' history is itself an ideological act,[132] one carried out by professional historians who want to legitimise what they do by redefining the boundaries around the discipline of history and thereby giving priority to what they are good at: constructing narratives based on archival sources and marginalising the rest. Supposedly 'radical' (that is, non-primary source) methods and philosophical concerns have thus been marginalised to the fringes of the discipline.

But, as the French historian Fernand Braudel has pointed out, 'historical narrative is not a method, or even the objective method *par excellence*, but simply a philosophy of history like any other'.[133] Jenkins concludes in the same vein:

> In fact liberal pluralism restricts its tolerances to those histories and historians who subscribe to the values of 'the academic' lower case. For if liberal pluralism accepts

129 Barker, *Britain in a Divided Europe*; E. Barker, *The British Between the Superpowers 1945–50* (London, Macmillan, 1983); N. Beloff, *The General Says No: Britain's Exclusion from Europe* (Harmondsworth, Penguin, 1963).

130 C. A. Pagedas, *Anglo-American Strategic Relations and the French Problem 1960–1963: A Troubled Partnership* (London, Frank Cass, 2000), p. 7.

131 Quoted in Callinicos, *Theories and Narratives*, p. 51.

132 K. Jenkins, 'Introduction: On Being Open About Our Closures', in K. Jenkins (ed.), *The Postmodern History Reader* (London, Routledge, 1997), pp. 1–30 (pp. 5–6).

133 Quoted in Callinicos, *Theories and Narratives*, p. 45.

that any sort of representation of the past is permissible ... then clearly other types of historiography such as upper case versions ... are not 'not history' but just 'different'. Consequently at this point lower case history has to lose its innocence and become as positioned and interested as any other history. In preventing just anything counting as history, a tolerant liberal pluralism in the lower case becomes an intolerant Liberal Ideology in the upper. Accordingly, what we have here is the ideologisation/politicisation of all histories.[134]

The cynic could even argue that the 'say it with documents' approach,[135] getting at what Watt describes as 'the real archival evidence',[136] or what G. M. Trevelyan termed 'the facts of history',[137] *is* positioned, because it can be taken as a manipulation of professional historians by the officials who choose and weed all the documents deposited in the PRO, giving them an artificially important place in British history, which, it could be argued, they feel they deserve after years of neglect in the press and on television.

Hence, the issue of whom to include in the historiography of Britain and Europe and whom to leave out is both a question of taste and of politics, reaching to the heart of the debates about how we view the discipline and how scholars interact with other narrators of the past, academic or otherwise. This book takes an inclusive approach to the literature, one that seems on a practical and theoretical level to best reflect the development of interpretations about contemporary history in Britain. Readers who only want to read about the development of the professional historical literature are advised to turn straight to Chapter 3, on the revisionist school; but it will soon be found that it is only by accounting for the earlier writing, the orthodox school, that the interpretations of the professional historians can be put into context.

It is the contention of this book, then, that there are three schools of writing about British European policy that offer competing interpretations of the history. They can be delineated through analysis of the sociological context within which they emerged and developed, which shapes the type of study that characterises each school, the methods the schools employ to access the past and the questions they ask of it. In this sense, it can be seen how historiography is a Foucauldian enterprise that attempts to uncover the 'discursive formations', the 'bodies of ideas and concepts which claim to produce knowledge about the world' and 'sketches out ... underlying discursive regularities and connects their production

---

134 Jenkins, 'Introduction', p. 15.
135 A term taken from A. Deighton, 'Say it with Documents: British Policy Overseas 1945–1952', *Review of International Studies*, 18:4 (1992), 393–4.
136 D. C. Watt, 'Demythologising the Eisenhower Era', in Louis and Bull (eds), *The Special Relationship*, pp. 65–85 (p. 72).
137 G. M. Trevelyan, *An Autobiography and Other Essays* (London, Longmans, Green and Co., 1949), p. 68.

and transformation to the broader social and political processes of which they are a part'.[138]

Different fields of inquiry, argues Ludmilla Jordanova, like the disciplines to which they belong, 'share intellectual preoccupations, and in this sense they are communities built around ideas of one kind or another, whose members are constantly conversing, in their writings as much as in their direct contacts'. She develops this line of argument two pages later: 'Just as modern societies need to be understood in terms of the structures, such as transport, banking and health services, which enable them to function, so academic disciplines need to be placed in the context of their support systems and institutional bases.'[139] Unfortunately, in Britain not much attention has yet been paid to the structural forces at work on historical interpretation, that is, the relationship between the workings of the academic industry and the fads and fashions within it that shape what subjects get studied and by what means. Even in the historiography of science, which at the last count boasted five models of change,[140] Jon Turney has argued that the sociological dimension has been frequently overlooked. 'There is still much to discuss, notably the role of communities of researchers, not just individuals, in building epistemic standards into scientific practice.'[141] The schools approach would seem to offer a promising way of pursuing this subject in more detail.

Conclusion

The logic behind this book can be explained using the words of Gabriel Spiegel:

> it is by focusing on the social logic of the text, its location within a broader network of social and intertextual relations, that we best become attuned to the specific historical conditions whose presence and/or absence *in* the work alerts us to its own social character and formation, its own combination of material and discursive realities that endow it with its own sense of historical purposiveness.[142]

Since, as the imperial historian C. A. Bayly points out, 'The writing of history can never be divorced from the making of history', it is worthwhile rethinking history as a means of elucidating the relationship between historians and the wider world.[143]

138 Howarth, 'Discourse Theory', p. 116. Hayden White also hits on the connection between historiography and discourse analysis in his 'Performance Model of Discourse', which regards discourse 'as an apparatus for the production of meaning rather than as only a vehicle for the transmission of information about an external referent': White, *The Content of the Form*, p. 42.
139 L. Jordanova, *History in Practice* (London, Arnold, 2000), pp. 1–3.
140 Richards, 'Theories of Scientific Change', pp. 203–16.
141 *The Times Higher Education Supplement*, 14 January 2000, p. 14.
142 Quoted in Callinicos, *Theories and Narratives*, p. 93.
143 C. A. Bayly, 'The Second British Empire', in Winks (ed.), *Historiography*, pp. 54–72 (p. 54).

The next three chapters trace the development of the historiography of British European policy on two levels. On the empirical level they show how the interpretation of events has changed over time, in response to one dominant community of writers being replaced by another. Challenges by historians to the conventional wisdom of a flawed British policy have resulted in more nuanced, sympathetic accounts of the history, which have been sustained in the most recent historiography, explored in the fourth chapter. On the theoretical level they seek to explain the mechanics by which the schools blossomed and then those by which the orthodoxy was replaced by revisionism and post-revisionism.

This is a complex process involving the interplay of various factors, turning especially on the work of key individuals and on the development of simplifying models, which in time become powerful discursive formations about the past. Undoubtedly there is more that might be said about this, but what emerges strikingly from the historiographical analysis of British European policy is that 'what might at first glance seem to be different interpretations of the same event are in fact arguments based on totally different constructions of a presumed event'.[144] That is a significant finding in itself. So let us now explore how the orthodox school defined and interpreted the history of British policy towards Europe.

---

144 Monas, 'Introduction', p. 2.

2 The orthodox school

Jordanova observes that 'fields build up their own traditions and by that very process spawn questions; these questions are less in the sources than the minds of those who study them'.[1] To understand the goals of the academic historians who came to the study of British European policy from the 1970s onwards, it is necessary to have prior awareness of the interpretation placed on British European policy by writers before them, by those first to the field: politicians, diplomats and journalists.[2] They are the people who have set the agenda, and their criticisms have provided the stimulus for much of the reassessment of Britain's aims and objectives in Europe that has been undertaken since.

Contemporary historians have used new sources and applied different methodologies to the study of British European policy. But the focus of their attention on the key stages in Britain's policy towards European integration has been shaped by what the first wave of writers said about that policy, and how they went about historicising it. This is not to denigrate those early accounts or to suggest that historiography inevitably advances to a better, more astute or more

---

1 Jordanova, *History in Practice*, p. 174.
2 British politicians are usually quick to go into print with their versions of what happened, though some are more informative than others. C. Attlee, *As It Happened* (London, William Heinemann, 1954); T. Benn, *Out of the Wilderness: Diaries, 1963-7* (London, Hutchinson, 1987); T. Benn, *Office Without Power: Diaries, 1968-72* (London, Hutchinson, 1988); Lord Boothby, *My Yesterday, Your Tomorrow* (London, Hutchinson, 1962); G. Brown, *In My Way: The Political Memoirs of Lord George-Brown* (London, Victor Gollancz, 1971); J. Callaghan, *Time and Chance* (London, Collins, 1987); B. Castle, *The Castle Diaries, 1964-70* (London, Weidenfeld and Nicolson, 1984); R. Crossman, *The Diaries of a Cabinet Minister: Vol. 1, Minister of Housing, 1964-66* (London, Hamish Hamilton and Jonathan Cape, 1977); R. Crossman, *The Diaries of a Cabinet Minister: Vol. 2, Lord President of the Council and Leader of the House of Commons, 1966-68* (London, Hamish Hamilton and Jonathan Cape, 1976); A. Eden, *Full Circle: The Memoirs of Sir Anthony Eden* (London, Cassell, 1960); D. Healey, *The Time of My Life* (London, W. W. Norton, 1990); E. Heath, *The Course of My Life: My Autobiography* (London, Hodder and Stoughton, 1998); Lord Home, *The Way the Wind Blows: An Autobiography* (London, Collins, 1976); D. Jay, *Change and Fortune: A Political Record* (London, Hutchinson, 1980); R. Jenkins, *A Life at the Centre* (New York, Random House, 1991); Earl of Kilmuir, *Political Adventure: The Memoirs of the Earl of Kilmuir* (London, Weidenfeld and Nicolson, 1964); H. Macmillan, *Tides of Fortune, 1945-1955* (London, Macmillan, 1969); H. Macmillan, *Riding the Storm, 1956-1959* (London, Macmillan, 1971); H. Macmillan, *Pointing the Way, 1959-61* (London, Macmillan, 1972); H. Macmillan, *At the End of the Day, 1961-1963* (London, Macmillan, 1973); D. Owen, *Time to Declare* (London, Michael Joseph, 1991); M. Stewart, *Life and Labour: An Autobiography* (London, Sidgwick and Jackson, 1980); H. Wilson, *The Labour Government, 1964-70: A Personal Record* (London, Weidenfeld and Nicolson and Michael Joseph, 1971).

truthful interpretation of events, for as Gwyn Prins has noted, 'The invention of tradition is neither surprising nor dishonest, especially not in cultures with no single criterion of truth.'[3] Rather, it is an insight into the dialogue historians are engaged in when they research and write their texts: with themselves, with their sources, with each other and with other writers who have worked in the field before them.

This chapter examines the genesis and development of the orthodox 'missed opportunities' interpretation of British European policy. It argues that the reason this perspective gained such a wide following in the literature was because of its attraction to a transnational assortment of individuals who had one related aim: to change the course of British foreign policy. It was thus fuelled by an array of politicians, civil servants, diplomats and journalists, working its way into the discourse of a smattering of academics from across Britain, Europe and the United States who all found something in it to support their view of a misguided or failing British foreign policy after the Second World War. In the international arena, the orthodoxy appealed to followers of Jean Monnet, both on the Continent and in the United States, who felt that it was wrong of British policy-makers to shun the supranational approach to integration embodied in the ECSC, the EDC and the EEC. They used the missed opportunities interpretation as a propaganda device to push a 'cautious and slow' Britain closer to the Continent.[4] In the domestic arena, the idea that Britain had missed opportunities in Europe spoke loudly to a host of politicians and journalists who became obsessed with the idea of British 'decline' in the 1960s,[5] and although they were hardly from the same mould as Monnet and his followers in terms of their view of the appropriate means and ends for European integration, they used orthodox terminology in a nationally-rooted critique of post-war British foreign policy.

To advance this case, the chapter is split into three main parts. The opening part examines the crux of the orthodox interpretation of British foreign policy: that Britain should have been 'in' Europe from the start. The second part analyses the major players in this school and the ways in which they have historicised the conventional wisdom; it shows that British European policy was received so critically because European federalists and British politicians both had axes to grind against successive governments. Before concluding, the final part assesses two theoretical issues that flow from this chapter: one is the applicability of

---

3 G. Prins, 'Oral History', in P. Burke (ed.), *New Perspectives on Historical Writing* (Cambridge, Polity Press, 1991), pp. 114–39 (p. 126).

4 P. Spaak, *The Continuing Battle: Memoirs of a European 1936–1966*, trans. Henry Fox (London, Weidenfeld and Nicolson, 1971), p. 142.

5 Tivey, *Interpretations of British Politics*, p. 132, notes that the declinism that swept through Britain in the 1960s had two stimulants, Suez (the strategic factor) and relatively slow growth (the economic factor).

employing the term 'school' to describe this group of writers; the other is the correlation between the form of history and its content. Historiographical interpretation, it suggests, is decisively influenced by the type of study written and the perceived audience for that text. It was not until the middle of the 1980s that a new wave of writers managed to break decisively from the orthodoxy, penning academic studies that refocused the history by asking new sets of questions of it. Small wonder, therefore, that this refocusing saw tired assumptions and interpretations put to the sword.

'Missed opportunities': historicising the conventional wisdom

Britain's approach to European integration since 1945 has not been well received. According to this view, Britain was and is an 'awkward' or 'reluctant' country that misguidedly remained aloof from the ECSC, the EDC and then the EEC, joining belatedly and without much enthusiasm in 1973. Thereafter, London has hampered the efforts of its partners to create 'ever closer union among the peoples of Europe',[6] preferring intergovernmental modes of co-operation which have had a 'damaging and distorting impact upon the relevance of federalism to the European Community'.[7] 'The story of Britain's relationship to the construction of Europe after 1945 is singularly unhappy', wrote Ralf Dahrendorf, a member of the European Commission at the time of the accession negotiations in the early 1970s, 'The story of Britain and Europe is calamitous.'[8]

    The reason for this tragedy is both economic and political. Taking the financial aspect first, Martin Dedman contends that the 'policy choice can be seen as a costly failure as the Common Market proved to be a more successful commercial venture than the UK's Commonwealth links'.[9] Politically, by reaffirming Britain's sense of difference from the Continent, not being 'in' at the start has led to decades of tension between Britain and the Community that has yet to be resolved. The idea that Britain is 'afraid' of the EU, communicated by the current European Commission President Romano Prodi in a speech in Oxford in April

---

6 The Treaty of Rome establishing the European Community was signed by six member states (commonly referred to as 'the Six'), Germany, France, Italy, Belgium, the Netherlands and Luxembourg. The full text of the treaty is at http://europa.eu.int/eurlex/en/treaties/dat/ec_cons_treaty_en.pdf.

7 M. Burgess, *Federalism and European Union: Political Ideas, Influences and Strategies in the European Community, 1972–1987* (London, Routledge, 1982), p. 2. Britain's intergovernmental approach to Europe is, notes David Allen in 'Britain and Western Europe', in Smith, Smith and White (eds), *British Foreign Policy*, pp. 168–92 (p. 170), of a 'fundamentally different order from that of its European counterparts'.

8 Dahrendorf, *On Britain*, p. 145.

9 M. J. Dedman, *The Origins and Development of the European Union 1945–95: A History of European Integration* (London, Routledge, 1996), p. 67.

2002, echoes the long-term tendency for Europeanists to stress British separateness from the Continent. Britain, he said, is 'constantly on the defensive, putting the brakes on, dragging its feet on vital issues, fighting a rearguard action that can hold up, but cannot stem, the tide of history ... But deep down we all know Britain is culturally and historically part of Europe.'[10]

This is a simple and compelling story about Britain's relations with the Continent; and the very phrase 'missed opportunities' has, by dint of repetition, become one of *the* most common critiques of British European policy among euroenthusiasts. It evokes myriad images about Britain in the world since 1945: not only decline but drift, indecision, illusions of grandeur, introspectiveness and myopia. A widely cited speech by the US Secretary of State Acheson at a student conference at West Point, New York in 1962 gathered together these various strands in a devastating critique that has been reverberating around establishment Britain ever since.

> Great Britain has lost an empire and has not yet found a role. The attempt to play a separate power role - that is, a role apart from Europe, a role based on a 'special relationship' with the United States, a role based on being the head of a 'commonwealth' which has no political structure, or unity, or strength and enjoys a fragile and precarious economic relationship by means of the Sterling area and preferences in the British market - this role is about played out.[11]

One way to demonstrate the pervasiveness of the orthodox interpretation and to elucidate more of its fundamental characteristics is to analyse how political cartoonists have depicted British European policy.[12] Graphic illustrations of political personalities and events are an under-used but potentially valuable source to both historians and historiographers,[13] because they offer sharp insights into the

---

10 Full text of his speech is at www.sbs.ox.ac.uk/html/news_article.asp?ID=80.

11 Quoted in G. Ball, *The Discipline of Power: Essentials of a Modern World Structure* (London, The Bodley Head, 1968), p. 69. The imagery Acheson evoked is apparent in a *Spectator* cartoon that directly refers to this speech, which is reprinted in J. Jensen, 'The End of the Line? The Future of British Cartooning', in *A Sense of Permanence? Essays on the Art of Cartoon* (Canterbury, The Centre for the Study of Cartoons and Caricature, 1997), pp. 11–22 (p. 19).

12 The Centre for the Study of Cartoons and Caricature, founded in 1975 at the University of Kent, at Canterbury, holds 85,000 original drawings that are being put into an online database that can be searched by cartoonist, name, date or subject. The Centre is now the base for a collaborative project, CartoonHub, funded by the Research Support for Libraries programme, and links the Centre's collections with those held at the London School of Economics Library, the John Rylands Library, University of Manchester and the National Library of Wales. See http://library.ukc.ac. uk/cartoons/main.html and http://library.ukc.ac.uk/cartoons/cartoonhub.html respectively. See also C. Seymour-Ure, 'The Centre for the Study of Cartoons and Caricature and the University of Kent', in *A Sense of Permanence?*, pp. 9–10.

13 Jordanova's opinion, *History in Practice*, p. 190, is that in too many history books' 'pictures become decorative add-ons, they are not integrated into historical argument'. For an example of how analysis of cartoon and media imagery can be used to illustrate historical arguments see S. Lee, *Victory in Europe? Britain and Germany since 1945* (Harlow, Pearson Education, 2001), pp. 72–3.

prevailing climate of opinion about a given issue at a particular moment in time. This however is a view that came under fire in a paper presented at the launch of CartoonHub on 13 May 2002, where one contemporary political cartoonist thought academic attention to cartooning to be distortive of a practice that does not lend itself easily to analysis in the same way that texts or speeches do. For the purposes of simplicity this opinion will not receive sustained attention here; but it does suggest that academics construct fields of study around certain assumptions and principles which may, or may not, be accepted in the wider world: 'The purpose of all this imaginative activity, of course, is one or both of two kinds of comment. The first is a definition or interpretation: 'this is what the Prime Minister is like'. The second, and stronger, in terms of the [cartoonist's] armoury's firepower, is a bolt of criticism (or, less often, approval) ...'[14] Cartoons, continues Colin Seymour-Ure, 'offer a type of comment – assertive, emotional and often with several layers of meaning ... The cartoon is thus an editorial in pictures.'[15] As Anthony Howard points out, however, the opinions expressed by cartoonists may not always coincide with the written editorial in a newspaper, but 'no one seems to mind even if it sends the pre-ordained editorial sky-high'.[16]

An examination of three cartoons, from the *Frankfurter Allgemeine Zeitung* in 1991, the *Evening Standard* in 1961 and the *Observer* in 2002 shows a marked stability in cartoonists' representation of the British approach to Europe, featuring a number of strands. The first is that Europe since 1945 has been 'on the move'; the second and third corollaries of the first: that Britain since the Second World War has been 'drifting' and that it has harmed its interests by being on the 'sidelines' of Europe.

Europe on the move

The first image invented by the missed opportunities school is that, through its integrative efforts from the 1950s, Europe has been 'on the move': hence the vehicle-oriented imagery, missed boats and missed buses. Monnet summed up this position in his memoirs, where he talks of Britain's first application to join the EEC as flow-

---

14 C. Seymour-Ure, 'What Future for the British Political Cartoon?', *Journalism Studies*, 2:3 (2001), 333–55 (335).

15 *Ibid.*, pp. 333 and 335. On p. 345 he notes that cartooning 'has become a distinctive part of what people expect in their paper; its practitioners have become long-serving stars and its methods draw on well-understood and deep-rooted conventions'. For cartoonists' views on their craft see the pieces by Nicholas Garland, Ralph Steadman, Steve Bell, Roger Law and Kevin Kallaugher in *A Sense of Permanence?*

16 A. Howard, 'Introduction' to *Twenty Years of Cartoons by Garland* (Edinburgh, The Salamander Press, 1984), first page (the book has no page numbers). For Michael Foot 'it is almost always the satirists who see things more clearly than anyone else', 'Introduction' to *Vicky's Supermac: Harold Macmillan in Cartoons by Victor Weisz of the Evening Standard* (London, Park McDonald, 1996), pp. 11–18 (p. 18).

2 'Looks like Robinson Crusoe
doesn't wish to be saved' (Lurie,
Frankfurter Allgemeine Zeitung,
1991)

ing from the need to find a role in the world: 'they would find it only by catching up
with the Europe that was on the move'.[17] In Britain, the Europeanists keenly
grasped the metaphor. The former Foreign Office junior minister Anthony Nutting,
for example, moaned that, with the ECSC, 'The first European bus had started on
its maiden trip with Great Britain waving a hand limply from the kerbstone.'[18]

The vehicular theme inspired many of the cartoonists working on this
theme, as the cartoon by Ranan Lurie (Figure 2), which first appeared in the
Frankfurter Allgemeine Zeitung, nicely demonstrates.

Although not drawn at the time (it appeared in the run-up to the Maastricht
negotiations), this image nicely captures the vehicular metaphor for 'Europe' that
was fashionable in the 1950s and 1960s. 'The New Europe' is depicted as a large,
brand-new, technologically advanced ship, apparently making easy progress
through the ocean to a brighter future somewhere off the frame of the picture.
Milward describes the separation of Britain from the Continent as being rooted
in different perceptions of state power influence in the international system, and

17 J. Monnet, *Memoirs*, trans. Richard Mayne (London, Collins, 1978), p. 452.
18 A. Nutting, *Europe Will Not Wait: A Warning and a Way Out* (London, Hollis and Carter, 1960),
    p. 32.

in doing so puts in words what the image of this ship is intended to convey. 'Early historical accounts of the Community divided politicians into those who still ... inhabited the benighted world of European nationalism and those around who[m] the great light had shone, the prophets of the new order.'[19]

Britain drifting

Extending the notion that Britain missed the chance to board the European boat at the start of its voyage, the second strand to orthodox historiography is that Britain would be left behind by Europe, in political, economic and strategic terms. According to Lurie's cartoon, it does not even *possess* a means of transport, it is directionless. Britain is represented as an island adrift in the sea and with no means of propelling itself in the same direction as Europe. The country is, moreover, represented as inward-looking, putting domestic concerns above internationalist ones (note the 'no entry' signs placed around its shoreline) and in a bad state of physical repair, a reference perhaps to the ailing British economy.

That the character standing on the island (a personification of the British people) is drawn wearing a union jack hat and standing next to a tattered union jack flag on the pole is a telling comment on Britain's nationalism and over-inflated sense of its place in the world. While proudly sporting the hat, the wearer fails to see that the flag is ripped and worn, past its sell-by date, going some way to support David Edgerton's claim that the 'historiography of modern Britain, especially Britain in the wider world, is dominated by one issue – "decline".'[20] 'Keep the pound' protestors sometimes wear the style of dress portrayed in this cartoon to make their point today. A photograph of a lone protester outside the Bank of England, taken in the aftermath of the launch of the euro, also shows him carrying a placard reading 'No surrender; stuff the euro; Rule Britannia'.[21]

Another cartoon, this time by Vicky in the *Evening Standard* in June 1961, the year Seymour-Ure labels the 'start of Britain's satire boom',[22] makes the point about 'drift' even more forcefully (Figure 3). Published two months before the launch of Britain's first application to join the EEC, the message is that Britain has reluctantly accepted that its future lies with Europe. One sees a disgruntled Harold Macmillan being towed along in a small boat without any oars, an image that conveys the impression of Britain reluctantly being pulled into Europe's

---

19 A. S. Milward, *The European Rescue of the Nation-State* (London, Routledge, 1992), p. 17.
20 D. Edgerton, review, 'Declinism, The Lost Victory, British Dreams, British Realities, 1945–50. By Correlli Barnett', *London Review of Books*, 18:5 (1996), 14–15 (14). Another who draws this conclusion is Peter Ghosh, review, 'How We Got Where We Are: Hope and Glory, Britain 1900–1990. By Peter Clarke', *London Review of Books*, 18:23 (November 1996), 18–19 (18).
21 *Daily Telegraph*, 3 January 2002, p. 10.
22 Seymour-Ure, 'What Future', 351.

THE EMIGRANT

3 'The emigrant' (Vicky, *Evening Standard*, 12 June 1961)

orbit. The ship pulling Britain along closely resembles the 'New Europe' boat that Lurie would later feature in his cartoon. Looking down on Macmillan are two influential European leaders, on the left President Charles de Gaulle of France and on the right the West German Chancellor Konrad Adenauer. 'To Europe' stickers adorn Macmillan's luggage, and he is being haunted by his words to Hugh Dalton in 1950, at the time the ECSC was established: 'Europe is finished, sinking. If I were a younger man, I'd emigrate to the United States.'

The comparison in size between the European and British vessels and – in other cartoons – between European leaders (especially de Gaulle) and British leaders is a further feature of cartooning about Britain and Europe. This mode of characterisation is most prevalent in cartoons about Britain's two applications to join the EEC by the likes of Emmwood in the *Daily Mail* in the 1960s. The obstacle in the way of Britain becoming a member of the EEC, de Gaulle, is usually shown to tower over the supplicants, Harold Macmillan and Harold Wilson, the latter often wearing a pointed 'D' hat standing for 'dunce'.[23]

Here, instead, we see one of the other regular features of cartooning about Britain and Europe. Prime Minister Macmillan is depicted as carrying with him

---

23 See for instance the cartoon featured on the cover of Daddow (ed.), *Harold Wilson and European Integration*, depicting a tennis match between de Gaulle and Wilson. The former has a tennis ball labelled 'Common Market' attached to his racket by a piece of string.

lots of 'baggage', suggesting that London was hamstrung in its efforts to enter the EEC by its past, its global commitments, especially the Commonwealth and the management of sterling as a worldwide reserve currency. De Gaulle in his speeches vetoing British membership of the EEC made much of Britain's wider ties that, he said, stymied the country's ability to act as a truly 'European' power, and Britain's reluctance to devalue sterling was often perceived as one of the key factors in the failure of Wilson's attempt to take Britain into the Community.[24] There is an Atlantic dimension here too. For the 'Europeanists in British public life', remarks David Watt, 'it has virtually axiomatic that our failure to 'catch the European bus' in the mid-1950s was almost entirely due to a national obsession with the special relationship.'[25]

Britain on the sidelines

The third image that appears in both orthodox historiography and political cartooning on this subject shows that Britain has always been on the sidelines of Europe expecting and, regularly, hoping that the schemes for unification on the Continent would fail (Figure 4).

This cartoon, published in the *Observer* at the time of the launch of the euro in January 2002, shows the contemporary appeal of missed opportunities discourse. Here, on the one hand, is the symbol of the euro, personified as a ski-jumper wearing pristine skiing clothes. It is launching itself down a ski-jump towards an adoring public below. Beside the ramp at a beer garden table, evidently not about to join the euro on its adventure, sits the British pound, dressed in the colours of the union jack. It is smoking, drinking beer from an English pub tankard and eating fish and chips. The overall impression gleaned from this cartoon, as with those previously examined, is of an awkward, disinterested, grumpy, unhealthy Britain refusing to get involved with the latest Continental scheme for closer integration.

However, the cartoonist, David Simonds, is not quite as gloomy in his prognosis for Britain. Waiting at the bottom of the ski-jump are a fire engine and an ambulance with stretcher-bearers ready to attend to the euro should its leap fail. He thus adds a note of caution that marks this image apart from those common in the 1950s and 1960s.[26] Cartoons of British European policy are illustrative of how

24 See also the cartoon in the *Economist*, 19 November 1966, p. 742, picturing Wilson attempting to drive through the 'gates' of Europe, manned by de Gaulle, in a car with a huge, unbalanced set of luggage teetering on the roof. The luggage is labelled 'east of Suez', 'devaluation' and so on.

25 D. Watt, 'Introduction: Anglo-American Relations', in Louis and Bull (eds), *The Special Relationship*, pp. 1–14 (p. 7).

26 Note also three shady civil service advisers sitting near the pound sign, an image reminiscent of the judgement common in the sceptic media in Britain (analysed in the introduction) that British European policy has been made 'behind closed doors'.

4 Untitled (David Simonds, *Observer*, 6 January 2002)

the British nation and British foreign policy have been perceived in the world after the Second World War.

The genesis of the orthodoxy

Political cartoonists, like the Europeanists whom they echo in their pictures, express the idea that the success of the federalist project compelled British governments, however reluctantly, to reorientate British foreign policy towards Europe. Separateness, backwardness, introspectiveness and history holding back Britain are all themes that run through these cartoons and which characterise orthodox historiography of British European policy as it emerged and developed from the 1950s onwards. Having explored the interpretation of orthodox writers, it is now possible to begin deconstructing the school with a view to finding out more about the underlying forces that have shaped it and the ways in which the past has been narrativised.

In a political science text on British foreign policy published in 1973, Joseph Frankel asked the question that spurred orthodox writers into action. 'How are we to explain Britain's neglecting to take a lead in Western European affairs when it was open to her in the later 1940s and in the 1950s? In retrospect, this seems to be the fundamental and most costly mistake in post-war policies'. His answer is that 'its causes must be sought in the faulty perceptions, anticipations and priorities of successive British governments'.[27]

The manner in which Frankel approaches this topic suggests that when approaching historical texts two crucial factors must be borne in mind. One is that there is a strong link between questions and answers in history: the reason for taking on a project will tend to shape the sources consulted and, ultimately, the conclusions drawn. The other is that there is a multiplicity of conscious and subconscious factors that mould how one approaches and researches a given topic. As Jordanova states, 'The models each historian finds appealing have a great deal to do with 'their' period, as well as with their own political, social and economic views.'[28]

To deconstruct Frankel's question, it betrays a host of assumptions that characterise orthodox approaches to the study of British European policy. His use of the word 'neglect' implies inattentiveness to or lack of interest in Europe; the idea that Britain could have taken a 'lead' presumes that the Continental integrationists would have sat by and allow Britain the freedom to drive integration down intergovernmental lines; that this can be classed the 'most costly mistake' of Britain's post-war policies is a value judgement with which not everyone would agree (what about Suez?); and using the word 'faulty' to describe the decision-making of successive governments is equally in need of context. The revisionist critique of the way in which orthodox writers approach the subject- matter is the subject of the next chapter, so no further comment is necessary at this stage. Already, however, one begins to see the connection between the reason for writing, which manifests itself in the type of study and target audience, and the interpretation placed on historical events.

Despite the obviously positioned nature of Frankel's interpretation, a function of the methodology he explicates here, what is striking is that in Britain

> the ways in which evidence has been found, selected and used, how authors have chosen a particular genre to write their work up in, which audiences they have targeted and the tacit assumptions upon which their work rests, tend to be obscured. A critical reader needs to be able to think through these issues, and one obvious step is to ask what kind of history any piece of writing constitutes.[29]

Unfortunately, given the pressures of time and the constraint of working to a word limit, it is unrealistic, even in a historiographic study, to expect to be able to uncover every single influence at work on the production of historical texts. Writing an 'anthropology of history', which 'makes sense of the practices and

---

27   J. Frankel, *British Foreign Policy 1945–1973* (London, Oxford University Press, 1975), pp. 233–4.
28   Jordanova, *History in Practice*, p. 14 of the preliminaries.
29   *Ibid.*, pp. 33–4.

ideas of a distinct group of people', is arduous enough. This is especially so when it covers the writing in a field over a long period of time, as is the case with this study,[30] where two methodological problems rear their heads.

The first is that, in theory, such a study entails a full biographic analysis of each historian: his or her formative experiences, political outlooks, connections and reasons for writing. This is difficult enough, even before one notes that biography as a genre is not without its critics, and is generally acknowledged to provide only partial answers to questions such as these: 'history of a sort' Monas calls it.[31] The second reason is that many of the writers in the field have now died, leaving only their published works and rarely their private papers, making for a constraint on the researcher hoping to deal with text as the product of the 'author' him- or herself. Hence, a collection of lengthy biographic representations of key players, that one might assume to be the goal of a historiographic study, might in fact pose many more questions than it proffers answers. It would be extremely lengthy and difficult to organise satisfactorily, because of the problems associated with weaving together the different strands of people's lives.

The problems associated with undertaking this kind of study are manifest from a glance at the website of an American organisation, Public Information Research (PIR), which one can use to identify social connections among politicians, academics, business people and journalists. The database can be searched by name, producing a 'social network' scatter diagram for that person showing all the other people and organisations the database finds them to have been in contact with in their public life. All the names appearing on the scatter diagram can in turn be searched. To take the example of two people featuring prominently in this chapter, the diagram for Miriam Camps shows her to have had over 40 known contacts in the political, economic and academic areas of life covered by the PIR; Jean Monnet had well over twice that number. Given the nature of human existence these would seem to be conservative estimates, to say the least.

But this is no reason to despair. The historiographer can at least begin the process of identifying the intricate networks of individuals who have contributed to a given field by locating writers and their work in the context of their time. This is what the following analysis seeks to achieve.

For the purposes of simplification, it can be argued that the orthodox school of writing on British European policy originated from six separable but by no means separate communities: the European federalists, their American backers, British federalists, journalists and instant historians from the period, the self-confessed 'Europeans' within the British political elite and other British critics displeased with the state of the nation in the 1950s and 1960s. Taking each in turn,

---

30 *Ibid.*, p. 15 of the preliminaries.
31 Monas, 'Introduction', p. 15.

one can see that the history they wrote served less the purposes of the reader than the writer. Orthodox historiography was at root political discourse originating from discontent with British foreign policy, and was written with more than an eye on changing the future.[32]

The founding fathers

The most obvious place to start in search of the origins of the orthodoxy on Britain and Europe is with the European federalists, for, as Alan Milward suggests, the literature on European integration 'is dominated by legends of great men. Most histories emphasise the role of a small band of leading statesmen with a shared vision.'[33] Within that category, the three dominant individuals are Jean Monnet, Robert Schuman and Paul-Henri Spaak.[34] They were not shy of publicising their achievements because, François Duchêne points out, they sought to reorganise Europe's political and economic structures, so they needed to spread their message widely; integrationist language was a crucial part of the project. 'With broad and active backing ... Monnet in effect made his vision of Europe the received wisdom. He is the tutelary deity of Brussels (and devil of Eurosceptics) today.'[35]

Monnet was a French economist whose formative political experience occurred while serving as Deputy Secretary-General of the League of Nations in 1919–23.[36] In a short biographic piece on Monnet by M. Albertini, tellingly entitled 'The Greatness of Jean Monnet' and appearing on the website of the Altiero Spinelli Institute of Federalist Studies, it is noted that, exasperated with its unanimous decision-making procedure, Monnet resigned from the League in 1923; 'the veto', he said, 'is the profound cause and at the same time the symbol of the impossibility of overcoming national egoism'.[37]

After the fall of France in June 1940 Monnet proposed a federal union between Britain and France. This never became reality but, in its proposal for common organisations for defence, foreign and economic affairs, the union

---

32 Pfaltzgraff, *Britain Faces Europe*, p. 7.

33 Milward, *The European Rescue*, p. 318.

34 Other key players who receive less attention include Robert Marjolin (who worked with Monnet on the Monnet Plan and was Secretary-General of the OEEC until 1955), Altiero Spinelli (who established the European Federalists Movement in 1943), Alcide de Gasperi (Italian Prime Minister and Foreign Minister 1945–54, afterwards becoming President of the ECSC) and Pierre Uri (economic adviser to the French Planning Commission 1947–52, Monnet's assistant and a senior official in the ECSC 1952–59).

35 F. Duchêne, 'Jean Monnet – Pragmatic Visionary', in M. Bond, J. Smith and W. Wallace (eds), *Eminent Europeans: Personalities Who Shaped Contemporary Europe* (London, The Greycoat Press, 1996), pp. 45–61 (p. 57).

36 *Ibid.*, p. 47.

37 www.eurplace.org/federal/monnet.html#greatness.

proposal shows the direction of his thinking.[38] The idea of 'union' is, indeed, deeply engrained in Monnet's approach to problem-solving and, as something of an epitaph for his life, Monnet wrote in his memoirs 'I have always been drawn towards union, towards collective action. I cannot say why, except that Nature made me that way.'[39] At a meeting with the British on 5 August 1940 he again showed his federal colours, urging 'The European states must constitute themselves into a federation.' By the time the war ended, it is said, Monnet's federalist, functionalist approach to integration was firmly entrenched, his view being that it was 'impossible for any European nation independently to plan for economic growth and prosperity'. The idea that Europe should federate was again at the heart of his talks with British Treasury officials at the end of April 1949.[40]

Moving on from considering his vision to his methods, the most plausible explanation for the repetition of his views in so many quarters would seem to be the sheer number of contacts he built up in the United States and on the Continent throughout his lifetime. His energy was directed towards persuading politicians of the merits of federalism, both directly through personal contact and indirectly, through 'men who cannot afford to make mistakes – bankers, industrialists, lawyers, and newspapermen'.[41] The use in his memoirs of phrases such as 'Action is urgently needed if Europe is not to let her opportunity pass by' (talking of the year 1956 when the Spaak negotiations leading to the founding of the EEC were in full swing),[42] shows the extent to which his own concentration on seizing apparent historical moments of opportunity has become the language of choice in orthodox historiography.[43] He also talks in this passage of this being 'a great new opportunity for Europe' which 'had to be seized'.

Schuman, Prime Minister of France for a short time in 1947–48, Foreign Minister 1948–53 and President of the European Parliament 1958–60 is, through his work with Monnet in founding the ECSC, also revered as one of the 'founding fathers' of European unity,[44] another 'apostle of supranationality'.[45] In a

---

38 www.europa-web.de/europa/011vkvjf/113ebw/monnet.htm.
39 Monnet, *Memoirs*, p. 221.
40 *Ibid.*, pp. 279–80.
41 *Ibid.*, p. 271.
42 *Ibid.*, p. 418.
43 See also p. 423, where he talks of bringing the problems of bringing the Common Market negotiations to fruition, 'Would the opportunity be lost?' and p. 432, where he asks 'Must [opportunities] be missed simply because they were not expected so soon?'
44 Born in the Grand-Duchy of Luxembourg in 1886, he was a German national, and then a French national when Lorraine reverted to French control in 1918. He obtained a doctorate in German law from Strasbourg University in 1912 and began his political career in the French National Assembly in 1919. This information from www.europarl.eu.int/ppe/tree/schuman/en/biography.htm. See also D. Urwin, review, 'The European Rescue of the Nation-State. By Alan S. Milward', *Journal of Common Market Studies*, 32:1 (1994), 112–13 (113).
45 Milward, *The European Rescue*, p. 329.

pamphlet commemorating the fiftieth anniversary of the 'Community Europe', Pascale Fontaine employs the hyperbole that traditionally accompanies Europeanist reflections on Schuman and the origins of European unity. 'On 9 May 1950, Robert Schuman made history by putting to the Federal Republic of Germany, and to the other European countries who so wished, the idea of creating a Community of pacific interests. In so doing he extended a hand to yesterday's enemies and erased the bitterness of war and the burden of the past.'[46] In his memoirs, Schuman did not hold back. Britain, he said, 'is ... out of principle and in all circumstances, hostile to all integration, in the sense that we understand it, to all federal structures ... That is why European integration might perhaps receive Britain's blessing, but only the spur of events seems like to compel its membership.'[47]

The third 'founding father', the former Belgian Prime Minister Paul-Henri Spaak, is most often commemorated for his efforts to found the EEC; but by that time he had already established his credentials as a 'good European'. He was the first chairman of the OEEC, where he had several run-ins with the British over the remit and powers of the Council of Europe (discussed further below).[48] He attended the Hague Congress of Europe in 1948, was twice elected President of the Consultative Assembly of the Council of Europe, in 1949 and 1951, and in 1952–53 was President of the General Assembly of the ECSC.

It was, furthermore, Spaak that proposed a meeting of the ECSC's Foreign Ministers 'to relaunch the European idea' in the wake of the collapse of the EDC.[49] Attending as Belgian Foreign Minister, he 'was a key figure at the 1955 Messina conference, where he ... was empowered to chair a committee which would examine proposals for a European Community'. The Spaak Report, as it became known, was accepted by the Six, and Spaak was entrusted with the task of drafting the EEC and Euratom Treaties.[50] On his death, the *Financial Times* wrote 'His

46 P. Fontaine, *A New Idea for Europe: The Schuman Declaration – 1950–2000* (Luxembourg, Office for Official Publications of the European Communities, 2000), p. 5. Milward, in his review, 'Robert Schuman: Homme d'État. By Raymond Poitevin', *Journal of Common Market Studies*, 26:2 (1987), 344–5 (344), notes that '[a]ll [previous lives of Schuman have been simple hagiographies'.

47 From the French, '[L'Angleterre] est ... par principe et en toute circonstance, hostile à toute intégration, dans le sens que nous y attachons, à toute structure fédérale ... C'est pourquoi l'intégration européenne recueillera peut-être sa bienveillante bénédiction, mais seule la contrainte des événements paraît susceptible de forcer son adhesion': R. Schuman, *Pour l'Europe*, 2nd edn (Paris, Les Éditions Nagel, 1964), p. 115.

48 Spaak, *The Continuing Battle*, pp. 197–8, 203–6 and 219–26. On resigning from the Presidency in December 1951, he rued that 'we [the delegates to the Strasbourg Assembly] have missed all our chances' to build a united Europe, p. 223.

49 R. Mayne, 'Schuman, De Gasperi, Spaak – The European Frontiersmen', in Bond, Smith and Wallace (eds), *Eminent Europeans*, pp. 22–44 (p. 42).

50 A. Blair, *The Longman Companion to the European Union since 1945* (London, Pearson Education, 1999), p. 252.

intense efforts to promote European unity earned him the title of one of the 'founding fathers of Europe'.'[51]

The activities of Monnet, Schuman and Spaak have given them a central place in the historiography of European integration. Today, European Studies departments in universities regularly endow suitably qualified academics with Jean Monnet Professorships, indicating the esteem in which he, in particular, is held among European integration specialists. Their discourse about grasping the opportunity to build a new Europe, free from conflict, has, in essence, become federalist discourse.

> The history of the Community was a struggle between the forces of light and darkness. For the European saints it was the moment of rejection of the old order which was exalted as the most important moment of their lives, the conversion on the road to Damascus expected of all the Community's labourers on earth, *including those who wrote its history.*[52]

Milward, however, adds a note of caution to this picture of a band of 'Eurosaints' saving Europe from itself.

One reason is that he dates their conversion to the idea of pooled sovereignty somewhat later than most. 'Like Spaak, Robert Schuman appears to have been indifferent to the question of European unity before the Second World War and to have been convinced only in 1948 that the interests of his country would be best served by some form of European union.'[53] Milward dates Monnet's conversion to supranationalism to 1948, in the wake of the American Congress passing Marshall Aid legislation and the Administration (ECA) preparing Western Europe for federation under the auspices of the OEEC. In this light, he suggests we look again at the 1945 Monnet Plan, which is erroneously portrayed as a harbinger of federalism in Europe: 'the goal of the original Monnet plan was thoroughly national'.[54]

The other reason he gives is that it was the Americans, not the Europeans, who drove the federalist project. The zeal with which Monnet and his friends pursued European federation in the 1950s and the key positions they took up within the Communities, has, Milward, says, distorted both their own and others' interpretations of their earlier attitude to nationalism and federalism in Europe.[55] Roger Bullen was of a similar view: 'The founding fathers of the European federal

51 Quoted in E. Barker, *The Common Market* (London, Wayland Publishers, 1973), p. 44.
52 Milward, *The European Rescue*, p. 319. Emphasis added.
53 *Ibid.*, p. 325. The word 'Eurosaint' is taken from W. E. Paterson, review, 'Eminent Europeans: Personalities WhoShaped Contemporary Europe. Edited by Michael Bond, Julie Smith and William Wallace', *Journal of Common Market Studies*, 35:3 (1997), 488–9 (488).
54 Milward, *The European Rescue*, p. 334. On the Monnet Plan see J. Killick, *The United States and European Reconstruction 1945–1960* (Edinburgh, Keele University Press, 1997), pp. 43–104.
55 Milward, *The European Rescue*, Chapter 6.

movement of the second half of the twentieth century have assiduously propagated a number of myths about the origins and purpose of integration.'[56]

Valid though Milward's and Bullen's concerns are, the most significant factor from the point of view of this study is that these key figures and the writing about them have been fundamental to the development of the orthodox school of writing on Britain and Europe. Judging by the language and images around which their arguments crystallise, one might even say that this is a metanarrative that contains its own techniques for marginalising alternative interpretations and downplaying sources of evidence that challenge the ideological predilection of the author. In the same way that David Howarth and David Marsland show Margaret Thatcher to have hegemonised evocative words and phrases to strengthen her position in the debate about the ills of social collectivism in the 1980s,[57] the Monnetists have a set of linguistic strategies that they employ in their critique of British European policy, which have borne upon the historiography in two ways.

Firstly, they have imputed integration history an inbuilt teleology. It is, for example, commonplace to imply that there was only one 'path to unity' in the aftermath of the Second World War, the federalist path that the likes of Monnet, Schuman and Spaak were treading ('only its length remains unknown),[58] a view 'based on the normative assumption that the path taken by the Six in the 1950s was not only successful but natural, and also morally superior to the British preference for trade liberalization within intergovernmental institutional structures.'[59]

The upshot of this view is that it is possible to draw unfavourable comparisons between the nationalist, short-sighted British and the luminaries of post-war integration.[60] Where they are the heroes of the integration story, the British are the villains.[61] Like German historians in the 1960s and 1970s who interpreted modern German history as a *Sonderweg* ('a historically unique departure from the apparently normal path of democratic virtue'), Britain's relations with the EEC have tended to be construed as an 'abnormal detachment from developments on the European Continent and – after 1945 – from European integration'.[62]

56 Bullen, review, 'Britain, France and the Unity of Europe 1945–1951. By John W. Young; The Foreign Policy of the British Labour Government 1945–1951. Edited by Ritchie Ovendale', *Journal of Common Market Studies*, 24:1 (1985), 77–8 (77).

57 Howarth, 'Discourse Theory', pp. 124–7 and *The Times Higher Education Supplement*, 3 March 2000, p. 20.

58 D. Brinkley and C. Hackett (eds), *Jean Monnet: The Path to European Unity* (Basingstoke, Macmillan, 1991); Monnet, *Memoirs*, p. 432.

59 Kaiser, *Using Europe*, p. 16 of the introduction.

60 For instance E. Dell, *The Schuman Plan and the British Abdication of Leadership in Europe* (Oxford, Oxford University Press, 1995) and Lord Jenkins of Hillhead's opening remarks in Bond, Smith and Wallace (eds), *Eminent Europeans*, preface, p. 7.

61 This point is well made in M. Forsyth, review, 'The Recovery of Europe: From Devastation to Unity. By Richard Mayne', *International Affairs*, 48:1 (1972), 100–1 (100).

62 Kaiser, *Using Europe*, introduction, p. 16.

The twin assumptions that the federal path was the correct one for Europe and that the British were wrong not to tread it run through accounts of British policy towards European integration by writers who concentrate on the life and works of the founding fathers and those who have followed in their footsteps. As Prodi put it in his Oxford speech: 'Britain's attitude to Europe contrasts with that of many of its European partners. It is a source of fascination, perplexity, and sometimes frustration elsewhere in Europe. Despite much progress over the years ... the UK's stance in Europe has too often been defensive. Arguing sometimes for things not to happen. But history did not stop.'[63] The continuity in attitude this demonstrates is evidence of three features of orthodox historiography of British European policy that recur throughout this chapter. The first is that orthodox historiography stems in large measure from live political debate about European integration and Britain's attitude to it after 1945. Monnet, Schuman and Spaak and their friends and colleagues examined in this chapter developed distinctive ideas about where western Europe should go after the Second World War.[64] They attempted to impose these on the European and international political, security and economic agendas, and in so doing hoped to persuade the British that the intergovernmental approach to integration was outdated. Lambasting British European and foreign policy after 1945 became intimately bound up with their selling of the European idea to converts and other potential awkward partners alike.

The second is that the orthodoxy tends to take on a crusading tone reminiscent, according to White, of much history-writing and biography: '[i]t seems possible to conclude that every historical narrative has as its latent or manifest purpose the desire to moralise the events of which it treats.'[65] Jordanova agrees that 'All historical accounts contain moral judgements, either implicit or explicit. History written for a general public is, by its very nature, likely to bring such judgements into prominence.'[66] This, Nigel Hamilton argues, is part and parcel of the writing of lives. 'Life *is* full of monsters and heroes ... we cannot blind ourselves to human nature.'[67]

Following on from this, the third feature of orthodox historiography is that it exhibits both descriptive and prescriptive dimensions. As Colin McInnes has

63 Quoted at www.europa-web.de/europa/011vkvjf/113ebw/monnet.htm.
64 Even Milward, who as we have seen argues that it was not until at least three years after the Second World War that their federal ideas became entrenched, admits in *The European Rescue*, p. 336, that despite the lack of consistency in Monnet's thinking before that time, 'This is in no way to suggest that a European federation did not become the lodestar of Monnet's political actions from that moment onwards.'
65 White, *The Content of the Form*, p. 14.
66 Jordanova, *History in Practice*, p. 162. For discussion of the politicised nature of public history see pp. 155 onwards.
67 N. Hamilton, 'The Role of Biography', in A. Seldon (ed.), *Contemporary History: Practice and Method* (Oxford, Basil Blackwell, 1988), pp. 165–9 (p. 167). Emphasis in original.

argued in another context, 'the line between description and prescription is a thin one. In describing we construct not only the possibility for action but also the nature and limits of that action.'[68] By describing what they saw as an obstructive, awkward British policy towards Europe, orthodox writers were attempting to influence the future course of that policy, rendering the 'history' contained in these works politically motivated propaganda. For Monnet and his band of Europeans, British European policy needed to be changed, and their contemporary criticisms of Britain, together with the publication of their memoirs and biographies by leading sympathisers, were key tools of diplomacy to that end.

Milward remarks upon the wide-ranging nature of their propaganda campaign by noting that '[T]heir associates have testified to so many conferences, spoken so frequently to the media, and given so many oral history interviews, all to the effect that the start of the Community was an act of conversion.'[69] The founding fathers have, therefore, to be the starting-point for any analysis of the historiography of Britain's relations with Europe, though their ideas and the policies that flowed from them were devised and shaped by many other people, not least the Americans. It is to the broader Cold War environment within which integration occurred that we now turn in an effort to gauge their wider impact.

America's Cold War warriors

The second community of writers driving orthodox historiography is made up of the American federalists, many of whom have personal connections with Monnet. 'It was on Monnet that the Americans mainly relied to sustain the momentum towards European integration and he was the man whom they often chose as a privileged interlocutor and interpreter of their plans to other governments.'[70] How and why did this close relationship develop? One reason was that European unity came early in the post-war years to be seen in Washington as an important adjunct to America's strategy of containing the spread of communism. Thus, for example, President Harry Truman announced the Truman Doctrine in March 1947. Ostensibly about the donation of American aid to Greece and Turkey, Truman extended the scope of the US effort 'to support free peoples who are resisting attempted subjugation by armed minorities or by outside pressures'.[71]

But this was about more than unity among the Europeans with the backing of the Americans; they wanted to be involved at all levels of the project. 'The US

---

68 C. McInnes, 'So Who Needs Doctrine Anyway?', paper presented to the British International Studies Association Annual Conference, December 2001, draft 4, version 2, pp. 4–5.

69 Milward, *The European Rescue*, p. 318.

70 *Ibid.*, p. 334.

71 Truman's speech is reprinted in B. J. Bernstein and A. J. Matusow, *The Truman Administration: A Documentary History* (New York, Harper and Row, 1968), pp. 251–6; this from p. 255.

favoured a more tightly knit Europe for a variety of reasons that included idealism (federalism would stop war) and a desire for control over the western project.'[72] Later in 1947, William Bullitt, a State Department official, summed up the line of thinking about a worldwide communist threat that, by becoming the accepted wisdom in Washington, had led to the Truman Doctrine. As one step to combat the spread of communism, Bullitt suggested a 'European Federation of Democratic States' that could 'face up to Russia'. On the surface a military project, economic and technical aid was part of his vision too, as they would help counter political instability in western Europe.[73] He found willing accomplices in men such as the Secretary of State Dean Acheson, who saw 'economic assistance [as] primarily a weapon in the struggle against Communism; the Marshall Plan primarily a program for achieving strategic, not economic, goals'.[74]

Political instability was a source of ongoing concern for Washington after the Second World War, as it heralded the prospect of the Communist Parties spreading their appeal in democratic countries deemed of vital strategic importance to the Americans. In France, the Communist Party (PCF) managed to poll well over 25 per cent of the vote in the two general elections held in 1946,[75] leading Jean Blondel to write in the 1970s that 'Those who in the late forties hoped that an improvement of living conditions would be accompanied by a substantial Communist decrease have been disappointed.'[76]

In Italy, the Communist Party (PCI) was a member of the three coalition governments formed between December 1945 and May 1947, along with the Christian Democrats (DC) and the Republican Party (RPI). Like Blondel for France, Paul Ginsborg is led to conclude for Italy that 'in 1945–8, it would seem wide of the mark to accuse the Communists of failing to make a revolution'.[77] David Hine is of the same opinion. 'With communist dictatorship in Eastern

---

72 A. Deighton, 'British–West German Relations, 1945–1972', in K. Larres (ed.), *Uneasy Allies: British–German Relations and European Integration since 1945* (Oxford, Oxford University Press, 2000), pp. 27–44 (p. 31). See also Ruane, *The Rise and Fall of the European Defence Community*, pp. 25–6.

73 S. E. Ambrose, *Rise to Globalism: American Foreign Policy 1938–1970* (Harmondsworth, Penguin, 1973), pp. 139–40. Chapter 5 incorporates a critical analysis of the origins of the Truman Doctrine.

74 M. J. Hogan, 'The Rise and Fall of Economic Diplomacy: Dean Acheson and the Marshall Plan', in D. Brinkley (ed.), *Dean Acheson and the Making of U.S. Foreign Policy* (Basingstoke, Macmillan, 1993), pp. 1–27 (p. 2). See in addition M. J. Hogan, *The Marshall Plan: America, Britain and the Reconstruction of Western Europe, 1947–1952* (Cambridge, Cambridge University Press, 1987), pp. 26–53 and A. Wilson and R. D. McKinzie, 'Oral History Interview with Dean Acheson, 30 June 1971', Truman Library, www.trumanlibrary.org/oralhist/acheson.htm, p. 3.

75 Figures from Table 1.1 in A. Stevens, *The Government and Politics of France* (Basingstoke, Macmillan, 1992), p. 25.

76 J. Blondel, *The Government of France*, 2nd edn (London, Methuen, 1974), p. 105.

77 P. Ginsborg, *A History of Contemporary Italy: Society and Politics 1943–1988* (London, Penguin, 1990), p. 83.

Europe an increasingly obvious fact of life, many Italians could be forgiven for supposing that the Communists were on the verge of a similar coup in Italy.' It was, he says, only the 'promise of American [Marshall Aid] assistance for a resolutely anti-communist Italian government [that] encouraged the DC to expel the Socialists and Communists from the Council of Ministers'.[78] Even in the spring of 1948, Hugh Wilford notes, the British Foreign Office was convinced that the Communists were poised for victory in the General Election, and put concerted propaganda efforts into trying to limit their appeal to Italian voters.[79] Washington shared London's fear and, as part of the strategy of the Central Intelligence Agency (CIA) was to subsidise non-communist left and centre parties in Western Europe, the Agency made payments to political groups that supported Alcide de Gasperi (another trusted 'European' in America's eyes) in that election.[80]

The strategic importance assigned to western Europe by Washington's Cold War warriors was reflected in the effort American intelligence agencies expended on building support for a federal Europe that would be a 'client' of the United States.[81] One intelligence historian, Richard Aldrich, has drawn attention to this dimension of America's strategy as follows:

> Covert operations are central to any understanding of events in post-war Western Europe ... American officials, trying to stabilize post-war Europe in the face of growing communist parties in France and Italy, assumed that this required rapid unification, perhaps leading to a United States of Europe ... The creation of a federalist United States of Europe was something of a holy grail for Washington.[82]

He goes on to argue that between 1949 and 1960, the CIA discreetly injected 4 million dollars into the European Movement, which had been founded at the Hague Congress in May 1948 and counted among its Presidents of Honour such individuals as Winston Churchill and Paul-Henri Spaak,[83] in an effort 'to drum

78 D. Hine, *Governing Italy: The Politics of Bargained Pluralism* (Oxford, Oxford University Press, 1993), p. 26. On p. 28 he notes that Italy received some 1.5 billion dollars from the Marshall Aid programme.

79 H. Wilford, 'The Information Research Department: Britain's Secret Cold War Weapon Revealed', *Review of International Studies*, 24:3 (1998), 353–69 (358–9).

80 *Ibid.*, p. 345. See also Milward, *The European Rescue*, pp. 332–3.

81 W. Wallace, review, 'Inside the Foreign Office. By John Dickie; The European Rescue of the Nation-State. By Alan S. Milward', *The Times Literary Supplement*, 30 April 1993, p. 25.

82 R. J. Aldrich, *The Hidden Hand: Britain, America and Cold War Secret Intelligence* (London, John Murray, 2001), p. 342. For a précis of his argument see R. J. Aldrich, 'European Integration: An American Intelligence Connection', in A. Deighton (ed.), *Building Post-War Europe: National Decision-Makers and European Institutions, 1948–63* (Basingstoke, Macmillan, 1995), pp. 159–79 (p. 159).

83 The national sections of the European Movement are coordinated by an international secretariat based in Brussels. The British section of the European Movement, created in 1949, works closely with groups within political parties and oversees the work of the Young European Movement. It is currently chaired by Ian Taylor, a Labour Member of Parliament. Its website can be accessed at www.euromove.org.uk/00_navigation%20frame.html.

up mass support for the Marshall Plan, the Schuman Plan ..., the European Defence Community and a European Assembly with sovereign powers.'[84]

The intelligence history sheds new light on the projects of Monnet, Schuman and Spaak, because it identifies them not as leaders in the movement for European unity but as pawns in a Cold War game played out by America and Russia. For writers such as Aldrich, the federal enthusiasts in Washington drove integration in Europe at least as much, if not more than, those in Brussels, Paris and Bonn. The relationship was certainly close, and it becomes harder to detect the leaders and followers as time goes on: but in the first post-war decade America, he suggests, made much of the running: 'Quite simply, the most enthusiastic federalist power in post-war Europe was the United States.'[85] Milward, as we have seen, sees a similarly nuanced picture. Monnet, he says, had chosen carefully whom he acquainted himself with in the United Sates, but makes the point that as 'American influence and leverage over Western Europe diminished, so too did Monnet's own power and influence in Paris'. This takes him nearer to Aldrich's position, that Monnet was in no way the master of his or Europe's destiny in the face of dedicated covert American assistance to Europe after 1947.[86]

With the Americans showing this degree of zeal for a united Europe, and supporting that policy with considerable investment, of a psychological, a political and a financial nature, it is no surprise that British reticence to join the early moves to unity has been criticised as hotly there as on the Continent. Of all the 'substantial obstacles' faced by the CIA in its efforts to federalise Europe, notes Aldrich, 'the biggest ... was London, which under both Labour and Conservative administrations staunchly resisted the idea of a federal Europe'.

British resistance took several forms. First of all, Attlee's Labour government made it plain that although it supported the idea of unity in Europe, it preferred the intergovernmental, not the federal mode of co-operation. As Foreign Secretary Ernest Bevin worked hard, for instance, to limit the powers of the Council of Europe at Strasbourg, and Labour kept Britain from participating in the ECSC. Second, Churchill, despite his playing a leading part in the founding and early years of the European Movement, his rhetoric about forming a United States of Europe and his having a strong affinity for the 'special relationship', led a Conservative Party that was deeply sceptical about the federal approach to unity. Both he and his son-in-law Duncan Sandys, the President of the European Movement, gradually lost their federalist fervour, and with it the confidence of the Americans, culminating in Sandys being deposed as President, to be replaced by 'Spaak's federalist element'.[87]

---

84 Aldrich, *The Hidden Hand*, p. 343.
85 *Ibid.*, p. 344.
86 Milward, *The European Rescue*, p. 334.
87 Aldrich, *The Hidden Hand*, pp. 349–51.

European integration seen in its intelligence context involved many more organisations, pressure groups and individuals than are normally written into the history. The European projects funded by the CIA have, for obvious reasons, not been mentioned in the memoirs or oral testimony provided by key players in Europe and America at this time. As an organisation it has been carefully written out of European integration history. Texts that do mention it tend to concentrate on its higher-profile work in overthrowing pro-Communist governments and replacing them with pro-Western ones, on its work against Russia and China in eastern Europe, Asia and Africa, for example.[88] CIA funds used in support of its European operations, although comparatively small by today's standards and the amount of money devoted at the same time to Marshall Aid, were channelled into all sorts of activities, even cultural ones, if they were deemed important enough in combating the appeal of communism to those in western Europe. This, says, Wilford, was a crusade to win the 'hearts and minds' of opinion-formers on a grand scale, not just those of the politicians and diplomats, but of the world's intellectuals, the media and the *literati* more widely.[89]

The moral and *matériel* support lent by the Americans to the federal project, coupled with British intransigence on this matter, explains why so many of them propagate the critical interpretation of British European policy in their memoirs. Even those Americans in the State Department, such as George Kennan, who warned against alienating the British by bullying them into accepting federalism, nonetheless saw minimum action by the United States as being to 'try gently to persuade Britain to move towards Europe'.[90] It is more usual, however, to find the first generation of post-war American policy-makers being openly hostile to London's stance on Europe. Six individuals stand out in this respect.

First of all, Dean Acheson, who was American Secretary of State 1941–45, Under Secretary of State 1945–47 and Secretary of State again 1949–53, and someone to whom Monnet, whom Acheson described in his memoirs as 'one of the greatest Frenchmen' and the 'brilliant originator' of the Schuman Plan,[91] had 'easy access'.[92] It is generally accepted that European unity was one of Acheson's pet projects and 'he had always ... proclaimed the American federal system as an

88 For instance W. Isaacson and E. Thomas, *The Wise Men: Six Friends and the World They Made* (New York, Touchstone, 1988), p. 574.

89 H. Wilford, "Unwitting Assets?' British Intellectuals and the Congress for Cultural Freedom', *Twentieth Century British History*, 11:1 (2000), 42–60 (43).

90 Aldrich, *The Hidden Hand*, p. 353.

91 D. Acheson, *Present at the Creation: My Years in the State Department* (London, Hamish Hamilton, 1969), pp. 76–7 and 707. See also the portrait by D. Brinkley, *Dean Acheson: The Cold War Years, 1953–71* (London, Yale University Press, 1992), especially pp. 76 and 187.

92 Milward, *The European Rescue*, p. 334.

exemplar to the world'.[93] Britain's rejection of the Schuman Plan was, he said in his memoirs, 'the greatest mistake of the post-war period'.[94] On top of implying that Britain lost out economically by not joining European schemes at the start, Acheson suggests that the tone and tenor of British foreign policy in 1950 convinced the Americans that they would have to look elsewhere for leaders in Europe, principally in Paris but also in Bonn; so it was also a strategic mistake.[95]

Ruane sounds a note of caution to the conventional wisdom by challenging the view that Acheson and his colleagues tried to 'lever Britain into membership of the EDC'. Their evaluation of British European policy was, he stresses, retrospective; *at the time*, according to briefing papers for meetings between Prime Minister Churchill, Foreign Secretary Eden and their American counterparts in January 1952, Acheson was happy for London to remain outside the EDC. Indeed, the documents suggest he claimed to 'fully understand the reasons why the U.K. objects to full participation'.[96] The divergence between the events themselves and how they have been remembered and written as history is a powerful reminder of the importance of words and language games in constructing the reality we now speak of as 'British European policy'. Like Milward on Monnet, Ruane points to discrepancies in their positions not explored by previous writers.

Secondly, one might point to George Ball, a 'like-minded thinker' and close associate of both Acheson and Monnet,[97] the latter the only person to have a chapter named after him in Ball's memoirs.[98] He 'had worked closely with Monnet on plans for the European Coal and Steel Community in the late 1940s and ... later represented it and several other Common Market agencies in America',[99] occupying the posts of Secretary of State for Economic Affairs and, from 1961, Under-Secretary of State with special responsibility for European affairs.

Significantly, Ball revealed that he was 'amanuensis and intellectual punching bag whenever [Monnet] came to the United States'.[100] His use of the word 'amanuensis' says a lot about the constant transmission of ideas between Monnet and key American policy-makers, for it has two meanings: a person who writes from dictation or copies manuscripts, and a literary assistant. Ball

93 R. D. Challener, 'The Moralist as Pragmatist: John Foster Dulles as Cold War Strategist', in Craig and Lowenheim (eds), *The Diplomats*, pp. 135–66 (p. 146).

94 Acheson, *Present at the Creation*, p. 387. Elsewhere he is quoted as saying that 'It was not the last chance for Britain to enter Europe, but it was the first wrong choice.'

95 Hogan, 'The Rise and Fall', p. 16. See also L. S. Kaplan, 'Dean Acheson and the Atlantic Community', in Brinkley (ed.), *Dean Acheson and the Making of U.S. Foreign Policy*, pp. 1–27 (pp. 32–5).

96 Ruane, *The Rise and Fall of the European Defence Community*, pp. 28–30.

97 *Ibid.*, p. 187. For the Frenchman's account of their long acquaintance see his *Memoirs*, pp. 227–8.

98 G. W. Ball, *The Past has Another Pattern: Memoirs* (London, W. W. Norton and Co., 1982), Chapter 6.

99 *Ibid.*, p. 187; Milward, *The European Rescue*, p. 334.

100 Ball, *The Past Has Another Pattern*, p. 95.

acted in the former capacity, implying that Monnet would come to Washington and dictate scripts and speeches for Ball to use, a role Barker alludes to when she says that

> While the politicians were on the public stage, in the wings there was Jean Monnet. He was always prompting and sometimes directing the politicians. He knew every-one of importance, was always on the move, and seemed to be everywhere at once … he was a sort of one-man international pressure group, persuading, manoeuvring and pushing forward politicians, top officials and business tycoons.[101]

Little wonder, then, that Ball was of much the same outlook as Monnet on the British question, although, as Ruane notes of Acheson, he did make some attempt to empathise with the situation facing British policy-makers in the post-war era.

Echoing Acheson's opinion that Britain had 'not yet found a role', Ball quoted Disraeli in his memoirs to advance the argument that the British 'failed to understand "the relative mediocrity of their circumstances"'.[102] Elsewhere he is less kind. 'Great Britain had not yet adjusted to reality; no longer an empire, it was now merely an island nation on which the sun not only set, but set every evening – provided one could see it for rain.'[103] The crux for him was that Britain should have boarded the European bus at the start of its journey. Looking back in the 1980s he believed that 'Had Britain joined the Schuman Plan at the outset, it could have taken the laboring oar in drafting the Rome Treaty that created the EEC, and the peoples of Western Europe might today be combining their ener-gies in a broader framework that could give real meaning to the concept of an Atlantic Partnership.'[104] For Ball, as for Acheson, the British approach to Europe had little to recommend it compared to the approach taken by the 'good Europeans', because it did not support his wider aim of achieving a Euro-Atlantic partnership in the defence and foreign policy fields.[105]

The third, fourth and fifth people one might examine in an attempt to under-stand the American critique of British European policy are the Dulles brothers, Allen Welsh and John Foster, and their sister Eleanor Lansing. Allen Dulles was a driving force behind many of the CIA's post-war 'cultural and labour activities' in Europe.[106] Long an 'enthusiast for covert operation,' he became head of the CIA in 1950 and with the help of Thomas Braden set up a new branch, the International Organizations Division, to co-ordinate the work of the disparate movements

---

101 Barker, *The Common Market*, p. 45.

102 Ball, *The Past Has Another Pattern*, p. 81.

103 *Ibid.*, p. 209.

104 *Ibid.*, p. 222.

105 G. Ball, *The Discipline of Power*, p. 57. The chapter before, pp. 39–56, provides further evidence of his affection for Monnet.

106 For his rather anodyne account of the aims and methods of the CIA see A. Dulles, *The Craft of Intelligence* (London, Weidenfeld and Nicolson, 1964).

America supported.[107] 'Many Americans working for the CIA', writes Aldrich, 'were either themselves liberals, idealists or determined federalists ... Others simply viewed American federalism as a model which should be exported.'[108] Leonard Mosley argues that from the CIA director's discretionary fund Dulles, a 'close friend of Monnet',[109] 'paid one member of the French cabinet $30 thousand a year for himself' and 'handed him $500 thousand to distribute among his fellow members' in order to bribe the French into ratifying the EDC treaty.[110] The rapid post-war expansion of CIA and State Department efforts to combat the spread of communism in Europe and elsewhere is also noted by Eleanor Dulles in a study of American foreign policy-making: 'Our personnel abroad increased, and our budget reflected the growing demands on our resources.'[111]

Allen Welsh's anti-communist zeal was matched by his brother John Foster Dulles, Secretary of State in the Eisenhower administrations of 1953 and 1956 until his death in 1959. By dint of his higher-profile position, John Foster has received more historiographical attention than either his brother or sister, who headed the Berlin Desk at the State Department from 1952 to 1959. Honoured as the *Time* 'Man of the Year' in 1954 for his efforts on America's behalf in the 'struggle with Communism',[112] John Foster was an 'old friend' of Monnet,[113] 'the longest, most intimate and deepest of Dulles' ties overseas', comparable only to his relations with Adenauer.[114]

By contrast, 'Dulles never quite understood the British as he did the French and the Germans', because 'Eden and the British never quite believed in the danger of Germany slipping away from the West, as Dulles and Adenauer did'.[115] This problem was made all the more acute because of poor personal relations between Eden and Dulles, hitting a nadir over the EDC. The latter, it is said, saw that 'Europe's urgent need was integration and that Britain opposed this; that British power was in serious decline, while America's superiority was indisputable'.[116] As

---

107 Aldrich, *The Hidden Hand*, pp. 345–6.

108 *Ibid.*, p. 344.

109 Milward, *The European Rescue*, p. 334.

110 L. Mosley, *Dulles: A Biography of Eleanor, Allen, and John Foster Dulles and their Family Network* (London, Hodder and Stoughton, 1978).

111 E. L. Dulles, *American Foreign Policy in the Making* (New York, Harper and Row, 1968), p. 125.

112 www.time.com/time/special/moy/1954.html.

113 Mosley, *Dulles*, pp. 56–7 and 448; M. A. Guhin, *John Foster Dulles: A Statesman and his Times* (New York, Columbia University Press, 1972), p. 214; R. Goold–Adams, *The Time of Power: A Reappraisal of John Foster Dulles* (London, Weidenfeld and Nicolson, 1962), p. 34; R. H. Immerman, *John Foster Dulles: Piety, Pragmatism, and Power in U.S Foreign Policy* (Wilmington, DE, Scholarly Resources Inc., 1999), p. 12.

114 R. Drummond and G. Coblentz, *Duel at the Brink: John Foster Dulles' Command of American Power* (London, Weidenfeld and Nicolson, 1961), p. 37.

115 Goold-Adams, *The Time of Power*, pp. 156 and 34.

116 T. Hoopes, *The Devil and John Foster Dulles* (London, Andre Deutsch, 1974), p. 166.

the 'greatest champion' of the EDC,[117] he bluntly 'laid part of the blame for the failure of the EDC at the British door,'[118] and continually railed against what he saw as 'British sabotage' of Europe's plans for integration.[119]

The final person in need of analysis to explain American antipathy towards British European policy is David Bruce, whom John Taft judged to be even more 'obsessed' by European integration than his Washington friends.[120] He was America's Ambassador to France, 1949–52, Special American Representative to the High Authority of the ECSC, 1953–54, Ambassador to West Germany 1957–59 and Great Britain, 1961–69 and a close associate of the CIA luminary Frank Wisner.[121] He was at least as in awe of Monnet as Acheson and Ball, cabling to Acheson that he saw in the Schuman Plan 'the most imaginative and far-reaching approach that has been made for generations to the settlement of fundamental differences between France and Germany'.[122]

Monnet, for his part, describes Bruce in his memoirs as an ambassador 'in the best American tradition' who, through his efforts to implement the Marshall Plan, helped bring about the 'preservation of democracy' itself.[123] Predictably, given that 'he became the most articulate American advocate of European integration', helping to swing Acheson behind the Schuman Plan,[124] Bruce's view of British European policy was that it was deeply flawed. But unlike Acheson, who tended to concentrate his criticisms on the rejection of the Schuman Plan, Bruce thought more along the Dulles' lines that the failure to create a European Army, for which Britain is often blamed, represented 'the greatest lost opportunity in modern European history'.[125]

What emerges from the above is that the Washington foreign, defence and intelligence policy-making circles in the first decade after 1945 were inhabited by a tight-knit group of individuals who shared certain key beliefs: that Europe could and should be remade on a federal basis, as the United States had been many years before; that European unity would serve the anti-Communist cause and lead

---

117 Ruane, *The Rise and Fall of the European Defence Community*, p. 42.

118 *Ibid.*, p. 159. On the contrast between Dulles's relationship with Eden and Dulles's relationships with Monnet and Adenauer see also Drummond and Coblentz, *Duel at the Brink*, pp. 37–9.

119 Drummond and Coblentz, *Duel at the Brink*, p. 59. On p. 197 they praise Dulles as the man who 'saved the Common Market' in the face of stiff British opposition in 1957.

120 Quoted in N. D. Lankford, *The Last American Aristocrat: The Biography of David K. E. Bruce, 1898–1977* (London, Little, Brown and Company, 1996), p. 213.

121 Aldrich, *The Hidden Hand*, p. 350. Bruce was well-versed in intelligence techniques, having served during the Second World War in the London branch of the Office of Strategic Services, America's first secret intelligence agency. See N. D. Lankford (ed.), *OSS Against the Reich: The World War Two Diaries of Colonel David K. E. Bruce* (London, The Kent State University Press, 1991).

122 The quotation is from Acheson, *Present at the Creation*, p. 382.

123 Monnet, *Memoirs*, p. 270.

124 Lankford, *The Last American Aristocrat*, pp. 221–2.

125 Quoted in J. Ramsden, review, 'N. Lankford, Aristocrat: The Biography of Ambassador David K. E. Bruce', *Contemporary British History*, 11:2 (1997), 166–8 (168).

in time to a Euro-Atlantic partnership in the fields of defence and security, politics and economics; and that, in shunning involvement in the unity project, British governments misguidedly placed the national interest above the interests of regional and global security.

This is not to deny that these people were in complete agreement about America's Cold War strategy, the end-state for Europe, and which methods should be used to reach it. A theme running through John Harper's article on the Americans and European unity is the clashes between Kennan, who saw the goal of American aid in political terms, and Will Clayton, Under Secretary of State for Economic Affairs, who saw it as economic.[126] He also reminds us that Acheson, who we have seen above was trenchantly critical of the British and British foreign policy, was 'sceptical of creating a 'United States of Europe'' but keen to apply supranational solutions to specific European problems, a nuanced view that reminds us of Ruane's addendum to our conventional picture of Acheson.[127]

But the broadly comparable way in which Acheson, Ball and Allen Welsh, John Foster and Eleanor Dulles, not to mention Charles Bohlen, John McCloy, Robert Lovett and Averell Harriman, interpreted the workings of the international system and the relationship of states within that system suggests something more than a random convergence of like-minded individuals. They were a community in more than just the sense that they inhabited the same policy-making environment because, as Jordanova reminds us, the word community 'does not just mean people living in the same location, but those voluntarily associating together, or linked in some significant way, that is, groups likely to have values and aspirations in common'.[128]

The main driving forces behind European integration and our subsequent interpretations of that process were, says Nigel Ashford, Monnet and his 'network of friends and colleagues who influenced US policy in favour of supranational European integration'.[129] The transference of ideas, concepts and plans for supranational European integration around America, France, Germany and Belgium in the years after 1945 goes a long way to explaining the historiographical entrenchment of the orthodox interpretation that Britain has been Europe's awkward partner. Whether one takes the traditional view of Monnet and the founding fathers as the source of inspiration, or the version favoured by intelligence historians, who see them acting on behalf of Washington and the CIA, it seems fair to argue that the relationship was formalised by the establishment of the American

---

126 J. L. Harper, 'In Their Own Image – The Americans and the Question of European Unity, 1943–54', in Bond, Smith and Wallace (eds), *Eminent Europeans*, pp. 62–84 (p. 67).
127 *Ibid.*, p. 70.
128 Jordanova, *History in Practice*, p. 179.
129 N. Ashford, review, 'Eisenhower, Kennedy and the United States of Europe. By Pascaline Winand', *Journal of Common Market Studies*, 33:2 (1995), 309–10 (309).

Committee on a United Europe (ACUE), set up in the summer of 1948 by Allen Dulles and William Donovan, founder of the Office of Strategic Services (OSS), to be 'the CIA's parent American body for European unity organisations'.

Its primary role was to fund European unity groups and it 'worked closely with US government officials involved with the Marshall Plan, particularly those in the Economic Cooperation Administration (ECA). But ACUE also had a fascinating East European dimension, which tied it into liberation and the volatile exile groups working with the CIA and Radio Free Europe.'[130] ACUE is not to be confused with Monnet's Action Committee for a United States of Europe, ACUSE, 1955–75, set up to harness the power of political parties and trade unions of the Six 'to persuade Governments to transfer more and more of their powers to common institutions', and described by Jean-Jacques Servan-Schreiber as a 'federal authority of the mind'.[131]

ACUE's first beneficiary was the European Movement, which has been discussed above. The second was the Bilderberg Group, founded in 1952 by Joseph Retinger (former Secretary General of the European Movement) and Prince Bernhard of the Netherlands, 'in response to the rise of anti-Americanism in Western Europe'. The Bilderberg Group sought to generate a Euro-Atlantic consensus on potential areas of conflict, such as atomic weapons, by bringing 'leading European and American personalities together once a year for an informal discussion of their differences'.[132] Aldrich argues that by 1956 ACUE, funded by 'US government subventions managed by the CIA', was spending so much money on these and similar projects that its Directors feared it would be publicly exposed.[133] Such was the role of the American Cold War warriors in revivifying Europe after 1945.

The British federalists

Martyn Bond, Julie Smith and William Wallace argue that 'personalities count in what is chosen, in which opportunities are seized or missed'.[134] For the federalists in Washington and on the Continent, Britain missed the European boat in the early 1950s, and their criticisms of British European policy that began to appear in the press and 'instant history' books in the 1950s and 1960s were efforts to convince the British of this. It is to the third group, the British federalists, that this chapter now turns in order to trace the channels through which Monnet's ideas

---

130 Aldrich, *The Hidden Hand*, pp. 359 and 343.
131 See Monnet, *Memoirs*, pp. 405–17, these quotes from p. 408. He prefers to call it, p. 409 'a multiplier of ideas'.
132 *Ibid.*, p. 369.
133 *Ibid.*, p. 366.
134 *Ibid.*, p. 13.

flowed into Britain, tapping into Michael Gehler's comment 'one should not underestimate the influence of the European federalists in setting up different ideas, concepts and programmes on European integration'.[135]

One of the major exponents of federalism in Britain has been the think-tank Federal Union, 'founded in 1938 to campaign for federalism for the UK, Europe and the world',[136] disseminating information widely 'to parliamentarians, business leaders and other opinion molders'.[137] In May 2001 the chairman of Federal Union, Sir Anthony Meyer, gave an address in which he highlighted the overlap between the federalist and the Europeanist agendas. 'We fully support the European Movement, of which most of us are anyway members, in its campaign for active British participation in the European Union; as we support Britain in Europe's campaign for British membership of Economic and Monetary Union when the conditions are right.'[138]

Federal Union has two immediately associated bodies. The Wyndham Place Trust was founded in 1960 'to work on the federal idea in a religious context'.[139] Of greater relevance to this study is the Federal Trust for Education and Research, an independent think-tank that was founded in 1945 by William Beveridge out of the idea that Federal Union 'ought to engage in educational work. Political action and propaganda had their part to play; but deeper and (in the best sense) more academic study, reflection, and research were essential too'.[140] Its constitution states that it 'acts as a forum in which the suitability of federal solutions to problems of governance at national, Continental and global level can be explored',[141] and in the year 2000 it proclaimed that is has 'made a powerful intellectual contribution to the *study of federalism* and in particular Britain's relationship to the emerging European Union'.[142] Two years later the wording had changed, from the

---

135 M. Gehler, review, 'Interdependence Versus Integration, Denmark, Scandinavia, and Western Europe, 1945–1960. By Thorsten B. Olesen', *Journal of European Integration History*, 3:2 (1997), pp. 100–2 (p. 102).

136 This quotation is taken from the Federal Union website, www.federalunion.uklinux.net/about.htm. A comprehensive official history has been written by R. Mayne and J. Pinder, *Federal Union: The Pioneers* (Basingstoke, Macmillan, 1990). For an early exposition of the merits of a federal union among states, see W. B. Curry, *The Case for Federal Union* (Harmondsworth, Penguin, 1939). He advocated, pp. 105–16, the independent control of foreign policy, the pooling of all armed forces, greater economic interdependence and international control of colonies, communications, currencies and civil rights laws.

137 Pfaltzgraff, *Britain Faces Europe*, p. 23.

138 www.federalunion.uklinux.net/news/chairmansmessage.htm. Accessed 8 February 2002.

139 Mayne and Pinder, *Federal Union*, p. 69.

140 *Ibid.*, p. 109.

141 'A Note for Friends About the Federal Trust' (London: The Federal Trust, October 1999), p. 1.

142 'The Federal Trust For Education and Research, Enlightening the Debate on Good Government' leaflet distributed at the Federal Trust and the Trans-European Policy Studies Association (TEPSA) conference, 'Consolidating EMU', London, 9 June 2000. Emphasis in original. As the publicity points out, The Federal Trust helped in 1974 to establish TEPSA, 'a network of like-minded institutes from all the countries of the enlarging European Union.'

study of 'federalism' to the study of 'democratic unity amongst states and peoples', perhaps reflecting growing unease about using the term publicly in Britain. What had not changed was the passage specifically referring to the study of Britain's relations with the EU,[143] and it credits the Federal Trust with bringing Britain 'into Europe' and leading 'the British section of the European movement to a federalist stand in the British political debate on the future of Europe'.[144]

Its activists have been drawn from a cross-section of society. As one of its members, and a historian of Britain and Europe, Uwe Kitzinger, put it:

> They came from a wide variety of backgrounds: one the son of a peer, another who left school at fourteen, one the son of a small tailor, another the son of a bank clerk, several with family origins on the Continent, some candidates or local councillors of the Labour, some of the Liberal and some of the Conservative Party, some full-time trade unionists, some lawyers, some in public relations, one who worked for the British Council of Churches, another for the *Economist*, several at universities or various research institutions.[145]

This, then, was a body with a strong chain of connections and a big will to shift elite opinion in favour of Britain taking the European route. Its numerous meetings, conferences and resulting literature, explains Robert Pfaltzgraff, 'enabled the idea of Common Market membership to be spread among newspaper editorial writers, Members of Parliament, and other persons capable, in turn, of influencing a broader segment of British opinion'.[146]

The current President of the Federal Trust is Sir Donald Maitland, Ambassador and Permanent Representative to the EEC 1975–79, and its Chairman is John Pinder, about whom more below. Its Council Members include British 'Europeans' such as Lord Cockfield, Sir Michael Palliser and Lord Roll of Isden, and also number amongst them people from the worlds of academia, economics, business and charity, together with the former Director of the European Movement and a special adviser to Downing Street's Policy Unit. The sprawling network of individuals belonging to or associated with Federal Trust supports the core argument advanced in this chapter that many writers in the orthodox school are bound by a shared desire to see Europe take the federal path

---

143 www.cix.co.uk/~fedtrust/aboutus_home.htm.

144 A. Bosco, review, 'European Unity and World Order: Federal Trust 1945–1995. By John Pinder', *Journal of Common Market Studies*, 35:2 (1997), 325.

145 U. Kitzinger, *Diplomacy and Persuasion: How Britain Joined the Common Market* (London, Thames and Hudson, 1973), p. 190. Kitzinger worked at the Economic Section of the Council of Europe between 1951 and 1958, and worked up through the University of Oxford between 1956 and 1976, before taking leave of absence in 1973–75 to work for Christopher Soames, then Vice-President of the European Commission. He sat on the National Council of the European Movement between 1974 and 1976 and was a member of the Royal Institute of International Affairs (RIIA) between 1973 and 1985: *Who's Who 2000* (London, A. and C. Black, 2000), p. 1153.

146 Pfaltzgraff, *Britain Faces Europe*, pp. 24–5.

to integration after the Second World War and a shared disappointment that Britain resisted this move in the post-war era.

Given their internationalist outlook and their declared aim of convincing the British that their future lies nearer to the heart of Europe, it is no surprise that members of the various federalist movements have been leading exponents of the orthodoxy on British European policy. Their concern is thus with what one of Monnet's biographers called the 'bottomless pit of a question' as to why the British 'were so resistant to European integration';[147] hence the pervasiveness of historical accounts that chastise politicians and civil servants whose 'misjudgements ... led their European policy so grievously astray'.[148]

The official historians of Federal Union, Richard Mayne and John Pinder, have, one reviewer mentions, themselves 'been for four decades loyal to the European construction'.[149] Mayne worked as an official in the ECSC, 1956–58, and in the EEC, 1958–63, and was personal assistant and speech-writer to Monnet in the period 1963–66. Pinder has been chairman of the Federal Trust since 1985 and earlier the press officer of Federal Union, 1950–52. He worked at the Economist Intelligence Unit (EIU), an organisation 'which included among its staff persons who were also members of Federal Union' in 1952–64 (rising to its Director of International Operations)[150] and was President of the Union of European Federalists, 1984–90.[151]

Both have published widely on European integration history; both are highly critical of Britain's policy towards European integration. Mayne argues that '[S]cepticism, based partly on lack of interest and partly on ignorance, was the characteristic reaction of British officials to the initiatives proposed by Monnet, Schuman and the Six.'[152] Pinder consistently issues 'a characteristically

---

147 F. Duchêne, *Jean Monnet: The First Statesman of Interdependence*, trans. Richard Mayne (London, W. W. Norton and Co., 1994), p. 208. He was also a Federal Trustee, Mayne and Pinder, *Federal Union*, p. 113.

148 *Ibid.*, p. 98. Another body of interest in the context of this study is the Regional Commission. Set up in 1956 it was 'a group containing the hard core of its supporters of the Monnet approach to Community-building', planning 'how to change British opinion and policy': Mayne and Pinder, *Federal Union*, pp. 146–7.

149 Bosco, review, 'Federal Trust 1945–1995. By John Pinder', *Journal of Common Market Studies*, 325.

150 Pfaltzgraff, *Britain Faces Europe*, p. 25.

151 *Who's Who 2000*, pp. 1390 and 1623. The EIU was set up in 1946 during Geoffrey Crowther's editorship, and provides 'country intelligence', from global macroeconomic forecasts to political and economic analysis. Further information can be obtained from its website at www.eiu.com. See also R. D. Edwards, *The Pursuit of Reason: The Economist 1843–1993* (London, Hamish Hamilton, 1993), pp. 902–6.

152 See Richard Mayne, review, 'The Price of Victory. By Michael Charlton', *International Affairs*, 60:2 (1984), 326–7 (327). Mayne's publications include *Postwar: The Dawn of Today's Europe* (London, Thames and Hudson, 1983); *The Community of Europe* (London, Victor Gollancz, 1962) and *The Recovery of Europe: From Devastation to Unity* (London, Weidenfeld and Nicolson, 1970).

well-argued appeal to British policy-makers to abjure their intergovernmental-ism',[153] and his judgement that Britain 'remained coldly aloof from the Europeans' ideas' has a distinctly Monnetist flavour to it.[154]

Their history of the 'pioneers' of Federal Union is interspersed with vitri-olic sideswipes about the post-war elite in Britain and its short-sightedness and crude negativity towards the Continent, an apt summary coming in a passage where they discuss the contribution made to the federalist cause by Jo Josephy, one of the founding directors of Federal Union. She was right, they argue, to be concerned that Britain 'would find herself perched precariously on the perimeter of a united Europe … But it was to be some time before British governments were to learn that lesson – if indeed they have'.[155]

Journalists and instant historians

Several journalists and instant historians have played vital roles in spreading the federalist message and promoting the European cause in Britain. Turning first to the journalists, Greenwood reminds us that 'until the 1970s the British press tended to be pro-Community',[156] a remark that is especially applicable to the *Economist*, a newsmagazine that (along with *Time* and *Newsweek*) 'had truly international circulation and would be cited without an identifier in almost any city on the globe'.[157]

Its European correspondents have consistently advocated closer British involvement in the process of European integration, and it is poignant that it is the only organ of the British press to be mentioned by name by de Carmoy in the

153 C. Brewin, review, 'Maastricht and Beyond: Building the European Union. By Andrew Duff, John Pinder and Roy Pryce', *Journal of Common Market Studies*, 34:1 (1996), 134. See for example J. Pinder, *Britain and the Common Market* (London, The Cresset Press, 1961), written in a four-week period finishing on the day Macmillan announced Britain's first application to the EEC, 'to show what membership would mean to us' (foreword).

154 J. Pinder, *Europe Against de Gaulle* (London, Pall Mall Press for Federal Trust, 1963), p. 68. For a restatement of his position see J. Pinder, 'Prewar Ideas of Union – The British Prophets', in Bond, Smith and Wallace (eds), *Eminent Europeans*, pp. 1–21, especially p. 119.

155 Mayne and Pinder, *Federal Union*, p. 94. A close associate of Mayne and Pinder, Roy Pryce, should also be included in analysis of the spread of the federalist message in Britain. He was Director of the Federal Trust, 1983–90 and previously Head of the Information Office of High Authority of the ECSC, 1957–60, and Head of the Joint Information Office of the European Communities, 1960–64. *Who's Who 2000*, p. 1664. His publications include *The Political Future of the European Community* (London, John Marshbank, 1962) and *The Dynamics of European Union* (London, Routledge, 1990).

156 S. Greenwood, review, 'Britain For and Against Europe: British Politics and European Integration. Edited by D. Baker and D. Seawright', *Journal of Common Market Studies*, 36:4 (1998), 603–4 (603).

157 E. R. May, 'The News Media and Diplomacy', in Craig and Lowenheim (eds), *The Diplomats 1939–1979*, pp. 665–93 (p. 666).

section of his 'Defence and Unity' dealing with Britain's turn to the EEC from 1959.[158] The same goes for Anthony Sampson, who noted that in the middle of 1960 'the press – headed by the *Economist*, which diplomats read – was becoming louder' in its support for an application to join the EEC.[159] What Sampson omitted to mention was that the paper's support for British entry to the EEC had been building for a number of years, and that in November 1955 it had issued this stark warning: 'Unless the British Government will say what it will do, not simply what it will not do, a time may soon come when it will find that it has missed a bus that it will wish it had caught.'[160]

Evidence on the meeting of minds between Monnet and his friends the Europeanists at the *Economist* is to be found in this passage from Monnet's memoirs, where he describes its editorials on Europe in the late 1940s (along with those in *The Times*) as 'admirable ... worthy of Jay's, Madison's and Hamilton's *Federalist Papers*. Re-reading all this, one has the feeling that so rich a current of thought could hardly fail to bring about European unity on the broadest front.' He goes on to say that when he came to London to generate support for the Schuman Plan, one of his first meetings was with an old friend Geoffrey Crowther, then editor of the *Economist*; 'afterwards, I could face my political contacts'.[161]

An illustration of the *Economist*'s disaffection with British foreign policy is to be found in its *Guide to the European Union*, first published in 1988 and reworked several times since. In the section dealing with the origins of the EU, Monnet is credited with being 'the most clearsighted and persuasive advocate' of supranational integration. Britain, it says, 'stood aloof' from the ECSC, 'having given the matter very little serious thought'.[162] Indeed, the case of Britain is deemed so problematic that Anglo-EU relations warrant examination as one of three 'special problems' explored in the 1994 edition, along with enlargement and 'the future'. Here, Dick Leonard says that the 'history of distrust' built up since the early days now contributes to the 'uneasy relationship' between Britain and the EU.[163]

Two *Economist* writers stand out in this respect: Christopher Layton and Miriam Camps. Christopher Layton is the son of Walter (Lord) Layton, who was a Federal Union activist, Vice-President of the Consultative Assembly of the

158 de Carmoy, 'Defence and Unity', p. 357.

159 A. Sampson, *Anatomy of Britain* (London, Hodder and Stoughton, 1962), p. 320.

160 *Economist*, 19 November 1955, pp. 633–4 (p. 633). The paper's 'internationalism', and thus its aversion to Britain's aloofness from the Continent, is set out in the official history by Edwards, *The Pursuit of Reason*, p. 44.

161 Monnet, *Memoirs*, pp. 283 and 306.

162 D. Leonard, *The Economist Guide to the European Union: The Original and Definitive Guide to all Aspects of the European Union* (London, Hamish Hamilton, 1994), pp. 3 and 5.

163 *Ibid.*, pp. 227–32.

Council of Europe, 1949–57 and editor of the *Economist* in the years 1923–39.[164]
Lord Layton (whom Spaak describes as a 'good European')[165] was a member of
various European federalist groups and 'a crucial link between the British section
of the European Movement and ACUE'.[166]

The younger Layton joined the EIU in 1953, and in 1954 took up the post
of 'Editorial writer – European Affairs', where he met Pinder, another EIU
employee, Duchêne, a close friend and biographer of Monnet, and 'other federalists in the EIU who had written in *World Affairs* about the blindness of Britain's
negative policy towards European integration'.[167] Layton, observes Ruth Dudley
Edwards in the official history of the newspaper, had 'been much involved with
his father in various abortive post-war manifestations of the European movement', and with Duchêne became 'another key foreign-department crusader for
Europe'.[168] 'European unity', Aldrich surmises, 'was a Layton family business,'[169] and what was Layton business was often *Economist* business.

Camps modestly described herself as the 'mother' of the OEEC.[170] She
was a foreign affairs officer in the American State Department, 1939–54,
specialising in problems relating to European economic co-operation and integration, and was involved in the development and implementation of the
Marshall Plan, the OEEC and the ECSC.[171] 'As a private citizen', notes William
Diebold, 'she wrote under the auspices of American and British research organizations and was recognized as a leading expert on the European Community
and especially Britain's relations with it.'[172] Two such organisations were
Political and Economic Planning (PEP), based in London, and the Ford
Foundation, based in Washington. The former (later renamed the Policy Studies
Institute, with Pinder as its Director from 1964–1985) sponsored Camps's

164 Edwards, *The Pursuit of Reason*, especially pp. 608–52. See also Mayne and Pinder, *Federal Union*, p. 147 and Lord Gladwyn, *The Memoirs of Lord Gladwyn* (London, Weidenfeld and Nicolson, 1972), p. 142.

165 Spaak, *The Continuing Battle*, p. 209.

166 Aldrich, *The Hidden Hand*, p. 359.

167 Mayne and Pinder, *Federal Union*, p. 153; Monnet, *Memoirs*, p. 456.

168 Edwards, *The Pursuit of Reason*, p. 923.

169 Aldrich, *The Hidden Hand*, p. 359.

170 M. Camps, 'Missing the Boat at Messina and Other Times?', in B. Brivati and H. Jones (eds), *From Reconstruction to Integration: Britain and Europe since 1945* (Leicester, Leicester University Press, 1993), pp. 133–43 (p. 133).

171 This biographic information is taken from 'Mount Holyoke College Archives and Special Collections, Manuscript Register, MS 0627', www.mtholyoke.edu/offices/library/arch/col/ms0627r.htm.

172 W. Diebold, 'Foreign Economic Policy in Acheson's Time and Ours', in Brinkley (ed.), *Dean Acheson*, pp. 233–55 (p. 244).

173 Ford Foundation Archives (hereafter FFA), 58–196, Officer Grant Request IA–60G, 1 April 1959. I am grateful to Geoffrey Warner for information about the activities of Political and Economic Planning.

investigations into the economics of European integration.[173] The latter expanded in 1950 from a 'local philanthropy in the state of Michigan' into 'a national and international foundation',[174] and provided extra funds on top of the money she received from Political and Economic Planning in support of 'a running evaluation of the common market and free trade area plans as they develop', the object being 'to comment on the progress made towards European economic integration and on the problems which appear to be emerging'.[175]

Her study of attitudes, she remarked in September 1957, 'would not simply be descriptive'. She proposed to 'evaluate the justification of the attitudes and ... speculate as to the implications for the future development of the free trade area'.[176] From the admittedly patchy records relating to her application, it appears she came under pressure under one month later from Joe Slater at the Foundation 'to concentrate on British attitudes toward and evaluations of the effects of the free trade area'. The works she subsequently completed bore the hallmarks of Slater's wishes and were incorporated into her proposal for grant renewal in March 1959. Here, she said she would seek to 'have some impact on the thinking from which policies emerge', involving a 'considerable amount of talking both formally and informally with those who shape policy and those who seek to inform public opinion'.[177]

She achieved her aim, building an impressive array of contacts, including Monnet, American businessmen, government officials, research writers and university professors. In Britain she came into regular contact with government officials, business groups, and 'the responsible British journalists who write on these questions'. In addition, she says, she briefed the Labour Party spokesman on Europe, John Edwards,[178] before every important debate on Europe in the House of Commons.[179]

---

174 www.fordfoundation.org/about/mission.cfm.

175 FFA, 58–196, Camps letter to J. E. Slater, undated but estimated to be June 1957.

176 FFA, 580–0063, Camps, memorandum to Martin Tank, 12 September 1957, p. 2.

177 FFA, Camps letter to Slater, 10 March 1959. She also revealed in *Britain and the European Community 1955–1963*, (London, Oxford University Press, 1964), preface, p. 7, that Frank Lee and other British civil servants had read the 'entire book in draft'. One of those, it later emerged, was Russell Bretherton, Britain's representative at the negotiations that led to the founding of the EEC. See M. Camps, 'Missing the Boat', p. 134.

178 Rt Hon L. John Edwards, MP for Blackburn (1945–50) and Brighouse and Spenborough (1950–59). He was a member of the British Delegation to the Council of Europe from 1955, its Vice-President from 1957 and Chairman of the Budget Committee of the Western European Union, 1955–58 and was elected president of the Consultative Assembly in April 1959. He died in November 1959. The obituary in the Labour Party Conference Report for 1959, p. 51, describes him as 'devoted to the cause of European integration'. Thanks to John Walker of the Labour History Archive and Study Centre for supplying me with this information. See also Stewart, *Life and Labour*, p. 85, who notes that Walker has a road named after him in Strasbourg.

179 FFA, Camps letter to Slater, 10 March 1959.

Praised by Mayne and Pinder as 'one of the shrewdest observers of Europe during this period,[180] Camps, like Layton, wrote for the *Economist* on European institutions at the time when the newspaper first began to voice the opinion that Britain was missing opportunities in Europe.[181] This theme would dominate her books, most notably *Britain and the European Community, 1955–63*, where she analysed, amongst other things, the 'misjudgement' that led to London's withdrawal from the 'major turning-point in the integration of Europe, the Messina process,[182] and Britain's subsequent efforts to come to terms with the EEC, culminating in the first application in 1961.[183] Camps and her peers have tended to see a combination of political, economic and personal failings, especially 'short-sightedness and national egoism' as reasons why Britain 'missed the European bus'.[184] Reviewing Camps's *Britain and the European Community* in 1965, S. C. Leslie wrote that she 'is, or was, a 'European' and her convictions are not concealed. Yet, he continued, 'this rarely leads to bias'.[185] Revisionist historians would strongly disagree.

Thus, it can be argued that appearances of the *Economist*'s 'neutrality' can be deceptive, and 'although each issue has traditionally opened with a proud statement of its independence ... on the European issue the newspaper was committed to a staunchly federalist line', with more than a few of its writers and editors coming from the network of 'dedicated federalists and those prominent in European organisations'.[186] Likewise, argues Wilford, with other publications: hence the scandal in Britain in 1967 when it was revealed that the London-based Anglo-American journal *Encounter* 'had, for a decade following its launch in 1953, regularly received covert subsidies from the United States Central Intelligence Agency'.[187]

The case of the *Economist* is significant in the context of the historiography of British European policy for two reasons. First of all, it highlights the degree to which discourses about European unity, and Britain's place on the fringes and then as part that process, are products of writers' backgrounds, their formative experiences, education, family and non-family relationships, jobs, other work

---

180 Mayne and Pinder, *Federal Union*, p. 143.
181 M. Camps, *Britain and the European Community*, preface, pp. 6–7.
182 *Ibid.*, pp. 47 and 28.
183 Her other texts include *What Kind of Europe? The Community since De Gaulle's Veto* (London, Oxford University Press, 1965) and *European Unification in the Sixties: From the Veto to the Crisis* (London, Oxford University Press, 1967).
184 Barker, *The British Between the Superpowers*, p. 230. She was Assistant Diplomatic Correspondent with Reuters, 1947–8, Diplomatic Correspondent for the BBC's European Service in 1949–65 and head of European Talks for the BBC 1965–9.
185 S. C. Leslie, review, 'Britain and the European Community 1955–1963. By Miriam Camps', *International Affairs*, 41:1 (1965), 121–2 (121).
186 Aldrich, *The Hidden Hand*, p. 359.
187 Wilford, '"Unwitting Assets?"', 42.

experience and political outlook. The second, follow-on, reason is that it sheds light on 'the social construction of historical knowledge, its production within communities, now of a fairly structured kind, that are rooted in institutions, nations, political groupings and so on'.[188] Writers such as Layton and Camps possessed multiple professional identities, moving in distinct but overlapping circles of power and influence. Equally at home in Britain, in America or on the Continent, they worked in various official and unofficial capacities, for government, newspapers and research organisations. The flow of federalist discourse around these channels was picked up on by British politicians keen to push the country closer to the Continent.

British euroenthusiasts

The federalist programme and the criticisms of British foreign policy that fell out of it struck a chord with the sentiments expressed by the euroenthusiasts in British political life, who thought as Monnet did about the need for Britain to be part of a supranational European project. It is they who make up the fifth group of writers one needs to analyse in order to comprehend the popularity of the orthodoxy about Britain and Europe.[189] Their careers brought them into close contact with key opinion-formers such as Monnet and the institutions he helped create, and allegations that the British missed opportunities or missed buses resonate throughout their accounts of British policy-making towards Europe. By dint of repetition, the discourse of missed opportunities has become the interpretative paradigm of choice for this generation of politicians in Britain.

Of these, five stand out.[190] One of the first to go to print was the diplomat Anthony Nutting, who served as Minister of State at the Foreign Office, 1954–56. *Europe Will Not Wait*, first published in 1960, encapsulated the conventional wisdom, and nearly rivals Camps's work in terms of its influence on the historiography. Of the early post-war years, he wrote 'There can be no

---

188 Jordanova, *History in Practice*, p. 199.

189 A large collection of oral evidence from the British policy-makers involved has been gathered in Charlton, *The Price of Victory*. Extracts from this have been published as M. Charlton, 'How and Why Britain Lost the Leadership of Europe (1): 'Messina! Messina!' or, the Parting of Ways', *Encounter*, 57:3 (August 1981), 8–22; M. Charlton, 'How (and Why) Britain Lost the Leadership of Europe (2): A Last Step Sideways', *Encounter*, 57:3 (September 1981), 22–35 and M. Charlton, 'How (and Why) Britain Lost the Leadership of Europe (3): The Channel Crossing', *Encounter*, 57:3 (October 1981), 22–33.

190 One might also refer to the words of the diplomat Nicholas Henderson, quoted in Sanders, *Losing an Empire, Finding a Role*, p. 73, 'We had every Western European Government eating out of our hand in he immediate aftermath of the war. For several years our prestige and influence were paramount … we could have stamped Europe as we wished.' Alec Douglas-Home also conveys this idea: 'we could have had the leadership of Europe but let it slip from our grasp'. He is quoted in D. Maclean, *British Foreign Policy since Suez, 1956–68* (London, Hodder and Stoughton, 1970), p. 507.

doubt that at that moment and for several years afterwards Great Britain could have had the leadership of Europe on any terms which she cared to name. If we had offered our hand it would have been grasped without question or condition.'[191] He cannot decide which of the ECSC, EDC or EEC episodes was the most damaging for the British, but is one of the few writers to put the EDC one on a par with the other two. Eden's creation of the Western European Union in the wake of the collapse of the EDC in 1954 was, he states, too little too late: 'I cannot avoid the unhappy conclusion that, had we done what we did even a few months sooner, we could have had the honour and good fortune to lead Europe, rather than just to rescue it; we could have a flagship not just a lifeboat.'[192] The second is the former businessman and Member of Parliament (MP) Edmund Dell, one of the British Labour Party members who rebelled against party instructions in October 1971 and voted for British membership of the EEC.[193] He wrote of Britain's 'abdication of leadership in Europe' when in 1950 it refused to join with the Six in founding the ECSC. 'Messina', he continued, 'gave the UK another chance but that too was missed.'[194]

Echoing their opinion is Roy Denman in his book *Missed Chances*. He was a member of the team negotiating British entry into the EEC in 1970–71, and then principal British negotiator in successive international trade rounds, before joining the European Commission in 1977 as Director of External Relations.[195] He too is scathing about post-war British European policy. 'In the euphoria of Allied victory in 1945, Britain could have had the leadership of Europe for a song. Britain missed that chance and almost every other since.'[196] To account for this tragedy, Denman rounds up the usual suspects: 'virtually all of Britain's postwar Prime Ministers with the exception of Edward Heath'.[197] 'With very few exceptions', he subsequently wrote, 'British politicians failed to understand this seismic shift in Continental Europe', brought about by the Second World War and manifested in the 'great revolution' instigated by Monnet and Schuman.[198]

191 Nutting, *Europe Will Not Wait*, p. 3.
192 *Ibid.*, p. 75.
193 *Guardian* obituary, 4 November 1999, http://politics.guardian.co.uk/politicsobituaries/story/ 0,1441,563453,00.html.
194 Dell, *The Schuman Plan*, p. 303. See also Alan Milward's review in *Journal of European Integration History*, 3:2 (1997), 99–100.
195 In 1975 he became Head of the European Secretariat in the Cabinet Office. After serving in the Commission as Director General for External Relations he served between 1982 and 1989 as Ambassador of the European Communities in Washington. On p. 1 of *Missed Chances* he sets out his argument as follows: Britain's decline in the twentieth century can be traced to 'a British failure to understand and deal with Continental Europe.'
196 Denman, *Missed Chances*, p. 2.
197 D. Leonard, 'Eye on the EU', *Europe*, 357 (June 1996), 3.
198 R. Denman, 'Joining the Euro', in R. Beetham (ed.), *The Euro Debate: Persuading the People* (London, The Federal Trust for Education and Research, 2001), pp. 79–86 (p. 82).

The Prime Minister who led Britain into the EEC in 1973 is of the same view. Much is made of the fact that Heath's maiden speech in the House of Commons concerned the necessity of Britain joining the ECSC, giving his approach an 'incremental symmetry' that concluded with his leading Britain into the EEC,[199] a fact not lost on Monnet.[200] In the interim he was a regular attender at Federal Trust conferences on Britain and Europe.[201] He takes the classic orthodox line in his memoirs that the Attlee government 'missed what proved to be the historic opportunity of taking part in the negotiations in 1950 which led to the formation of the EEC' and that the British 'grievously underestimated the importance of the Messina Conference'.[202]

The final example of Europeanists in Britain who espoused the orthodoxy was Roy Jenkins, one-time President of the European Commission. He attacked the architect of Britain's first application to join the EEC, Harold Macmillan, for only 'belatedly seeing the light', part of his broader charge that British policy-makers have refused to take the country 'wholeheartedly into Europe'.[203] The charges that British European policy after 1945 has been misguided and the parallel search for scapegoats by the British euroenthusiasts indicate a strong affinity between their views and those of the four other communities examined before them in this chapter. The sixth and final group is altogether more eclectic.

Other British critics

The orthodoxy on Britain and Europe has not been the sole preserve of those associated with the federal project, although it does account for the great bulk of the literature. An additional reason why the orthodox interpretation of British European policy became so deeply entrenched within British elite attitudes was that it could so easily be adapted to suit any agenda. It has attracted a wide variety of adherents, from federalists and Europeanists to domestic critics within British politics, pursuing personal vendettas against the leading architects of postwar British foreign policy.

Nutting, Dell, Denman, Heath and Jenkins have thus been joined in their condemnation of British policy by contemporaries who have fewer Europeanist

---

199 Young, *This Blessed Plot*, p. 221. As Heath wrote in his memoirs, 'My views on the subject had been on the record since 1950', Heath, *The Course of My Life*, p. 356. See also J. Campbell, *Edward Heath: A Biography* (London, Pimlico, 1994), pp. 115–16 and George, *An Awkward Partner*, pp. 47–50.

200 Monnet, *Memoirs*, pp. 455–7.

201 Mayne and Pinder, *Federal Union*, pp. 112–14.

202 Heath, *The Course of My Life*, pp. 355 and 201.

203 R. Jenkins, 'Foreword' in Mayne and Pinder, *Federal Union*, p. 8. Jenkins is held in very high regard by Europeanists abroad. See, for example, Prodi's speech in Oxford in April 2002, www.sbs.ox.ac.uk/html/news_article.asp?ID=80.

credentials, but who, through their critical reports on British European policy, deserve to be located alongside the federalists as originators of the orthodoxy about Britain and Europe. It is important to note, however, that these are of a qualitatively different mindset about the underlying principles of integration. That the 'Tory Strasbourgers' Robert Boothby, David Maxwell Fyfe and Harold Macmillan propagate the conventional wisdom at all is evidence that personal relationships, not just ideological and political outlook, can have important bearing on the historicisation of past events.

Boothby, a British delegate to the Consultative Assembly of the Council of Europe 1947–57, lamented that in 1945 'Britain could and should have taken the undisputed leadership of a united Western Europe … We did nothing.'[204] He repeated this in a second volume of memoirs, published sixteen years later. 'In 1949 Britain could have had the leadership of a united western Europe on its own terms.'[205] David Maxwell Fyfe, Home Secretary and then Lord Chancellor in Churchill's 1951–55 administration, was also of the opinion that the 'enthusiasm among Europeans for our leadership met with a blank hostility' from Eden and the Foreign Office.[206] Harold Macmillan, the architect of Britain's first application to join the EEC, also turned his sights on Eden, contrasting the 'time and effort' he (Macmillan) devoted to 'various aspects of the European Movement' with the 'rather frigid sentiments' towards Europe expressed by Eden in 1951.[207]

These commentaries reveal how politicians' reputations often assume mythical quality and become the stuff of unchallenged conventional wisdom. Eden is not a fondly remembered Prime Minister. His association with the Suez crisis has meant his going down in history 'as the prime minister who steered the ship of state onto the rocks'.[208] In the European arena he, along with Churchill, attracts much of the blame for the demise of the EDC at the hands of the French in 1954, the argument being that this was a 'litmus test of the Conservative Government's enthusiasm for Europe, and of Eden's in particular'.[209] Politics is a fickle business, and foreign secretaries and prime ministers often make as many enemies on their way to the top as they do friends, so it is important to remember 'how personality and personal enmity influence the rise of individual politicians', says Nick Crowson.[210] Boothby, Maxwell Fyfe and Macmillan make no

204 Boothby, *My Yesterday, Your Tomorrow*, p. 73.
205 Lord Boothby, *Recollections of a Rebel* (London, Hutchinson, 1978), p. 219.
206 Kilmuir, *Political Adventure*, p. 186. See pp. 177–89 for an exposition of his wider views on the subject.
207 Macmillan, *Tides of Fortune*, pp. 225–7 and 463.
208 A. J. P. Taylor, introduction to S. Aster, *Anthony Eden* (London, Weidenfeld and Nicolson, 1976).
209 Greenwood, *Britain and European Cooperation*, p. 50.
210 N. J. Crowson, review, 'Backbench Debate within the Conservative Party and its Influence on British Foreign Policy, 1947–58. By Sue Onslow', *Contemporary British History*, 11:4 (1997), 133–4 (133).

secret of their dislike of Eden in their memoirs, and this has shaped their treatment of his European policy accordingly – so much so that, Kevin Ruane notes, like 'missed opportunities' discourse, the view that Eden was resistant to a 'pro-European' policy has become 'almost an historiographical orthodoxy' in its own right.[211]

However, he continues, the orthodoxy that the evil Eden quashed Boothby's, Maxwell Fyfe's and Macmillan's ambitions for Britain in Europe 'has begun to be questioned'.[212] They all support their critique of Eden's European policy by drawing a distinction between the apparently encouraging speech Maxwell Fyfe gave about the EDC at Strasbourg on 21 November 1951 and the speech Eden gave later that evening on the same subject in Rome.[213] Maxwell Fyfe, for example, records that his speech 'created an excellent impression' and Nutting, who likewise claims that the speech was well received, supports him. Eden, the story goes, merely confirmed in Rome his 'hostility' to the European project, leading to the 'sense of betrayal' they later felt.[214]

The flaw in their argument has been pointed out by Eden himself and by many of his biographers.[215] To argue that Eden's speech was the antithesis of Maxwell Fyfe's is, they claim, a distortion of the evidence. David Carlton remarks that only through 'selective quotation' have those with an interest in denigrating Eden made Maxwell Fyfe's speech seem so forthcoming, noting that Macmillan only cites the following extracts of the Strasbourg speech in his memoirs: 'I cannot promise full and unconditional participation but I can assure you of our determination that no genuine method shall fail for lack of thorough examination which one gives to the needs of trusted friends.' Carlton continues by pointing out that 'what Macmillan did not admit was that the speech *as a whole* was open to an interpretation that did not please the non-British 'Europeans''. To this end, he quotes Peter Calvocoressi's damning analysis, that Maxwell Fyfe merely 'told the Consultative Assembly that it was quite unrealistic to expect Great Britain to join a European federation and held out no hope that Great Britain might establish anything more than some minor form of association with a European Defence Community'.[216]

Dutton agrees that 'there was no difference in substance between the messages conveyed by the two men' and cites the uncomplimentary verdict by former French premier and 'convinced European' Paul Reynaud, who, speak-

---

211 Ruane, *The Rise and Fall of the European Defence Community*, p. 8.
212 *Ibid.*
213 Boothby, *My Yesterday Your Tomorrow*, pp. 83–4; Boothby, *Recollections of a Rebel*, p. 220; Macmillan, *Tides of Fortune*, p. 463.
214 Kilmuir, *Political Adventure*, pp. 186–7; Nutting, *Europe Will Not Wait*, pp. 40–6.
215 Eden, *Full Circle*, p. 33.
216 D. Carlton, *Anthony Eden: A Biography* (London, Allen Lane, 1981), p. 309. Emphasis added.

ing after Maxwell Fyfe but before Eden, was reportedly 'strongly critical of our attitude'.[217] Historians have tended to support their version of events, rather than those of Boothby, Maxwell Fyfe and Macmillan. 'Maxwell Fyfe might insist that Britain was 'not closing the door'', noted Charlton, 'but Eden spoke for the reality – no fundamental changes in the British position of "close association"'.[218] John Young considers that the Home Secretary's speech went 'no further than the much vilified [Labour Foreign Secretary Herbert] Morrison had done in September in expressing the desire to associate with the Six'. Maxwell Fyfe's words were, he continues, not just frostily received by Reynaud, they were 'condemned by Belgium's Paul-Henri Spaak as "disappointing" and "derisory"'.[219]

Spaak recalled in his memoirs that Macmillan's views on Europe were classically British, but that he 'clothed his arguments in somewhat more elaborate language'.[220] Hugo Young summarises the revisionist perspective with the argument that Macmillan was a 'European only of his time and place, which is to say a tormented and indecisive one',[221] a view that accords with Tratt's laconic assessment that, on the issue of Europe, Macmillan was 'not what we would call today a conviction politician,'[222] and Jenkins's judgement that, if not so Churchillian in his vacillations over Europe, Macmillan was only 'partially a European'.[223]

Part of the explanation for this divergence of views about who are and who are not the 'Europeans' in British politics flows from the amorphous and constantly changing conceptions of what the term means in Britain, and what it is perceived to mean abroad.[224] What further complicates matters is that British politicians are prone to rapid changes of mind on the subject. To take one less well-known example (away from, say, Harold Wilson, who was renowned for his vacillating stance over Europe in the 1960s and 1970s), it has been found that one of the most virulent sceptics of the Thatcher years, Nicholas Ridley, addressed the Federal Trust in 1969 on the merits of approaching federalism 'through the

---

217 D. Dutton, *Anthony Eden: A Life and Reputation* (London, Edward Arnold, 1997), pp. 293–4.
     Spaak's reaction is given on p. 295. See also V. Rothwell, *Anthony Eden: A Political Biography,*
     1931–1957 (Manchester, Manchester University Press, 1992), p. 198.
218 Charlton, *The Price of Victory,* p. 148.
219 Young, *Britain and European Unity, 1945–1999,* p. 35.
220 Spaak, *The Continuing Battle,* pp. 219–21.
221 Young, *This Blessed Plot,* p. 115. See also Greenwood, *Britain and European Cooperation,* p. 50;
     Ruane, *The Rise and Fall of the European Defence Community,* pp. 20–6.
222 Tratt, *The Macmillan Government,* p. 13.
223 R. Jenkins, *Churchill* (London, Macmillan, 2001), p. 856. Spaak, *The Continuing Battle,* p. 211.
224 On the other side of the debate, Kenneth Morgan has commented on the variation in meaning of
     'Eurosceptic' in British politics since the 1960s, in K. O. Morgan, *Callaghan: A Life* (Oxford,
     Oxford University Press, 1997), p. 393.

front door, not the back door'.[225] Boothby and his conspirators might have been more sympathetic to European unity than Eden, but that is not to say their ideas, especially concerning Britain's leadership of the Continent, were any more likely to appeal to the federalists at that time than the line pursued by Eden. What their recollections show is how the orthodox school is riven with, and driven by, politics in all its forms. From the deep ideological divisions over the future of international politics that swayed federalist thought to the personal animosity that fuelled criticisms of Eden's European policy by British politicians, this section has lent much support to Geoffrey Barraclough's argument that 'The history we read, though based on facts, is, strictly speaking, not factual at all but a series of accepted judgements.'[226]

Content and form

That contemporary history deals with events within living memory and that many of the people involved with them are still alive and publishing their version of what happened, means that arguments about the past are often still raging in the present. The historiography of Britain's European policy is one example of this ongoing 'battle for history' among a variety of commentators on the past.[227] This section will begin by reflecting on the implications of labelling the writing examined above a 'school' and go on to analyse the correlation that seems to exist between the type of study one writes and the interpretation one places on events. Biography, memoir, autobiography and academic history (which can in turn be broken into subcategories such as official and unofficial biography, textbook and monograph history and so on), all shape history debates; but each makes different methodological demands on its writers, and this crucially affect the interpretation(s) they place on past events.

Is it possible to label the fairly diverse array of writers analysed above a 'school'; and what, if it is, does it imply to say that a writer belongs to such a school? In another context, Stoker argues that it is misleading to use the word 'school' to describe competing methods of studying political science. The term 'school', he observes, 'creates an exaggerated sense of cohesion and order within

---

225 Mayne and Pinder, *Federal Union*, p.187. On p.165 they observe that Max Beloff gave a lecture at the 1961 Easter Seminar of the Cambridge Federal Union group. He later contributed a chapter to Martin Holmes's edited volume, *The Eurosceptical Reader* (Basingstoke, Macmillan, 1996). Mark Stuart notes the transformation in the attitude of Lord McAlpine, who was once an enthusiast for European integration but who joined James Goldsmith's Referendum Party in the 1990s, in *Douglas Hurd, The Public Servant: An Authorised Biography* (Edinburgh, Mainstream, 1998), p. 415.

226 Quoted in Carr, *What is History?*, p. 14.

227 This term is taken from J. Keegan, *The Battle for History: Re-fighting World War Two* (London, Pimlico, 1997).

the various sub-divisions' of the discipline and he therefore prefers the looser label 'approach'. The different approaches he identifies within political science, normative theory, historical institutionalism, behavioural analysis, rational choice theory, feminism and discourse analysis

> guide practitioners towards different ways of doing political science. They answer questions about the core subject matter to be addressed; the mode by which evidence should be obtained; the nature of the theoretical enterprise that should be undertaken; and offer diverse and underlying assumptions about the nature and dynamics of politics.[228]

While dismissive of the label 'school', he nonetheless argues that each 'approach' identifies its own subject-matter, has a distinctive methodological orientation, possesses different perspectives on state politics, entails contrasting theories about the world and has a different status within the discipline.[229]

His uncertainty about using the term 'school' goes a long way to supporting the argument advanced in the last chapter that there is no settled definition of the term within academia. Most writers take the Stoker line that schools or approaches imply cohesion, a commitment to a theory, a method, an interpretation or, better still, all three. To reinforce this point, one might refer to the work of the international relations theorist Tim Dunne, who in 1998 published a study of the 'English school' of writers on international relations. He asserts that writers belonging to this school have three things in common: a common agenda, a broad interpretative approach and the same theoretical underpinnings. Significantly for us here, he argues that schools contain writers linked by 'family resemblances'. Members of a school do not have to adhere rigidly to a single interpretation of historical events; instead, there are 'aspects of their thinking which are interwoven and distinct'.[230] Dunne's definition echoes that of Roger Epp, who, in an article on the same topic published in the same year, argued that 'any identifiable intellectual tradition or school is known by the dilemmas it keeps. It can be understood as an extended answer to a set of questions which, in turn, shape it in ways that open up certain types of inquiry and preclude others.'[231]

If the term 'school' is indeed flexible enough to incorporate writers with similar but not the same views, but who are bound intellectually by a common agenda and a common theoretical framework ('the dilemmas they keep'), then it seems fair to argue that the writing in this book can be categorised into schools, for four main reasons.

---

228 G. Stoker, 'Introduction', in Marsh and Stoker (eds), *Theory and Methods*, pp. 1–18 (p. 7).

229 *Ibid.*, pp. 10–11.

230 T. Dunne, *Inventing International Society: A History of the English School* (Basingstoke, Macmillan, 1998), pp. 5–6.

231 R. Epp, 'The English School on the Frontiers of International Relations', *Review of International Studies*, 24:1 (1998), 47–63 (50).

The first is that (the final category of British contributors apart) the wave of writers explored in this chapter has a common agenda: the advance of the federalist cause in Europe. It is this idea that shapes their view of the world and that shapes their outlook on Britain as the awkward partner. Federalism is the 'theory' that underpins their speeches and writing about contemporary historical events; federalism is the value they cherish most highly. The second is that orthodox historiography has a recognised 'status' in the field of British European policy, as Stoker suggested was the case with different traditions within political science. The missed opportunities interpretation has provided the stimulus and the agenda for the academic attention one now sees being paid to developments in British European policy. The third reason why these writers can all be placed in a school is because the links among them indicate more than just a heterogeneous or loosely coordinated attack on nationalism in the post-war era. The federalist agenda has been a by-product of considerable economic and political support given to the process of European integration by the Americans. An initially small but relatively tight-knit transnational network of individuals has managed to distribute their views widely, resulting in the development of a common identity, rooted in a 'communal memory' and, to purloin a phrase from Ian McBride, a 'distortion of the past for their own purposes'.[232]

The final reason why these writers can be labelled a school requires reference to Dunne's 'family resemblances'. Human families do not generally consist of individuals who look identical and, despite some similarities, members of family units do not all act in exactly the same way, or have the same behavioural idiosyncrasies and character traits. This way of conceiving of schools is useful because it removes the requirement for writers belonging to them to produce accounts of the past that are either the same or even very similar, and this limited similarity would seem to be a feature of the orthodox school of writing on Britain and Europe. It has already been shown that politicians such as Boothby, Maxwell Fyfe and Macmillan did not hold the same views on European integration as Monnet and his friends. Their accounts of Britain's missed chances are driven by domestic political and personal concerns and have little or no grounding in federalist thinking, but they do still voice the conventional wisdom about events, and therefore have to be classed in the same school as the federalists.

What this implies in turn is that schools of writing in contemporary history crystallise around interpretations more than they do around methods and theories which, and this goes for the historical profession generally, are as infrequently studied as they are acknowledged. For 'theories and methods' in political science one could substitute 'worldview and sources' in the realm of contemporary history.

---

232 Publicity for I. McBride, *History and Memory in Modern Ireland* (Cambridge, Cambridge University Press, 2001).

These *act* as theories but are not *articulated* as such, and for that very reason are usually of greater interest to the historiographer than the historian, for the former – more than the latter – is intrinsically concerned with explaining how pivotal moments in history become historicised in the way that they do, 'investigating the ways in which they have been recalled, commemorated and mythologised'.[233]

An example one might employ in support of the argument that schools can house differing viewpoints without having their overall cohesion damaged is to look at the diversity of opinions among orthodox writers about which was the greatest opportunity missed by Britain. Some writers do not decide one way or the other, casting the entire period as a tragedy of missed opportunities.[234] For writers such as Dell and Nutting, the refusal to enter the Schuman Plan talks was the most significant chance missed.[235] Those who focus, like F. S. Northedge, on the defence, security and Cold War dimensions of European integration place greater weight on Britain's lack of support for the EDC, which, they feel, was more in Britain's immediate security interests than the Schuman Plan had been.[236] For a greater proportion of writers Britain's failure to be a founder member of the EEC in 1955–57 was the most costly mistake, resulting as it did in a rift that was harder to heal and has had the most damaging implications for the British in coming to terms with Europe and for the Europeans in coming to terms with a Britain consistently sniping from the sidelines.[237] Historiographical schools are flexible enough to incorporate divergences on detail among their members, as long as they agree on the broad interpretation of events.

Genre

It would also appear that schools are driven by different genres of writing. From the above, it can be evinced that the orthodox school is characterised by a wide

233 *Ibid.*
234 Charlton, talking to an array of policy-makers, comes to this conclusion in *The Price of Victory*. See also P. Hennessy, 'The Attlee Governments, 1945–1951', in P. Hennessy and A. Seldon (eds), *Ruling Performance: British Governments from Attlee to Thatcher* (Oxford, Basil Blackwell, 1987), pp. 28–62 (p. 47); Denman, *Missed Chances*, especially p. 184 and Barker, *Britain in a Divided Europe*, p. 152.
235 Dell, *The Schuman Plan*, p. 5; Nutting, *Europe Will Not Wait*, p. 34.
236 F. S. Northedge, *Descent from Power: British Foreign Policy 1945–73* (London, George Allen and Unwin, 1974), pp. 152–3.
237 Bullock, *Ernest Bevin*, pp. 777–90; Camps, *Britain and the European Community*, p. 45; Frankel, *British Foreign Policy*, p. 319; A. Seldon, 'The Churchill Administration, 1951–55', in Hennessy and Seldon (eds), *Ruling Performance*, pp. 63–97 (p. 87); J. Barnes, 'From Eden to Macmillan, 1955–59', in Hennessy and Seldon (eds), *Ruling Performance*, pp. 98–149 (pp. 129–30); Lamb, *The Failure of the Eden Government*, p. 101; F. Roberts, 'Ernest Bevin as Foreign Secretary', in R. Ovendale (ed.), *The Foreign Policy of the British Labour Governments, 1945–1951* (Leicester, Leicester University Press, 1984), pp. 21–42 (pp. 34–5); D. Reynolds, 'The Origins of the Cold War: The European Dimension, 1944–1951', *Historical Journal*, 28:2 (1985), 497–515 (512).

number of types of study: political memoir, biography, autobiography, instant history and oral testimony, to name the most prominent. The contrasting reasons for the members of each school putting pen to paper in the first place impact upon the place Britain's policy towards Europe holds in the overall narrative in a number of subtle but important ways.

The first is, quite simply, that the genres of literature that have given rise to the conventional wisdom, especially political memoirs, do not have as their focus British European policy *per se*. Political memoirs and associated forms of reflection on the past are not exclusively concerned with the European question, often exposing more about the thinking of the federalists on the Continent, in America and in Britain than they do the developments they purport to describe, and tend therefore to say more about how *they* thought and conceived of European integration than about how the *British* went about constructing European policy.

In such works, the history of Britain's European policy is in many respects treated as something of a side issue, referred to in two or three lines that generally incorporate refrains of missed opportunities, missed boats, or missed buses or to the effect that Britain has been playing catch-up in Europe. This is especially true of British politicians, who tend not to specialise in specific areas of competence during their careers. If they hold Cabinet posts at all, it is common form that they can be appointed with no prior background, expertise or even interest in any of the departmental briefs they are handed. More often than not it is the personal as opposed to the political situation that gets explored in memoirs, prompting R. K. Middlemas's judgement that political recollection can too often be dull and uninformative in terms of bringing new light to bear on long-running debates. 'Some parts of [Macmillan's memoirs] read like extracts from the Annual Register, or from the lengthy Foreign Office briefs which Bevin used to read out in the House of Commons.'[238] A. J. P. Taylor was characteristically colourful in his opinion: 'Old men drooling about their youth? No!'[239]

The second way in which genre impinges on historical interpretation is that a large proportion of British politicians have neither the time nor the interest, even with the aid of a team of researchers and ghostwriters, to devote much attention to Europe, when the conventional wisdom has been established for a number of years. It is easy to forget for scholars who organise their studies around the defining theme of British European policy, that for policy-makers in the 1950s the European question was not high on their agenda. The sad fact for Europeanists and students and historians of British European policy is that most of them simply did not take a keen interest in Europe in the 1950s, and only marginally more so

---

238 R. K. Middlemas, review, 'Tides of Fortune, 1945–1955. By Harold Macmillan', *International Affairs*, 46:3 (1970), 568–9 (568).

239 Quoted in Prins, 'Oral History', p. 114.

in the 1960s when it was thrust on to the political scene with successive British applications to join the Community. The emerging Cold War, relations with Russia, America, China, the Commonwealth, Greece, Turkey, Aden, Malaysia, Cyprus, the Middle East, Rhodesia and South Africa, not to mention domestic political issues, all impinge on the time devoted to the European question in political memoirs. The Conservative Chancellor Rab Butler's declaration that he was 'bored' with European integration by the time of the Messina conference, and that Foreign Secretary Eden was 'even more bored than I was' are telling insights into the apathy about Europe in the corridors of Whitehall in the 1950s.[240]

The third reason why genre affects interpretation draws on the symbiotic relationship between political memoir and political biography. When writing political biography there regularly occurs, notes Mark Steyn, a 'morphing of biographer and subject', so that the interpretation placed on events by the subject can often become the accepted interpretation of the biographer.[241] This should not come as a startling revelation given the origins of biography as a literary form. 'For much of its history [biography] was largely hagiographic, recording the saintly practices of genuine or putative saints.'[242] Published a year after the Foreign Secretary's death, Francis Williams's biography of Bevin, subtitled *Portrait of a Great Englishman*, would seem to be one obvious example of this tendency in Britain.

It is too simplistic to tar every life portrait with the same brush, however, for as Nigel Hamilton asserts, biography takes on 'multitudinous forms and genres ... as the way we look at real lives and have looked at them throughout history'.[243] As a result, one needs to be aware that different forms of biography offer different amounts of scope for interrogating the subject's worldview and stories about the past. It is immediately possible to distinguish between official and unofficial biography as genres in their own right.

In the case of 'official biography' the reasons for the uncritical reception of the subject's views are not hard to locate. Often sponsored by the subject or his or her relatives, the official biographer is under immense pressure to confer honour on the individual whose life is being written, especially if he or she is still alive and has commissioned the biography to be written in the first place. In the case of a deceased subject, on what subjects the book covers and in what depth,

240 He was Chancellor of the Exchequer between October 1951 and December 1955. Quoted in Charlton, *The Price of Victory*, p. 195.

241 M. Steyn, review, 'Is Hillary Hurting? Hillary's Choice. By Gail Sheehy', *Sunday Telegraph*, 19 December 1999, p. 18. See also Walker, 'Historians and Cold War Origins', p. 224: 'As is usually the case in biographies, most cold war scholars sympathised with the positions espoused by their subjects.'

242 Elms, *Uncovering Lives*, p. 3.

243 N. Hamilton, 'In Defence of the Practice of Biography', *Contemporary British History*, 10:4 (1996), 81–6 (86).

especially on personal matters, the biographer will, by law or out of respect, have to bow to the demands of the family, the 'keepers of the flame', who in some cases may wish to be actively involved throughout the research process.[244] 'Part of the implicit understanding in 'official' biography', explains Ben Pimlott, 'is that the author should be counsel for the defence'.[245]

Adopting a hagiographic or uncritical approach can, then, either be planned or be something that happens unconsciously. Take the example of Alistair Horne's two-volume portrait of Macmillan, which relies heavily upon 'copious papers' and hours of interviews with the former Prime Minister.[246] Pimlott's verdict is that 'Horne comes perilously close to going native ... Macmillan's snobbery spills on to the author.'[247] To be fair to Horne, he does admit that a disadvantage of spending so long in the company of Macmillan is that it lowers one's resistance 'to falling totally under the spell of one of the most fascinating political figures of the twentieth century'.[248] Pimlott's charge is, however, indicative of the scorn that is often poured on official biographies, which, it is claimed, represent the views of the subject rather than critically analysing them.[249]

'Unofficial biography' itself is a category that can be broken down into sub-units for analysis. First, there are pen-picture sketches of politicians written at the time they rise to prominence, which act as publicity about the subject or instant judgements on important events in their careers. These have tended to be written by other politicians about their friends or mentors in the business.[250] Then, there are critical accounts by political opponents of the subject, written to warn the

---

244 Coined by I. Hamilton, *Keepers of the Flame: Literary Estates and the Rise of Biography* (London, Pimlico, 1992). In Elms, *Uncovering Lives*, p. 30, it is characterised as the 'Defender of the Faith' thesis.

245 Pimlott, *Frustrate Their Knavish Tricks: Writings on Biography, History and Politics* (London, Harper Collins, 1994), p. 26. On the need to preserve political reputations after the death of the subject because of family pressures see p. 155.

246 A. Horne, *Macmillan, 1894–1956: Volume 1 of the Official Biography* (London, Macmillan, 1988), preface p. 12; A. Horne, *Macmillan 1957–1986: Volume 2 of the Official Biography* (London, Papermac, 1991).

247 Pimlott, *Frustrate Their Knavish Tricks*, p. 28.

248 Horne, *Macmillan* Volume 1, preface p. 12.

249 In addition to Horne's works see K. Harris, *Attlee*, 2nd edn (London, Weidenfeld and Nicolson, 1995), D. R. Thorpe, *Alec Douglas-Home* (London, Sinclair-Stevenson, 1996) and P. Ziegler, *Wilson: The Authorised Life of Lord Wilson of Rievaulx* (London, Weidenfeld and Nicolson, 1993).

250 R. Jenkins, *Mr Attlee: An Interim Biography* (London, William Heinemann, 1948); M. M. Krug, *Aneurin Bevan: Cautious Rebel* (London, Thomas Yoseloff, 1961); W. Rees-Mogg, *Sir Anthony Eden* (London, Rockliff, 1956); Lord Moran, *Winston Churchill: The Struggle for Survival* (London, Constable, 1966); A. Sampson, *Macmillan: A Study in Ambiguity* (London, Allen Lane and Penguin, 1967); N. Fisher, *Harold Macmillan* (London, Weidenfeld and Nicolson, 1972); G. Hutchinson, *Edward Heath: A Personal and Political Biography* (London, Longman, 1970); M. Laing, *Edward Heath: Prime Minister* (London, Sidgwick and Jackson, 1972). See also Aster, *Anthony Eden*; K. Young, *Sir Alec Douglas-Home* (London, J. M. Dent and Sons, 1970); P. M. Williams, *Hugh Gaitskell: A Political Biography* (London, Jonathan Cape, 1969).

public about the flaws in their existing or potential leaders. Figures such as Tony Benn and Harold Wilson have inspired several such books since the 1960s, the latter then becoming the subject of a fawning response by one of his friends.[251] As political polemic these are again of comparatively limited value to the contemporary historian in terms of their reconstruction of events, but invaluable as insights into how politicians were portrayed at the time they were in, or about to assume, power.

The scope for unofficial biographers to interrogate their subjects thus depends on the era, the relationship of author to subject and the reason for him or her putting pen to paper. Even given this greater degree of latitude compared to the official biographer, John Campbell, the unofficial biographer of Heath and Thatcher, maintains that, on the whole, the biographer is limited to restating the politicians' own versions of events, often already in print. 'In my experience it is usually a waste of time interviewing politicians who have written their memoirs, because all they ever do is repeat what they have written; and much the same I think applies to historians.'[252] Jordanova agrees: 'To write a convincing biography the author needs a certain measure of sympathy with their subject, and they are likely to identify more or less strongly with that person – this is true of all historical projects.'[253]

All this makes political diaries, memoirs (what John Grigg calls those 'monumentally egocentric' studies),[254] autobiographies and witness accounts fraught with danger as sources of contemporary history. The human memory is less than perfect. Forgetfulness and loss of memory mean that policy-makers cannot always remember with precision the course of events in which they were involved, sometimes decades ago. 'There are', notes Prins, 'certain sorts of memory which may be forever irrecoverable because of the manner of their loss.'[255] In the case of the civil servants and politicians who have contributed to the development of orthodox historiography, criticism, apologia and self-justification are enmeshed in their assessments of the key events in British European policy. On the one hand, civil servants tend to take what Mayne calls the *mea culpa* approach,[256] discussing what more they could have done to promote a constructive, forward-looking foreign policy for Britain. They are also more reticent about publishing their views, which

251 R. Lewis, *Tony Benn: A Critical Biography* (London, Associated Business Press, 1978); D. Smith, *Harold Wilson: A Critical Biography* (London, Robert Hale, 1964), pp. 11–12 and P. Foot, *The Politics of Harold Wilson* (Harmondsworth, Penguin, 1968). For the response see E. Kay, *Pragmatic Premier: An Intimate Portrait of Harold Wilson* (London, Leslie Frewin, 1967).

252 Written correspondence from John Campbell, 6 March 2000.

253 Jordanova, *History in Practice*, p. 162.

254 J. Grigg, 'Policies of Impotence', *International Affairs*, 48:1 (1972), 72–6 (73).

255 Prins, 'Oral History', p. 126.

256 Mayne, review, 'The Price of Victory. By Michael Charlton', *International Affairs*, 60:2 (1984), 326–7 (327).

tend to gain public attention through their presence at academic conferences and witness seminars. On the other, politicians are equally as much concerned with the allocation of blame and with stressing the value of their own contributions, seamlessly extending the personal animosity they felt for other decision-makers, as the example of Eden shows, into a critique of European policy.

But this is being kind. Decision-makers also suffer from 'intentional' memory loss,[257] a reminder that 'forgetting is about something real'.[258] Austen Morgan's damning judgement is representative of the majority verdict on political memoirs: 'Politicians belong to that special class of liar who seem to be genuinely unable to discriminate between special pleading, the suppression of material evidence, and outright falsification of the record.'[259] Their memoirs and autobiographies tend to range from the bland to the controversial as a means of obscuring their own personal involvement with sensitive issues and to sell books. Newspaper editors naturally prefer literary atom bombs to hand grenades, and controversy over dull and verbose recollection, although books by 'big-name' politicians usually get published either way. Memoirs, autobiography and eyewitness testimony might relegate discussion of the European policy process below personal vitriol and entail obfuscation of important or controversial episodes; but that is because their authors write not for historians but for themselves, the public, their contemporaries and their successors.

Interpretation

Taking official and unofficial biography together, one can draw out two principal reasons why these works voice the conventional wisdom about Britain and Europe. The first turns on the questions biographers ask of their subject and therefore of history itself. 'Most modern biographies', observes Pimlott, 'for all their revelations of promiscuity and personal disorder, have barely departed from the Victorian, and medieval, tradition of praising famous men. Nowhere is this more true than in the comparative backwater of political biography.'[260] The issue of Europe tends to be treated only spasmodically, and only then in the context of the 'big' decisions that were made in London. The rejection of the Schuman Plan, the turn from the EDC, the withdrawal from Messina, the failure to win over de Gaulle: these are the major themes around which debates among orthodox writers crystallise, because for them they constitute the historical problem that needs explaining. Other policy innovations either go unmentioned or are devoted only the occasional line.

257 Seldon, 'Interviews', pp. 6–7.
258 Appleby, Hunt and Jacob, *Telling the Truth about History*, p. 267.
259 Morgan, *Harold Wilson*, p. 389.
260 Pimlott, *Frustrate Their Knavish Tricks*, p. 154.

One should expect this, because these are expansive studies. Ranging over a lifetime's political work will naturally lead to gaps and distortions in the history. A caveat here is the growing trend amongst academic biographers to write what can be called 'contextualised biography', so that they contribute to the revisionist turn in the historiography as opposed to the orthodoxy. The major feature of this genre is that biographers split their subject's life into themes rather than chronologically, as demonstrated by Dutton's work on Eden, which is grouped in chapters entitled 'Eden and the dictators', 'Eden and Chamberlain', 'Eden and the United States', 'Eden and the Russians', 'Eden and Europe' and so forth. This permits more analytical weight to be attached to particular issues that might otherwise be glossed over or excluded altogether.

Pimlott highlights the second reason why biography as a genre often supports the orthodoxy about events. 'Publishers, reflecting public taste, continue to want orthodox lives spiced with colourful details, of orthodoxly famous people: the best contracts go to those who provide them.'[261] Yet those details rarely extend deeper than tastes, habits and personal likes and dislikes. Biographers seeking to employ psychoanalytical insights to explain the actions and behaviour of their subjects are held back by the tradition of political biography in Britain, which has tended to shy away from bringing Freudian analysis to bear on writing lives.[262] There are various possible reasons for this.

White argues that, because psychoanalysis was originally devised for the study of neurotics and psychotics, it 'appears to be a mistake' to try to deal with historians, thinkers, writers or politicians in the same way. 'After all, a neurotic is one who by definition is unequipped to sublimate successfully the obsessions which constitute the complex that determines the structure of his personality.' In the case of the writers White analysed (for example, Karl Marx and Alexis de Tocqueville) psychoanalysis might be helpful in accounting for their interest in certain kinds of problems, 'but it would do little to help us understand the specific forms of their works, the specific relations between theory and data which exist in them, and the appeal that these works have for those publics whose psychological proclivities differ from those of the authors'.[263]

It seems, moreover, that historians do not deem it sufficiently 'scholarly' to concentrate too heavily on sexuality and personal relationships as explanations of political behaviour. This might be accepted in biographies of film stars, pop stars and television actors, but is deemed too reminiscent of the 'tabloid newspaper treatment of modern politics and politicians' to be incorporated into

---

261 *Ibid.*, p.159.
262 S. Friedlander, *History and Psychoanalysis: An Inquiry into the Possibilities and Limits of Psychohistory*, trans. S. Suleiman (New York, Holmes and Meier, 1975).
263 White, *Metahistory*, p. 431.

biographies.[264] The formative experiences of politicians are thus usually treated as adjuncts to explanations of behaviour rooted in political caste or ideology. There might be a case to be made that there has not been *enough* experimentation with Freudian analysis, which, Pauline Croft argued in 1996, was in 'irreversible decline'.[265] Judicious use of methods designed to uncover the source of political action from personal backgrounds, while no more testable than other influences, would be a new and interesting departure in British historiography, adding to our understanding of the body politic. Returning to Hamilton, he pointed out in 1996 that some universities in Britain had started to offer undergraduate and postgraduate courses on the practice of biography which might replenish interest in 'discredited' approaches to the writing of political lives.[266] But for the time being traditional methods of researching and writing the lives of politicians in Britain look set to stay, popular as the finished product is among the political, academic and publishing communities, and so well do they sell in high-street book hops. The orthodoxy might only stretch so far, but as far as political biography goes, it seems to be far enough.

Intentional and unintentional memory loss or forgetfulness thus combine with methodological problems flowing from having to organise a morass of material into a coherent whole to create texts that, from the historian's perspective, rarely cover the relevant theme in sufficient depth. The perceived audience for such works necessitates the production of a different kind of history from that favoured by professional or academic historians: expansive, looser, sweeping texts as opposed to dense narratives about specific themes over shorter periods. On this evidence, it would seem possible to elicit a relationship between the *form* of history and its *content*.

Conclusion

Live political debate about Britain's place in the world in the post-war era has worked its way into the historiography of British European policy through the development of the orthodox school. To ascertain the process by which this occurred it is necessary to account for the rapid spread of federalist thinking about the best form for European integration after 1945. By the 1950s and 1960s, Monnetist discourse incorporating phrases such as 'missed opportunities', 'missed boats' and 'missed buses' conjured such powerful pictures about Britain's

---

264 P. O'Brien, 'Is Political Biography a Good Thing?', *Contemporary British History*, 10:4 (1996), 60–6 (62).

265 P. Croft, 'Political Biography: A Defence (1)', *Contemporary British History*, 10:4 (1996), 67–74 (72). For an overview of the insights historians can garner from psychohistory see Burke, *History and Social Theory*, pp. 114–18.

266 Hamilton, 'In Defence of the Practice of Biography', p. 82.

policy towards the integration project that it crept almost without notice into media and public discourses about Britain and Europe. Political cartooning, political memoirs, biographies, press reporting of British foreign policy and instant histories have been replete with such imagery, even in the face of evidence to the contrary.

Three main conclusions flow from the preceding analysis. The first is that language and discourse play powerful roles in the development of historiographical interpretations. This chapter has shown how the charge of missed opportunities has been used by a variety of people for a variety of ends. It is unfortunately easier to posit that this happens than to diagnose why, because it is tricky to explain precisely why myths, sayings or particular words and phrases become the vocabulary of the conventional wisdom about events. Future researchers might wish to engage psychologists and literary theorists in the search for answers.

What can be established through historiographical analysis of the literature is that succinct or memorable words and phrases act as simplifiers of a complex world. In a global society where we are bombarded with information at an alarming rate we cannot hope to understand or remember the detail in everything we hear, see and read.[267] What we do remember are strong images and pithy descriptions of personalities and policies, and these images have been ably provided by the missed opportunities discourse, which signifies, variously, economic decline, foreign policy drift, aloofness from the Continent, xenophobia and political mismanagement. Hill's words are therefore most apposite here. 'Long-established perceptions and conventional wisdoms', he writes, 'can become more or less objective parts of an individual's environment.'[268] The rhetorical construct of missed opportunities has acted as a readily accessible model for those wishing to affect the future by reinterpreting the past. What R. Palme Dutte refers to as 'official myths' have, 'by dint of incessant repetition [been] presented and often accepted by many sincere people ... as the Gospel truth'.[269]

The second conclusion is that orthodox discourse has generated an internal logic of its own; it is ideologically weighted, but not displayed as such. In much the same way, the language that the sceptics use in support of their arguments against Britain's adopting the euro or entering deeper into the process of integration has taken on meanings of its own. Words and phrases such as 'sovereignty', 'independence', 'keep the pound', 'federalism', 'Brussels' and 'bureaucrats' do not on their own prompt negative thoughts about the integration project. But when woven together into eurosceptical discourse about European unity they take on

---

267 The need to simplify events so that the historian can 'order' historical facts is taken up in B. Southgate, *History: What and Why? Ancient, Modern, and Postmodern Perspectives* (London, Routledge, 1996), pp. 63–4.

268 Hill, 'The Historical Background', p. 30.

269 R. Palme Dutt, *Problems of Contemporary History* (London, Lawrence and Wishart, 1963), p. 38.

entirely new layers of meaning that are functions of the discursive webs within which they hang. What these words symbolise to the user and signify to the listener or reader is more important in shaping perception in the euro debate than any meaning they convey outside that context.

The final conclusion one might draw from this chapter is that historical texts are multilayered, complex constructs that prioritise some facts over others, ask some questions but not others, and cleverly submerge potentially conflicting bodies of evidence or opinions beneath the one most favoured by the author. Even an influential orthodox writer such as Camps made time in her seminal text to highlight the political, strategic and economic differences between Britain and the Continent that go a long way to explaining why successive governments in London did not feel able to integrate the country in a supranational organisation.[270] It is the aim of the next chapter to examine how these inconsistencies were exploited by the academic historians who founded the revisionist school in the 1980s. The historiography of British European policy, it will be argued, changed fundamentally when this new generation of writers came to the field, asking new questions of the past and bringing new sources to bear upon it.

---

270 Camps, *Britain and the European Community*, especially pp. 3–19.

3 The revisionist school

In the natural sciences, the reasons for conducting experiments and the laws, theories and models that spring from them are not plucked out of thin air nor generated in an intellectual vacuum. Taking the example of Charles Darwin's search for a theory of species change, Richards writes that:

> he did so in a conceptual environment formed partly of ideas stimulated by his *Beagle* voyage and partly of ideas acquired from his grandfather, from [Jean-Baptiste] Lamarck, and from a host of authors he read between 1836 and 1838. These ideas not only determined the various problems against which successful hypotheses were selected, but they also initially fixed the restraints on the generation of trial solutions.[1]

The same, according to Thomas Kuhn, is true of history: 'The historian' … always picks up a process already underway, its beginnings lost in an earlier time. Beliefs are already in place; they provide the basis for the ongoing research whose results will in some cases change them; research in their absence is unimaginable though there has nevertheless been a long tradition of imagining it.'[2] Jordanova makes a similar point about the need to understand the intellectual traditions within a given field if one is to satisfactorily explain why historical interpretations are established and revised over time. Academic works, she says, 'are parts of elaborate conversations with other historians, living and dead. They are also conversations with governments, political parties, interest groups and so on.'[3] 'No historian', writes Munslow, 'can work in ignorance of previous interpretations or emplotments in the archive'.[4]

The British public and populist media remain largely unaware, or apathetic about, the steady campaign of persuasion that orthodox writers on British European policy have been engaged in. Academics, by contrast, have seen fit to engage with the debate about Britain and Europe sparked by the first school of writers and are still doing so.[5] Indeed, so deeply have they been reacting against the interpretation put on historical events by orthodox writers, and by association the analytical framework in place to describe events, that by the year 2001 the

---

1 Richards, 'Theories of Scientific Change', p. 223.
2 Kuhn, 'The Road since *Structure*', p. 235.
3 Jordanova, *History in Practice*, p. 1.
4 Munslow, *Deconstructing History*, p. 176.
5 S. Lee, review, 'Bullying Bonn: Anglo-German Diplomacy on European Integration, 1955–1961. By Martin P. C. Schaad', *Cold War History*, 3:1 (2002), 168–9 (169).

very attempt to use the vehicle metaphor of 'missed buses', formerly the phrase-
ology of choice, to describe Britain's approach to the Continent was now being
met with disdain. As the reviewer of Alex May's volume on British European
policy put it, 'My only criticism would be of the theoretical approach taken in the
concluding chapter which continues the overused "train" metaphor of a "federal-
ising" EU with Britain being left behind.'[6] It is to the academic historians' collective response (the 'conversation' they have been having with their predecessors)
that this study now turns, in an effort to trace historiographical developments
from the 1980s.

This chapter seeks to uncover the culture of academic scholarship on Britain
and Europe, defined as the 'taken-for-granted values, attitudes and way of behav-
ing, which are articulated through and reinforced by recurrent practices among a
group of people in a given context'.[7] It asks why academic historians have
disagreed so vehemently with the 'missed opportunities' interpretation. The
answer is that their contrasting interpretations are the result of their asking different questions of the history, writing different genres of work and using different
sources of evidence. The revolt against the tendency to plot Britain's European
policy as a tragedy for the country is a direct function of the way in which the
study of Britain and Europe has emerged as a sub-field of contemporary history
within higher education.

The academic treatment of this subject-matter, what might be called its
'disciplinisation',[8] has led to the history of British European policy being rewrit-
ten, based, characteristically in the field of international history, on newly
released primary sources. This, more than anything else, has been responsible for
the development of a new, revisionist interpretation; hence Thompson's view that
'Quite clearly the character of historiographical production cannot be separated
from the institutions in which it takes place, the constraints, demands and imperatives which are placed upon the producers as well as their relationship with their
audiences, both actual and potential.'[9]

To advance this case, the chapter is split into four main parts. The first
elucidates the key interpretative disparities between the orthodox and revisionist schools of writing on British European policy. The second traces the reasons
for this turn in the historiography. It begins by highlighting the considerable

6 R. Keitch, review, 'Britain and Europe Since 1945. By A. May', *Journal of Common Market
   Studies*, 38:1 (2000), 183.
7 Becher and Trowler, *Academic Tribes and Territories*, p. 23.
8 This term will be dissected later in this chapter, but in essence means the adoption of a subject (in
   this case Britain's approach to European integration) for study at university level and what that
   entails in terms of how the history is conceived, taught about and narrativised. Thompson, *What
   Happened to History?*, p. 72, prefers the term 'institutionalisation'.
9 Thompson, *What Happened to History?*, p. 71. The generational aspect of historiographical evolution is well brought in in another context by Bayly, 'The Second British Empire', pp. 60–71.

potential for this shift to have occurred sooner than it did, by highlighting that much of the evidence now used by revisionist historians was available to, but ignored by, orthodox writers, and suggests that it has taken the passing of time and the sustained attention of a community of like-minded diplomatic historians to fully draw out and exploit the inconsistencies in earlier works. The third part continues to account for the rise of revisionism by putting this wave of writing in its sociological context. Academics, it finds, have been de-bunking the conventional wisdom for all sorts of reasons, which are often only vaguely articulated, but which have radically altered how the history of Britain's relations with Europe has been conceived and studied. The final section explores the reasons why the PRO is the archive of choice for British historians working in this area.

The evidence presented in this chapter indicates that, in historiography, authorial identity is all important in determining how one appropriates the past and turns it into history. This identity helps determine what sources are consulted, which 'facts' are pulled from them and which ignored, which prioritised and which quietly dropped, which receive analytical weight and which are skimmed over peremptorily. As Kuhn and his followers have suggested about science, the cultural dimension is essential to any understanding of historiographical evolution.

Challenging the received wisdom

What emerges strongly from analysis of some of the most potent criticisms levelled at the orthodoxy by historians is that they find it seriously flawed both as a methodology and as a framework for accessing what happened in the past. In an article that has set the tone for much of the scholarly reconsideration that has occurred since, John Kent and John Young declared in 1989 that want they wanted to develop a 'new perspective' on British European policy that sought not to explain failure but to understand what impelled policy-makers to make particular decisions.[10]

The crux of their interpretation is that Britain did not miss any opportunities, chances, boats or buses in Europe in the 1950s because, at the time, British policy-makers did not perceive that there were any opportunities to grasp or vehicles to board. They echoed Jan Melissen and Bert Zeeman, who had, two years

---

10   J. Kent and J. W. Young, 'British Policy Overseas: The "Third Force" and the Origins of NATO – In Search of a New Perspective', in B. Heuser and R. O'Neill (eds), *Securing Peace in Europe, 1945–62: Thoughts for the Post Cold War Era* (Basingstoke; Macmillan, 1989), pp. 41–61. Interviews with John Kent, 16 April 2002 and Geoffrey Warner, 30 April 2002, have revealed that another doctoral research candidate was working on the 'Western union' concept at the same time, but that he never completed, nor was his work ever published.

earlier, summarised the growing belief among historians that 'Britain did not miss the European bus, it just declined to board one that was going in the wrong direction.'[11] Christopher Hill's 1988 judgement that it is 'pointless to spend too much time berating dead or ennobled Prime Ministers for missing the boat'[12] reflected the growing unease among historians through the 1980s and 1990s about the tendency by orthodox writers to work uncritically to European and American agendas when considering British European policy.[13] It culminated in the 1990s with Brian Harrison's judgement that what lay behind the missed opportunities interpretation was an 'over-personalised, present-oriented "who was to blame and how can we do better next time?" agenda'.[14]

Revisionist historians have thus been unpicking two key assumptions of orthodox historiography. The first concerns Britain's willingness to be part of the European project Monnet and Schuman devised; the second concerns the country's ability to be involved, let alone lead the process as some domestic critics suggested was possible.

Willingness to join Europe

Dealing first with Britain's willingness to join the federalist project, revisionist historians argue that orthodox writers overlook the low level of enthusiasm for Europe in the corridors of Whitehall and Downing Street. By doing so, they mix the positive assertion that British Prime Ministers *could* have taken Britain into European integration with the normative one that they *should* have. As early as 1969, Robert Pfaltzgraff noted that while it was 'fashionable' at that time to criticise British foreign policy 'for having failed to give priority to European integration' this judgement rests on hindsight. To Whitehall policy-makers in 1945–56, 'Britain's international role … resembled more that of a superpower

---

11 Melissen and Zeeman, 'Britain and Western Europe', p. 93.
12 Hill, 'The Historical Background', p. 45. See also Watt, 'Introduction', p. 7.
13 The evolution of this strand of thinking can also be traced in the following texts: A. Seldon, *Churchill's Indian Summer: The Conservative Government, 1951–55* (London, Hodder and Stoughton, 1981); D. C. Watt, *Succeeding John Bull: America in Britain's Place 1900–1975* (Cambridge, Cambridge University Press, 1984); J. W. Young, *Britain, France and the Unity of Europe 1945–1951* (Leicester, Leicester University Press, 1984); G. Warner, 'The Labour Governments and the Unity of Western Europe, 1945–51', in Ovendale (ed.), *The Foreign Policy of the British Labour Governments*, pp. 61–82; S. Croft, 'British Policy Towards Western Europe: The Best of Possible Worlds?', *International Affairs*, 64:4 (1988), 617–29; J. Kent 'Bevin's Imperialism and the Idea of Euro–Africa, 1945–49', in Dockrill and Young (eds), *British Foreign Policy*, pp. 47–76; A. Deighton, 'Missing the Boat: Britain and Europe 1945–61', *Contemporary Record*, 4:1 (1980), 15–17 and J. Kent, 'The "Western Union" Concept and British Defence Policy, 1947–8', in R. J. Aldrich (ed.), *British Intelligence Strategy and the Cold War 1945–51* (London, Routledge, 1992), pp. 166–92.
14 B. Harrison, review, 'R. Coopey, S. Fielding and N. Tiratsoo (eds), The Wilson Governments 1964–1970', *Contemporary Record*, 7:2 (1993), 490–1 (490).

than her Continental neighbours.'[15] Lord Beloff was equally convinced: 'it is hard to see how any British government ... could have accepted entering upon such a venture [as the EEC]'.[16] Thus, says John Charmley, 'Those who cleave to the "lost opportunities" myth show, by doing so, an inadequate appreciation of the situation in which Britain found herself in 1950–1.'[17]

Building on these alternative perspectives, revisionist writers suggest that the choice about whether or not Britain should join schemes such as the ECSC, the EDC and the EEC was not as clear-cut as orthodox writers would have us believe, such were the main tenets of government policy (of both parties) and the climate of public opinion in Britain in the early post-war years. Here, the charge that key decision-makers were exceptionally 'anti-European' has been rebuffed by the argument that British Prime Ministers and Foreign Secretaries were simply the most visible part of what John Barnes calls a 'broad consensus within Whitehall which recognized the growing importance of Europe to Britain but which was not prepared to narrow its horizons to Europe alone'.[18]

Looking at the British from Monnet's perspective there were, notes Sean Greenwood, 'no real "pro-Europeans"' in Whitehall in the 1950s, despite their later pleas to the contrary [recall the opinions of the 'Tory Strasbourgers' examined in the preceding chapter]. Few at the time advocated joining integrative efforts in the 1950s; only later did they claim they did'.[19] Hugo Young agrees that the most vocal critics of European policy in the 1950s were hypocritical. Harold Macmillan, he writes, like many of his generation, was a 'European only of his time and place, which is to say a tormented and indecisive one'.[20] The 'anti-reputation of British leaders', argues David Reynolds, 'is unsupportable when applied to the individuals in question, even before one takes into account the people propagating the myth, many of whom had much the same perspective on European integration'.[21]

Ability to lead Europe

The second assumption against which revisionists have reacted concerns Britain's *ability* to lead Europe. Even had Britain wanted to join the integration process at

15 Pfaltzgraff, *Britain Faces Europe*, p. 3.

16 Lord Beloff, *Britain and European Union: Dialogue of the Deaf* (Basingstoke: Macmillan, 1996), p. 55.

17 J. Charmley, *Churchill's Grand Alliance: The Anglo-American Special Relationship 1940–57* (London, Hodder and Stoughton, 1995), p. 247.

18 Barnes, 'From Eden to Macmillan', pp. 98–149 (p. 131). His view is supported in Burgess and Edwards, 'The Six Plus One', p. 413 and Dutton, *Anthony Eden*, p. 307. See also Kaiser, *Using Europe*, pp. 43–4.

19 Greenwood, *Britain and European Co-operation*, p. 78.

20 Young, *This Blessed Plot*, p. 115.

21 D. Reynolds, review, 'J. W. Young (ed.), The Foreign Policy of Churchill's Peacetime Administration, 1951–55', *International Affairs*, 65:1 (1989), 144.

the outset, they assert, it would have faced difficulty in dominating the agenda to the extent that critics in Britain suggested it could:

> The truth of the matter was seen when Britain *did* try to take the lead in Europe: Bevin tried to 'lead' Europe after 1948, but was unable to prevent the Schuman Plan; Eden tried to establish institutional co-operation with the Six through the 1952 'Eden Plan', yet, as Spaak put it, Europe by this time was in a 'whole hog mood'; British proposals were only 'half-way houses'.[22]

The flaw in the 'leadership of Europe' thesis is, concurs Tratt, that Britain could not have persuaded the Six to go down the intergovernmental route to unification at that time. She quotes Monnet's warning to Roger Makins and Edwin Plowden in a meeting that took place shortly before the launch of the ECSC: 'if we were not prepared to accept the objective of a federal system in Europe', Makins recalled Monnet saying, 'they didn't want us in'.[23]

Moreover, the Six were not waiting idly for Britain to take the lead, bereft of ideas on how to proceed. They were adept at negotiating considerable advances exogenous from British input, as the launch of the Messina process and the subsequent Spaak negotiations so soon after the collapse of the EDC demonstrated. Such attempts to shift the focus away from supposed British failings reflect international historiography of European integration, which reminds us that the EEC and the EU have been carefully tailored to meet the domestic needs of French and German national interests. William Hitchcock even sees a plot to exclude Britain from European affairs in the early 1950s. 'Through the means Monnet had devised, France could capture the diplomatic initiative from the Anglo-Americans, subvert British objections to Continental unification schemes, and strike a bargain with Germany on a bilateral basis: equality of rights in exchange for a balance of power.'[24] Also on the subversive side, Robin Edmonds and Walter LaFeber saw Paris attempting to exclude Britain *and* America from European affairs.[25]

The British view of Monnet's intentions tends to be more sanguine. 'The idea of a French "plot" goes too far ... Rather it seems that British membership was not a priority for Monnet.'[26] For Max Beloff, in a contemporary study

22 Young, *Britain and European Unity, 1945–1999*, pp. 53–4. Emphasis in original.
23 Tratt, *The Macmillan Government*, p. 209.
24 W. I. Hitchcock, 'France, the Western Alliance and the Origins of the Schuman Plan, 1948–1950', *Diplomatic History*, 21:4 (1997), 603–30 (628).
25 R. Edmonds, *Setting the Mould: The United States and Britain, 1945–1950* (Oxford, Oxford University Press, 1986), pp. 210–11; W. LaFeber, *America, Russia, and the Cold War 1945–1992*, 7th edn (New York, McGraw-Hill, 1993), p. 86. See also R. Aron, 'The Historical Sketch of the Great Debate', in D. Lerner and R. Aron (eds), *France Defeats EDC* (London, Thames and Hudson, 1957), pp. 2–21 (p. 3) and Winand, *Eisenhower, Kennedy*, p. 23.
26 Young, *Britain and European Unity, 1945–1999*, p. 30. See also Warner, 'Ernest Bevin and British Foreign Policy, 1945–1951', in Craig and Loewenheim (eds), *The Diplomats 1939–1979* pp. 118–19 and Tratt, *The Macmillan Government*, p. 27.

written with the help of conversations with leading American policy-makers towards Europe, Monnet acted on the belief that the success of integration 'would inevitably lead in the end to Britain coming in'.[27] But in the meantime, Monnet wrote in his memoirs, the Schuman Plan had got Europe 'on the move. Whatever the British decided would be their own affair.'[28]

By attacking the twin pillars of orthodox historiography, that Britain could have joined Europe's integrative efforts and that it could have led them, revisionist historians have treated the subject in what more than one reviewer has described as a 'broadly sympathetic' way.[29] One of the major consequences has been the rehabilitation of key policy-makers, and especially post-war Prime Ministers and Foreign Secretaries, who, according to the conventional wisdom, were blindly negative to the idea of Europe and Britain's involvement in it. By contrast, writes Anne Deighton, 'it is a fallacy to believe that Britain turned her back on Continental Europe during the fifteen years or so that followed the Second World War'.[30] Tratt repeats Deighton almost word for word: 'This is not to say, though, that the British government turned its back on Europe completely after the Second World War.'[31] There is, says Young of the Attlee administrations, 'far more [to them] ... than the error of "missing the European bus"',[32] the orthodoxy intentionally obscuring a more subtle, reflective British approach to Europe.

Revisionist historians have thus been attempting to fill in the gaps in our understanding of the stimuli behind, and formation of, post-war British foreign policy, giving, argues George Wilkes, a clearer perspective on events:

> The weight given to the UK's mistakes in historical accounts has had some unfortunate side-effects: historians have tended to pass quickly over important episodes in British–Six relations which did not involve conflict, and have been more concerned to explain the inadequacy of the motivation or vision behind British European policies than to analyse their causes and effects thoroughly.[33]

Hill would agree: 'It is not enough in the late 1980s to recite a list of apparent failures in British foreign policy since the last war and to link them to an inability

---

27 Max Beloff, *The United States and the Unity of Europe* (London, Faber and Faber, 1963), p. 58.
28 Monnet, *Memoirs*, p. 306.
29 M. Hopkins, review, 'Britain and European Unity 1945–1992. By John Young', *International Affairs*, 70:4 (1994), 811. Nicholas Rees uses the same word to describe Greenwood's interpretation in his review, 'Britain and European Co-operation Since 1945. By Sean Greenwood', *International Affairs*, 69:4 (1993), 792–3 (792).
30 Deighton, 'Missing the Boat', p. 15.
31 Tratt, *The Macmillan Government*, p. 11.
32 Young, 'Britain and "Europe": The Shape of the Historiographical Debate', p. 210.
33 G. Wilkes, 'The First Failure', p. 4.

to let go of past attitudes and commitments.'[34] Margaret Gowing also has little sympathy for 'counter-factual history – what might have happened but didn't'.[35] As in the process of painting a picture, the orthodox school covered the canvas with broad sweeps of the brush. Revisionists see their role as filling in the detail, adding new characters to the scene and depicting the shape of existing ones more sharply, helping to give the picture of Britain's relationship with Europe its perspective.

But although the revisionists have been taking a more sympathetic approach to British European policy, they do not totally avoid criticising British policy-makers. They centre most of their attacks on the 'clumsiness' of British diplomacy towards Europe, which, they say, damaged the presentation of British policy abroad.[36] Ill-judged speeches and badly-phrased diplomacy served to hamper British foreign policy-makers in their efforts to chart a course that would suit British interests but would not appear to be inimical to the European project. Of Eden, for example, Young writes that 'his tone too often gave the appearance of being anti-European'.[37] Anthony Adamthwaite lambasts British diplomacy during the second application to join the EEC.[38] Furthermore, revisionists have been known to engage in the 'missed opportunities' debate. Young, for example, arrived in the first edition of *Britain and European Unity* at the conclusion that the years 1955–57 represent the period when the most serious opportunities were missed, though by the second edition he had dropped the judgemental portion of that sentence.[39]

Thus criticisms of British policy-makers are not altogether absent from revisionist accounts; but in terms of their weighting within those texts they form a much smaller proportion of the narrative, in much the same way that in orthodox texts, opportunities to rehabilitate or sympathise with policy-makers are either passed up altogether or given minimal attention. The schools operate on two sides of the same historiographical coin, orthodox writers prioritising some facts and events, revisionists others. It is to the origins of revisionism and the reasons why revisionists prioritise different sets of facts and events that the chapter now turns, in an effort to trace the birth and development of the revisionist school.

34 Hill, 'The Historical Background', p. 33.
35 M. Gowing, 'Nuclear Weapons and the "Special Relationship"', in Louis and Bull (eds), *The Special Relationship*, pp. 117–28 (p. 125).
36 Young, *Britain and European Unity, 1945–1999*, p. 51.
37 Young, *Britain and European Unity, 1945–1999*, pp. 37–8. See also Greenwood, *Britain and European Co-operation*, p. 78 and Kaiser, *Using Europe*, pp. 42–3.
38 A. Adamthwaite, 'John Bull v. Marianne, Round Two: Anglo-French Relations and Britain's Second EEC Membership Bid', in Daddow (ed.), *Harold Wilson and European Integration*, pp. 151–71 (p. 169).
39 Young, *Britain and European Unity, 1945–1992*, p. 52; Young, *Britain and European Unity, 1945–1999*, pp. 48–9.

The genesis of revisionism

Dating precisely the origins of revisionist historiography is not easy for two
reasons. It is tricky first of all because this is not a zero-sum game, whereby the
emergence of a new school of writing necessarily meant the extinction of its pred-
ecessor. One would not expect politicians writing from a Europeanist perspective
now, such as Michael Heseltine and Leon Brittan, to disavow their view of missed
opportunities just because the majority of academics writing in the field do so.[40]
Blair's Birmingham speech demonstrated that in these quarters the orthodox
school remains alive. It is just that it does not now receive the kind of unques-
tioning reception among historians that it used to, and it has now to coexist with
a growing number of works that deconstruct its underlying assumptions.

     The second reason why dating the emergence of revisionism is problematic
is that there is no single moment or text to which one can point and say 'that was
when the revisionist school was born'. The transgression of the boundaries
between the orthodoxy and revisionism has been a more subtle process, which
occurred gradually from the 1970s onwards, and is not one that lends itself to
analysis in terms of dates. So although it is possible to argue that one school of
writing has supplanted another, this is neither to deny the continued existence of
the orthodox interpretation nor to claim that revisionism can be dated back to a
particular point in time.

Sowing the seeds

To reinforce the point that chronological boundaries between schools of writing
are not easy to draw, one can analyse the date and content of a variety of works
that contained what are labelled in this book the 'seeds of revisionism'. The use
of the word 'seeds' draws upon Kuhn's argument about the natural sciences, that
'Often a paradigm emerges, at least in embryo, before a crisis has developed far
or been explicitly recognised.'[41] It taps into the idea that history texts are multilayered and contain allusions to alternative interpretations of the past without
expanding on them, so as not to challenge the dominant interpretation put on the
past by the author.

     Orthodox historians went some way to giving us what has since become the
alternative interpretation; but it was something of an accidental development, if
it was acknowledged at all. Compared to the full-blown revisionism that emerged

---

40 M. Heseltine, *Where There's a Will* (London, Hutchinson, 1987), pp. 255–74; L. Brittan, *A Diet of
    Brussels: The Changing Face of Europe* (London, Little, Brown and Company, 2000), where on
    p. 191 he bemoans the 'mistake' of 'not being there' when the Common Agricultural and Common
    Fisheries Policies were set up.
41 Kuhn, *The Structure of Scientific Revolutions*, p. 86.

later, and bearing in mind that orthodox historians led their accounts of British European policy with the 'missed opportunities' thesis, they cannot be considered in and of themselves revisionist texts. What will become apparent below is that historiographical evolution is brought about not just by the consultation of new sources or by new methods of research being used to access the past, but through the willingness of individuals, working alone or in groups, to break out decisively from the interpretative mould set by their predecessors in the field.

There are two threads in the literature that display the pattern of revisionists drawing out and developing the unresolved interpretative tensions latent within earlier texts: the Third Force conception of British foreign policy under the Labour governments of Clement Attlee, and British policy towards European integration under the Churchill and Eden governments. Taking each in turn, it will be shown that, before the decisive break occurred in the middle of the 1980s, there had been rumblings of discontent among historians about the prevailing orthodoxy, but that it took the study of British European policy, to become an area of academic inquiry in its own right to prompt the emergence of a self-aware revisionist school of writing.

Turning first of all to the foreign policy of the Attlee governments, 1945–51, in two articles, published in 1982 and 1984 respectively, John Baylis gave academic voice to the prevailing orthodoxy that Attlee's Foreign Secretary, Ernest Bevin, was largely uninterested in promoting co-operation between Britain and Europe. He used the fishing metaphor that the Dunkirk and Brussels Treaties, signed in 1947 and 1948 respectively,[42] were 'sprats' to lure the American 'mackerel' into the defence of the West.[43]

Penned at a time when Ronald Reagan and Margaret Thatcher were stoking superpower tensions, the view that a British politician had moulded the post-war security environment to the benefit of the West already had many adherents, and Baylis was not the first to go in search of the reasons behind what Kenneth Morgan calls 'the majesty of [Bevin's] overall grand design' of entangling America in the defence of Western Europe.[44] Just as Monnet and Schuman are revered in Europeanist circles as the architects of European unity, Bevin, the argument went, could reasonably be lauded as one of the fathers of the Euro-Atlantic partnership embodied by NATO.[45]

---

42 The Dunkirk Treaty was signed by Britain and France, the Brussels Treaty by the same two countries plus Belgium, the Netherlands and Luxembourg.

43 J. Baylis, 'Britain and the Dunkirk Treaty: The Origins of NATO', *Journal of Strategic Studies*, 5:2 (1982), 236–47; J. Baylis, 'Britain, the Brussels Pact and the Continental Commitment', *International Affairs*, 60:4 (1984), 615–29.

44 K. O. Morgan, review, 'Ernest Bevin. By Alan Bullock; The Diary of Hugh Gaitskell 1945–1960. Edited by Philip Williams; Breach of Promise. By John Vaizey', *The Times Literary Supplement*, 11 (November 1983), pp. 1243–4 (p. 1244).

45 A useful overview of this debate can be found in R. Frazier, 'Did Britain Start the Cold War? Bevin and the Truman Doctrine', *Historical Journal*, 27:3 (1984), 715–27.

With the Foreign Secretary himself saying that 'It is given to so few men to see their dreams fulfilled',[46] the view that NATO was his crowning achievement had long provided fodder for hagiographic biographies of the Foreign Secretary.[47] It was also appealing to key members of the political and defence establishments in Britain: to civil servants,[48] to Bevin's Labour colleagues,[49] and to Conservative opponents,[50] all of whom praised the Foreign Secretary for saving Western civilisation from the Communist menace. This establishment perspective worked its way into the official history of British foreign policy in the aftermath of the Second World War.[51] Amongst its writers there was, Bradford Perkins observes, 'broad satisfaction with the foreign policy of the Labour government'.[52]

For the very reason that Bevin received such widespread establishment acclaim, this view was also propagated by socialists and communists who believed that Labour had needlessly entangled Britain in the Cold War against a Russian ally the Attlee government should have been able to deal with constructively. They compared the Foreign Secretary unfavourably with the man who

46 Quoted in G. Warner, 'The British Labour Government and the Atlantic Alliance, 1949–1951', in O. Riste (ed.), *Western Security: The Formative Years* (Oslo, Norwegian University Press, 1985), pp. 247–65 (p. 263).

47 Notably Williams, *Ernest Bevin*, pp. 266–7; Roberts, 'Ernest Bevin as Foreign Secretary' and M. Stephens, *Ernest Bevin: Unskilled Labourer and World Statesman 1881–1951* (Stevenage, SPA Books, 1985), pp. 109–24.

48 I. Kirkpatrick, *The Inner Circle: Memoirs of Ivone Kirkpatrick* (London, Macmillan, 1959), p. 205; A. M. Browne, *Long Sunset: Memoirs of Winson Churchill's Last Private Secretary* (London, Indigo, 1996), pp. 59–60 and Nutting, *Europe Will Not Wait*, p. 21. On the military side see Montgomery of Alamein, *Memoirs* (London, Collins, 1958), p. 511.

49 On this issue even Herbert Morrison stood 'firmly behind the hard line of his old enemy Bevin': B. Donoghue and G. W. Jones, *Herbert Morrison: Portrait of a Politician* (London, Weidenfeld and Nicolson, 1973), p. 433. See in addition Attlee, *As It Happened*, p. 171; Healey, *The Time of My Life*, p. 114; H. Wilson, *Memoirs: The Making of a Prime Minister 1916–64* (London, Weidenfeld and Nicolson and Michael Joseph, 1986), p. 125; Harris, *Attlee*, p. 295 and B. Pimlott (ed.), *The Political Diary of Hugh Dalton, 1918–40, 1945–60* (London, Jonathan Cape, 1987), linking remarks, p. 469.

50 On the Conservative side see Eden, *Full Circle*, p. 5; Macmillan, *Tides of Fortune*, pp. 132–3; Aster, *Anthony Eden*, pp. 90–1; Rees-Mogg, *Sir Anthony Eden*, p. 99; R. R. James (ed.), *Chips: The Diaries of Sir Henry Channon* (London, Penguin, 1970), entry for 20 August, 1945, the occasion of Bevin's first major speech as Foreign Secretary, p. 502.

51 The official history runs to a number of volumes: R. Butler and M. E. Pelly (eds), *Documents on British Policy Overseas*, 1:1, 1945 (London, HMSO, 1984); R. Bullen and M. E. Pelly (eds), *Documents on British Policy Overseas*, 1:2, 1945 (London: HMSO, 1985); R. Bullen and M. E. Pelly (eds), *Documents on British Policy Overseas*, 1:3, 1945 (London, HMSO, 1986); R. Bullen and M. E. Pelly (eds), *Documents on British Policy Overseas*, 1:4, 1945 (London, HMSO, 1987); M. E. Pelly and H. J. Yasamee (eds), *Documents on British Policy Overseas*, 1:5, 1945 (London, HMSO, 1990); M. E. Pelly and H. J. Yasamee (eds), *Documents on British Policy Overseas*, 1:6, 1945–1946 (London: HMSO, 1991); H. J. Yasamee and K. A. Hamilton, *Documents on British Policy Overseas*, 1:7, 1946–1947 (London, HMSO, 1995).

52 B. Perkins, 'Unequal Partners: The Truman Administration and Great Britain', in Louis and Bull (eds), *The Special Relationship*, pp. 43–64 (p. 46).

would probably have been in his position had the Conservative Party won the 1945 general election, accusing him of being even 'less conciliatory than Eden would have been' in dealing with Russia.[53] Baylis's articles were thus indicative of many British and American histories of post-war British foreign policy written before the 1980s.[54] The enduring appeal of this interpretation can be seen from its appearance in Paul Kennedy's 1985 book on British foreign policy, where he said 'Bevin's chief aim was to bind the United States more closely to the defence of Europe' and in Hugo Young's verdict over a decade later that the Foreign Secretary was 'Britain's first peacetime Atlanticist'.[55]

There are disputes among these writers about the specifics of Bevin's foreign policy. The most obvious one concerns the timing of Bevin's conversion to the idea of luring Washington into a long-term defence commitment to Europe. For some, such as Frank Roberts and Elisabeth Barker, Britain's withdrawal from Greece and Turkey is evidence of a 'tricky plan' developed in 1947 for this purpose.[56] Ritchie Ovendale also posits that America began to retreat from isolationism after 1947 because of Bevin's 'tactical' manoeuvres in the Mediterranean.[57]

53 Krug, Aneurin Bevan, p. 102. For further expression of this opinion see D. N. Pritt, The Labour Government, 1945–1951 (London: Lawrence and Wishart, 1963), Brivati, Hugh Gaitskell, p. 166 and M. Foot, Aneurin Bevan: A Biography, Volume 2, 1945–1960 (London: Davis-Poynter, 1973), p. 32. For analysis see E. J. Meehan, The British Left Wing and Foreign Policy: A Study of the Influence of Ideology (New Brunswick, Rutgers University Press, 1960), pp. 30–4; J. Schneer, Labour's Conscience: The Labour Left 1945–51 (London: Unwin Hyman, 1988); L. D. Epstein, Britain: Uneasy Ally (Chicago, The University of Chicago Press, 1954), p. 81 and W. Knight, 'Labourite Britain: America's "Sure Friend"? The Anglo-Soviet Treaty Issue, 1947', Diplomatic History, 7:4 (1983), 267–82 (267–8).

54 The historical backdrop to a Chatham House Study Group report on the WEU and the Atlantic Alliance, published in 1955, reflects the official line that 'From the beginning British foreign policy aimed at the inclusion of the United States and Canada in a European security system': Britain in Western Europe: WEU and the Atlantic Alliance (London and New York, Royal Institute of International Affairs, 1955), p. 8. On the American side see T. H. Anderson, The United States, Great Britain, and the Cold War 1944–1947 (Columbia, University of Missouri Press, 1981); Camps, Britain and the European Community, p. 21; W. C. Cromwell, The United States and the European Pillar (Basingstoke, Macmillan, 1992), pp. 1–2; R. M. Hathaway, Ambiguous Partnership: Britain and America, 1944–1947 (New York, Columbia University Press, 1981), p. 270; L. S. Kaplan, 'An Unequal Triad: The United States, Western Union, and NATO', in Riste (ed.), Western Security, pp. 107–27 and LaFeber, America, Russia, and the Cold War, pp. 51–80.

55 Kennedy, The Realities Behind Diplomacy, p. 367; Young, This Blessed Plot, p. 31. Other writers who have pursued this line include Barker, Britain in a Divided Europe, pp. 117–27; Charlton, The Price of Victory, pp. 53–66; Frankel, British Foreign Policy, pp. 186–237 and 284–97; Northedge, British Foreign Policy, pp. 46–58; R. Ovendale, 'Britain, the U.S.A. and the European Cold War, 1945–8' History, 67 (1982), 217–35; R. Ovendale, 'Introduction', in Ovendale (ed.), The Foreign Policy of the British Labour Governments, pp. 1–17; A. Shlaim, Britain and the Origins of European Unity 1940–1951 (Reading, The Graduate School of Contemporary Euroepan Studies, 1978), pp. 68–115 and Sked and Cook, Post-War Britain, pp. 50–76.

56 Roberts, 'Ernest Bevin as Foreign Secretary', p. 33; Barker, Britain in a Divided Europe, p. 68.

57 R. Ovendale, The English-Speaking Alliance: Britain, the United States, the Dominions and the Cold War (London, George Allen and Unwin, 1985), p. 60.

For others, Britain's defence retrenchment in the region was more a matter of economic exigency and not tied to a master-plan, Bullock cautioning that 'such Machiavellian cunning does not ... seem to have been in Bevin's character'. Frankel suggests instead that Bevin had made his mind up much earlier, in 1945, when 'alignment with the United States seemed "natural" for a number of reasons': America was the only potential supplier of the economic and defence assistance Britain needed; it was easy to continue the habit of peacetime co-operation, especially in the intelligence arena, that had begun during the war; and building a European Third Force seemed an increasingly distant and 'utopian' prospect after 1945 as superpower disagreements became the norm in international relations rather than the exception.[58]

Disagreements on specifics, however, do not detract from the broad thrust of the orthodox interpretation of Bevin's foreign policy. 'The consensus view', note Kent and Young, 'stresses the significance of the Atlantic Alliance ... and interprets it as being, from the first, the ultimate goal of Britain's Foreign Secretary.'[59] The offshoot was that the building of a Third Force in Europe, to stand between the superpowers, did not feature highly, if at all, in Bevin's post-war thinking about British foreign policy. Michael Howard expressed it as follows: 'Discussions about a possible European 'third force' were multiple and diverse, but so far as I know no-one, during those post-war years, conceived of such a force as distinct, separate and potentially hostile to the United States. It was always visualised as existing within a general area dominated by American influence.'[60]

This concentration on the strategic dimensions of the Attlee governments' foreign policy, at the expense of the Europeanist Third Force elements, might well have been the result of the study of international relations in the 1980s being dominated by the security, defence and political implications of the Cold War. The motivation behind these studies was to discover the role Britain and NATO played in the origins of the Cold War; Britain's approach to European integration was not nearly so high on the agenda of international historians at this time, which was often taken as coterminous with London's Cold War strategy.

The transition between schools

Even as orthodox historiography held sway, however, there were some texts that had begun to question whether Bevin and his Labour Cabinet colleagues

---

58 Bullock, *Ernest Bevin*, pp. 41–2; Frankel, *British Foreign Policy*, pp. 186–7. See also LaFeber, *America, Russia, and the Cold War*, p. 52 and Northedge, *British Foreign Policy*, p. 58.

59 Kent and Young, 'British Policy Overseas', p. 41.

60 M. Howard, 'Introduction', in O. Riste (ed.), *Western Security*, pp. 11–12 (p. 12). For a restatement of this position see Lee, *Victory in Europe?*, pp. 51–2.

were so neglectful of the European dimension of British foreign policy. Three historians stand out in this respect: Victor Rothwell, Alan Bullock and Geoffrey Warner.

Rothwell was among the first in Britain to use documents released to the PRO under the Thirty Year Rule, and the bedrock of his analysis was achieved using Foreign Office papers. In his 1982 book *Britain and the Cold War*, he agreed with the reasoning behind what was later to become the revisionist interpretation, that Bevin was more interested in co-operating with Europe than had been assumed, but, importantly, he did not mention the concept of the Third Force by name:

> Bevin remained devoted to the concept of some type of West European unity, formal or informal, under British leadership, both because he did not think that the Americans could be relied upon permanently to defend Western Europe and aid it economically and because he did not want Western Europe in general, and Britain in particular, to become merely an appendage of American power.[61]

A year later, Bullock built on the foundations Rothwell had laid for a reassessment of Bevin's foreign policy in a biography of Bevin that included analysis of his private papers. For him, ideas about building a Third Force were the preserve of the 'Keep Left' group of Labour MPs, and consequently they did not gain much of a hearing at Cabinet level. The Foreign Secretary, Bullock argues, 'never allowed himself to be misled by the illusion of a Third Force', although he refers a number of times throughout the biography to the depth and longevity of Bevin's thinking on the subject – which might be seen as something of an unresolved contradiction within the text.[62]

Moving historians nearer what is now the revisionist interpretation of the Third Force was Geoffrey Warner, in a series of articles on Anglo-French diplomacy, British foreign policy and European integration. In the first, published in 1971, he wrote that, slowly through 1947, the British began to view the Dunkirk Treaty 'as a possible nucleus of a wider European and indeed Atlantic grouping directed against the threat of Communist aggression' and that 'it would be a mistake to view the Brussels Treaty solely in military terms' as it contained provisions for economic, social and cultural co-operation among the signatories.[63] In an article published in 1984, coincidentally the same year as Baylis's study of the origins of the Brussels Treaty, Warner argued that the Foreign Secretary *had* envisaged creating a Third Force, but that: 'Bevin certainly seems to have been thinking in terms of what later became known as the "dumb-bell" concept of the Atlantic relationship, i.e., a partnership between two equals: the United States on

---

61 Rothwell, *Britain and the Cold War 1941–1947*, pp. 443–4.
62 Bullock, *Ernest Bevin*, p. 416 See also pp. 318, 396, 491–5, 520–9 and 632.
63 Warner, 'The Reconstruction and Defence of Western Europe', pp. 261–2.

the one hand and a British-led Western Europe (perhaps the colonial territories and possibly even the Commonwealth) on the other.'[64]

Hard on the heels of Warner interrogating the tired assumptions concerning Britain's early post-war foreign policy came a series of articles by John Kent and John Young. For them it was an even clearer-cut case of Bevin's wanting to construct a Third Force that would be independent of both superpowers, but being forced by the exigencies of economics and defence to play the American card in 1949. Like Warner, they say the Foreign Office documents detailing the Permanent Under-Secretary's Committee's deliberations on 'European Policy' in 1949–50 (where 'the main purpose was to throw cold water upon any suggestion that Western Europe, with or without the support of the Commonwealth, could form a "Third Force", independent of both the United States and the Soviet Union'),[65] should not blind us to Bevin's enthusiasm for building a Third Force at earlier times. His ambition, they argued,

> reflected a mixture of British power-political aspirations, economic requirements and ideological predilections. It embodied a major British role in the first rank of global powers, post-war economic recovery and a middle democratic socialist way between the harsh and conflicting ideologies of unfettered American capitalism and repressive Soviet Communism.[66]

Warner has since published further support for this firmer interpretation of Bevin's Third Forcism in an article quoting Bevin's intentions of building 'a new Commonwealth without regard for America or Russia'. The British Empire, the Foreign Secretary told newspaper correspondents in March 1946, 'isn't going to be either the 49th [American] State or the 17th [Soviet] Republic'.[67]

'Full blown' revisionism

How and why did Warner, Kent and Young arrive at this firmer interpretation of Bevin's intentions? There appear to be four principal reasons, which together shed a good deal of light on the key differences between the revisionist and orthodox

---

64 Warner, 'The Labour Governments', p. 79. See also Watt, *Succeeding John Bull*, p. 121.

65 This Committee was set up by Bevin in February 1949 and was intended to act as the equivalent of the State Department's Policy Planning Staff, to advise the Foreign Secretary on long-term policy issues. Warner, 'The British Labour Government', p. 248 and Warner, 'Bevin and British Foreign Policy', p. 116. See also more recently Saki Dockrill, *Britain's Retreat from East of Suez: The choice between Europe and the Wider World?*, p. 12.

66 Kent and Young, 'British Policy Overseas', pp. 64–5. See also Kent, 'Bevin's Imperialism'; J. Kent, 'The "Western Union" Concept' and Young, *Britain and European Unity 1945–1999*, pp. 6–25.

67 The first quotation here is from a biographer of the former editor of *The Times*, Donald McLaghlan, the second from the diaries of Sir Pierson Dixon, Bevin's Private Secretary, both in Warner, 'Ernest Bevin and British Foreign Policy', p. 108.

schools of writing on Britain and Europe. At the heart of their analysis lies the desire to get beyond the hindsight-driven accounts of their predecessors. NATO, they say, should not be seen as the goal of Bevin's foreign policy from the outset. Not people instinctively inclined to accept conventional wisdoms,[68] Kent and Young see the orthodoxy as a convenient myth:

> which submerges the efforts to develop a new imperial system beneath the rhetoric of saving Western civilisation from the Communist menace. As such it is more a reflection of Foreign Office efforts to present British foreign policy as ... enlightened, liberal and altruistic rather than an accurate portrayal of the ideas and policies of political and official elites.[69]

Playing upon Bevin's 'success' in helping found NATO overlooks, they say, his failure to create a Third Force, because the Washington Treaty was for him a second-best, not the goal at which he single-mindedly aimed after 1945.

The foundation of their interpretation, and the second factor in its development, was the assiduous reading of primary source documentation in the PRO. Bevin's interjections in Cabinet discussions, his speeches to the House of Commons, the wording of the Dunkirk and Brussels Treaties and the movement of key reports and memoranda around Whitehall were all being examined for the first time, and were used extensively in support of their re-reading of British foreign policy. In March 1948, to take one example, Bevin is quoted as saying to Cabinet: 'We should use US aid to gain time, but our ultimate aim should be to attain a position in which the countries of W. Europe would be independent both of the US and the Soviet Union.'[70]

To take another, Kent and Young contrast the 'sprat to catch a mackerel' thesis, and the associated orthodox emphasis on the politico-military dimensions of the Dunkirk and Brussels Treaties, with the wording in those treaties. Offering an interpretation strongly reminiscent of Warner's, the signatories, they remind us, proposed to develop co-operation in a larger number of areas than simply defence:[71] 'The fact that the Brussels Treaty was followed one year later by the conclusion of the North Atlantic alliance should not lead us into the error of supposing that it was intended primarily as a military pact, still less that it was no more than bait to entice the United States into a commitment to defend western Europe.'[72]

The release of primary sources has led other historians down the same path, if not quite so far, and, now that revisionism has become dominant in the field, it

---

68 Interview with Kent.
69 Kent and Young, 'British Policy Overseas', p. 58.
70 Cited in Kent, 'Bevin's Imperialism', p. 70.
71 Kent and Young, 'British Policy Overseas', pp. 46–7; Kent and Young, 'The "Western Union" Concept', pp. 169–70; Young, *Britain and European Unity 1945–1999*, pp. 16–19.
72 Warner, 'The Labour Governments', p. 66.

too is beginning to find itself the subject of deconstruction by the next generation of scholars. Using newly declassified sources pertaining to the Information Research Department (IRD), the intelligence historian Hugh Wilford echoes Kent and Young's verdict that Labour ministers set about building a Third Force in Europe, only to abandon hope of achieving it by the end of 1948 and that, by 1950, the idea had completely 'succumbed to the concept of an Atlantic alliance'. In the course of the article, however, he waters down this claim through analysis of the fervent anti-Communism of the civil servants and politicians in charge of the IRD. Given their persistent anti-Communist propaganda efforts, he says, 'it is questionable whether the Labour ministers who charged IRD with advertising the Third Force were ever themselves sincerely committed to that concept'.[73]

The third factor explaining the rise of revisionism concerns the broader reassessment of the politics of the Attlee governments that has accompanied it. So-called socialist governments were, revisionists argue, in fact highly imperialist in outlook. Attlee provided 'philosophical justification' for the Third Force in his New Year's Day broadcast to the nation in 1948,[74] while Bevin said he wanted to create a 'Euro-African bloc' as a means of regaining a measure of independence from America after its loan to Britain in 1945 and Marshall Aid in 1947.[75]

'If properly developed', he told the French foreign minister Georges Bidault in November 1947, the huge resources in western Europe and their territories in Africa 'amounted to more than either the Soviet Union or the United States could muster, and should enable Western European Powers to be independent of either'.[76] Co-operation with countries such as Belgium, moreover, would offer strategic benefits in the form of raw materials necessary to the manufacture of atomic weapons: 70 per cent of the world's uranium supply was estimated to lay in the Belgian Congo at this time.[77] Bevin's enthusiasm for the Third Force was publicly stated in the House of Commons on 22 January 1948 in a speech regarded by the 'good European' Paul-Henri Spaak as 'an historic event', although typically this is followed a page later by the rueful remark that neither Bevin nor his successors showed 'such courage' in helping to promote the cause of European unity afterwards.[78]

Hence, to suggest that the Third Force idea was only the preserve of 'prominent intellectuals' among Labour left-wingers such as G. D. H. Cole or Richard

---

73 Wilford, 'The Information Research Department', pp. 354, 356 and 368.
74 Young, *Britain and European Unity 1945–1999*, p. 16.
75 Kent, 'Bevin's Imperialism', p. 56. See also Rothwell, *Britain and the Cold War*, p. 449; Hogan, *The Marshall Plan*, p. 111; Greenwood, *Britain and European Cooperation*, pp. 16–17 and 21 and Warner, 'The Labour Governments', pp. 64–6.
76 Quoted in Warner, 'Bevin and British Foreign Policy', p. 112.
77 Kent, 'Bevin's Imperialism', p. 55; Young, *Britain and European Unity, 1945–1999*, pp. 10–12.
78 Spaak, *The Continuing Battle*, pp. 142–3.

Crossman,[79] or 'some European politicians',[80] or that Bevin's approach was merely a 'flirtation'[81] overlooks, revisionists argue, the widespread appeal of the idea within British, American and European policy-making circles in the late 1940s. Key officials in the Foreign Office and the State Department, many members of the Conservative opposition and establishment press organs such as *The Times* are all thought to have favoured the Third Force concept. This, say Kent and Young, was a 'wide-ranging consensus'.[82]

The final and perhaps the most compelling factor in the rise of revisionist historiography is associated with the genre of writing that allowed the new inter-pretation of Labour's foreign policy in 1945–51 to become the norm: academic historiography. For the purposes of analysis, this factor can in turn be split into three: the focus of revisionist studies, periodisation, and the allure of the Third Force as a new model for understanding post-war British foreign policy.

Rothwell and Bullock were not interested exclusively in Bevin's policy towards European integration nor, for that matter, in the Labour government's general attitude towards Europe in the post-war era. The former reflected the tenor of earlier historiography in concentrating on Britain's role in the origins of the Cold War, while the latter wrote a biographical study that had many of the expected additional targets, not least that of understanding Bevin's personality and his relations with Cabinet colleagues, the Prime Minister, the Labour Party and his foreign counterparts. The European aspect of Bevin's foreign policy was downgraded accordingly.

This provides a strong contrast with Kent and Young's work, which concentrated almost exclusively on the idea of the Third Force, playing up the European dimension of British foreign policy accordingly. Using new sources, bringing out the imperialist dimensions of Labour's foreign policy and re-read-ing speeches and treaties that had been in the public domain for many years, but had hitherto been ignored or overlooked by historians, they managed to reinterpret British European policy under the Attlee administrations as being intrinsically concerned to bring about European integration, but abandoning this stance as ultimately unattainable when it became clear that the political, economic and strategic obstacles in the way of a Third Force were too high to overcome and when for security reasons the turn to America seemed the only

79 Frankel, *British Foreign Policy*, pp. 236–7; Bullock, *Ernest Bevin*, pp. 395–6.
80 Dell, *The Schuman Plan*, p. 115.
81 A. Adamthwaite, 'Britain and the World, 1945–9: The View from the Foreign Office', *International Affairs*, 61:2 (1985), 223–35 (228).
82 Kent and Young, 'British Policy Overseas', p. 51. See also Hogan, *The Marshall Plan*, pp. 41 and 113; J. L. Gaddis, 'The United States and the Question of a Sphere of Influence in Europe, 1945–1949', in Riste (ed.), *Western Europe*, pp. 60–91 (p. 70) and Winand, *Eisenhower, Kennedy*, pp. 15–18.

way to combat the perceived threat from Russia and to rebuild British prestige on the world stage.

Turning next to the issue of periodisation, it is noteworthy that Rothwell's study terminated in 1947, *before* 1948, when Kent and Young argue that the Third Force conception was at its apogee in the Foreign Office. The closure of Rothwell's study could be due to any number of factors: chance, the lack of time to consult the archives for another year, or the publishers wanting a certain length of book. The crux is that, whatever Rothwell's sources may have been, and despite his belief that primary documentation allows the best access to the past, the shut-off point for his study militated against his examining evidence for what has since become the crucial year in this particular story. Consequently, he never felt comfortable about actually naming the Third Force as a distinct and definable aspect of Bevin's thinking.

Put this way, historiographical interpretation can be seen to be a function of decisions made by historians about how to organise their research and writing and where to begin and end their narratives. One writer who does focus on the issue of periodisation is Jordanova, who is led to conclude that the construction of historical texts is a complex, multidimensional process: 'a subtle blend of diverse elements such as the sources selected, the manner of their use, the context in which the historian works, their training, commitments and prejudices'.[83]

Finally, let us turn to the harder-to-measure but nonetheless significant impact of labelling. It has been argued by Kaplan that labelling theories and concepts can have powerful repercussions on their acceptance by scholars, who are inherently conservative with a small 'c' in terms of the credence they give to new concepts, theories, interpretations and ideas about the past. [84] And as one commentator on Foucault described his attitude to labels and labelling: 'names … don't matter so much in themselves; rather, their meaning comes from the ways in which they are articulated and deployed by various interests within the flow of power relations'.[85]

Kent and Young not only *described* Bevin's Third Force concept, but they also *named* it as such. They did this, importantly, in the *titles* of their articles too. This strategy, it seems, played a significant role in persuading the historical community at large that here was a new way of understanding post-war British foreign policy. It gained further weight within the field because they juxtaposed the Third Force interpretation against earlier approaches, naming the writers against whom they set their new reading of the history, and thus clearly

---

83 Jordanova, *History in Practice*, p. 107. For her discussion of periodisation see Chapter 5, pp. 114–40.

84 Morton A. Kaplan, *On Historical and Political Knowing* (London, The University of Chicago Press, 1971), p. 83.

85 Danaher, Schirato and Webb, *Understanding Foucault*, p. 94.

marked out the territorial boundaries between the 'old' and the 'new'. In an academic world in which fads and fashions play crucial roles in generating adherents to new concepts, interpretations and theories, this undoubtedly was a factor, perhaps even the most important one. This chapter now moves on to examine in more detail the broader historiographical impact of early revisionist work on Bevin's foreign policy.

The spread of revisionism

Adherents to this new approach came both from the next generation of scholars and from among established scholars, even those who formerly had adhered to the orthodoxy, providing support in the discipline of history for an observation made about the natural sciences: 'Prestige accrues predominantly to those whose discoveries prove fruitful as a basis for further work by other scientists.'[86] Of many potential examples of the growth in appeal of the revisionist interpretation amongst historians, two stand out: subsequent literature on the foreign policy of the Attlee governments and subsequent literature on Britain's approach to Europe in the 1950s.

In terms of British foreign policy under Attlee, analysis of the work of four historians will suffice to show the dramatic impact of revisionism. The first two are the postgraduate research students Martin Francis and Charles de Brabant, who cited writers such as Kent and Young as key influences on their (unpublished) work in 1989 and 1992.[87] Unsurprisingly, their interpretation of Britain's approach to European integration had a strongly Third Force flavour to it. The doctoral supervision process in Britain is one of the mechanisms by which ways of seeing the world are passed on from generation to generation, so it is no surprise to find students new to the field unhesitatingly adopting the newest interpretation on the block.

The third example is the American academic Peter Weiler, who published a biography of Bevin in 1993. Given the tenor of earlier biographical representations of Bevin and his foreign policy, by Alan Bullock, Mark Stephens and Frank Roberts, one might have expected Weiler to praise the Foreign Secretary for saving Western civilisation by signing the North Atlantic Treaty (NAT). Writing at the turn of the 1990s, however, Weiler was apprised of the revisionist turn in scholarship and took seriously Bevin's rhetoric about wanting to build a Third Force in Europe. He contextualised his research using the revisionist literature which had taken a grip of the field, resulting in an account that balanced Bevin's

---

86 F. Reif, quoted in Becher and Trowler, *Academic Tribes and Territories*, p. 84.
87 C. P. A. de Brabant, 'Anglo-French Colonial Co-operation Principally in West African Affairs, 1943–1954' (Oxford University M. Litt, 1989); M. Francis, 'Labour Policies and Socialist Ideals: The Example of the Attlee Government, 1945–51' (Oxford University PhD, 1992).

concern with security against what was now regarded as his genuine interest in building a 'Euro-African bloc' in the period 1945–9.[88]

The fourth and most memorable example is John Baylis.[89] By the time he published *The Diplomacy of Pragmatism* in 1990 he had, Jay Wagner noted, changed his 'emphasis and interpretations', being less sure that his earlier interpretation of NATO being a success story for Bevin held true.[90] Not now the view that Bevin single-mindedly wanted to entangle America in the defence of Western Europe after 1945. Instead, he directly referred to writers such as Kent and Young to argue that Bevin was more interested in European co-operation and colonial exploitation than he had previously thought. The signing of the NAT, he said, was an admission that the building of a European unit between the superpowers had failed, and not a credit to one man's skill and diplomatic vision. One can see further evidence here of the historiography being propelled by the interpretative fads and fashions of the time, together with the unstructured way in which new historiographical interpretations become the accepted wisdom among communities of scholars. Had Baylis remained unaware of Kent and Young's contributions he might well have continued to uphold what Eric Hobsbawm calls the 'mythical halo' that hangs over the 1945–51 Attlee administrations.[91]

The second example of the rapidity with which the new approach to British European policy spread throughout academe concerns Britain's policy towards European integration in the 1950s. The previous chapter showed how the orthodoxy was dominant until the 1980s, serving a number of political purposes in Britain, America and on the Continent. Yet, at the same time, competing interpretations of British European policy were rarely absent from the literature. In 1963, the *Observer* journalist Nora Beloff published a book exploring Charles de Gaulle's first veto on British membership of the EEC in 1963. Analysing the history of the Schuman Plan negotiations she noted that, despite Conservative criticisms of the Labour government for not joining, 'neither side of the house could have accepted a supranational High Authority'.[92] She echoed the views a year earlier of Northedge, who analysed the considerable political, economic and ideological gaps that existed between Labour's plans for Britain and the supranational Europe envisaged by the 'founding fathers'.[93]

88 P. Weiler, *Ernest Bevin* (Manchester: Manchester University Press, 1993), pp. 144–87.
89 J. Baylis, *The Diplomacy of Pragmatism: Britain and the Formation of NATO, 1942–49* (Basingstoke, Macmillan, 1993).
90 J. Wagner, review, 'The Diplomacy of Pragmatism: Britain and the Formation of NATO, 1942–49. By John Baylis', *International Affairs*, 69:4 (1993), 781–2 (781).
91 Referred to in Hennessy, 'The Attlee Governments', p. 29.
92 Beloff, *The General Says No*, p. 58.
93 Northedge, *British Foreign Policy*, pp. 134–45.

The 1970s witnessed further expressions of dissatisfaction with missed opportunities discourse, and this is particularly evident in an article by Keith Sainsbury, published in 1977. Critics, he says, charge Britain with a lack of 'European faith'. 'It is the writer's view, however ... that Britain was not psychologically ready to "enter Europe" in 1955, and that her interests and commitments were then probably irreconcilable with the essential European concept. This was certainly the general view at the time.'[94]

But it was the 1980s that saw the orthodoxy come under sustained attack, with direct rebuttals of its epistemological and methodological underpinnings becoming commonplace. In 1981 Anthony Seldon suggested that hindsight is a major factor in the construction of missed opportunities discourse, noting à la Northedge that 'there were formidable difficulties' to be overcome before Britain could take the European route, 'not least the Commonwealth'.[95] Six years later he was to make much the same point about the politicisation of the history by 'self-styled Europeans' such as Boothby and Maxwell Fyfe.[96] In the interim, the distinguished Foreign Office official John Colville made a rare departure from the official norm with these words: 'People now talk as if there were great opportunities missed. I doubt there were those opportunities. Nobody wanted that particular [European] solution.'[97] That same year, 1983, Elisabeth Barker put Britain's missed chances partly down to 'short-sightedness and national egotism', but went on to argue that the result was also due to the fact that London 'was simultaneously trying to start up the NATO bus, keep a hand on the emergency brakes of the Korean bus, and steer clear of a disastrous collision with Russia or China or both.'[98] In 1985 Jeremy Moon explored the role played by Europe in British politics before and at the time of the Schuman Plan announcement, concluding that, as in Whitehall, there was little attention to the Europe question in the country at large.[99] Melissen and Zeeman's 1987 article in *International Affairs*, tellingly subtitled 'Opportunities Lost?' was an indication of how far historians had come in the 1980s in deconstructing the orthodoxy.

The tone of these studies, and scholars' increasing willingness to take issue with the conventional wisdom mark the 1980s as the decade when the revisionist school of writing on Britain and Europe was born. Interviewed about their perceptions of the growth of interest in British European policy in the 1970s and

---

94 K. Sainsbury, 'Selwyn Lloyd', in A. Shlaim, P. Jones and K. Sainsbury (eds), *British Foreign Secretaries Since 1945* (London, David & Charles, 1977), pp. 117–43 (p. 124).

95 Seldon, *Churchill's Indian Summer*, p. 427.

96 Seldon, 'The Churchill Administration'.

97 Quoted in Charlton, *The Price of Victory*, p. 23.

98 Barker, *Britain in a Divided Europe*, p. 230.

99 J. Moon, *European Integration in British Politics 1950–1963: A Study of Issue Change* (Aldershot, Gower, 1985), pp. 68–112.

1980s, Geoffrey Warner pointed out that there were people writing in this area in the 1970s, himself included. John Young agreed, adding, however, that he did not really begin to feel part of an academic community on this subject until the middle of the 1980s, until those early works had been published and the networks of like-minded historians began developing alongside them.[100]

By the end of the decade, dissatisfaction had spiralled to such an extent that writers such as Sean Greenwood were beginning to turn the tables on the ortho-doxy by arguing that 'the "missed opportunities" were not those of the British, but rather those of Monnet', quoting Young's 1984 book on Anglo-French rela-tions to support his argument: 'By excluding Britain from the Schuman Plan, the cost of Monnet's tactics was a limited Europe, of only six nations, based on bureaucratic functional lines rather than an evolving, living, political organism, covering a wide area of Europe, such as Bevin had always hoped to create.'[101] In a series of articles and books in the 1980s and 1990s Young set about drawing together the previously disparate criticisms of the conventional wisdom. In 1988 he reassessed Britain's policy towards the Schuman Plan, arguing that it is 'unfair' to level charges of missed opportunities at British policy-makers because of the then widespread consensus about the need for a global role for Britain both among politicians and in the country – the same factors cited by earlier writers.[102]

A year later, he attacked critics of Churchill's policy in the 1950s by suggesting first of all that his European policy was not without its 'positive aspects', although the sense of a missed opportunity *vis-à-vis* the creation of the EEC comes through quite strongly in this article.[103] Together with his work with Kent on the Third Force and the publication of the textbook *Britain and European Unity*, Young's contribution, especially the section entitled 'Lost Opportunities?' at the end of Chapter 2, where he dissects the fault-line between early and later writers on this subject, has to be seen as one of the vital ones in terms of the devel-opment of a full-blown revisionist perspective on the history. He has been widely footnoted in later texts, and has supervised and been the external examiner for several students who have written doctoral dissertations on contemporary British foreign policy, thus setting the agenda both formally and informally for much of the historiography that has been published since.

Sean Greenwood's mirror-image deconstruction of the missed opportunities interpretation in *Britain and European Co-operation*, which appeared a year before Young's textbook, in 1991, is an example of the rapid spread of revisionist

100 Interviews with Warner and Young, the latter on 16 May 2002.
101 Greenwood, *Britain and European Cooperation*, p. 39; Young, *Britain, France and the Unity of Europe*, p. 166.
102 John W. Young, The Schuman Plan and British Association, in Young (ed.), *The Foreign Policy of Churchill's Peacetime Administration 1951–1955* (Leicester, Leicester University Press, 1988), pp. 109–34.
103 Young, '"The Parting of Ways"?', especially p. 218.

ways of thinking around the academic community throughout the 1980s. Other scholars, notably David Reynolds, were quick to join them in vigorously debunking the conventional wisdom. The latter goes so far as to argue that Britain did not need the Europeans in 1955–56 because it 'was exerting itself as a power more energetically than at any time outside the world wars, certainly far more than its Victorian heyday'.[104]

There is no single year to which one can point as the year that saw one school replace the other: they have always coexisted, to a greater or lesser degree. One is on firmer ground in terms of identifying writers who have been central to the interpretative shift in the historiography. The emergence of revisionism, while relatively limited in the 1960s and 1970s, picked up pace in the 1980s and culminated in the 1990s with the publication of the first textbooks on Britain and European unity. That revisionist writers have, in the main, been drawn from the academic historical community indicates once more that historical interpretation is a function of the genre of work. It is necessary, therefore, when attempting to explain the rise of revisionist historiography, to examine the institutional context within which it emerged, because this has shaped both how the past has been accessed by these writers and how they have conceived the field of British European policy.

The effects of 'disciplinisation'

There are a number of reasons why contemporary historians have been keen to attack the conventional wisdom about Britain and Europe, of which two stand out: the tendency, in-built within the scholarly enterprise, to de-bunk orthodoxies, and the consultation of primary sources. Both can be seen as products of what can be labelled the 'disciplinisation' of the study of contemporary history and, consequently, of British European policy throughout the 1980s. Before exploring them in detail, it is necessary to explain what the word 'disciplinisation' means in the context of historiography and why it has been used in this study.

It is commonly used to reflect how Foucault understood the term 'discipline' and how Hayden White applied it to the professionalisation of the study of history in the nineteenth century.[105] Foucault argued that the term 'discipline' has two meanings that are intricately interwoven with the concepts of 'power' and 'power relations'. On the one hand, he said, discipline is a verb, 'to discipline'

---

104 He uses as evidence conscription, the continental commitment, the intensive development of the Commonwealth, the sterling area, the nuclear programme, high defence spending and a strong economy. Britain, he states, was 'less than a superpower' but 'more than the "queue" of Europeans': Reynolds, *Britannia Overruled*, p. 198.

105 See also Thompson, *What Happened to History?*, pp. 72–5.

someone, for example. On the other, discipline is a noun, relating to 'a body of skills and knowledges'. We speak, for example, of the variety of disciplines one needs to master to become a musician, or a professional sportsman or woman. Crucially, however, we also speak of *academic* disciplines such as history, sociology, politics, chemistry, mathematics and so on. To be a student at school or university we must enter into different academic disciplines and gain certificates and degrees that provide the credentials that will help make us suitable for various posts in later life.[106]

Making one's way in academic fields involves becoming recognised and valued in that field by acquiring the requisite skill-sets to be a valuable member of that community and more importantly, to be *recognised* as such. '[T]his process is, according to [Stephen] Toulmin, one of enculturation ... What principally gets inherited ... is not a disembodied set of mental concepts but particular constellations of explanatory procedures, techniques, and practices that give muscle to the explicating representations and methodological goals of science.'[107] Written about becoming a member of a scientific discipline, Richards's description of the initiation that takes place is equally applicable to the processes undergone to become a member of any academic discipline. It might be likened to joining a club: 'To be admitted to membership of a particular sector of the academic profession involves not only a sufficient level of technical proficiency in one's intellectual trade but also a proper measure of loyalty to one's collegial group and adherence to its norms.'[108]

According to Becher and Trowler, the key characteristics of a discipline (bearing in mind their caveat that they will vary from discipline to discipline – some are more cohesive, tightly knit and possess less permeable boundaries than others), are both tangible and intangible, and include a shared sense of belonging, the awareness of neighbouring disciplinary territories, the existence of 'idols' (or 'big-names'), distinct discourses, traditions, customs, practices, transmitted knowledge, beliefs, morals, forms of communication and rules of conduct.[109] Their understanding of disciplines brings through their socially constructed nature, and as Burke argues, it is helpful to take disciplines 'as distinct professions and even subcultures, with their own languages, values and mentalities or styles of thought, reinforced by their respective processes of training or "socialization"'.[110] Richards, again deploying scientific terminology, judges them to be 'like evolving biological populations, that is, like species. Each discipline has

---

106 The ideas and quotes informing this paragraph are drawn from Danaher, Schirato and Webb, *Understanding Foucault*, pp. 50–1.
107 Richards, 'Theories of Scientific Change', p. 219.
108 Becher and Trowler, *Academic Tribes and Territories*, p. 47.
109 Based on *Ibid*. For discussion of how to 'get on' in academia see Chapters 4–6.
110 Burke, *History and Social Theory*, p. 3.

certain methods, general aims, and explanatory ideas that provide its coherence over time.'[111]

White used Foucaultian thought to inform his account of the professional study of history in the nineteenth century, published in 1974 as *Metahistory*. For him, history was steadily 'academized' across western Europe during this period, as evidenced by the establishment of Chairs in history at the University of Berlin in 1810 and at the Sorbonne in 1812. At the mid-way point in the century he notes that the 'great national journals of historical sciences are set up', *Historische Zeitschrift* in 1859, *Revue Historique* in 1876, *Rivista Storica Italiana* in 1884 and, finally, the *English Historical Review* in 1886. He therefore intertwines 'professionalisation' with 'disciplinisation', seeing the latter as a product of the former. In practice, he argues, it entailed a number of processes: the formation of a 'clerisy' for the promotion and cultivation of a socially responsible history, the training and licensing of apprentices, the maintenance of standards of excellence, the running of the 'organs of professional communication' and the establishment of scholarly journals as vehicles for the dissemination of findings.[112]

The concept of disciplines is thus not only useful in describing and explaining the methodological, epistemological and ontological contrasts between the disciplines of history, politics, chemistry, physics and sociology as they exist today, but is also applicable when it comes to explaining how specialisms grow and develop under the aegis of those disciplines, and, through an understanding of Foucault and White's work on disciplines, what one has to do to make oneself valued in a given field. So, just as one can explore the growth of disciplines on a 'macro' level, one can also use that apparatus for exploring the emergence of sub-fields within those disciplines – knowledge production on the 'micro' level.

Drawing on Foucault and White, the term 'disciplinisation' is employed in this study to denote the process by which academics have drawn up boundaries around the subject of British European policy and made it into a clear sub-field of the discipline of contemporary history. These boundaries are not necessarily meant in a formal sense, in that they are not intentionally excluding individuals or groups from participating in the study of this subject. Rather, the notion of boundaries is meant to suggest the way in which the study of a given topic develops its own momentum, its own sets of questions and methods of study, its own implicitly understood intellectual traditions and, underlying all this, its own deeply entrenched sets of power relations, revolving around networks of communication centring on journals such as *Contemporary British History* (formerly *Contemporary Record*), key individuals and key institutions. The discursive formations that have grown up with these developments, particularly the words

111 Richards, 'Theories of Scientific Change', p. 219.
112 For more on this see White, *Metahistory*, pp. 136–8 and Burke, *History and Social Theory*, p. 6.

and phrases used to deconstruct the conventional wisdom about missed opportunities, have been the glue that holds the school together, moulding how these academics 'behave and how they "see" the world'. Just as the orthodox school of writing developed a momentum of its own, with its own language, points of reference and modes of thinking about the past, the revisionist school likewise has readily identifiable features that are a function of the social context within which its members live and work and through which they have developed and defined their own identities and those of their specialism.

> The historian and history 'speak' from different places ... The historian speaks from a credentialised position within a public institution such as a museum, archive or university. The historian may engage in fieldwork and archival search, but it is the protocols and procedures of the institution which will shape how history will be written, and how the different historical events will be fitted together to form a coherent vision.[113]

The processes by which disciplines and sub-disciplines and sub-fields of study are born and evolve are a large part of the explanation for historiographical evolution in the context of history-writing by scholars. But this leaves two important questions unanswered: what does the world academics construct look like, and what, precisely, is the glue that holds fields together – is it made of personal relations, or is there more to it than that? By homing in now on the drivers behind the academic search for knowledge and the methodological consensus within this field, it can be seen how this is a world rooted in a common vision about Britain's post-war political history and shared expectations about how to access the past. It is a community in every sense of the word.

Debunking conventional wisdoms

One aspect of historiography that has regularly been commented upon is the constant process of interpretation and re-interpretation of events, personalities and so forth. Historical events regularly seem to undergo treatment that follows the form of a Hegelian dialectic: thesis, antithesis, synthesis.[114] 'It is not without significance', Geoffrey Elton remarked wryly, 'that the one historian among the ancients for whom no-one has a bad word seems to be Asinius Pollo, of whose writing nothing survives.'[115] Human beings are inquisitive, investigative and argumentative, and academia in particular possesses, Raymond Morrow and

---

113 Danaher, Schirato and Webb, *Understanding Foucault*, p. 101.
114 For details see Danaher, Schirato and Webb, *Understanding Foucault*, pp. 99–100 and White, *Metahistory*, p. 124. For an example of how the dialectic approach has informed the historiography of post-war British decline see H. Jones, 'The Post-War Consensus in Britain: Thesis, Antithesis, Synthesis?', in Brivati, Buxton and Seldon (eds), *The Contemporary History*, pp. 41–9.
115 Elton, *The Practice of History*, p. 2.

David Brown note, an 'inherently competitive character',[116] making scholars especially prone to taking issue with established traditions and received wisdoms.

This is not a new observation. Thomas Fuller, analysing the fluctuating interpretations of Richard III's legacy throughout the seventeenth century, compared historians with 'birds ... who cannot rise except it be by flying against the wind, as some hope to achieve their advancement by being contrary and para-doxal in judgment to all before them'.[117] Donald Watt goes a step further: he main-tains that it is *necessary* for the historian to rail against earlier writers as a means of correcting the inherently flawed judgements put about by the 'first wave of writers [in a field] ... that curious mélange of backward-looking commentators, political fixers, myth-makers and second-guessers whose initial occupation of the field makes the job of the professional historian so much more difficult.'[118]

Surveying the words of Fuller and noting the fact that revisionism is 'in-built' in the historical profession (the editors of the autumn 1978 edition of *History Workshop* said that historians are 'suspicious of orthodoxy'),[119] Southgate is led to the view that 'contrariness of that kind remains as an important motiva-tor in historical research.'[120] This tradition also led Elton to comment that the only certainty in history is that 'there will be more said and that, before long, others will say it'.[121] Robert Rhodes James alluded to the same point at the beginning of his biography of Eden: 'There will be further and different assessments. This is in the nature of historiography. "Definitive" biography is no more attainable than "definitive" history.'[122] Historiographical evolution can in this context be taken as one of scholarship's givens. One explanation for an event or events is bound to be met with suspicion by a host of critics, who will propose alternatives.

It is possible to construe in three ways this tendency of human beings, and academics in particular, to revise the past. The first is to see it as the product of changing times, of developments in the present affecting society's view of its past. According to this view, the revising of history is part of an ongoing search for a past that can be used in the present to help construct a better future. Contemporary history is especially susceptible to the changing climate of opinion, with disci-plinary fads and fashions driving changes in the way the past is represented.[123]

---

116 R. A. Morrow and D. D. Brown, *Critical Theory and Methodology* (London, Sage, 1994), preface, p. 14. See also Carr, *What is History?*, p. 124.

117 Quoted in Southgate, *History*, p. 69.

118 Watt, 'Demythologising the Eisenhower Era', p. 72.

119 'History and Theory', editorial, *History Workshop*, 6 (1978), 1–6 (1).

120 Southgate, *History*, p. 69.

121 Elton, *The Practice of History*, p. 63.

122 Robert Rhodes James, *Anthony Eden* (London, Weidenfeld and Nicolson, 1986), preface, p. 14.

123 Bayly, 'The Second British Empire', p. 67, remarks that the 'younger generation of the 1960s pulled [Imperial] scholarship in the direction of fashionable regional studies and anthropologically informed history. But contemporary politics did exercise a subtle influence.'

In this context, it might be tempting to see the growth of interest in British European policy in the 1980s as representative of a Europe-wide surge in academic interest in the integration process brought about by the *rélance* of the Community that took place in that decade. In response to what was widely seen as EEC stagnation in the 1970s, the passing of the Single European Act (SEA) in 1986 generated heated debates about the direction of Community reform and compelled reconsideration of where the Community was heading as an international organisation. In Britain, the Europe question had special relevance in the light of the role it played in deepening splits within the Conservative Party in the course of the decade. A paradox began to emerge between Prime Minister Margaret Thatcher's championing of the Single European Market and her increasingly hard line with the pro-European members of the Cabinet and the workings of the Commission in Brussels.[124] That she put her signature to the SEA after the resolution of the bitter dispute over Britain's contribution to the EEC budget and soon afterwards lambasted the EEC in her Bruges speech as 'a European super-state exercising a new dominance from Brussels'[125] implies a degree of tension between her actions towards Europe and her words about it, which merely served to exaggerate the impression that Britain was Europe's 'awkward partner'.

The second way of interpreting constantly changing perspectives on the past involves being more cynical and draws on the academic impetus to revisionism captured in Fuller's and Watt's words above. Here, one is forced to confront the idea that the reinterpretation of history serves personal and career ends: 'there are surely few social scientists who are unaware that the very choice of which projects to carry out involves some kind of value choice, if only with respect to what interests them or to what advances their professional career (or to some other criterion)'.[126] Kaplan's further observation about the development of scientific knowledge is just as applicable to the development of historical knowledge, picking up as he does on the observation that those newest to a field of study are usually the most innovative:

> scientists, particularly theoretical scientists, seem by psychological inclination to be disposed to reject established beliefs. The incentives for this to operate upon young scientists would seem greater than upon older scientists, who have become members of the scientific establishment … [I]t is easier for a young scientist to establish his reputation by means of a theoretical innovation than by building on the work of an established figure. All these considerations would make it more likely that young, rather than old, scientists would be innovators.[127]

---

124 Forster and Blair, *The Making of Britain's European Foreign Policy*, p. 23.
125 M. Thatcher, *The Downing Street Years 1979–1990* (London, HarperCollins, 1996), p. 745.
126 Kaplan, *On Historical and Political Knowing*, p. 130.
127 *Ibid.*, pp. 13–14.

Becher and Trowler explain this phenomenon by reasoning that 'Those who have as yet made no major intellectual commitments have little to lose by investing in potentially high-risk, high-profit commodities', while those with more established reputations have a greater propensity to want to safeguard the prevailing status quo in a certain field.[128]

Expanding on this theme, Beloff argued that:

Young people seeking to get their foot on the academic ladder in history as in other disciplines must show their capacities for research. While some topics for these arise from the overall view and requirements of the young researcher, supervisor or patron ... it is probable that more attention will be paid to his work if it is of a kind to challenge accepted notions.[129]

All such views help prop up the argument that academic life involves co-operation with others working in one's field, but also a degree of competition with them.[130] One way to get your work noticed is to present a new interpretation (not necessarily a radical one) or to uncover documents that bring new light to bear on an existing problem, displacing history from an innocent search for truths about the past and locating it instead in its temporal and sociological environments, an activity that serves the needs and aspiration of the historian rather than those of the past.

Two points might be made in response to this cynical view of academic historiography. One is that one can admit some element of personal interest in writing and re-writing history without at the same delegitimising academic history as a form of historiography. There may be personal, career and other concerns about self-advancement or aggrandisement at play in what gets studied and how by historians, but so there are in all forms of historical inquiry: academic, journalistic and political. The world and our understanding of it are socially constructed, and that goes for natural science as much as it does for history and the other humanities.

The other response is to test this claim against what historians have to say about how and why they construct history in the way they do. Here, one discovers that even though historians are not shy about admitting the key role played by such considerations in terms of what they study and how, caution is needed about asserting that historiography is the product only or even mainly of the individual historian's personal ambitions. There is at least as much evidence in this study to suggest that the pursuit of contemporary history is in Britain inextricably linked to the release of primary sources; and it is to the methodological dimensions of 'disciplinisation' that we now turn.

---

128   Becher and Trowler, *Academic Tribes and Territories*, p. 99.
129   Beloff, *An Historian*, p. 32.
130   On which point see Becher and Trowler, *Academic Tribes and Territories*, pp. 118–22.

The PRO and historical scholarship

In the section of *Metahistory* dealing with the professionalisation of history, White explained that the methods of instruction given to aspirant historians were those of the German historian Leopold von Ranke. They 'consisted essentially of an injunction to use the most refined philological techniques for the criticism of historical documents, combined with a set of statements about what the historian ought *not* to attempt on the basis of the documents thus criticized'.[131] Even if this did not entail the 'archive fetishism' that some critics of the primary source historical method have since implied it did (White points out that the artistic elements of historiography remained important at this time, especially in terms of the presentation of findings), the nineteenth century saw Enlightenment empiricism become deeply entrenched in the practice of history. The goal was to uncover 'what actually happened' in the past by 'letting the documents speak for themselves'.[132]

While it is an oversimplification to suggest that historical instruction in Britain today has not moved on at all, there is certainly something in the argument that the professional community of historians in Britain remains deeply wedded to primary sources as the cornerstones of historical knowledge. 'Without archives', notes Thompson, 'historians are all but helpless.'[133] Certainly this would appear to be the perception amongst historians of British European policy: 'The assurance with which professional historians after Ranke had assumed that immersion in the sources would assure a perception of the past that corresponded to the past has long been modified. However, historians have not given up the basic commitment to historical honesty that inspired Ranke.'[134]

When asked about the impetus behind her work on Britain and European integration, Deighton said that:

> I don't think [the] relaunch of [the] EC is a reason as much as the availability of documents. The Thirty Year Rule plays such a powerful role in the generation of contemporary historical research ... I certainly don't remember being infected by some kind of passion for Europe as the SEA was being negotiated! Indeed, it is worth remembering that, at the time, the possible impact of the SEA was under-estimated.[135]

Young was of the same mind, and, while acknowledging that 'academic interest only really picked up c[irca] 1984–85 as the EEC itself recovered from the doldrums of the 1970s', he did not feel that political events explain the whole

---

131 White, *Metahistory*, p. 136. Emphasis in original.
132 *Ibid.*, pp. 141–2.
133 Thompson, *What Happened to History?*, p. 85.
134 Iggers, *Historiography*, p. 144.
135 Email correspondence with Deighton, 6 May 2000.

story. The form of his scholarship, he said, was very much a function of the available sources: 'It fitted into my interests in the origins of the Cold War as an undergraduate *and* it was an area just opening up in the archives (so no-one could beat me to it).'[136] He also remarked that: 'I started off seeing the Cold War as a focus to my PhD in 1979 but realised in 1980–81 – long before any revival of the EEC – that the unity theme was essential to Anglo-French relations, and completed in 1982 with that focus,'[137] showing something of the haphazard process by which academic sub-fields originate and develop. One exception to this rule is Geoffrey Warner, who keenly admits to being a 'Europhile' of long standing and whose work in the field has been stimulated by his passion for the integration project.[138] Nonetheless, his research methodology has involved where possible the scrutiny of documentation released by the government under the Thirty Year Rule, tested against oral history and analysis of press opinion.

The correlation between sources and historians' attention to a given period has been identified by Kevin Jefferys, who associates 'revisionist historians with full access to official records at the Public Record Office'.[139] In the early stages of his 1978 book on Britain and European unity, Avi Shlaim, Deighton's doctoral supervisor, wrote that 'The writing of authoritative history of this subject cannot precede, it can only follow, the opening of the official papers for research ... [My] interpretation is necessarily tentative in that it is not underpinned by primary sources.'[140] His view has been taken seriously by his successors in the field, and follows a long line of exponents of primary-source history working to the maxim 'no documents, no history',[141] or, put another way, '[T]he seeker after the truth has often to delve in documents and archives.'[142]

Why have primary sources had such a hold over the study of contemporary history in Britain? Why is the PRO so often the first port of call for aspirant historians and doctoral candidates working in the field of history? The obvious answer is that for the person dealing with the British government's policy on a set issue, the PRO is indispensable because it is home to the state record of government deliberations. But that is by no means the end of the story, at least not for those with an interest in unpicking the fabric of historiography in Britain. It will be argued here that there are four additional reasons that need to be borne in mind.

---

136 Email correspondence of 27 January 1999. Original emphasis.
137 Email correspondence with Young, 8 May 2000.
138 Interview with Warner, 30 April 2002.
139 K. Jefferys, review, 'The Myth of Consensus: New Views on British History, 1945–64. Edited by Harriet Jones and Michael David Kandiah', *Contemporary British History*, 11:1 (1997), 157–8 (157).
140 Shlaim, *Britain and the Origins of European Unity*, p. 4.
141 Beloff, *An Historian*, p. 10. See also M. Beloff, *New Dimensions in Foreign Policy: A Study in British Administrative Experience 1947–59* (London, George Allen and Unwin, 1961), p. 12.
142 Palme Dutt, *Problems of Contemporary History*, p. 38.

The first three operate on the methodological and epistemological levels and encompass the argument that the PRO suits a historical community trained to recover documentary evidence about the past using broadly Rankean techniques. The fourth takes us into the realms of cost–time effectiveness, those practical considerations that underpin much academic research but which have been routinely ignored by analysts of historiography.

It has been observed that only a small proportion of all government documentation survives the weeding process to make it to the shelves of the PRO, prompting the former director of the Institute of Contemporary British History (ICBH), Harriet Jones, to wonder 'to what extent we are being given enough material to understand the subject'.[143] Moreover, Thompson points out,

> before the historian even gets to [archival evidence] it has been classified, arranged and put in order by other hands, and so another layer of selectivity has been interspersed between the initial selectivity on the part of the consciousness who generated the documentation and the further selectivity of the historian which the historian will inevitably exercise in dealing with it.[144]

'Truth', Foucault argued, 'is a thing of this world: it is produced only by virtue of multiple forms of constraint ... Each society has its regime of truth, its "general politics" of truth ... [recognising] the status of those who are charged with saying what counts as true.'[145] His emphasis on truth as a 'regime', functioning as part of a set of norms, conventions and attitudes held at a given time, is one of the reasons why the regime of truth produced by historians has been severely questioned since the 1970s.

Such concerns do not worry archive-based historians. The prime reason for the privileged place of the PRO is that the sources therein, empiricists argue, offer us the chance of producing narratives that correspond directly with a now absent past. The PRO is complicit in reinforcing this belief and is unashamedly positivist in advertising itself as the place to find out about Britain's past: 'Centuries of history at your fingertips' it proudly proclaims in one of its advertising brochures. 'The Public Record Office', it continues, 'is the archive of the United Kingdom. The records and images of a nation are preserved on its 167km of shelving, from the Domesday book to the latest Government papers to be released to the public.'[146]

Behind the rhetoric of this glossy advert lies a telling observation about how the historical community and, indeed, Western societies at large, view the role of

143 Harriet Jones, review, 'Bob Boothby: A Portrait. By Robert Rhodes James', *Contemporary Record*, 6:2 (1992), 403–4 (404).
144 Thompson, *What Happened to History?*, p. 87.
145 Foucault in interview with Alessandro Fontana and Pasquale Pasquino, quoted in P. Rabinow (ed.), *The Foucault Reader*, pp. 72–3.
146 PRO introductory brochure, distributed at PRO academic induction days.

'facts' and 'evidence'. 'Integrity, the search and respect for truth' are the fundamental goals of a civilised society, said an article in the *Times Higher Education
Supplement* in the year 2000.[147] Newspapers are replete with portraits of celebri-
ties revealing 'the truth' about their lives. In courts of law, people fight to have
their version of 'the truth' upheld; either that or they fight to have a previously
accepted judgement of 'the truth' overturned. In this process, lawyers rely on
cases carefully constructed out of eyewitness testimony, business records, records
of telephone conversations, video evidence and so on, all of which is disputed by
their opponents. Complaints are regularly to be heard that legal teams 'twist' the
words of the defendant, of witnesses and the accused to suit their view of what
happened at a particular time and place. In brief, what they do is attempt to
construct on the basis of fragmentary evidence and conflicting accounts a believable story about the past, incorporating stories about people's beliefs, actions and
motivations.

For historians, one of the most believable versions of 'the truth', if not 'the
truth' itself, is most likely to be found in the papers on the shelves of the PRO.
Despite growing awareness since the 1970s of the challenge to history from
philosophy and literary theory there lingers, Iggers argues, the conviction that the
historian deals 'with a real and not an imaginary past and that this real past,
although accessible only through the medium of the historian's mind, nevertheless called for *methods and approaches* that followed a logic of inquiry'.[148] The
key phrase here is the italicised portion 'methods and approaches'. The discipline
of history in Britain sets great store by the pursuit of 'facts' in the PRO mainly
because they are testable, that is, written down: 'the real historical world ... has
to be established through a reading of the documentary and other fragments which
the real world of the past has left behind'.[149] The historian can assert that in the
margin of a particular document the British Foreign Secretary had commented
'X', and he or she can do this safe in the knowledge that others can go and check
the veracity of this claim. Stoker's observation about political science is equally
applicable to history: 'different approaches ... emphasise different types of
evidence, but none denies the *need* for evidence'.[150] Thus PRO evidence suits not
only the empiricist historian researching a doctorate but the demands of his or her
examiners in the discipline, who have to verify that the student has mastered the
relevant techniques, and done so using sources that the discipline deems to be
worthy.

The PRO is, therefore, the archive of choice for many historians working
in the field of British European policy. History written without 'facts' obtained in

---

147 *The Times Higher Education Supplement*, 14 January 2000, p. 16.
148 Iggers, *Historiography*, p. 15. Italics added.
149 Evans, *In Defence of History*, p. 112.
150 Stoker, 'Introduction', pp. 3–4. Emphasis in original.

the PRO could be dismissed as a form of bias, a pungent critique usually reserved for reviews of political memoir and biography, which lament their 'superficiality and super-abundance'.[151] Not only do PRO sources appeal to historians as sources of evidence in and of themselves, they seem in addition to offer better access to the 'truth' about what happened in the past *relative to other sources of contemporary history*, including the media, oral testimony, political diaries and memoirs, autobiography, private papers and the record of parliamentary debate contained in *Hansard*.

Take Grigg's verdict on instant history, especially that penned by politicians, what he calls 'auto-hagiography'. He judges that 'there are degrees of partiality, and any account of a practising politician, given either by himself or by someone he has authorised, must necessarily [involve] partiality to an exceptional degree'. 'Memoirs', he continues, 'make the worst of all worlds, being less reliable as source material than diaries or other strictly contemporary documents, while lacking any of the credentials of objective history'.[152] Evans is just as dismissive: 'most people, unless they are politicians, go to some trouble to make sure that they do express themselves in a reasonably consistent and non-contradictory way'.[153] They both echo the opinion of Graf von Schwerin, who was of the opinion that memoir writers 'often wrote with the benefit of hindsight, not of the facts as they actually happened, but of the role they wished history to record of them in relation to the events in question, often allowing themselves the license of adjusting the facts'.[154]

If Hennessy's verdict is representative, historians do not trust the press any more than they do politicians' memoirs: 'historians are likely to find newspapers poor witnesses to much contemporary history'.[155] Even respected organs such as *The Times* and the *Economist* are not deployed as much as they could be. Put simply, British historians do not accord the same degree of respectability to the press as they do to the PRO as a source of historical evidence. In terms of ranking sources of contemporary history in terms of their perceived reliability, the

---

151 J. Hollowell, review, 'Callaghan: A Life. By Kenneth O. Morgan', *Contemporary British History*, 11: 4 (1997), 129–33 (129).

152 Grigg, 'Policies of Impotence', 72–3. Works on Harold Wilson provide interesting exceptions to the hagiographic tendency of British political biography, one reviewer noting an 'anti-Wilson tirade'. See K. Jefferys, review, 'Harold Wilson. By Austen Morgan; Harold Wilson. By Ben Pimlott', *Contemporary Record*, 7:1 (1993), 198–200 (198). The literature on Wilson's governance of Britain is also explored in O. J. Daddow, 'Introduction: The Historiography of Harold Wilson's Attempt to Take Britain into the EEC', in Daddow (ed.), *Harold Wilson and European Integration*, pp. 1–36.

153 Evans, *In Defence of History*, p. 112.

154 Quoted in E. Fursdon, *The European Defence Community: A History* (London, Macmillan, 1980), p. 3.

155 P. Hennessy, 'The Press and Broadcasting', in Seldon (ed.), *Contemporary History*, pp. 17–29 (p. 22). He uses as his example media accounts of Britain's relations with the EEC.

press and broadcast media would seem, at best, to be on a par with, or perhaps even below, memoirs and witness histories, all of which are well below publications by other historians in terms of their perceived reliability as sources on the past. It is well known, argues Christopher Phipps, that the 'printed text has come to enjoy [an] assured status of certainty, authority and reliability' and that, especially, 'books have become trustworthy disseminators of knowledge'. The work that goes into the writing, refereeing and printing of books apparently renders them more reliable purveyors of knowledge because they deliver an 'authority, veracity and textual reliability [which] have had to be grafted on over time through the concerted, often thwarted, efforts of author and printer'.[156] Newspapers do not have the same appeal to scholars labouring under the notion that 'scientific' and 'scholarly' are synonymous.[157]

Book reviews that stress the fallibility of interpretations on periods for which primary material is not available reinforce the caution with which historians generally approach writing about the post-Thirty Year Rule period. To take one example, of Young's *Britain and European Unity* George remarked that 'While the treatment of the early period is reliable, Young's foray into more contemporary scholarship does not enhance his reputation as a scholar.' He was similarly scathing about Greenwood's *Britain and European Co-operation*: 'his judgements are more questionable the nearer the book approaches to the present,'[158] highlighting his opinion that it is harder to evaluate the immediate past because of fewer reliable, that is, primary sources.

That the PRO's sources are thought to offer direct access to the past sheds light on the second reason why it is so widely used by historians: most of its sources are written by the individuals whose thought processes historians are trying to unravel, and so aid their ability to empathise with them. The use of 'empathy' is at the heart of revisionist historiography on Britain and Europe, which concentrates on the predicament decision-makers found themselves in over Europe and attempts to understand how they saw the world and how they went about devising a policy for Britain on the back of their perceptions. Employing the documentary method is an explicit attempt to see through the hindsight and recreate how the world looked from Whitehall in the 1940s, 1950s and 1960s. Joyce Appleby, Lynn Hunt and Margaret Jacob capture this methodological prescription well: 'scholars in the practical realist camp are encouraged to get out of bed in the morning and head for the archives, because they can uncover

---

156 C. Phipps, review, 'The Nature of the Book: Print and Knowledge in the Making. By Adrian Johns', *The Times Higher Education Supplement*, 3 March 2000, p. 32.

157 Morrow and Brown, *Critical Theory and Methodology*, p. 4.

158 S. George, review, 'Britain and European Unity, 1945–1992. By John W. Young', *Journal of Common Market Studies*, 33:2 (1995), 306–7 (307); S. George, review, 'Britain and European Co-operation Since 1945. By Sean Greenwood', *Journal of Common Market Studies*, 31:1 (1993), 128.

evidence, touch lives long passed and "see" patterns in events that might other-wise remain inexplicable'.[159]

Danaher, Schirato and Webb describe the process as representing the view that 'historical events occurred as a consequence of the various motivations of different historical actors. Accordingly, it is the duty of historiography to work through these motivations and recreate the thought patterns and feelings of the significant historical figures.'[160]

How exactly do PRO sources help the historian empathise with past subjects? Historians use empathy as a way of 'getting inside the heads' of the people whose legacy they are studying. That legacy is, Brivati points out, embod-ied in the policy discussion that survives in the memos and notes now in the PRO.[161] But it is even more than that: it is the sometimes illegible scribbles in the margins of policy documents; it is the irascible comments to colleagues or offi-cials. It is, in sum, what Brivati terms 'the ordinary humanity' epitomised by these off-the-cuff remarks that have been left to us to historicise.[162] For diplomatic historians these are the building-blocks of which accounts of Britain's relation-ship to the Continent must be built, not bland critiques based on hindsight and political prejudice. When Hopkins stated that Young's was one of the first 'sympa-thetic' accounts of Britain and Europe, he might equally have said it was one of the first 'empathetic' accounts.[163]

Physically handling original documents gives the impression that one is, literally, 'bringing history to life'. This may seem unduly romantic but it is impor-tant in terms of understanding what historians actually do. The sources in the PRO help them build a bridge between the present and the past, because, while it is impossible to retrieve the past by physically reliving the events as they unfolded, at least these sources offer some mechanism by which to read what are considered to be vital elements of it, and so to relive the past mentally. The approach scholars have taken to their study of PRO records, instilled in them by the historical train-ing they have received in British universities, has, they hope, replaced the ideolog-ical dogma displayed by orthodox writers in their discourse on Britain and Europe.

The third reason why the PRO dominates the attention of professional histo-rians is bound up with the volume of evidence it houses: there is always the chance of finding something 'new'. It can be argued that the choice of topics for doctoral and other forms of advanced research is strongly determined by pragmatic as well as academic concerns, which Young alluded to when he talked about consulting the

---

159 Appleby, Hunt and Jacob, *Telling the Truth about History*, p. 251.
160 Danaher, Schirato and Webb, *Understanding Foucault*, p. 102.
161 B. Brivati, 'Cd-Rom and the Historian: Information Technology and the Writing of History', in Brivati, Buxton and Seldon (eds), *The Contemporary History Handbook*, pp. 471–8 (p. 477).
162 *Ibid.*
163 See Note 29 above.

archives first so no one could beat him to it. Scholars are not shy of admitting that they become involved in particular research areas because they or their supervisors suggest that there is a lacuna in the literature, or because to do so might open up more career doors at a later stage, or because funding bodies are looking sympathetically on that particular domain at that particular time. The reasons vary from scholar to scholar; but there is an in-built drive within the academic world to produce something original.

What 'original' means varies from discipline to discipline, but in history it seems to involve one of two things: either bringing a new interpretation to bear on a given theme or uncovering previously overlooked or hidden sources of evidence. Both help build one's reputation, boost one's attractiveness in terms of publishing and considerably advance one's career profile in the broader academic community, in the process adding to our stock of historical knowledge. The twin demand for evidence and originality is a potent mix, and historians have the luxury of the PRO in their attempts to respond to that demand. Its shelves play host to numerous documents and papers on all spheres of political, economic, social and family life in Britain. Hence, using PRO sources offers the attraction that one may uncover a previously undiscovered or unscrutinised source. If not, there is enough extra evidence to hold out the prospect that one will be able to bring a new perspective to an existing area of historical inquiry.

The final reason why the PRO has such a hold over revisionist historiography takes us away from the arena of epistemology and methodology and into the pragmatic considerations of historians: time and money. Whatever is said about different generations of historians possessing different methods or theoretical perspectives on how best to undertake the study of history, one cannot avoid discussing the impact of research cost-effectiveness when it comes to explaining what academic historians do, in an era of increasing financial belt-tightening at governmental, university and departmental levels.

On the time side, Harriet Swain commented in the year 2000 that the whole community of academics had become 'obsessed by research ratings'.[164] The pressures on scholars to fulfil the demands of their departments for a high research profile and a top rating in the Research Assessment Exercise (RAE) are well known.[165] Long gone, sadly in the opinion of some, are the days when academics could sit in their ivory towers cogitating for a decade on a *magnum opus*. The emphasis now is on the RAE cycle of churning out articles and monographs, preferably of the single-author variety, putting historians, like their counterparts in other disciplines, under pressure both from funding bodies and departments to produce publishable articles and monographs in the shortest time possible.

164 *The Times Higher Education Supplement*, 17 March 2000, p. 20.
165 A point taken up in Jordanova, *History in Practice*, pp. 23–4.

Doctoral research students are under similar pressure to confer honour on their supervisors and satisfy the requirements of PhD research criteria within a three-year period, when external sources of funds run dry and departments are threatened with financial penalties for non-submission of theses. We explored above how historians rank PRO sources above other sources in contemporary history in terms of their perceived reliability. In addition, the PRO must appear relatively attractive compared to other sources of evidence, because a vast amount of material can be gathered in a few days. Once the ordering procedures have been fully mastered and note-taking is being conducted at the optimum rate, it is possible in two or three days to glean enough material to write for up to two months.[166] Compare this to the time it takes to amass two months' writing out of oral interviews or newspapers, even if, like *The Times*, they are fully indexed. The only source comparable in terms of cost-effectiveness is secondary books and articles; but in the field of contemporary history – as opposed to historiography – it is rarely acceptable to use secondary texts as primary sources when there is such an array of primary documentation waiting to be devoured. 'New' or 'original' research is usually equated with primary source research.

The ordering in the RAE of single-authored works above edited volumes might, moreover, presage a downgrading of the kind of teamwork on history that some historians have suggested is the most appropriate route to take in search of more rounded, comprehensive accounts of the past. This would be especially applicable to books examining foreign policy formation, when edited volumes offer the greatest chance of gathering together experts from across the countries involved in a single collection. Deighton, writing on the origins of the Cold War, has speculated that 'for historians, the sheer quantity of new archival material ... now ironically raises questions about whether a total history that recounts and explains the beginnings of the Cold War could be written at all, unless by a multilingual team of historians'.[167] In America, Elizabeth Cobbs Hoffman has remarked that 'It baffled me that historians, whose *raison d'être* is to see connections between events, could see little connection between the United States and the rest of the world', but such are the external pressures at work on the production of historical texts, that the *limits* on the narrative power of the story are not the focus of the historian, and opportunities for collaboration often have to be passed up.[168]

---

166 I am grateful here to Richard Aldrich for sharing his PRO experiences with me.
167 Deighton, 'The Cold War in Europe', p. 93.
168 E. C. Hoffman, 'Diplomatic History and the Meaning of Life: Towards a Global American History', *Diplomatic History*, 21:4 (1997), 499–518 (499). This theme is picked up in S. Collini, *English Pasts: Essays in History and Culture* (Oxford, Oxford University Press, 1999), where, on p. 36, he argues that 'future narrators of "our island story" will probably opt for forms that are more essayistic, more frankly selective, more visual, and perhaps in some ways more overtly polemical and self-reflective as well'.

On the funding side, it is, quite simply, cheaper to visit the PRO than it is to use these competing sources. It is expensive to travel all over the country or the world interviewing eyewitnesses and other commentators, especially when the volume of evidence one gleans can be disappointing. Likewise, private papers are crucial historical sources; but because they are spread around the country this makes them less appealing to the cash-strapped scholar or research student than the files readily accessible on the shelves of the PRO. As Jordanova puts it, 'The costs of travelling to work on sources of which there are no copies ... should not be underestimated.'[169] Other sources of contemporary history suffer, moreover, from differing levels of accessibility and copyright laws. It can be costly and time consuming to cite them and difficult to gain permission from the family to quote directly from them. The PRO is near London, so it is relatively easy to get to, and one can scrutinise a large quantity of material there in a short space of time. Along with the time factor, therefore, the financial underpinnings of historical research have to be considered crucial component parts of any explanation for why Kew remains central to the pursuit of history in Britain.

Given that the PRO holds the place it does in historiography in Britain for a combination of intellectual and practical reasons, it seems that the production of history has to be viewed as a process that operates on two levels. On the first level one needs to account for the first three reasons given above: the PRO houses the 'official' record of events, it enhances one's ability to empathise with historical characters and there is always the chance of discovering a new source of evidence. On the second, personal level, one finds equally compelling explanations for why the PRO has been so important to the study of contemporary history in Britain: it is cost-effective. Resources in history are scarce, as they are in many sections of the academic world and the country at large, as is demonstrated in Britain by the ongoing debates about how to equip and retain manpower in the armed forces, to pay for the National Health Service, to fund the railways and to supply schools and teachers with sufficient materials and classroom assistance. In an area of research in which funds are tight and publication deadlines pressing, PRO sources hold out an attractive way of writing an original study in a short space of time. Add to that John Kent's opinion that, before research into contemporary British history really took off in the later 1980s, the PRO provided a meeting place for like-minded historians, especially those working outside London,[170] and it can be seen that it has

---

169 Jordanova, *History in Practice*, p. 24.
170 Interview with Kent. The ICBH was predicated on the assumption that there should be a place where historians could meet and discuss their work, in addition to the informal networking that occurred in the PRO and at conferences. Scholars attend such gatherings, Harvey Kaye notes, for 'the most basic of human reasons – to see old friends, have a few drinks together, share a good meal and tell a few tales ... Conventions afford annual reunions': *The Times Higher Education Supplement*, 18 February 2000, p. 9.

played and continues to play an important role in binding a sometimes disparate body of academics together in a vibrant research community.

Conclusion

Paul Anand has commented that 'Perhaps science is like riding a bike – thinking deeply about the process, as opposed to the performance, just does not help.'[171] Although writing about science, he conveys a scepticism about thinking about the microfoundations of research that, this study contends, is to the general long-run detriment rather than the benefit of academia. In history, where scholarly 'performance', taken as the content of the books, articles and other publications produced by scholars, is a direct function of 'process', and where historiographical analysis is fairly thin on the ground, the need is especially pressing. Explaining the spread of revisionist historiography, like the spread of the orthodoxy before it, entails explaining how communities of research originate and evolve and how the participants in those communities build networks and transfer ideas, methods, concepts and language within those structures. In sum, it involves explaining how interpretations become the conventional wisdom and how conventional wisdoms are overthrown and replaced by new ones: how knowledge communities rise and fall.

The core finding of this chapter is that the process of research into British European policy by academic historians has had a significant impact upon the way they have interpreted that policy. Historians have been involved in scrutinising new sources and re-interpreting existing ones to produce a sustained attack on the conventional wisdom about the history of Britain's relations with Europe, albeit by privileging 'those subjects for which orderly documents exist'.[172] What this does in turn is to support the major argument of this book, that the interpretation of historical events is a socially constructed phenomenon, generated by different communities of writers at different times in response to a variety of stimuli. Historiographical analysis of the literature suggests that Foucault's concepts of power-knowledge and discipline, echoed in White's focus on academisation and disciplinisation, are not to be dispensed with as tools for understanding the structural forces at work on the production of historical belief-systems. The way in which the study of British European policy became a focus for historical research in its own right through the 1980s, and the way historians have used their documents, resulted in seismic shifts in how the sub-field has been conceived and written about.

---

171 P. Anand, review, 'A Manual of Model Behaviour: Models as Mediators: Perspectives on Natural and Social Science. Edited by Mary S. Morgan and Margaret Morrison', *The Times Higher Education Supplement*, 17 March 2000, p. 26.

172 Monas, 'Introduction', p. 12.

There are three additional conclusions that can be drawn from this chapter. The first is that analysis of the interpretative shift that occurs when one school replaces another in a field of writing illustrates that historical texts are complex, mulitlayered phenomena, replete with internal contradictions and tensions. The historiography of British European policy has witnessed revisionist historians using new sources and methods. But they have, crucially, built their interpretations on foundations already laid in orthodox texts, which tended to mingle analysis of alternative interpretations in with the dominant one that British policy and policy-making was flawed. Revisionists weight their accounts quite differently, extending analysis of the competing interpretations of British policy suppressed by, but never entirely missing from, orthodox texts.

Steve Smith argues that one of the French philosopher Jacques Derrida's main goals was to 'to show how there is always more than one reading of any text' and that a 'double reading' can be a profitable way of deconstructing histories.[173] This is not to assert that *anything* can be read into texts, but is an extremely prescient remark on the density and complexity of historical narratives, the subtle but nonetheless detectable internal inconsistencies of interpretation and argumentation within narratives: 'The fact that authors do not intend all that they say does not render their intentions uninteresting or irrelevant; it merely highlights the subterranean quality of many of the influences that play upon word choices.'[174]

The second conclusion is that the distinction between secondary and primary sources is not an easy one to draw. The deconstruction of historical texts acts as a reminder that the conventional boundaries drawn by historians between different types of source are arbitrary, especially since on the back of those boundaries the founders of the discipline (and their disciples today) attribute greater reliability to some sources over others.

Primary sources, such as those contained in the PRO, are riddled with problems as sources of history for three reasons. To begin with, someone in a position of power and influence wrote them for someone else in a position of power and influence, so that the historical context of their production will have shaped what was said and how. Next, it can be argued that they survive to make it to the shelves of the PRO or a private paper collection for a reason: perhaps they support the officially approved version of events or justify a particular action or decision, or rehabilitate a particular individual. Finally, they are worked up into historical stories by historians, who themselves have their own agendas and reasons for writing. Carr's words go some distance to making the point that histories are the

173 S. Smith, 'New Approaches to International Theory', in J. Baylis and S. Smith (eds), *The Globalisation of World Politics: An Introduction to International Relations* (Oxford, Oxford University Press, 1997), pp. 165–90 (pp. 182–3).
174 Appleby, Hunt and Jacob, *Telling the Truth about History*, p. 267.

product of historians working on texts to produce other texts and hence to the problem of making a rigid distinction between primary and secondary sources:

> No document can tell us more than what the author of the document thought – what he thought had happened, what he thought ought to happen or would happen, or perhaps only what he wanted others to think he thought, or even what he himself thought he thought. None of this means anything until the historian has got to work on it and deciphered it.[175]

In a discipline that sets such store by primary-source history, it would be useful to see greater reflection by practitioners on the problems associated with using these as sources and a greater acceptance of different forms of accessing the past. This might entail redrawing the disciplinary boundaries of history, so is not something that will happen imminently. It is surely worthwhile, however.

The third conclusion one can draw from the preceding analysis is that historiography, the putting of pen to paper or finger to keyboard, is the historian's final act in a long tale that involves a raft of choices along the way: choices about what to study, how to study it, where to study it, which sources to use, how to organise one's findings and where to publish them. Evidence is not simply 'found' in the documents, it is moulded in crucial ways by the historian who chooses how to narrate the past. It is, moreover, the historian who approaches the archives with implicit theories about how to access and represent the past and preconceived ideas about what he or she might find there, formed out of reading material already published about a given subject. The next chapter takes up these themes in more detail through examination of current developments in the historiography of British European policy.

---

175 Carr, *What is History?*, p. 16.

4   The historiography in current perspective

The preceding chapters have examined the origins and development of the orthodox and revisionist schools of writing on British European policy. The aim of
this chapter is to trace trends in the historiography since the middle of the 1990s
and to assess the extent to which they represent a break from or a continuation
of the earlier literature. The first part shows how a new generation of historians of British European policy have been concentrating on two themes: the
negotiations about setting up a Free Trade Area (FTA) in western Europe in the
mid to late 1950s and the applications by the two Harolds, Macmillan and
Wilson, to take Britain into the EEC in the 1960s. It is argued that this literature broadly represents a continuation with revisionist historiography. It is heavily influenced by evidence gleaned from primary sources in the PRO, and it
continues to deconstruct the conventional wisdom about British policy, so it is
methodologically and ontologically in tune with the accounts analysed in the
last chapter.

The second part explains how new directions in the historiography add
credibility to philosophical claims that historical interpretations are not, and
cannot be, arrived at by letting the sources speak for themselves, but are
crucially influenced by how historians organise their material into a coherent
story. Here, the focus is on how, despite broad similarities, the second generation of historians has begun to break free from both orthodox and revisionist
conceptions of the past by injecting elements of chaos and uncertainty into their
narratives. They stress, for example, how the earlier schools artificially impose
order on what they perceive to be a chaotic, disorderly process of foreign-policy-
making in London. The current historiography of Britain's relations with Europe
thus continues to provide fertile ground on which to consider not just the nature
of the conflicting interpretations of events themselves but also the nature
and practice of contemporary history. Both themes will be taken up in the
concluding chapter.

An emerging post-revisionist synthesis?

The most prominent development in the historiography of British European
policy since the mid-1990s has been the emergence of what can be described
as a post-revisionist interpretation of the motivations behind 'Plan G', the British
proposal for a European Free Trade Area announced by Macmillan in October

1956. The major exponents of this approach have been the historians Wolfram Kaiser, James Ellison, Liz Kane and Martin Schaad.[1] Prior to exploring the reconfiguration of the history that has flowed out of this development, it is of course necessary to establish what a 'post-revisionist' interpretation is.

In terms of a definition, it is useful to return to Cold War historiography where, Gaddis found, conflicting orthodox and revisionist interpretations were eventually brought together to form 'a third stage ... in the historiography'.[2] J. Samuel Walker expanded on this, defining post-revisionism as 'a new consensus' or 'synthesis' that 'draws from both traditional and revisionist interpretations' to present what he called an 'even-handed' explanation of the beginning of the Cold War.[3] Brian McKercher, studying the writing of American foreign relations in the inter-war years, found the same pattern: 'the developmental historiographical typology of the work in the United States mirrors that of the Cold War: the evolution of an orthodox school, the emergence of a revisionism that questioned the methodology and basic assumptions of the older school, and the advent of recent post-revisionist analyses.'[4] Deighton neatly summarises their assessments by suggesting that a post-revisionist interpretation stems from the synthesisation of 'two antithetical approaches'.[5]

The significance of the emergence of post-revisionism in the historiography of Britain's relations with Europe will become clear through analysis of the process by which it has been reached. Writers belonging to the orthodox school used what Nora Beloff called the 'officially approved metaphor' that the FTA would act as a 'bridge' between the states involved in setting up the Common Market and the remainder, led by Britain, who wanted closer but not supranational integration in Europe.[6] Indeed, Tratt shows how the language of building 'bridges' between Britain and the EEC states built a momentum all of its own, the

---

1 Kaiser, *Using Europe*, Chapter 3; J. R. V. Ellison, 'Perfidious Albion? Britain, Plan G and European Integration, 1955–1956', *Contemporary British History*, 10:4 (1996), 1–34, now incorporated in Ellison, *Threatening Europe*, parts 1 and 2; L. Kane, 'European or Atlantic Community?: The Foreign Office and "Europe", 1955–1957', *Journal of European Integration History*, 3:2 (1997), 7–33; E. Kane, 'The Myth of Sabotage: British Policy Towards European Integration, 1955–6', in E. du Réau (ed.), *Europe des Élites? Europe des Peuples? La Construction de L'éspace Européen 1945–1960* (Paris, Presses de la Sorbonne Nouvelle, 1999), pp. 291–301; M. Schaad, 'Plan G – A "Counterblast"? British Policy Towards the Messina Countries, 1956', *Contemporary European History*, 7:1 (1998), 39–60. See also K. Steinnes, 'The European Challenge: Britain's EEC Application in 1961', *Contemporary European History*, 7:1 (1998), 61–79 and Tratt, *The Macmillan Government*, pp. 11–54.

2 Gaddis, 'The Emerging Post-Revisionist synthesis', 172.

3 Walker, 'Historians and Cold War Origins', pp. 207 and 227. See also Melanson, *Writing History*, pp. 214–15.

4 McKercher, 'Reaching for the Brass Ring', 567.

5 Deighton, 'The Cold War in Europe', p. 83.

6 Beloff, *The General Says No*, p. 84.

paradox being that despite its prevalence in Whitehall in the late 1950s, ministers and officials were far from translating the aspiration into anything approaching a coherent or credible policy.[7]

The official justification for proposing a FTA was later repeated in the memoirs of major players such as Macmillan, who held the posts of Foreign Secretary and then Chancellor of the Exchequer in the years 1955–57, when the proposal emerged and was accepted by Whitehall as the plank on which British European policy would be based for the foreseeable future. In *Riding the Storm* he put forward this innocent version of Plan G: 'I was anxious that the Free Trade Area ... should develop an institutional basis within which the ideals of United Europe could be fostered and developed.'[8] He reiterated this in his next volume, claiming that Plan G was proposed 'with the hope of bridging the gap which threatened to develop between two groups of European powers, and thus preserving, in a vital field, the concept of European unity'.[9] Alistair Horne's official biography reiterated Macmillan's line that Plan G 'would provide an institutional link with the EEC', further evidence perhaps of the morphing of subject and writer that can occur during the writing of biographies.[10]

Officials in London were doubly piqued that the Six agreed to negotiate a FTA only then to publicly criticise the British proposal. Reginald Maudling, Chair of the OEEC negotiations on the FTA, lamented in his memoirs that 'it had been explicitly agreed by the heads of the French and German Governments that as soon as possible after the signature of the Treaty of Rome, negotiations occurred should take place to bring Britain and the other Western European nations into a system of European free trade.'[11] Nutting was also rueful, believing the EEC states to have reneged on their agreement at the time of the signing of the Treaty of Rome to come to an agreement with the British over the FTA, pointing out that the British were willing to make many concessions on the FTA, yet 'still the French were not satisfied'.[12]

Policy-makers in London formed a close relationship with instant historians of this period who, although as we have seen were on the whole critical of British European policy, took the official government line on this issue. Camps, noting the deal to undertake FTA negotiations after the signing of the Treaty of Rome, sowed the seeds of later controversy when she wrote that Plan G was 'not

---

7 Tratt, *The Macmillan Government*, pp. 34–5, 48, 50 and 61–2.
8 Macmillan, *Riding the Storm*, p. 441. Prime Minister Anthony Eden was quiet on the subject in his memoirs.
9 Macmillan, *Pointing the Way*, p. 44.
10 Horne, *Macmillan: Volume 2*, p. 30. For further details see Horne, *Macmillan: Volume 1*, pp. 385–7.
11 R. Maudling, *Memoirs* (London, Sidgwick and Jackson, 1978), pp. 68–9.
12 Nutting, *Europe Will Not Wait*, p. 98. See also Keith Sainsbury, 'Harold Macmillan', in Shlaim, Jones and Sainsbury (eds), *British Foreign Secretaries*, pp. 110–16 (p. 113).

maliciously conceived'.[13] Another contemporary observer, Barker, also took the view that Plan G was a defensive reaction forced on London by the creation of the EEC on the Continent. 'In the end, a FTA seemed the only course open to Britain.'[14]

Continental Europeans were, by contrast, virulently critical of this new development in British policy. Monnet asked and answered his own question on the subject. 'Did anyone want Britain once again to dominate Europe from the outside? ... That was what would happen if we abandoned the rules of the Community to embrace the empiricism of the Free Trade Area.' He went on to query 'the spirit in which [British initiatives] were conceived'.[15] Spaak too charted what he saw as growing 'hostility' by Britain towards the Messina process from the end of 1955. The FTA proposal, he said, made it 'increasingly difficult for me to work with the British' because it would have 'submerged the Common Market' in 'a much more modest enterprise which offered no prospect of a European political union'.[16]

French Foreign Minister Maurice Couve de Murville echoed his sentiments, castigating Plan G as a 'desperate move in order to prevent the entry into force of the Rome Treaty'.[17] As so often, therefore, he echoed Charles de Gaulle – not known for agreeing often with Monnet's views on integration – who voiced the dominant Continental perception of British European policy at this time by remarking in his memoirs that Britain's initiatives 'were calculated to submerge the Community of the Six at the outset in a vast FTA together with England and eventually the whole of the West'.[18] His was a telling criticism, given George's observation that in preferring Plan G to the supranational approach to integration 'Britain risked appearing as the mouthpiece of the United States', bolstering de Gaulle's suspicions of *les Anglo-Saxons* and reinforcing his impression of Britain's 'subservience to the United States'.[19]

Plan G has received similarly short shrift amongst the Europeanists in Britain. Jenkins describes it as 'a foolish attempt to organise a weak periphery

---

13 Camps, *Britain and the European Community*, pp. 140–1 and 510. See also M. Schulte, 'Industry Politics and Trade Discrimination in West Germany's European Policy 1957–1963' (London School of Economics Ph.D., 1996), pp. 93–127.

14 Barker, *Britain in a Divided Europe*, p. 153.

15 Monnet, *Memoirs*, pp. 449–50.

16 Spaak, *The Continuing Battle*, p. 236.

17 Couve is quoted in Charlton, 'How (and Why) 2', p. 33. See also R. Marjolin, *Architect of European Unity* (London, Weidenfeld and Nicolson, 1989), pp. 317–22.

18 C. de Gaulle, *Memoirs of Hope: Renewal 1958–62*, trans. Terence Kilmartin (London, Weidenfeld and Nicolson, 1971), pp. 179–80. Continuing that theme in his January 1963 press conference, during which he vetoed Britain's first membership application, the General said that 'as they were unable from the outside to prevent the European Community from being born, they now intended to paralyse it from within': Quoted in de Carmoy, 'Defence and Unity', p. 358.

19 George, *An Awkward Partner*, p. 27.

against a strong core' and Heath is still irked by Britain's persistent inability to see the political dimensions to integration, which rendered the essentially economic FTA contrary to the objectives of the Six.[20] Monnet's old friend Mayne summed up the Europeanist perspective on Plan G with the remark that the FTA would have dissolved the EEC 'like a lump of sugar in an English cup of tea', a view that according to Barker was widely held amongst members of the European Commission at that time.[21] The *Economist* remains as critical as ever. In its *Guide to the European Union* Dick Leonard writes that 'the UK initiative in founding the European Free Trade Association ... in 1959 was widely seen as a spoiling device to reduce the impact of the EEC which had been established the previous year'.[22]

Professional historians have tended to be split on the issue. Charlton was persuaded by the British officials and politicians he interviewed into placing a gloss on British policy, seeing it as a 'last attempt by Britain to square the circle with the Continental Europeans and Britain's traditional interests in the Commonwealth by an alternative design for European co-operation'.[23] Others, while sympathising with the plan from the point of view of protecting Britain's vital economic interests, give more weight to the Europeanist perspective that it did not go far enough in terms of pooling sovereignty to appeal to the Europeans.

Milward, for example, says that, although this was a 'dramatic policy change', the British proposal was intricately designed exclusively to serve the British and contained none of the 'links to national reconstruction which the EEC had incorporated', meaning that Plan G was greeted coolly on the Continent. Furthermore, he continues, many in London hoped it 'would appeal to German opponents of the common market of the Six, to all in Belgium and the Netherlands anxious about a Franco-German hegemony, and [would help] to win American support by offering a larger framework for integration than the Six and one in which Britain would be a leading member.'[24] Given the disputes about economic policy in the German government between the free-traders led by Minister for Economic Affairs Ludwig Erhard and the integrationists led by Chancellor Konrad Adenauer, it is easy to see how suspicion of British policy developed and spread around Adenauer and his network of contacts in Washington and Paris.[25]

---

20 Jenkins, *A Life at the Centre*, p. 105; Heath, *The Course of My Life*, p. 202.
21 Mayne, *The Recovery of Europe*, p. 252; Barker, *The Common Market*, p. 75.
22 Leonard, *The Economist Guide to the European Union*, p. 227.
23 Charlton, 'How (and Why) 2', p. 24. See also M. Pinto-Duschinsky, 'From Macmillan to Home, 1959–64', in Hennessy and Seldon (eds), *Ruling Performance*, pp. 150–85 (p. 163); Maclean, *British Foreign Policy*, p. 80 and R. Holland, *The Pursuit of Greatness: Britain and the World Role, 1900–1970* (London, Fontana, 1991), p. 286.
24 Milward, *The European Rescue*, pp. 429–30.
25 S. Lee, 'German Decision-Making Elites and European Integration: German "Europolitik" during the Years of the EEC and Free Trade Area Negotiations', in Deighton (ed.), *Building Post-War Europe*, pp. 39–54. See also Lee, *Victory in Europe?*, pp. 78–84.

This has led a good many more historians, consulting Foreign Office, Cabinet and Prime Ministers' papers, to extend Milward's interpretation of Plan G as a malicious British initiative. As Young put it: 'Rather than the policy of 1951–4 based around benevolence and non-involvement, London now seemed opposed to the efforts of the Six and prepared to play an active role against them.'[26] In Lamb's opinion, Plan G was a diversion 'which the British hoped to keep going for some time to prevent the Six agreeing to a formal treaty'.[27] Greenwood, footnoting Lamb's book, saw it as a 'spoiling tactic'.[28] Clearly the writers adopt differing postures – some are more acerbic than others – but the essence is the same. 'The view that "the period of British hostility to the plans of the Six was short-lived" is not easy to sustain in the light of recent research.'[29]

In the 1990s a band of historians arrived at an interpretation that blended elements of the sympathetic and critical perspectives on British policy to make a post-revisionist 'balanced judgment', as one of them described it.[30] Consulting in addition to the files from the political departments of government those from the Treasury and Board of Trade, they argue that a malicious policy in 1955 had, by 1957, mutated into a genuine policy of co-operation with the Continent. Ellison, for instance, wrote 'Plan G evolved from consideration of a counter-initiative to the Common Market in Autumn 1955 but ... it eventually became an attempt to come to terms with the Six',[31] later contesting that this is 'an historical question too complex to lend itself to condemnation or vindication'.[32]

Kaiser agrees that although Plan G 'retained a destructive function for some time' it did 'undergo an astonishing functional metamorphosis during 1956'.[33] Richard Griffiths and Stuart Ward are not quite as kind, arguing that by October 1957, when negotiations on the FTA started, 'The British had modified their position somewhat but not in crucial areas'[34] – evidence of the interpretative nuances that exist in all schools of writing: they are not monolithic. However, the central contention of the third wave of historians is that the motivations behind Plan G became less malicious towards the Six during 1956, and it is worth noting that

---

26 Young, *Britain and European Unity 1945–1999*, pp. 44–5. See also Young, '"The Parting of Ways"?', 217.
27 Lamb, *The Failure of the Eden Government*, p. 95.
28 Greenwood, *Britain and European Co-operation*, p. 68.
29 *Ibid.*, p. 67.
30 Schaad, 'Plan G', 59. See also Ludlow's brief post-revisionist synthesis in *Dealing with Britain*, pp. 26–9 and Reynolds, *Britannia Overruled*, pp. 216–19.
31 Ellison, 'Perfidious Albion?', p. 1.
32 Ellison, *Threatening Europe*, p. 222.
33 Kaiser, *Using Europe*, p. 61.
34 R. T. Griffiths and S. Ward, '"The End of a Thousand Years of History": The Origins of Britain's Decision to Join the European Community, 1955–61', in R. T. Griffiths and S. Ward (eds), *Courting the Common Market: The First Attempt to Enlarge the European Community 1961–1963* (London, Lothian Foundation Press (1996), pp. 7–37 (p. 13).

they explicitly employ the *language* of American Cold War post-revisionism to mark their contribution to the historiography, self-consciously setting themselves against earlier work in the field, marking territory and suggesting why they disagree with the bolder polemics of their predecessors.

Revising revisionism

In an earlier study, I argued that it represented the genesis of a new school in its own right, a post-revisionist school of writing on British European policy following the orthodox and revisionist schools.[35] On reflection, it seems that may have been overstating the case. The two schools identified in this study can be used, and are intended to be used, as explanatory frameworks within which to analyse the first fifteen years of British European policy after 1945. The Plan G literature is more limited in terms of what it seeks to understand, applying to one specific issue as opposed to the longer course of Britain's policy towards European integration after the Second World War. The significance of the emergence of a post-revisionist interpretation is, therefore, that it signals a step-change in the evolution of revisionist historiography, though it is too early to tell if it heralds a decisive break from it. At the very least, it is a sign that the revisionist school has entered a new phase in its development. This, it seems, is second-generation revisionism.

Indeed, at the level of interpretation, the third wave of writing is deeply influenced by revisionist historiography. Many post-revisionist historians remain convinced that the aim of sabotaging the nascent EEC (the revisionist interpretation) lingered in many quarters of Whitehall, even *after* agreement had been obtained that Plan G should be an effort to accommodate British interests with those of the Europeans. They draw special attention to the parts played in the drama by Macmillan and the President of the Board of Trade, David Eccles, both of whom, they say, harboured pernicious ambitions for the FTA until spring 1957.[36] But, Ellison continues, 'despite recent historical judgement to the contrary, the British government was not intent on breaking the Common Market in spring 1957' and the personal motives of key individuals should not be read as indicative of broader Whitehall opinion.[37] This really does seem to be a question of an interpretative shift within the revisionist school – a matter of emphasis – as opposed to the type of fundamental disagreement over the longer course of Britain's attitude to integration that might presage the displacement of the orthodoxy by revisionism in the field of British European policy.

35 O. J. Daddow, 'Rhetoric and Reality: The Historiography of British European Policy, 1945–2000), Chapter 3.
36 Ellison, 'Perfidious Albion?', pp. 27–8; Kaiser, *Using Europe*, p. 74; Griffiths and Ward, '"The End of a Thousand Years of History"', p. 13.
37 Ellison, *Threatening Europe*, p. 116.

However, as Kuhn pointed out in the context of the natural sciences, it only takes one or two studies to revise the way specific issues within a discipline are viewed before the dominant paradigm or way of viewing the world can be destabilised and, in the long run, even dislodged by a new paradigm that reconfigures the discipline by changing scientists' perception of the problems to be solved and the most appropriate ways of solving them. Putting this into historiographical terms, and remembering that this study deals not with an entire discipline but a sub-field of the discipline of history, it is important to bear in mind the part played by revisionist writing on the Third Force in destabilising the consensus about Britain and Europe that had dominated the field until that time. The reassessment of British European policy it entailed quite rapidly became the 'normal' way for academics to approach this topic from the late 1980s, and it can be said to have been one of, if not the, crucial factors in prompting the birth of revisionism on Britain and Europe.

If it is far from clear-cut whether this is a new school or a revision of revisionism, there are nonetheless two more readily identifiable characteristics of post-revisionist historiography. One is that new directions in the historiography highlight the growing overlap between economic and political history, the other that the history of British foreign-policy is increasingly being set in its wider international perspective.

Putting economics into political history

Reviewing Kaiser's *Using Europe* for *Contemporary British History*, Kane argued that 'The strengths in this book are to be found in its economic sections. Kaiser's use of both Treasury and Board of Trade files makes a valuable contribution to the knowledge of the British policy making machinery in this period as well as providing a thorough understanding of the economic background of British policy.'[38] Her assessment that the study of new sources is sufficient grounds on which to recommend a history book has a long tradition in academe, which sees historical works as incrementally adding to our stock of knowledge about the past. Eclecticism *vis-à-vis* sources is also often judged to result in interpretative eclecticism, and so some works are commended for that reason.[39]

But why *has* the consultation of documentation relating to policy-making in the economic departments been a relatively recent departure in the historiography of British European policy? This appears to be a combination of intellectual choice and methodological pragmatism on the part of the historians new

---

38 E. Kane, review, 'Using Europe, Abusing the Europeans: Britain and European Integration, 1945–63. By Wolfram Kaiser', *Contemporary British History*, 11:4 (1997), 134–6 (136).

39 Gaddis, 'The Emerging Post-revisionist Synthesis'.

to the field, shedding a good deal of light not just on the pursuit of history, but on the glass barriers that have built up between history and its neighbouring disciplines.

Frankel provides one explanation for the relative separation between economics and politics within the study of diplomatic history in Britain after the Second World War, rooting his argument in the post-war conception of international relations as governed by political and diplomatic rather than trade relations: 'The last war was an all-out national effort in which security completely overrode economic considerations; security continued to overshadow them during the early period of the cold war and they gradually shifted to the foreground of British foreign policy only in the 1960s.'[40] His words serve as a reminder that orthodox historiography was popular at a time when the threat of the Cold War turning 'hot' and the need to safeguard national security against the perceived threat of Communism and, potentially, armed attack by the Soviet Union were the dominating characteristics of the international system and the study of international relations. Economic considerations were, it seems, simply less important to the politicians and historians of the time.

A second explanation concerns Whitehall machinery, and is that in policy-making terms there has long been a divorce between the economic and the political departments of government, highlighted by William Wallace: 'The separation of foreign economic policy from the traditional concerns of foreign-policy has been deeply embedded in British policy and practice.'[41] For practitioners and historians of this epoch the reality was of a decision-making process in which, Beloff observed, the Treasury and Foreign Office were rivals. Back as far as the 1930s, he argued, the Treasury was of the view 'that economic affairs were its concern alone and that the Foreign Office should be confined to the more traditional spheres of diplomacy'.[42] Historians of the constitutional role of the Treasury in the foreign-policy process have also arrived at this assessment. George Peden, for example, notes that members of many Whitehall departments, especially the Foreign Office, have tended to emphasise the Treasury's 'meanness'.[43]

---

40 Frankel, *British Foreign Policy*, p. 255.
41 Wallace, *The Foreign Policy Process in Britain*, p. 156. See also Beloff, *New Dimensions in Foreign Policy*, pp. 23–4; A. Adamthwaite, 'Introduction: The Foreign Office and Policy-Making', in Young (ed.), *The Foreign Policy of Churchill's Peacetime Administration*, pp. 1–28 (p. 17).
42 Quoted in Wallace, *The Foreign Policy Process in Britain*, p. 170. See also Clarke, 'The Policy-Making Process', p. 87.
43 G. C. Peden, *British Rearmament and the Treasury: 1932–1939* (Edinburgh, Scottish Academic Press, 1979). He continues the theme of the practical and academic separation of economics from other spheres of government activity in G. C. Peden, *British Economic and Social Policy: Lloyd George to Margaret Thatcher*, 2nd edn (London, Phillip Allen, 1985).

Even *within* the political departments of government, separation rather than integration has traditionally been the order of the day. In the field of foreign affairs, for example, the Commonwealth Relations Office and the Colonial Office were separate departments until 1966, when they merged to create the Commonwealth Office, the new department being separate from the Foreign Office until they merged in 1968 to form the Foreign and Commonwealth Office. Since coming to power in 1997, Blair's rhetoric about trying to create 'joined-up government' must be seen in the context of ruling parties looking to create efficient methods of modern mass government.

Having said that, when politicians and officials *did* publicly acknowledge the confluence of economics with politics in the making of foreign-policy historians of Britain and Europe also paid them attention. This has been especially apparent in the literature on Britain's applications to join the EEC, which devotes as much time as both Macmillan and Wilson did in their speeches on the subject to explaining the economic causes of Britain's turn to Europe. David Sanders summarises the place they gave economics in their rhetorical construction of British European policy by arguing that: 'At the decision-making level, the crucial factor was the apparent benefit which it was believed EEC membership would bestow on the British economy; at the structural level, the major causal influence was the autonomous shift in the pattern of Britain's external trade – away from the Empire and towards the Commonwealth'.[44] The months spent publicly haggling about trade issues at the negotiating table in Brussels merely served to exaggerate the impression, one that British Prime Ministers have cherished, that British European policy is driven by economic, not political, factors.

A third factor that might explain why these historians have been engaged in more nuanced thinking about the economic component of the political and vice versa is the development of the concept of 'interdependence' within the study of international relations. Roger Tooze describes the concept as follows: 'Interdependence as it has developed in the post-war system makes the policy and conceptual distinction between "foreign" and "domestic" and between "political" and "economic" largely redundant, mainly because of the interpenetration of national economies and the centrality of economic and welfare goals to the continued legitimacy of contemporary governments.'[45] Comparing the weight attached by Tooze to the economic determinants of foreign policy with that attached by

---

44 Sanders, *Losing an Empire, Finding a Role*, p. 136. See also Beloff, *The General Says No*, pp. 90–136; Camps, *Britain and the European Community*, p. 231; Beloff, *Britain and European Union*, p. 63; Frankel, *British Foreign Policy*, p. 224; Northedge, *British Foreign Policy*, p. 304 and Sked and Cook, *Post-War Britain*, p. 169.

45 R. Tooze, 'Security and Order: The Economic Dimension', in Smith, Smith and White (eds), *British Foreign Policy*, pp. 124–45 (p. 132).

Frankel in the earlier quotation, one can discern a sea-change in political science treatments of the international system that surely influenced historians, evidence of the subconscious stealing and adaptation of ideas, models and concepts that regularly goes on between disciplines. Of course, it is difficult to measure how much historians were affected by the surge of interest in the economic causes of political behaviour and foreign-policy decisions. But with the post-war surge in the popularity of economic history, with all that that entails in terms of the accompanying academic paraphernalia (university courses, research centres, journals, conferences, networks and so forth), one can argue that diplomatic historians became more attuned through the 1980s to assessing the commercial context of British European policy.

Yet it must also be considered that economic factors were more or less forced upon revisionist historians by the nature of the events they were investigating: Britain's European policy was in the early days led by economic considerations. As Young explains, by the middle of the 1950s it was the Treasury and the Board of Trade that 'dominated the key committees looking at European policy', and that to overlook the economic inputs to foreign-policy was to misconstrue how that policy was made and treated in Whitehall.[46] This feature of London's policy-making towards Europe, notes Sabine Lee, 'reflects the perception [in Britain] of the integration process as primarily an economic issue'.[47]

They were picking up on an overlap between economics and politics that economic historians had for obvious reasons already identified, one most evident in the literature on the devaluation of sterling in September 1949. Many early texts only alluded to the foreign-policy consequences of devaluation in passing.[48] Studies of the key Labour actors at the time reinforced that approach,[49] and it was reaffirmed at a 1991 witness seminar on devaluation when Edwin Plowden, the Treasury's Chief Planning Officer and Chairman of its Economic Planning Board, was tackled on the extent to which decision-making on the value of sterling was

46 Young, *Britain and European Unity 1945–1999*, p. 42.

47 Lee, *Victory in Europe?*, p. 79.

48 For example, Barker, *The British Between the Superpowers*, pp. 156–60; Gilmour and Garnett, *Whatever Happened to the Tories*, p. 29; K. O. Morgan, *Labour People: Leaders and Lieutenants: Hardie to Kinnock* (Oxford, Oxford University Press, 1989), pp. 171–2; Morgan, *The People's Peace: British History 1945–1990* (Oxford, Oxford University Press, 1990) pp. 73–4; Northedge, *British Foreign Policy*, p. 40; Sked and Cook, *Post-War Britain*, pp. 36–7.

49 Brivati, *Hugh Gaitskell*, pp. 84–6; Williams, *Hugh Gaitskell*, pp. 195–203; C. Bryant, *Stafford Cripps: The First Modern Chancellor* (London, Hodder and Stoughton, 1997), pp. 24–34; Bullock, *Ernest Bevin*, pp. 704–66; A. Cairncross and B. Eichengreen, *Sterling in Decline: The Devaluations of 1931, 1949 and 1967* (Oxford, Basil Blackwell, 1983), pp. 129–52; A. Cairncross (ed.), *The Robert Hall Diaries 1947–53* (London, Unwin Hyman, 1989), pp. 1–99; Dell, *The Schuman Plan*, p. 34; Donoghue and Jones, *Herbert Morrison*, pp. 446–7; Foot, *Aneurin Bevan*, pp. 269–77; Harris, *Attlee*, pp. 434–6; Jay, *Change and Fortune*, pp. 185–91.

influenced by the political waves devaluation might make abroad. 'To be honest', he admitted bluntly, 'I don't think they played much part.'[50]

Only after 1984, when Scott Newton published an article in *Economic History Review* on the relationship between Britain's sterling crisis in 1947 and London's response to the Marshall Plan, did the foreign-policy significance of devaluation start to come to the attention of diplomatic historians. The crisis, he argued, dealt a fatal blow to those in the Attlee Cabinet hoping to go it alone with a European Third Force separate from the Americans.[51] He followed it up with two further articles on the same subject in the *Review of International Studies* and the *Journal of Imperial and Commonwealth History* that helped raise further the profile of economics within the historiography of British European policy.[52] His analysis of the link between economic and political factors in the making of British foreign policy would soon help inform Kent and Young's thinking on the centrality of the concept of the Third Force within British foreign policy. Since we have already seen the impact of their work on the historiography, by association we must also recognise the role Newton's work played in providing impetus to their reassessment of Britain's post-war foreign-policy strategy.

There are a number of intellectual reasons, therefore, why the second generation of academic historians of British European policy have been searching the files of the economic departments stacked in the PRO as well as the files of the political departments. But, as ever with historiography, we must also consider the pragmatic reasons for using these sources which are equally compelling, and perhaps even more so.

The choice of which documents to consult and which to ignore turns on the relative weighting assigned by historians to two considerations. The first concerns the historian's perspective on who and what the drivers were of the events that have become the accepted version of the history. This will determine the country or countries that are the focus of attention, the particular departments of state involved and the key individuals within those departments whose actions, beliefs and motivations need exploring as a means of telling that historical story. In theory, the historian will search through as much surviving primary source material as he or she can to understand how policy was made, by whom and for what ends.

However, in making this judgement the historian must also weigh up the relative costs and benefits of consulting sources that have already been

---

50 P. Hennessy, 'Witness Seminar: 1949 Devaluation', *Contemporary Record*, 5:3 (1991), 483–506 (502). See also Pimlott (ed.), *The Political Diary of Hugh Dalton*, pp. 450–7.

51 C. C. S. Newton, 'The Sterling Crisis of 1947 and the British Response to the Marshall Plan', *Economic History Review*, 37:3 (1984), 391–408.

52 S. Newton, 'The 1949 Sterling Crisis and British Policy Towards European Integration', *Review of International Studies*, 11:1 (1985), 169–82; S. Newton, 'Britain, the Sterling Area and European Integration, 1945–50', *Journal of Imperial and Commonwealth History*, 13:3 (1985), 163–82.

historicised as opposed to those that have yet to be examined. Second-generation revisionists may have felt it more worth their while from a career point of view to search previously unopened files, because there is greater chance that they will find something to say about the past that their academic forebears had not already said. With the files of the Cabinet, Prime Minister and Foreign Office having been trawled, the search for a new interpretation and new sources of evidence has taken the second generation of academic historians down previously untravelled paths. It can be argued that the archives of the economic departments have been searched for reasons of exigency as well as for intellectual reasons.

Post-revisionist historiography has, for a combination of reasons, been putting more and more economics into the history of Britain's relations with Europe. A second characteristic of this literature is that it makes the reader well aware of the international setting of British diplomacy. This is especially the case when considering the literature on Britain's two applications to join the EEC in the 1960s.

The international dimension

Working on official British sources newly released to the PRO and in archives in countries such as France, Germany, the United States and Australia, historians of the entry bids are involved in a detailed reconstruction of the individual, departmental, governmental, non-governmental, interest group, media and international influences behind Britain's efforts to join the EEC.[53] Just as it confirms primary sources as the paragon of historiographical virtue, therefore, the writing of Britain's applications to join the EEC also displays the trend towards taking greater account of the international context within which British foreign-policy is devised and launched.[54]

As Klaus Larres explains, 'the multiplicity of internal and external factors of influence which shape the behaviour of contemporary European nations has to be taken into account when considering the nature of the relationships among these highly industrialized and intensively networked countries.'[55] The growing

---

53 For instance Wilkes (ed.), *Britain's Failure to Enter the European Community* and Daddow (ed.), *Harold Wilson and European Intregration*.

54 John Young's recommendation, in 'Britain and "Europe"', pp. 207–8, that international historians need 'to consider evidence from beyond Britain on this question, the attitudes and policies not only of the other EEC states ... but also of the European Commission ...; Britain's partners in the Commonwealth and ... in the European Free Trade Area; and of the United States' is a reminder that broadening perspectives tend for international historians to go hand in hand with 'balanced and comprehensive views'. See also Gaddis, *Now We Know*, pp. 282–3 and Monas, 'Introduction', p. 14.

55 K. Larres, 'Introduction: Uneasy Allies or Genuine Partners?', in Larres (ed.), *Uneasy Allies*, pp. 1–24 (p. 2).

attention to the myriad inputs to the foreign-policy process, other than the actions and decisions of members of the Whitehall policy-making elite, can be seen at work on the historiography in three ways.

First, in the focus on the ambiguous signals transmitted to Britain by key actors within governments of the Six, especially France, who, it has been found, sent mixed messages to British governments about the country's immediate chances of succeeding in joining the EEC. With these in mind, charges that Britain's diplomacy towards Europe was fatally flawed – while still apparent in the literature – have been balanced against analysis of the damage these ambiguous and often contradictory diplomatic communications from the Continent inflicted on the perception of policy-makers in London of when and how to launch the applications. Tratt's analysis of the origins of Britain's first EEC application shows how far historians have taken the idea that this is a story that needs telling on an international, rather than a national, basis. 'The British initiative announced by Harold Macmillan on 31 July 1961 sprang over-whelmingly from relationships and interactions in the external international environment.'[56] Her use of the word 'overwhelmingly' signifies the degree to which she feels the application was brought about by pressures in the international arena as well as at national level.

The second way in which we see a growing international dimension to the historiography is in the attention now being paid to the role of the European insti-tutions themselves, the Council of Ministers and the Commission, in shaping the reaction of the six EEC states to British moves on Europe in the 1960s. In this context, the tactics adopted by Britain and the EEC states during the Brussels negotiations in 1961–63 have come to be seen as significant barriers to Britain's entry to Europe, as have the actions of European member states and the Commission during the second application.[57] Here, the role of other applicants to the Community in shaping London's strategy has also been considered. Countries such as the Republic of Ireland, almost entirely absent from previous histories of developments in the 1960s, are now being shown to be vital to our understand-ing of the tactics used by Britain in its assaults on 'fortress Europe'. Co-applicant states are also shown to have had an effect upon the way the applications were treated by the Brussels institutions and in member states' capitals.[58]

---

56 Tratt, *The Macmillan Government*, preface, p. 10. See also pp. 7–8 of the main text and the conclud-ing chapter, especially p. 197, for further discussion of this point.

57 Ludlow, *Dealing with Britain* and N. P. Ludlow, 'A Short-Term Defeat: The Community Institutions and the Second British Application to Join the EEC', in Daddow (ed.), *Harold Wilson and European Integration*, pp. 133–50.

58 For example J. Toomey, 'Ireland and Britain's Second Application to Join the EEC', K. Böhmer, 'Germany and the Second British Application', both in Daddow (ed.), *Harold Wilson and European Integration*, pp. 227–42 and 211–26 respectively.

The third and final way in which the international setting has become more deeply embedded in the recent historiography also concerns developments in the world beyond the EEC and how they affected the politics of the British applications. Here, historians continue to focus on the obstacle put in Britain's way by de Gaulle and the so-called 'special relationship' with the United States. But they have extended those lines of inquiry to include analysis of the role the applications played not just in strengthening the 'friendly five' against the machinations of Gaullist France (the European context) but in holding Atlantic security structures together when, in the mid-1960s, France had withdrawn its forces from NATO's integrated command structure. By launching the second application, it has been argued, 'the Wilson government had not only met its own objectives, but also those of the Johnson administration'.[59]

The main significance of the development of what might tentatively be referred to as a post-revisionist school of writing on British European policy is that it displays elements of continuity with revisionist historiography, but also elements of change from it. Methodologically, the continuation from first-generation revisionism is clear: these studies are based on primary-source evidence, collected and organised into densely footnoted diplomatic histories. The differences operate mainly on the interpretative level.

The first is that there is a noticeably greater reticence amongst second-generation revisionists to judge the rights or wrongs of British European policy. By drawing attention to the uncertainty and complexity involved in constructing foreign policy in the domestic and international environments, they absent themselves from some of the more virulent moral and ethical pronouncements that characterise orthodox works and the response they have engendered in revisionist literature. They are not entirely absent from the histiography, however. Ellison remarks on the 'detrimental effect that British diplomacy had upon its own European policy' when it came to winning acceptance for the FTA strategy abroad;[60] Kaiser has been scathing about the motivations behind the first application, which he sees as 'appeasement' of the Americans;[61] and Adamthwaite is ultra-critical of George Brown as Foreign Secretary under Wilson: 'surely the worst Foreign Secretary of the century', he calls him.[62]

The second difference is the tendency to see Britain as a weaker player in the international system than even the revisionists did. It is becoming more

59 J. Ellison, 'Dealing with de Gaulle: Anglo-American Relations, NATO and the Second Application', in Daddow (ed.), *Harold Wilson and European Integration*, pp. 172–87 (p. 183).

60 Ellison, *Threatening Europe*, p. 230.

61 W. Kaiser, 'To Join or not to Join? The "Appeasement" Policy of Britain's First EEC Application', in Brivati and Jones (eds), *From Reconstruction*, pp. 144–56.

62 Adamthwaite, 'John Bull v. Marianne', p. 169.

common for British historians to work with their colleagues abroad, for example at conferences and on edited collections, and for them to travel to study foreign sources in Europe, the United States and elsewhere, these working habits adding new perspective to the study of British foreign-policy. But two additional factors may explain the phenomenon.

One is the temporal distance that exists between the second generation of historians and the past they describe. In most cases they were not living through the events as they happened but have been living instead with the consequences, quenching some of the passion of earlier accounts. The other is that Britain is not now widely regarded as a major player in the international system, compared, for instance, to what it was in the Victorian heyday of the 'jolly old Empire' and the pre-Suez era. Seeing Britain as one of a number of second-rank actors behind the United States has made it easier for historians to reinterpret Britain's past policy as subject to the comings and goings of international diplomacy and somewhat less under the direct influence of British policy-makers. Historians are becoming increasingly aware that British policy through the 1960s relied on winning the hearts and minds of the 'friendly five' EEC states – and especially Germany – as a way of pressuring France, in the figure of de Gaulle, into permitting British entry. Here is more evidence of historiography's being contingent upon the passing of time, and of events in the present affecting our attitudes towards the past. The focus of the next section is on three broader issues to emerge from the study of recent developments in the historiography, all of which reinforce philosophical arguments that historical interpretations are contingent as much on the historian as on his or her sources.

Post-revisionist narrativisation

The roots of the interpretative shift brought about by new treatments of Plan G and Britain's applications to join the EEC have been shown to lie in a combination of new sources being studied, a reappraisal of the role Britain has played in the world since 1945 and a younger generation of historians coming to the field, once removed from the events they seek to reconstruct. The aim of this section is to analyse the broader implications of these developments, which are three in number.

The first is that this generation of writers seems to have taken on board some of the concerns occupying 'post-ist' philosophers of history. Their stories about the past are neither as coherent nor as neatly tailored as those of orthodox and revisionist writers, and by injecting a sense of messiness into the past they seem to be questioning whether historical events unfolded in a way that can be captured by conventional forms of chronological narrative. The second implication concerns the role of the historian in constructing the past for us through periodisation, which, it can be shown, dramatically shapes the interpretation placed on events in the past. The third develops the argument developed in Chapter 1 concerning the influence of genre on interpretation, concentrating on the role played by textbooks in accidentally generating post-revisionist interpretations of the past. Again, therefore, the *form* of history is deemed to be integral to its *content,* and so it seems that there is more to recommend 'post-ist' claims about the practice of history than the defenders of 'proper' history would have us believe.

Destabilising narrative history

The first observation to emerge from this analysis of post-revisionist interpretations of British European policy is that some historians do appear to be taking seriously deconstructionist questions about why we write history and why we cast it in narrative form. This is the thrust of White's critiques of modernist history, echoing Foucault and forcefully reappraised in the British philosopher Alun Munslow's *Deconstructing History.*[63] Before assessing the extent to which post-revisionist historiography exhibits this trait it is important to clarify what narrative is and what the problems with it are held to be.

Narrative, writes Munslow, is a 'structure of explanation used to account for the occurrence of events and human actions'.[64] For Jordanova, it is 'an account, or narration of events, in the form of a story or a tale.'[65] In other words, it is a vehicle for understanding the past through the colligation and presentation of evidence culled from the available sources, put into chronological order and told as a chronological story. Going back to Munslow, 'A historical narrative is a discourse that places disparate events in an understandable order ... Such a narrative is an intelligible sequence of individual statements about past events and/or the experiences of people or their actions, capable of being followed by a reader while he/she is pulled through time by the author towards the conclusion.'

Deconstructionist historians have two main problems with narrative as a historical method. The first is that these narratives rarely contain analysis of the assumptions held by the historian about what it is that informs their view of causality, be it politics, race, gender, class, culture, coincidence, accident or whatever, and how they have set about emplotting the past. Narratives are, argues Munslow, more than the sum of their parts. The individual pieces of evidence are virtually meaningless until they are woven into story form, and it is in the weaving that the historian injects his or her personality and presumptions into the past.[66]

---

63 The problem of narrative as a method of telling historical stories is introduced on pp. 9–14 and expanded on pp. 140–62.
64 Munslow, *Deconstructing History*, p. 186.
65 Jordanova, *History in Practice*, p. 214.
66 Munslow, *Deconstructing History*, p. 10.

Falling out of this, the second problem concerns the telling of a historical story when perhaps there is none to tell. The questions of history posed by Munslow are an instructive way to approach this problem: 'Is it possible that the past unfolded as a particular kind of narrative the first time around and can we recover it more or less intact, or are we only selecting and imposing an emplotment or story line on it derived from our own present?'[67] Louis Mink, White and Jenkins, he notes, are adamant that 'we do not live stories but only reconstruct our lived experience in story form', so there is, he concludes, no 'discoverable *original* emplotment'.[68] Combine with that the words of Danaher, Schirato and Webb, and one has the crux of the postmodern challenge to history. 'Against this synthetic view of history ... Foucault conceives of history in terms of plurality – a multiple number of events that are as often and as much in conflict with one another as they can be held together.'[69]

The orthodox school of writing was denigrated by academic historians because it simplified the past for political ends and for seeing a teleological pattern in the history through from the origins of integration to some future end state from which Britain was, and is, wrong to diverge. But academic history, while different in terms of the sources it uses, still relies on emplotting the past as a narrative, a sequential series of events that challenges the discourse set in place by the 'missed opportunities' interpretation of British European policy, albeit by casting the history using the same chronological template.

For one current historian, Ellison, the imposition of a second narrative on the past by the revisionist school is just another attempt to impose order on British foreign policy when there was none, or very little; hence his development of the post-revisionist synthesis that refuses to articulate a firm answer to the question of whether Britain was trying to sabotage the EEC negotiations in 1955–58. That his work is punctuated with references to the ambiguous attitudes to Europe held by policy-makers such as Macmillan and Eccles even after the FTA proposal morphed into an attempt to coexist with the Common Market is an indication that he hopes to disrupt orthodox *and* revisionist ways of interpreting the history and an indicator as to why he finds judging the policy in the usual historiographical terms so difficult.

> The evolution of my ideas was really inspired by the inconsistency that I saw between the literature (pre-Schaad and Kaiser) and the documents I was reading at the PRO. It seemed to me that the development/implementation of policy was too complex to be either purely an attempt to associate with the Six, or, an effort to delay/deter/sabotage ... their efforts.[70]

67 *Ibid.*, p. 5.
68 *Ibid.*, pp. 9 and 11. Emphasis in original.
69 Danaher, Schirato and Webb, *Understanding Foucault*, p. 100.
70 Email correspondence with Ellison, 1 March 2000.

The disparate views within and between departments can, he implicitly suggests, only tendentiously be called a 'policy', for the very notion of a policy implies a strategy or coherence that was lacking in Downing Street and Whitehall at that time. Ellison is thus constructing a third narrative of events, centring on seeing disorder in what may or may not have been an orderly process of foreign-policy-making in London – something akin to a Chaos Theory of British European policy.

The work of the 'post-ist' writers presents a potent challenge to diplomatic historians and biographers who, as we have seen already, do in the main organise their material chronologically. In the reconstruction of politicians' lives, for example, a narrative is drawn up based on patterns discerned in the actions and supposed thoughts of the subject through birth, childhood, adolescence, adulthood and old age. Politicians' memoirs similarly look back on events and cast them in story form: 'I did this and then I did that.' The reason it is such a challenge is that it gets to the heart of many of the current concerns about history as a discipline, with its own distinctive methods and claims to knowledge about the past. Human beings relive their pasts through stories, and these serve a variety of national, cultural, political, and personal ends. The key questions concern the extent to which those stories are fabricated, and the extent to which they refer to actual happenings.

If one sides more with the former than the latter view, that histories are as much made by the narrator as lived by the subject(s), one must also explore why we emplot our lives and our history in story form, thereby imposing order on disorder. The desire to regulate our experiences in this way is, notes Munslow, 'a product of our own age's preoccupation with understanding the nature of our seemingly chaotic lives'.[71] In an era when we are bombarded with information at an alarming rate and through a variety of visual and aural media, stories offer us simplified versions of reality that we can use to inform our decisions about what to do and how to behave in the various circumstances. The human brain's limited capacity to organise and store all that information means some of it has to be filtered out altogether and the rest managed into a body of data that is accessible and instantly recognisable to us when we want to retrieve it at a later date. Stories are ways of going about undertaking this process in a fast, low-effort way.

It is important to note here that this is not to accuse historians of routinely lying or fabricating stories about the past, though that too is not unknown. Dismissing postmodern approaches to history on this basis is to misrepresent, perhaps intentionally, the nature of the critique of narrativisation as a method of representing the past. It is, instead, a means of stressing the point made by

---

71 Munslow, *Deconstructing History*, p. 13.

Jordanova, that 'For most people, historians tell stories, not in the sense that they make things up, but in the sense that their accounts of the past are structured and gain plausibility in the same manner as other narratives.'[72] Making evident the similarities between history and other forms of knowledge production, academic and otherwise, takes away the mystery that shrouds history as a pursuit and opens it up as a legitimate focus of study, not just to philosophers and historiographers, but to sociologists, critical theorists and theorists of language.

Periodisation

In addition to disturbing narrative modes of historiography, the second implication to be drawn from the post-revisionist turn in the historiography concerns the interaction between the historian and his or her sources. The consultation of archives has provided the evidential basis of revisionist and post-revisionist historiography; but it has been demonstrated that it is the historian who manipulates the sources into an interpretation, it is the historian who chooses where to start and stop historical narratives, and it is the historian who determines which sources of the many available to him or her will form the bulk of the interpretative insights presented in the text. 'To define a beginning in historical terms', writes Saville, 'involves a complex study of the past and its leverage upon the present',[73] and the process of composing stories has itself an integral role to play in shaping historians' perspectives, because that is where the choices about what 'counts' as relevant and irrelevant material come to the fore. Hence, Southgate argues, 'the "facts" we select as significant, the way we interpret them and compose them into a coherent and meaningful whole – these historical procedures will derive from the very personal character of the individual historian'.[74]

The disputes over Plan G bring out the full force of this finding, and it is especially apparent in the work of Liz Kane. Like Ellison, she used primary sources, concentrating her attention on the archives of the Foreign Office's Western Organisation Department and publishing her findings in two articles. On previous trends in the historiography her methodology might suggest that she would offer a revisionist or post-revisionist interpretation. Not at all. She marries primary sources to an orthodox interpretation, exonerating the British from charges of sabotage. In 'The Myth of Sabotage', published in an edited collection in 1999, she claims that

> It is ... possible to interpret that the British decision to establish a free trade area was not a decision to sabotage the common market ... but to improve relations with

---

72 Jordanova, *History in Practice*, p. 156.
73 Saville, *The Politics of Continuity*, p. 1.
74 Southgate, *History*, p. 67.

the Six and associate with the Messina plans. Indeed, far from attempting to destroy the work of the Six, the British government knew that the free trade area improved the chance that the common market would be formed.[75]

The words 'it is possible' at the beginning of this quote do most of the work for us in highlighting the argument that there are usually a number of competing interpretations that can be placed on a given historical event. The sympathetic interpretation she arrives at rests on references to developments in British foreign-policy in 1956–57 and especially on a sympathetic appraisal of Selwyn Lloyd's 'Grand Design' of January 1957, which she had explored in greater detail two years earlier in an article for the *Journal of European Integration History*. The 'Grand Design' advocated closer British co-operation with Western Europe in three ways: first, association with the Six in the non-supranational framework of the WEU as a means of promoting defence co-operation by meeting the costs of thermo-nuclear arms development; second, support for the OEEC as the main instrument for economic co-operation in Europe; and finally a General Assembly for Europe to replace all existing assemblies, including future Six power institutions and existing bodies such as the Council of Europe, the WEU and NATO.[76] This, she argues, is evidence that Britain was trying to come to terms with the EEC, not destroy it, as the Europeanists maintained.[77]

Looking at the contents of the Grand Design in isolation from its origins and impact abroad, and assigning most weight to the period 1956–57: these are the main reasons why she clings to the orthodox 'not maliciously conceived' interpretation of British policy at this time, and why she is critical of writers such as Kaiser for placing undue emphasis on the Foreign Office's strategy towards Europe between June and December 1955. This is exactly the period in which writers such as he, Ellison, and Schaad all say that the evolution of British policy towards Europe in the form of the FTA proposal needs to be understood.

It was at that time, they contend, that the Europeans sensed a switch in British strategy from benevolent neutrality to active opposition to their schemes, a perception that coloured their reaction to Selwyn Lloyd's proposals. 'The search for a new British initiative in Europe which eventually produced the FTA proposal had its origins in the Eden government's Autumn 1955 decision to block the development of a European Common Market.'[78] Put in this context, Ellison comments, 'it seemed to the Europeans that 'the "Grand Design" did just the opposite at a time when [they] hoped the Suez experience would turn

---

75 Kane, 'The Myth of Sabotage', p. 291.
76 Kane, 'European or Atlantic Community?', pp. 92–7. For further details of the Grand Design see Ellison, *Threatening Europe*, pp. 97–103.
77 The politico-military elements were not sanctioned by Cabinet, but Lloyd's second and third proposals were, and were presented to the WEU Council on 26 February 1957.
78 Kaiser, *Using Europe*, pp. 48–54; Ellison, 'Perfidious Albion?', 3; Schaad, 'Plan G', 44–7.

Britain towards Europe'.[79] The timing of the Grand Design could hardly have been worse, given that at that point the Messina powers were working to complete the negotiations on the Treaty of Rome. It contained none of the supranational principles that guided the work of the Six, and so could easily be seen as an 'alternative', even if the Foreign Office did not now see it, or want it to be seen, as such.[80]

Additional support for the argument that the past is constructed through narratives rather than found naked in the archives by the historian is to be found in the work of Ruane on an earlier issue: the agonising international efforts to create the EDC. Conventional scholarly accounts of the international disputes over German rearmament and the associated rise and fall of the EDC, he points out, focus on the period from October 1950, when the Pleven Plan was announced, to August 1954, when the French National Assembly failed to ratify the EDC Treaty, thus killing it. This, he says, is accepted to be the 'EDC crisis'. Yet the ensuing five weeks, which saw fevered efforts in the West to devise a solution to the problem of safely rearming Germany, culminating in the formation of the Western European Union (WEU), were no less significant. What that crisis lacked in length it more than made up for in severity, and his suggestion is that we place the EDC 'in its proper perspective, as a prelude to crisis rather than a crisis in and of itself'.[81] Hence, Ruane writes *in* to the historiography events that had previously been routinely overlooked by historians, exploring the diplomatic exchanges that had previously been written *out* of the field we know as British European policy, his choice of where to start and – in this case – stop his particular narrative in turn shaping his interpretation of what constituted the 'EDC crisis'.

What both these examples show is that it is the historian who brings history to life. It is the historian who is responsible for choosing which sources to consult and how to marshal the evidence taken from them into the history we read in historical books and articles. This process involves more than putting a series of 'facts' into chronological order, as in a chronicle. For it is at this stage that the historian has to select those 'facts' and what he or she considers to be the most telling pieces of evidence; and it is the historian who prioritises certain events and perspectives over others. Periodisation is important here, because how far back one goes in search of an understanding of a given event has, the example of Kane suggests, a significant impact on how an event is subsequently historicised.

It is not simply that contrasting interpretations are the product of different 'facts' being used by different writers, but that the same 'fact', which, defined

79 Ellison, 'Perfidious Albion?', 21.
80 Ellison, *Threatening Europe*, p. 103.
81 Ruane, *The Rise and Fall of the European Defence Community*, p. 5.

liberally, incorporates speeches and other oral and written sources, is put to different uses by historians according to the length of their narrative, the goal of their study and how important they judge it to be in relation to all the other 'facts' they seek to compress into story form. It is not therefore the 'facts' used by writers, but the way in which these 'facts' are *interpreted* and organised into narrative form that determines the positioning of writers with respect to a given historiographical debate. To say that one has a 'method' of research utilising this particular body of evidence does not even begin to explain the complex intellectual, psychological and neurological processes in the brain which combine to form historians' ultimate interpretations of events. The historian enters into a conversation with his or her sources at all stages in the pursuit of history: first in terms of the choice of topic, then in terms of how to study it, then in terms of what evidence is taken from those sources, then in terms of where the history starts and stops, and finally in terms of how the different pieces of evidence are weighted within that story.

Textbook history

The final observation to be drawn from the post-revisionist turn in the historiography, and one that underlies much of what has been discussed above, is that the type of study written has a strong impact on the interpretation of the past. This is particularly true of textbook histories, which pose an array of methodological problems for their authors, and can lead to the unwitting exposition of balanced, post-revisionist interpretations. Jordanova summarises the textbook tendency towards post-revisionism as follows. 'Because textbooks generalise, synthesise and seem to speak with one authority, they can be somewhat bland. Since they seek to be fair, and uncontentious, the sparkle, the sense of what the stakes are in divergent views of the past, sometimes gets lost.'[82]

The main feature of textbook histories is that they are required, in David Cesarani's words, 'to be reasonably up to date, clear and accurate',[83] and can date fairly quickly as new research is published and new historiographical interpretations come to the fore. One example from the field of British European policy is David Gowland and Arthur Turner's *Reluctant Europeans*. In the introduction they show their awareness of the changing historiographical landscape by writing that 'Britain has not played a uniformly laggardly role in the EC/EU',[84] a direct, if un-referenced, allusion to the revisionist school of writing that excuses British decision-makers from the crude charges of negativity traditionally

82 Jordanova, *History in Practice*, p. 19.
83 D. Cesarani, review, 'When Hens and Hitler do not Mix', *The Times Higher Education Supplement: Textbook Guide*, 25 February 2000, p. 6.
84 Gowland and Turner, *Reluctant Europeans*, p. 4.

levelled against them. On Plan G the interpretation they put forward is, it comes as no shock given the reference to Ellison, that it was not as offensive as the Europeanists assumed. Under the influence of Kaiser a few pages later, however, they shift to a less sympathetic posture.[85]

To take a second example, the contrasting interpretations Young places on the motives behind Plan G in his articles and books on Britain and Europe show the way in which the perceived audience for a textbook alters the author's presentation of historical events. His 1989 'The Parting of Ways' article gave academic impetus to the view that Plan G was inspired by a wish to 'sabotage' the EEC. Four years later, in *Britain and European Unity*, he viewed the FTA proposal in more orthodox fashion. His approach now was, in the words of one commentator, to view Plan G as 'a sincere, if naïve, attempt to redefine trade relations with Europe'.[86] In the second edition his sympathetic appraisal of Plan G has been partially offset by reference to Ellison and Kaiser, who touch on the lingering malevolence towards the EEC harboured in some British policy-making circles.[87]

This tendency by textbook writers to waver between the critical and the sympathetic perspectives on Plan G can be put down to the need to cram a quantity of material into a relatively limited space. Young explained that the interpretative fluctuations in his work over time fell out of the exigencies of writing a textbook on Anglo-European relations since 1945 as opposed to an article specifically on policy development in a short period:

> As to the Macmillan full-length book, well there I'm conscious that, although I've a right to express a view on certain issues, I'm also presenting a snapshot of current thinking on the issues, so at times my own views get blended in with those of others – or sometimes I just set out opposing interpretations and don't really resolve them. In doing the second edition … I've been very aware of time constraints and sometimes, quite simply, haven't had time to think my own views through.[88]

Reviewers of other textbooks have made this point. Scott Lucas commented on Young's book on Britain in the twentieth century that: 'Inevitably, in a book of 250 pages covering 100 years there are going to be oversights.'[89] Deighton's review of Walter Laqueur's *Europe in Our Time* betrayed a similar worry: 'the reader is left wondering whether the territorial scope of the book is not too ambitious, and its time span too long'.[90]

---

85 *Ibid.*, pp. 107 and 112.
86 Schaad, 'Plan G', 42–3.
87 Young, *Britain and European Unity, 1945–1999*, pp. 44–8.
88 Letter from Young, received February 1999.
89 W. S. Lucas, review, 'Britain and the World in the Twentieth Century. By John W. Young', *Contemporary British History*, 11:3 (1997), 125–6 (125).
90 A. Deighton, review, 'Europe in Our Time: A History, 1945–1992. By Walter Laqueur', *International Affairs*, 69:1 (1993), 149.

As the most commonly read of educational books, it is important to be aware of the particular requirements placed upon writers of textbook histories. 'There is a certain innate conservatism in the very notion of a textbook', notes Jordanova, 'not just in terms of content, but in pedagogic philosophy'.[91] The balanced or inconclusive interpretation of history they present is as much accidental as chosen, is arrived at for a combination of practical and methodological reasons, and they do not always manage to capture the battles that have been fought within disciplines to have particular interpretations accepted as the conventional wisdom. The demands made of textbook writers are becoming greater, as are the *types* of textbook on offer, so it is not a feature of the historiography that will imminently disappear.[92] As Steven Gunn has asked: 'Should they try to cater for both A-Level students and undergraduates in need of an introduction, when the demands of A-Level now include formal exercises in the interpretation of primary sources and a structured understanding of historiographical change?'[93]

Manchester University Press's 'Documents in Contemporary History' series shows that the emphasis in textbooks is increasingly towards letting *students* decide on the most appropriate interpretation from the range of options set out for them by the editor,[94] a trend being repeated in other disciplines, such as mathematics, where 'It is now seen as desirable for students to take responsibility for their own learning.'[95] The requirement for textbooks to be written according to the principle of 'say it with documents' suggests on the one hand the continuing lure of primary source material, while on the other there is the impression that such series have been affected by postmodern reflection on the interpretative content of history. It is as if letting the documents speak for themselves will circumvent postmodern concerns about history by ignoring historians' roles in the construction of stories about the past. Yet where is the reflection on how the primary sources were chosen, or analysis of their limitations as factual sources about the past? Thumbing through Baylis's *Anglo-American Relations Since*

91 Jordanova, *History in Practice*, p. 18.

92 *Ibid.*, pp. 19–20.

93 S. Gunn, review, 'Short on Pope-Burning', *The Times Higher Education Supplement: Textbook Guide*, 25 February 2000, p. 6.

94 See for example J. Baylis (ed.), *Anglo-American Relations Since 1939: The Enduring Alliance* (Manchester, Manchester University Press, 1997); S. Brooke (ed.), *Reform and Reconstruction: Britain After the War, 1945–51* (Manchester: Manchester University Press, 1995); S. Greenwood (ed.), *Britain and European Integration Since the Second World War* (Manchester, Manchester University Press, 1996). As the précis to these books makes plain, it 'is a series designed for sixth-formers and undergraduates in higher education: it aims to provide both an overview of specialist research on topics in post-1939 British history and a wide-ranging selection of primary source material'.

95 N. Steele, 'Method is More than the Sum of its Parts', *The Times Higher Education Supplement*, 17 March 2000, p. 38.

1939, there is on pages 16 to 17 a brief statement on how the sources were chosen but no lengthy commentary. Greenwood's *Britain and European Integration* contains no notes on sources at all.

The demands now being placed on textbook writers will exaggerate the problems that have always faced them in trying to convey the historiographical conflicts that have taken place between different generations and different schools of writing. It is important to be aware of this when it comes to assessing the drivers of post-revisionist readings of the past which, though usually balanced, are so out of choice rather than accident. The latter reason better explains why textbook writers present synthesised accounts of the past:

> textbooks present a viewpoint which, by the very nature of the genre, readers are discouraged from contesting, whereas a monograph, that is, a specialised scholarly study presenting the findings of original research to those who are pretty expert already, can evaluate diverse approaches to a subject, and acknowledge the depth of intellectual dimensions, even if, in the end, it puts a particular case with a distinctive type of authority.[96]

Given that textbook writers balance out competing perspectives on the past they might be classed 'post-revisionist'. But it is a different (implicit) form of post-revisionism than the (explicit) form of post-revisionism contained in the articles and sections in books on Plan G and the FTA in the historiography of British European policy. In journal articles and monographs there is more space and research time to articulate responses to the methodological problems raised by acknowledgement of competing accounts of he past. As Ellison has explained:

> I was also motivated by a sense of historiographical evolution more generally. For those of us writing now, US Cold War historiography has taught that extreme arguments are just that; sophistication in explanation and balance in judgment have proven to be scholarly watchwords in post-revisionism in general. I can't say that this was in my mind like some kind of dogma, but it was definitely a consideration.[97]

The consultation of new sources has gone hand in hand with an *a priori* awareness that the existing debate or method of narrating the past is flawed, confirming the judgement of this book that evidence drawn *from* sources is but a small part of the reason why historians arrive at the interpretations they do. What they take *to* them is at least as if not more significant in determining the interpretation ultimately placed upon past events. Amongst other things, historians

---

96 Jordanova, *History in Practice*, p. 19.
97 Email correspondence with Ellison, 1 March 2000. Schaad is also well aware of the debate among orthodox and revisionist writers, as the introduction to his 'Plan G' article shows. The importance of historiographical awareness to the development of post-revisionism is also alluded to in J. Kent, review, 'The End of Superpower: British Foreign Office Conceptions of a Changing World. By Stuart Croft', *Contemporary Record*, p. 478.

approach the primary sources already possessing views about the current state of the literature, concepts and theories about how the world worked in the past, the concerns of the present and a number of reasons for writing history in the first place, which are bound up with their positioning in the broader infrastructure of the sub-field. Analysis of textbook methodologies, and a comparison of them with the methodology that produces explicit, historiographically-aware post-revisionism is a stark reminder that history never comes to us in unadulterated form.

Conclusion

The principal conclusion to emerge from the above analysis is anything but firm, and is that, at this stage, it is problematical to predict what impact the post-revisionist turn in the historiography might have on the wider study of British European policy. The historiography may well develop in the coming years to reflect the reconfiguration of narrative portended by post-revisionism. But all judgements about whether it will develop into a school to rival the orthodox and revisionist schools must, at this relatively early stage, be tenuous and open to future adjustment.

Kaplan points out that 'new' theories tend to operate in a smaller domain; but there is no reason why they should not become accepted in other areas, spreading their influence across a field of research.[98] In theory, the methodological innovations introduced to the study of the history of Britain and Europe by post-revisionist writers could be transposed into other themes in this field, which in time would lead to a picture of post-war foreign-policy decision-making in Britain that is at the same time more internationally orientated and less cohesive in terms of narrative structure. It would be one that stresses the dithering of British policy-makers, their reluctance to make decisions and, on the European question, a dearth of attention to the issue, supporting Hennessy's argument that post-war British politics has been a story of 'muddling through'. In short, it would be a *messier* picture of British European policy.

This interpretation does not lend itself easily to narrativisation in terms of chronological ordering of events, because it suggests that to charge the British either with malicious intent or with being more sympathetic to European integration is to overlook the key point that 'the British' is a term open to definition. Commonly it refers to the British government's policy towards European integration. Broken down, that government consists of a host of individuals and departments, all of which are influenced by a range of pressures, especially the mood-swings, attitudes and in-fighting of the leading actors within. These individuals in turn have their interests shaped by the particular department or

98 Kaplan, *On Historical and Political Knowing*, p. 17.

organisation for which they work, which has vested interests to protect and agendas to push.

By demanding closer attention to agency-driven explanations of British European policy, post-revisionist historiography reminds us that the definition one ascribes to a given things or event has a great leverage over how historical events are interpreted. 'Whitehall' and 'the British government' are, they stress, composed of such a variety of different individuals and agencies, infiltrated by a plurality of outside interests, that, while nominally responsible, policy-makers were not necessarily in full control either of the policy that emerged from Whitehall or over how it was implemented. They also had a severe lack of time and motivation to think through the consequences of their actions, and their statements on the subject were often contradictory as a result. This messier picture of British foreign-policy-making may or may not be a more accurate representation of the past. What is clearer is that it portends major shifts in the texture of future narratives about Britain and Europe.

Conclusion: historians and historiography

'Judged as philosophy, works of history are likely to seem weak. Judged as history, works of philosophy are likely to seem irrelevant.'[1] Allan Megill's comment on the history–philosophy frontier casts light on the mutual suspicion that has come to characterise dealings between historians and philosophers since the upsurge in postmodernist thinking in the 1970s. It is important to comprehend the factors that have gone into driving a wedge between history and philosophy, one significant one being departmentally-based structures within academia that encourage 'artificial alienation and distance between even closely-related special-ities on either side of a boundary'.[2]

The artificiality of the separation between disciplines identified by Becher and Trowler is relevant here because it calls into doubt current ways of thinking about the 'nature of history' debate in Britain. Stereotyping the debate about the nature and status of history as a battle between 'historians' and 'postmodernists' obfuscates more than it enlightens, although to use the words of Ralf Dahrendorf it is 'very British indeed' to put debates such as this into zero-sum terms.[3] These misleading terms house several shades of thinking; but the subtleties of those positions, the potential for overlap and the existence of zones of agreement among philosophers and historians tend to get overlooked in the general stream of invec-tive that has come to characterise their dialogue on the subject. Depicting the issue in zero-sum terms generates a level of antagonism and vitriol that obscures the relevance of the 'history debate' to all scholars with an interest in history, philos-ophy and the micro-foundations of knowledge in its broadest sense.[4]

The reason is that the work of the two communities is not mutually exclu-sive but complementary, the borders between them not impermeable put porous. The disciplinary structures currently in place do not leave much room for the potential areas of overlap to emerge and be studied as areas of investigation in their own right, not least because there is little room in the market for scholars who classify themselves as 'philosophers of history'. Which kinds of department

1 Quoted in Becher and Trowler, *Academic Tribes and Territories*, p. 60.
2 *Ibid.*, p. 63.
3 Dahrendorf, *On Britain*, p. 13.
4 P. Finney, International History, Theory and the Origins of te Second World War', *Rethinking History*, 1:3 (1997). 357–79. The problems of defining the debate along biopopular lines form a major theme of his conference paper. 'What historians Actually Do: Politics, Historiography and Writing the Road to War in 1939/41'. European Social Science History Conference, The Hague, 2 March 2002.

are they suited to, and which departments have anything other than a passing interest in the subject?

In the United States, there is an established forum for the exchange of views among philosophers and diplomatic historians in the pages of *Diplomatic History* and its associated e-mail discussion list, H-DIPLO.[5] In a book first published in 1992, Burke remarked that 'explicit discussion of the relation between postmodernism and history has scarcely begun'.[6] Thankfully that situation is changing – if slowly. New journals in Britain, such as *Rethinking History*, may in time come to perform a similar function in Britain; but as things currently stand the potential for mutually beneficial cross-fertilisation of ideas and evidence is stymied by the way the debate is conducted. Inquiry into the research and writing of history cannot remain on the fringes of the discipline of history, or be left to intellectual historians, students of historiography or philosophers alone.

A major obstacle standing in the way of the kind of exchanges that would be advantageous rather than acrimonious is that academics are increasingly limited from experimenting with interdisciplinary methodologies and concepts by the nature of the job. What philosophers could see as a wilful disregard might in some, even many, cases merely be a reflection of the multitude of pressures at work on the construction of historical texts. Historians in the current climate, like all academics, 'are likely to find themselves "overextended, underfocused, overstressed, underfunded", in the words of one North American university principal'.[7] Student contact hours are increasing, the search for resources is taking more and more time and the pressures to convey honour on one's department in an increasingly competitive global academic market are growing, so they rarely have the time, even if they have the inclination, to dwell on the gaps in their understanding of the past and alternative interpretations that could be placed upon the events they describe. The lacunae in our knowledge may well be where philosophers wish us to dwell, but at present historians accrue more professional kudos by publishing about the events the documents suggest did unfold, however flimsy this approach might be epistemologically and difficult to achieve methodologically. As Thompson points out, the full impact of the 'publish or perish' syndrome brought about by the RAE in British universities has yet to be discovered, but it does seem to be inhibiting the scope for innovative historical research, teaching and writing.[8]

The 'reasoned detachment preferred by most academics' and the production of what Elton called 'just ordinary sound history' is what historians aspire to,

5 Finney, 'Still "Marking Time"?', 292–4.
6 Burke, *History and Social Theory*, p. 121.
7 Quoted in Becher and Trowler, *Academic Tribes and Territories*, p. 17.
8 Thompson, *What Happened to History?*, pp. 71–95.

because it legitimises their claims to produce knowledge that has veracity and explanatory power.[9] But this does not conform to the picture of knowledge production that has emerged in epistemological philosophy, which stresses its tendentious nature. The rethinking of history that entails, viewing it not as a 'special' or separate discipline of inquiry that exists in an intellectual vacuum but as part of a broader social discourse driven by power, influence and economics, reminds us of the prescience of White's view that 'one of the things one learns from the study of history is that such study is never innocent'.[10]

It is the challenge his view presents to a discipline that has been professionalising itself for over one hundred years that has sparked the acrimonious exchanges we now see, for historians feel their discipline to be under attack from a line of philosophical thinking that threatens the very foundations on which their individual reputations as credible purveyors of knowledge rest. 'Historians and historical theorists', writes Willie Thompson 'work in well-nigh separate disciplines in spite of the energetic efforts of postmodernist historians ... to effect a junction.'[11]

This book has sought to test some of the most contentious philosophical claims about the nature and practice of history through critical analysis of a given body of historical literature. It accepts in doing so that to a greater or lesser degree all philosophising about history has the capacity to antagonise certain sections of the historical community – so to say 'most contentious' is perhaps unnecessary, since they are all contentious in one way or another. The unequivocal answer to the question of whether philosophers have anything to tell historians about their craft, is 'yes, they do'. The answer to the question of whether historians should feel threatened by such inquiry into the ontological, epistemological and methodological foundations of their research is a resounding 'no, they should not'.

History, it has been argued, is a socially constructed phenomenon. Although this might sound a shocking way to treat a subject founded on the empiricist principle of objectivity, it is hardly a surprise, seeing that it is written by human beings. It is not the product of the primary sources, but the product of the imagination of the historian who reads them. Writing history entails an ongoing search for a story about the past that fulfils a number of needs, not least those of the historian and his or her perceived audience. In an effort to promote critical self-reflection and a more refined understanding of the past in the present, this study advocates that historians must take seriously philosophers' assertions that history is a construction, that emplotment and narrativisation are issues that affect our

---

9 *Daily Telegraph*, 27 April 2002, p. 14; *History Workshop 6*, editorial, p. 1.
10 White, *The Content of the Form*, p. 82.
11 Thompson, *What Happened to History?*, p. 68.

interpretation of the past, and that writing history is a political act.[12] History serves its writer, not the other way around, and one does not have to be 'fluent in Derridese' to recognise the fact.[13]

This concluding chapter reflects on some of the most prominent themes to emerge from the book, and suggests where future research in the historiography of British European policy may most profitably be undertaken. The first part explores the strengths and weaknesses of the historiographic method set down in the book. Clearly there are flaws in this approach, not least in the construction of a narrative about how the writing in this field has developed at a time when narrative is under attack from 'post-ist' thinkers. Nor is it claimed that this is a totally comprehensive survey of the available literature (works by non-British and non-American writers do not feature heavily) nor that it is the *only* way of treating the literature. Weighed against the benefits, however, the deficiencies are shown to be less of a burden, because it provides an accessible model through which to explore the growth of knowledge communities in the discipline of history, which have yet to receive the detailed attention they deserve.

The second part explores how the historiographical debate about Britain and Europe has been played out among scholars and former policy-makers, arguing that, contrary to the aims of the orthodox school of writers, it has had little impact either on media and public discourses about Europe or on the political agenda. Blair's embrace of the 'missed opportunities' thesis may or may not be a signal that things are about to change. The final part sets down a future research agenda for historiographers working on this and other sub-fields of history, highlighting potential ways forward both vertically and horizontally. Vertically, more work needs to be done on the workings of the academic industry in Britain, which would shed light on the ways ideas and concepts become orthodoxies; horizontally, it would be interesting to see if this is a special case by testing the extent to which other historiographical disputes exhibit properties similar to those found in the historiography of British European policy.

Those opposed to (or suspicious of) historiography will no doubt take issue with this book for three principal reasons. The first operates on the most general level, and is that historiography as a scholarly pursuit is a form of navel-gazing implying, says Perez Zagorin, 'infinite regress, because the historians who investigate the premises and politics of historical interpretations will need ... to have

---

12 Bayly, 'The Second British Empire', p. 71, concludes his article with the words 'Imperial history has always been intensely political.'

13 Peter Novick, quoted *ibid.*, p. 63. Some of the language and terminology used by philosophers is, admittedly, complicated for the uninitiated, though certainly not all, but it is insufficient to dismiss postmodern history or the philosophy of history more generally on the grounds that it is merely jargon. There are a number of writers on key thinkers such as Foucault and Derrida who 'translate' the more obscure parts of their writing as a way in to their work.

their own politics of interpretation investigated by other historians, and so on ad infinitum'.[14] In response it is worth reminding readers that this book is not a call for historians to stop writing history: 'no one is suggesting that all historians should suddenly abandon all other projects to devote themselves entirely to critical historiography'.[15] Historiographical studies of this type are intended to sit alongside histories, rather than replacing them.

The knock-on criticism would be summed up in the question: why should we trust historiographers any more than we should trust professional historians and other contributors to historical knowledge? The answer, of course, is that we cannot, although the word 'trust' is not meant pejoratively. Historians do not, usually, intentionally distort evidence, misread sources or present interpretations that they know to be false. Saying one does not trust a historical text is not therefore slandering historians. It is, rather, a reminder that they cannot tell *the* truth about what happened in the past, but *a* truth, and a call to open up historical texts to historiographical analysis by placing works of history in their social and cultural contexts.

The shortcomings of the diplomatic historians' reliance on documentary evidence is revealed in Rodney Lowe's critique of Lamb's claim that 'the release by the Public Record Office on 1 January 1994 under the Thirty Year Rule of the final official archives relating to the Macmillan Government enables historians to write the truth'.[16] This, Lowe notes, 'is of course nonsense'; the reason he gives is that 'By no means all the documents were released in 1994.'[17] Even before considering the source-based problems associated with historiography, one has to consider the limits on accessing the 'truth' about the past that come from the research methodology and the historian's predilections in terms of source selection, interpretative framework and theories about how the world works. Writing history with the aim of achieving some kind of apocalyptic objectivity is, at best, a futile ambition and at worst insincere to the reader; and in this respect historiography is no different from history in terms of its limitations as a source of knowledge.

Historiographers do not and cannot possess sounder claims to comprehensiveness than any other writers of books or articles, a point well made by Richards, who notes that the study of historiography 'may itself be regarded as a scientific enterprise, involving evidence, hypotheses, theories and models', and so equally liable to flux and challenge from other writers with different methodologies and conceptual frameworks.[18] History is the narrative of past events and

---

14 Quoted in Finney, 'Still "Marking Time"?', 307.
15 *Ibid.*, 305.
16 Lamb, *The Macmillan Years*, p. 1.
17 R. Lowe, review, 'The Macmillan Years, 1957–1963: The Emerging Truth. By Richard Lamb', *Contemporary British History*, 10:2 (1996), 239–41 (240).
18 Richards, 'Theories of Scientific Change', p. 203.

historiography is a narrative about those narratives. To assert that there are multiple ways of viewing the past and that those ways need further analysis is to imply that those studies are in turn open for scrutiny, and I welcome what Munslow refers to as the 'deconstructive consciousness' being brought to the epistemology and methodology employed in this book, just as I recommend its being bought to the study of the past.

Whether this leads, as Zagorin suggests, to 'infinite regress' turns on how one views the aims of the historiographical enterprise compared to those of the historical, for, as Frank Ankersmit has pointed out, a step back is not necessarily regressive. 'The wild, greedy, and uncontrolled digging into the past, inspired by the desire to discover a past reality and reconstruct it scientifically, is no longer the historian's unquestioned task. We would do better to examine the result of a hundred and fifty years' digging more attentively and ask ourselves more often what all this adds up to.'[19] His words are poignant now, when the trend is towards greater and greater numbers of history texts: 'more academic works of history were published between 1960 and 1980 than in all previous time'.[20] If the continual outpouring of histories of the First World War, of Hitler's role in inspiring and conducting the Second World War and the origins and development of the Cold War is a reliable indicator, it seems historians are no nearer quenching their thirst for dissecting the past in minute detail. The public, furthermore, are equally keen on reliving the past, judging by the interest in the numerous documentaries on terrestrial television about history, and the popularity of the satellite channels dedicated to history and biography (one academic, speaking off the record, has quipped that the 'Biography Channel' should be renamed the 'Hitler Channel', such is its concentration on the Second World War). If there is found to be a similar yearning for historiographical studies why, in the interests of critical self-reflection, not encourage it as a method of understanding the historical imagination and the forces at work on historical interpretation and re-interpretation?

The third potential critique of this study concerns the way it has emplotted the history of the writing on Britain's relations with Europe in narrative form. Having alluded throughout this book to the concerns raised by philosophers about telling a chronological story that distorts or underplays the messiness of the past, is this study not open to exactly the same charge, that it has narrativised the historiography into a coherent story when in fact the waves of writing neither existed in the first place nor succeeded each other in the temporal fashion described above? Of all the criticisms, this is the most difficult to provide a compelling response to, yet most in need of one. It should be pointed out first of all that, yes, the historiography has intentionally been presented in

19 Ankersmit, 'Historiography and Postmodernism', p. 152.
20 Becher and Trowler, *Academic Tribes and Territories*, p. 14.

narrative form. The extent to which that form is the product of a preconceived conception about historiographical progression thus becomes critical, for if historians can be accused of collecting evidence that suits preconceived social, political or other theories about how the world works, and worked in the past, then much the same applies to historiographers.

So: has this book been constructing a story about a body of literature that has not evolved in story form; has it imposed patterns where none exist? The answer is that this is most definitely a construction of the author's making. But while fully accepting the criticism that narrativising the historiography is to over-simplify the evolution of the literature on this subject (and has overlooked some texts altogether) the point also needs to be made that it has not posited a firm date when one school replaced another, nor has it been suggested that the emergence of one school has led to the extinction of the other. It can therefore be argued that, within the limits of the narrative form, this historiographical inquiry has attempted to explain the evolution of the literature chronologically while draw-ing attention to the haphazardness of the processes by which schools of writing are born and evolve. It has attempted to inject a degree of instability into the simple 'orthodox then revisionist then post-revisionist' model by drawing atten-tion to the constructed nature of schools of writing and by concentrating a large portion of the analysis in each chapter on their origins.

The three weaknesses in the critical historiographical method identified above are not fatal to the cause of critical historiography *per se*. The first two are offshoots of wider academic debates about the role of historians and the value of different forms of knowledge production, and are therefore more easily dispensed with than the third, which gets to the heart of the methodology used in this study as well as the form in which the evidence has been presented. It has to be admit-ted that, at the end of the day, this third objection is an insuperable one; but there are still a number of useful conclusions that can be drawn from this book, among which four stand out.

Rethinking the history debate

The first conclusion is that the history debate in Britain needs remoulding. No longer is it useful to talk about 'bias', or 'prejudice', or finding out the 'truth' about the past, or in any other similar hackneyed terms about the nature of history. Even those historians steeped in the empiricist tradition acknowledge that their accounts can never be entirely accurate, complete or without preju-dice of some form. Marwick, for instance, advances what he calls the 'Marwick 20 percent rule', which states that 'at least 80 per cent of what a scholarly histo-rian writes is likely to be soundly based – but the reader should always be ready to reject up to 20 per cent, which can be due to bees in the bonnet, sycophancy towards a patron, the desire to be in fashion, humble error, or various other reasons.'[21] If up to one-fifth of a historians' work is subject to the various influences Marwick identifies, could not one-fifth of works of history usefully be devoted to reflecting on how the text has been penetrated and moulded by those influences and or the consequent ramifications for interpretation? The parameters of the history debate could, with this in mind, usefully be moved from incorporating discussion of whether there is bias in historical texts to discussion of what *kinds* of biases are involved, for that is where some of the more demanding intellectual work has yet to be undertaken. As important as it is, debating the veracity of history is something of a red herring that has precluded us from separating the 'old' debate from the 'new' one, and my redefinition of the debate sits somewhere between the modernist and postmodernist versions set down by Munslow in *Deconstructing History*, where he states 'The most important question, then, is not the dog-eared modernist one of whether history is an accurate science, but the postmodernist one of how and why when we write about the past, we cast it in a particular form.' [22]

The advantage of following this new agenda is that it assumes the positioned nature of historical knowledge, rather than spending time justifying it as a claim about historiography: 'The deconstructive consciousness willingly acknowledges the sublime nature of the past – its literal meaninglessness, its lack of centre, and its consequent lack of truth – while mainstreamers still insist on asking what was the past really like and, through dint of professional archival research, believe they can get closer to its truthful reality.'[23] In other words, where conventionally the reliability or truth content of historical knowledge has been the focus for attention, the new approach would take as its point of departure the essential unreliability of that form of knowledge and would explore the reasons for it.

One of the most promising ways of doing that is through critical historiographical analysis and analysis of the social construction of history. Here, the political, cultural, institutional and economic dimensions to history are allowed to flourish within a framework that seeks both to understand and to explain why interpretations of history rise and fall over time. 'It is in this sense an adventure in the history of ideas, the study of how a subject has been written about, how trends and interests in research have changed, how public events, world affairs, and so simple a matter as the opening of an archive shapes the way in which writers explore the past.'[24] On our travels in this book we have found that the gathering and presentation of historical evidence are critically affected by a host of

---

21 Marwick, *The New Nature of History*, p. 49.

22 Munslow, *Deconstructing History*, p. 5.

23 *Ibid.*, pp. 146–7.

24 Winks, 'Preface', p. 13.

factors that are crucial to any understanding how history works for different individuals and different groups of writers, undermining once and for all the idea that history can be written 'for its own sake'. The idea that the past exists and can be studied independently of the historian and his or her imagination, position within academia, working environment, political persuasion or time of writing is simply untenable given the evidence presented above.

White says that philosophy of history 'is a commentary not only on the historical record but also on the activity by which a given encodation of the historical field can be permitted to claim the status of knowledge'.[25] Bearing this in mind, the second conclusion to be drawn from this book is that the construction of schools of writing is a promising way of testing the claims about the nature of history put forward by philosophers of history. By making the activity of historians and the ways they go about writing their texts the focus of attention, schools serve as useful devices for applying the philosophy to the history. If this oversimplifies the literature, then so be it: that is the aim of a model, to simplify reality as a way of enhancing our understanding of it.

The schools approach, adapted from Cold War historiography, has shown bodies of writing to develop because certain ideas and ways of viewing the past become accepted wisdoms among writers with shared goals and outlooks. Indeed, we are now in a position to elicit four characteristics of schools of writing. The first is that different schools ask different sets of questions of the past. The orthodox interpretation arose in the late 1950s and was sustained through to the 1980s by journalists, diplomats and politicians reflecting on Britain's apparent economic and political decline as a global power after 1945. It should not come as a shock, then, that they produced accounts that read like lists of 'guilty men', because they were – in the main – Euroenthusiasts, attempting to find an answer to the vexed question of where Britain had gone wrong *vis-à-vis* European unity.

Academic writers working to different agendas have driven the revisionist and now the post-revisionist interpretations of British European policy. Europeanists or not, they have refocused the history and, unencumbered by the need to explain away failure, they have tried instead to understand the dynamics of British European policy, grounding their accounts in primary-source documentation. Their interpretations have been significantly shaped by the agenda of the first school, because they have felt compelled to reply to its stinging criticisms of British European policy; so it is crucial to recognise that, although they are asking new questions and employing a different methodology, the structure within which writers in the second and third schools operate is to a large extent set by the first.

25 White, *Metahistory*, p. 428.

The second characteristic is that there are leaders who found the school and who are responsible for how it evolves and the avenues of research down which it travels. The part they play in prompting a Kuhnian *gestalt switch* that changes the way the past is conceived as an object for study is analogous to that played in teams by the people the sports psychologist Willi Railo refers to as 'cultural architects … people who are able to change the mindset of others. They are able to break barriers, they have visions.'[26] In the case of the orthodox school, one *could* point to Jean Monnet and British Europeans in the 1950s. But the real leader of this school, the true 'founder of discursivity' in the Foucauldian sense, appears to be Miriam Camps. Not only was she responsible for bringing academic integrity and a British audience to Monnet's views (hence the number of times she is footnoted in academic tracts and the memoirs of diplomats and politicians), but it was in her work that one sees the establishment of the language and terminology of 'missed chances', 'missed opportunities' and 'missed buses', which have come to characterise orthodox historiography.

The origins of the second school appear to lie in the work of John Kent, John Young, Geoffrey Warner and Anne Deighton. Their reconfiguring and rewriting of the history of Labour's foreign policy in the aftermath of the Second World War is evidence that an anomaly had been observed in the ability of those politicians and diplomats first to the field to satisfactorily explain British European policy. Contrary to the conventional wisdom of a set of negative and apathetic government policies towards European unity, here was a reading that highlighted a constructive, even a proactive policy in many respects. The master–apprentice nature of doctoral research supervision is just one of the most obvious ways in which theories and concepts have been handed down from those first in the field to their successors. Younger historians and those new to the area have been asking if both the orthodox and revisionist schools obscure as much as they reveal; hence the emergence in the later 1990s of what might in time become a third, post-revisionist school of writing, strongly rooted methodologically in revisionism but differing from it on an interpretative level and in terms of how the narrative about the past is constructed.

The third characteristic of schools of writing is that the seeds for their flowering are often sown years before they develop into full-blown schools, echoing Kuhn's judgement that the foundations for alternative perspectives on the world are often latent in a particular paradigm, but not fully recognised by those who work in it. The sympathetic judgement of British European policy developed by the revisionists was portrayed as a brand new departure in the literature. However, the seeds of revisionism, as they have been labelled, lay sown but unwatered until

---

26 Quoted in *Observer*, 19 May 2002, www.observer.co.uk/worldcup2002/story/0,11031,718176,00. html.

the mid-1980s, when Kent and Young probed more deeply into this area. At that point, there began 'the extraordinary investigations that lead the profession to a new set of commitments'.[27] Camps acknowledged that the interpretation she offered could be challenged by recourse to PRO sources. But having looked at the files she concluded nonchalantly that they contained little information about Britain's policy towards Europe that she did not already know – a reminder that it is not the sources that tell historical stories, but that they only speak through the historian.[28] Assuming that she looked at the same documentation to which the revisionists turned in constructing their accounts, at least in the early years, her words suggest that there is a strong link between membership of a school and how one manipulates and interprets historical evidence. Camps approached the official documentation with one mindset, Young, Kent and their successors with a quite different one. Not surprisingly, they emerged from the PRO with contradictory views of how and why events unfolded as they did.

This ties in neatly with the fourth characteristic of schools of writing: they are usually the product of younger researchers or those new to a field. The example of Camps's approach to the primary documentation is a good one to expand upon in this respect. Max Planck observed that 'a new scientific truth does not triumph by convincing its opponents and making them see the light, but rather because its opponents eventually die and a new generation grows up that is familiar with it'.[29] According to Kuhn, 'the men [sic] who achieve these fundamental inventions of a new paradigm have either been very young or very new to the field whose paradigm they change'.[30] Perhaps Camps's resistance to the alternative interpretation was due to the fact that her reputation was founded on the missed opportunities thesis, and that as an elder stateswoman in the field it was more than she could bear to overturn her entire ideology and worldview, a reminder that 'What a man [sic] sees depends both upon what he looks at and also upon what his previous visual-conceptual experience has taught him to see.'[31]

Her popularity among former policy-makers in Britain and the privileged position she carved out for herself in the historiography grants her works the paradoxical air of being 'unofficial official histories'. New academic researchers have no such reputations to maintain or consistency of views to uphold, and in terms of originality there is everything to gain from being controversial. Yet it would be both unfair and an oversimplification to say that the development of historical

---

27 Kuhn, *The Structure of Scientific Revolutions*, p. 5.
28 For another account based on primary sources but that sits well outside the interpretation offered by the revisionist school, see M. Deavin, 'Harold Macmillan and the Origins of the 1961 British Application to Join the EEC' (London School of Economics Ph.D., 1996).
29 Quoted in Kuhn, *The Structure of Scientific Revolutions*, p. 151.
30 *Ibid.*, p. 86.
31 *Ibid.*, p. 113.

interpretations is all about reputation-building. Away from the personal invest-
ments at stake in historiography, one has to view the generational aspect of historiographical progression in terms of the introduction of new questions, new
methods, new sources and new ideas to the study of history. This less cynical view
seems according to preliminary findings better to explain both why new
researchers come to the field and how they conceive of their objects of study and
the most appropriate methods to employ in the pursuit of history.

The third conclusion to emerge from this book is that despite the philosophical challenge to the modernist conception of history, primary sources remain
the bedrock of historical research in contemporary Britain. Here, more so than in
America if the impact of Vietnam on Cold War scholarship is a reliable indicator,
the opening of official records and the moves to promote the study of contemporary British history appear to have been of greater significance to the emergence
of revisionist literature on this subject than any feeling for 'Europe' on the part
of academics in the 1980s. If one wanted to find evidence to support the latter
judgement, it might be found in comparative perspective by looking at what
happened in Denmark at the time the SEA was being negotiated. Until 1985, notes
Knud Erik Jørgensen: 'The unspoken assumption was that "reluctant Europeans"
do not need to do research [into European integration] ... Research on the EC was
a latecomer to the social sciences in Denmark.'[32]

While it might have raised the profile of the study of European affairs, this
view of the external environment prompting research into contemporary history
has to sit alongside a more compelling explanation for the growth of interest
among historians in Britain: the declassification of official government documentation relating to British foreign policy after the Second World War. As the
section on the PRO in Chapter 3 argued, accounting only for political issues and
the prevailing climate of opinion is to overstate the role of external factors in
determining the routes down which historiography travels. While the Europe
question was one of the stimuli behind the growth of interest in post-war British
history, it was neither the sufficient nor the necessary condition for the historiographical evolution that occurred at that time.

Coming after the conclusions on the merits of schoolifying history as a
means of explaining historiographical evolution, this conclusion about the significance of primary sources serves as a reminder that history in Britain remains a
conservative discipline, with a small 'c', a product perhaps of the 'entrenched
conservatism' within academia more generally.[33] History is rooted in modernist
conceptions of how to access the past and represent it in textual form, and there

32 K. E. Jørgensen, 'European Integration as a Field of Study in Denmark', *Journal of Common
    Market Studies*, 33:1 (1995), 157–62 (157).
33 Becher and Trowler, *Academic Tribes and Territories*, p. 97.

are serious problems in asking historians to take more seriously philosophical concerns about the practice of history that they see, correctly or otherwise, as 'radical'. Lack of time, lack of interest and what is perceived as excessive jargon are just some of the reasons why historians have been reticent about dwelling on their craft to the same degree as philosophers and intellectual historians. The irony of this inattention to the microfoundations of what they do is well captured by Gerald Izenberg: 'For historians to avoid considering certain linguistic theories just because they couldn't continue to work as they have if the theories are true, is hardly a comfortable position to take from a discipline which prides itself on the rationality of its procedures.'[34]

Looking at the disciplinary reasons why historians are sceptical about philosophising about their craft, because it threatens their identity as purveyors of authoritative narratives about the past, allows one to draw a fourth conclusion from this study: the concept of 'political history' has a double meaning. In its conventional sense it is taken to mean the sub-field of history dealing with the history of political events, personalities and policies and is associated with the history of political parties, ideologies and given strands of governance: foreign policy, colonial policy, welfare policy, education policy and so on. The political history penned by the writers explored in this book concentrates on Britain's troubled relationship with the continental process of integration embodied in the early moves to integration, the ECSC, the EDC and the EEC, now embodied in the EU.

But much more significant from the perspective of the historiographer is the second meaning, which takes the writing of history to be a political act. Orthodox historiography of British European policy would at first glance represent the most obvious manifestation of this, incorporating works by politicians, diplomats, civil servants, journalists and other instant historians. The language they employ reflects the highly politicised nature of their discourse: they are not just describing events and processes, but trying to change things by writing what they do. The multiple identities they assumed during their careers – some were alternately diplomats, broadcasters, journalists and writers, some sometimes all at the same time – makes the exploration of the ebb and flow of ideas around these networks a complex yet ultimately rewarding exercise in terms of understanding how theories, ideas, and forms of language enter into mainstream political discourse and history books and how they become elevated to the status of conventional wisdom.

The revisionist and post-revisionist schools are also deeply imbued with politics: the politics of scholarship. It may come through more opaquely, and is as much implied as openly acknowledged in books and articles; but the academic

---

34 G. N. Izenberg, 'Text, Context, and Psychology in Intellectual History', in Kozicki (ed.), *Developments in Modern Historiography*, pp. 40–62 (p. 42).

literature on British European policy has been representative of a wider push towards bringing the study of contemporary British history in general and European integration history in particular to a bigger audience. The establishment of the University Association for Contemporary European Studies (UACES) in 1968 and the ICBH in 1986 are two examples of the multifarious ways in which the academic study of given history is a highly politicised process at all levels, revolving around the construction of formal and informal networks of contact.

UACES was set up, its newsletter of July 1968 said, to promote teaching and research in contemporary European studies across the disciplines of law, economics, politics and 'recent history'; to maintain and foster links between British universities and those in other countries 'as well as with such other bodies as may be thought fit'; to provide help towards the promotion of study in these fields; and to foster coordination of teaching and research. Its Annual General Meeting and Committee meetings, then held at Chatham House, brought together a number of university academics, including people who have written widely on Britain and Europe, notably Uwe Kitzinger and Roy Pryce, then at Oxford University and the Centre for Contemporary European Studies respectively. The minutes of the AGM held on 24 January 1969 record donations to the Association in the period from February 1968 to 21 January 1969 by, amongst others, the ECSC.[35]

The origins of the ICBH lay in the observation that epoch-changing post-war developments were being overlooked by history curricula at all levels of education in Britain, which only extended to the outbreak of the Second World War. Its founders were acutely aware of the need for greater attention to be given in Britain to the 'Europe' question, and they tapped into a plentiful supply of work that was already under way in this area. Many key names in the field have deep connections with the Institute, and although it is too simplistic to attribute the growth of interest in British European policy to the founding of institutions and organisations such as these (just as it is an oversimplification to put it down to the growth in the EEC's own momentum after the signing of the SEA) there was what Hennessy describes as a 'benign confluence' of developments in the middle of the 1980s that raised the profile of European integration history across the educational spectrum in Britain.[36]

The ways in which academics define their work in terms of earlier writing in the field, the methods they use, their sources and the formal and the informal networks of contact they build and within which they work are offshoots of the disciplinisation that has occurred in this area. So, where instant history is highly

---

35 I am grateful to Sue Jones for supplying me with copies of the minutes of the AGM and the first newsletter, number 0, July 1968. For details on its current activities see www.uaces.org.
36 Telephone interview with Hennessy, 12 May 2002.

politicised for obvious reasons, academic history is at least as political, if for different reasons: there are interests at stake, bandwagons of 'international academic fashion' to be launched and jumped on,[37] agendas to be pushed and personal goals to fulfil. Some or all of these can be achieved by writing academic history.

Situating historiography in its broader academic, social and cultural settings presents a strong argument for seeing the writing of history as an industry. Like an industry it has a real and a perceived market. These may or may not coincide but in the latter case enthusiasm for the product can be generated if it is marketed carefully enough. Like an industry, it has a competitive edge, with individuals and groups jostling to have their product marketed as the 'best', or, in history's case, the most authentic or credible product. And like an industry, it operates according to the rules of the market-place, with market forces to account to and all that entails in terms of publicity and the commercial dimension, both in terms of selling what is written and in attracting students to learn about it in places of further and higher education.

Policy-relevant history

The conclusions drawn from this study have so far been theoretical, concerning as they do the strengths and weaknesses of the historiographic method, the drivers of schools of writing and the nature and practice of contemporary political history; but there are two additional conclusions that emerge from this book. One should be of interest to political scientists, and is again theoretical, and the other to policy-makers, and so is of practical value.

The first concerns the role of language and discourse in constructing identities. Language plays a crucial role in how we perceive and react to events and people. Its importance is made all too clear by looking at the way in which historians rail against philosophers such as White who talk of their texts being 'fictions' or 'myths'. From the historians' perspective, these terms seem to imply that philosophers are denigrating their texts as fabrications or lies, when all that they are attempting to do is to access the truth. The term 'myth' as used by anthropologists such as Bronislaw Malinowski is not pejorative, and pertains to 'stories with social functions',[38] a definition that should act as a counter to some of the knee-jerk reactions about philosophy by historians.

For if one accepts the arguments set down in this book, writing history is an enterprise with deeply rooted social and political functions, whether the author be a politician, a journalist or an academic. 'In other words, the boundary between

---

37 Bayly, 'The Second British Empire', p. 68.
38 Burke, *History and Social Theory*, pp. 101–3.

fact and fiction, which once looked firm, has been eroded in our so-called
"post-modern" era. (Alternatively, it is only now that we see that the boundary
was always open.)'[39] Postmodern philosophy might not be telling historians
anything new about history. It does however tell historians things they do not
necessarily want to hear, and to make matters worse it does so more stridently.
More importantly, it equips us with a greater array of intellectual tools that we
can use to explore the foundations on which the discipline of history has been
constructed.

Other disciplines, such as political science, already have traditions of debating such issues and mechanisms in place to facilitate that process. Thomas
Christiansen, Knud Erik Jørgensen and Antje Wiener have written that 'the
constructivist project explicitly raises questions about social ontologies and social
institutions, directing research at the origin and reconstruction of identities, the
impact of rules and norms, the role of language and of political discourses'.[40]
They go on to argue that 'If the study of identity formation is accepted as a key
component of constructivist research, the role of language and of discourses
becomes crucial.'[41]

The goals of historiography and the constructivist project would therefore
seem to be mutually reinforcing, because historiography is an exercise in uncovering the constructed nature of historical texts and the ties, both linguistic and
social, that bind writers together in communities whose identities rest on shared
views about how the world works, on a common language and on networks of
power and influence, a point that feeds off Clifford Geertz's opinion that 'the
terms through which the devotees of a scholarly pursuit represent their aims,
judgements, justifications and so on, seems to me to take one a long way toward
grasping what that pursuit is all about'.[42] The overlap between constructivism and
historiography thus offers a good deal of scope for mutually beneficial exchanges
of ideas between historians and political scientists about the making of British
foreign policy and the construction of the 'European idea'.

This point was explored in Chapter 1, and does not need further elaboration
here. It is more useful to explore the fillip historiography gives to discourse analysis as a means of explaining political change. Missed opportunities discourse
and the mechanisms by which its message has been spread have been shown to
be integral in bonding together like-minded individuals in communities, creating
a shared sense of belonging and helping to define 'the other': those individuals
and states who did not share the enthusiasm for a supranational Europe after 1945.

---

39 *Ibid.*, p. 127.
40 Christiansen, Jørgensen and Wiener, 'Introduction' *The Social Construction of Europe*, p. 12.
41 *Ibid.*, p. 15.
42 Quoted in Becher and Trowler, *Academic Tribes and Territories*, p. 46.

The key words and phrases around which these groups of writers coalesce are not merely reflecting or mirroring an external reality: they are part of the process of creating that reality, a process to which Miriam Camps referred when she wrote that

> the line between what is actually happening today and what it is hoped will be happening tomorrow is frequently obscured by those people who have been most closely involved in the 'making of Europe'. This mixing of hopes with reality has been, in part, a deliberate tactic designed to generate the support that success, or complete confidence in success, attracts. In part it has also been the inevitable by-product of the enthusiasm and sense of commitment which has been shared by most of those who were concerned with the drafting of the Treaties of Paris and Rome.[43]

Reading between the lines of her statement, she is admitting not simply to writing *about* the European project, but that, through her writing, she has been a vociferous advocate *of* that project. The language games played out by politicians, diplomats and commentators are part of the bargaining and consensus-building that goes on among actors with different perceptions of what Europe is, different perceptions of what is in their immediate individual, group and national interests and different visions of how the EU should function and where the limits of its legislative competence should be.

To take another well-known example – Conservative Party policy towards Europe in the early 1990s – Rey Koslowski notes that 'the Major government insisted on keeping all references to federalism out of the Maastricht Treaty. Despite all the psychic rewards this victory in Treaty drafting may have brought to the British, it did not alter the reality of the new federal aspects of the polity that the Treaty constituted'.[44] Major's stance was shaped by the history of the Conservative Party's attitude towards European unity, which in turn was, and still is, bound up with how they construe Britain's past and define the country's identity with respect to 'Europe'. His policy demonstrated the routinised efforts by Britain to 'tone down' the supranational, Commission-led aspects of integration in favour of the intergovernmental approach, and was not merely a passive expression of 'scepticism', but was actively geared to changing the long-run course of the integration programme or, at the very least, keeping Britain out of the 'first rank' of integrators.

So words and speech-acts do seem to construct reality and shape policy in critical ways. Returning to the predicament Blair finds himself as he tries to persuade the British people of the merits of joining the single currency, raised in the Introduction, it is pertinent that he has employed the language of the

---

43 Camps, *What Kind of Europe?*, preface, p. 1.
44 Koslowski, 'Understanding European Union as a Federal Polity', p. 40.

federalists ('missed opportunities' and the 'illusions' that have detrimentally affected Anglo-European relations) to bolster his case. Nor is he the first Prime Minister to employ this lingo in an effort to convince the domestic and international audiences that Britain's future is with Europe. Nora Beloff quotes a speech Harold Wilson made to the European Parliament at Strasbourg in January in 1967 in the run-up to the second British application:

> History and the young generation will condemn beyond any power of ours to extend or excuse, the failure to seize what so many of us can clearly see now as a swirling, urgent tide in man's affairs. If we do fail, I want it to be understood, the fault will not be at Britain's door. But the cost, and above all the cost of missed opportunities, will fall, in an increasing measure, on everyone [*sic*] of us.[45]

Whether Blair can force this discourse to become, so to speak, the accepted currency among journalists, and therefore raise the profile of the contemporary events he uses to show the myopia of Britain's position is another matter, for it will be in competition with all the other terms that, for the British, have more resonance, 'federalism', 'sovereignty', 'Brussels bureaucracy', 'keep the pound', 'controlling our own affairs', 'not being run by Europe', 'superstate' and so forth. As Andrew Gamble and Gavin Kelly describe the problem facing the Prime Minister, 'Despite the very real integration which has taken place in the last 30 years, British public opinion seems no nearer to accepting the legitimacy of the semi-sovereignty game which the EU inaugurated.'[46]

In the political arena this has become a battle of words and phrases more than a substantive discussion of Britain's place in the world; when the latter issue does figure, it usually relies on equally ambiguous arguments about the threat 'Europe' poses to the Anglo-American 'special relationship'.[47] In the economic arena, naturally, the euro debate has a greater foothold in the financial costs and benefits of being part of a centrally-managed eurozone, mainly because of the Chancellor's insistence on Britain meeting the 'Five Tests' before Britain gets to vote on joining the single currency ('tests which demonstrate the central importance of economics to our decision'),[48] because of the ongoing debates about the viability of a single interest-rate for Europe and the problems the stability pact

---

45 N. Beloff, 'What Happened in Britain after the General said No', in P. Uri (ed.), *From Commonwealth to Common Market* (Harmondsworth, Penguin, 1968), pp. 51–88 (p. 73).

46 Gamble and Kelly, 'Britain and EMU', p. 107. See pp. 108–13 for analysis of the implications for the debate of the key terms 'Keep the Pound', 'Join the Euro' and 'Wait and See'.

47 For discussion of the haziness of the term 'special relationship' especially as it applies to relations between Britain and America with respect to Europe see O. J. Daddow, 'Britain, America and European Integration: Exposing the Cracks in the "Special Relationship"', in A. Alexandre-Collier (ed.), *La 'Relation Spéciale' Royaume-Uni/États-Unis: Entre Mythe et Réalité* (Nantes, Éditions du Temps, 2002), pp. 66–82.

48 Gordon Brown, speech to Labour Party conference in Blackpool, 30 September 2002. His speech is in full at www.labour.org.uk/gbconfspeech/.

causes and may cause in the future to members and aspirant members of the euro-zone. But it interlocks with political discourse about Europe, and Blair is severely constrained by the legacy of his predecessors' reluctance and/or inability to change discourses about 'Europe' in Britain, and he is proceeding cautiously on the assumption that 'To worship European unity publicly can be a dangerous proposition in the British debate.'[49] Perhaps for this reason 'Europhile' pronouncements by British Prime Ministers tend to be fairly sporadic.

Even allowing for the argument that there are severe problems in deter-mining who are the opinion-formers and who are the followers, the apparently unmitigated failure of orthodox writers' programme for changing British concep-tions of theirs and Europe's identity is striking. Like John Major at Maastricht, British leaders remain wedded to the concept of 'Europe à la carte', picking and choosing the bits they wish to be involved with and refusing to join as whole-heartedly as the enthusiasts have consistently urged since the 1950s.[50] Judged in terms of public discourse about Britain and Europe, the EU and the euro, it appears it will take more than isolated outbursts of 'Europeanism' to change deeply entrenched attitudes. The failure of 'missed opportunities' discourse to make anything but a marginal difference to the mainstream debates about Europe in British political culture is both a stark warning and grist to the mill of those same writers, who suggest that, 'Studying the remarkable similarity of identity-related statements by British party elites from the 1950s to the present, it seems as if the longer old ideas about political order remain unchallenged, the more room for manoeuvre narrows.'[51]

Why has mainstream British discourse about Europe been so consistently negative over time? Finding the answer could potentially take a book in itself, so the discussion here will be limited to five of the most obvious reasons why. First of all, there is the view that politicians have not wanted to debate the 'pro' side publicly and with the media, because they risk splitting their Cabinets and parties if they do. 'The adversarial system [of government] and the accountability of politicians to a partially informed electorate, together with the potentially emotive nature of the issue, militated against openness', says Tratt of the 1960s. Her words could reasonably be applied to any era.[52] That the issue of 'Europe' cuts across the party divide means that election results, Cabinet manoeuvrings and back-bench politics have shaped when Prime Ministers open the issue up for debate and when they seek to keep a lid on it. More often than not they err on the side of

---

49 Marcussen *et al.* 'Constructing Europe?, p. 116.
50 P. Catterall, 'Conclusion', in Daddow (ed.), *Harold Wilson and European Integration*, pp. 243–52 (p. 246).
51 Marcussen *et al*, 'Constructing Europe?' p. 117.
52 Tratt, *The Macmillan Government*, p. 195. See also p. 102.

caution, and even when they command a large parliamentary majority, leaders fear a slide in opinion poll ratings if they are bruised by an intra-party spat over Europe.

The second reason is that the issue of Europe has become associated with the question of leadership, so strongly that Prime Ministers have found it easier to make a decision not to decide 'until the time is right'. Macmillan's and Wilson's hesitant shifts towards the entry bids in 1961 and 1967 are testimony to the delicate balancing act involved, and even a zealot such as Heath made little attempt to sell the idea of 'political Europe' to the British people. Blair's Birmingham speech, while at the time considered a dramatic leap forward, might in time prove to be but a blip in the normal course of the debate about Europe in Britain. William Wallace's call in 1979 for 'a considerable effort of leadership' to be put into bringing home to the public 'the strength of the constraints under which British governments are now forced to operate, and the unreality of established myths of British independence' has not yet been heeded.[53]

The third reason for the persistence of eurosceptic discourse in British politics is the treatment of the Europe issue by Blair's predecessors. Liberal Democrat peer Shirley Williams, now Baroness Williams of Crosby, has pointed out that governments have usually attempted to manage the 'Europe question' by presenting it as an economic rather than a political issue, reflecting the view of most British politicians 'who saw the EEC very much as just that, a common market integrating for economic and trade purposes'. This tactic, she says, is evidence that political leaders strive to stifle wider and potentially more disruptive political debates about Britain's role in the world, its relations with the United States and bilaterally with its European neighbours. 'Perhaps Whitehall keeps tests and conditions on its mantelpiece, as cooks keep jelly moulds, there to be used for any purpose.'[54]

Quality of leadership is one thing, however, quality of the led quite another. The fourth reason why the propagandists for Europe have not made the impact on the public they might have liked is that, in the main, large sections of the British press perceive it to be in their interests to peddle the sceptic as opposed to the enthusiast line. We not only get the politicians we deserve, we deserve the media we read, it seems. The sceptic press hide behind the slogan that they reflect the public attitude, concentrating on what they see as an interfering 'Brussels bureaucracy' and an undemocratic policy-making process as reasons why Britain should save the pound. What the enthusiasts see as reasons to be in the EU to reform it – its democratic deficit, corruption, economic problems resulting from a single

---

53   Quoted in Dahrendorf, *On Britain*, p. 134.
54   Baroness Williams of Crosby, 'Foreword', in Daddow (ed.), *Harold Wilson and European Integration*, pp. 10–13 (p. 11).

interest rate and other economic problems of administering the eurozone – sceptics see not as a point of departure for a debate about the merits and weaknesses of the organisation, but, in extreme cases, as reasons to withdraw from it.

Clashing media and political agendas mean that governments have persistently had trouble in finding discursive modes of portraying 'Europe' in ways that strike a chord with a public steeped in imperial and military history. Despite the resonance of the missed opportunities interpretation to certain sections of the academic, policy-making and intellectual communities in Britain, the United States and western Europe, popular memory in Britain attaches greater significance to earlier periods and themes in history, with which they are usually more familiar through schooling, and which, apparently, require less of an effort to understand. The media reflect and reinforce this predilection for history as the history of great events and personalities.

Wars and conflicts are also easier to empathise with because of the visual dimension. The public consciousness is aroused by film and televisual portrayal of battles, for which there is a large volume of footage. They have also given rise to large amounts of witness history, and they have a human dimension expressed most clearly in the form of war poetry, which has been widely studied in British schools. The reporting of British European policy is thus burdened with the easy assumption that Britain is a 'sceptic' nation and that good Prime Ministers will reflect that in their unfortunate but necessary dealings with 'Brussels'. Interviewers and reporters let politicians get away with such glib generalisations because they also want to get away with making them.

A fifth reason why missed opportunities discourse has had so little impact is that it runs counter to Britain's national culture of seeing the country as a great global actor, rather than a regional power, a perception successive Prime Ministers have done little to alter in their speeches, if not their policies. For if one believes the revisionist interpretation of the history, then all Prime Ministers have on the surface been hesitant about Europe, yet pursued, or been compelled to pursue, to a considerable degree, integrationist policies that belie their rhetoric. Attlee's so-called socialist Labour government was both highly imperialist and committed to pursuing formal means of integration with France and the other Brussels Treaty signatories while it could; Wilson and Macmillan both applied to take Britain into the European Economic Community; Thatcher signed the Single European Act. The major disappointment from the Europeanist perspective was Churchill's prevarication over the question of unity in 1951–55. What this suggests is a break between what Prime Ministers say they are doing and what they actually do in terms of British foreign policy. If it is done intentionally then it is a cunningly devised policy; if it is unintentional, or forced on them by the Foreign Office, then it is less so, and takes us back to questions about leadership. With important changes now under way in the teaching of contemporary history in schools, it will be interesting to see the extent to which attitudes to Europe change, or not, over the coming decades.

So there is another, academic side to the story of Britain and Europe; but the revisionist historians' interpretation that British politicians have in practice been more involved with the plans for continental unity than they let on (and that they regularly belie with their actions what they say in public) has not until now been a common feature of the debate about the European question, and this hints at a reluctance by academic historians to make their findings relevant to policy-makers and the media. The reason would seem to be deeply rooted within the discipline: 'Historians commonly prefer to avoid relating their scholarly concerns to contemporary affairs, on the grounds that generalization from one situation to another is highly suspect.'[55] Still, this is startling at a time when the idea of 'knowledge for its own sake' has come under fire from governments in both the United States and Britain, and when 'there has been an increasing emphasis in government policy and rhetoric on the vocational functions of HE [Higher Education], in terms both of its role in supplying qualified students for the professions, industry and commerce, and in terms of its research function.' If the media and politicians are to be criticised for ignoring the past, some blame for that must go to historians who fail to bring their work to a wider audience than other historians. History, it might therefore be argued, is too important to be the preserve of academics alone.

In an endeavour to fill the void on this subject between academics and practitioners, one might highlight two reasons why the enthusiasts can take heart from the history books on this subject. The first is that when they have taken a lead, Prime Ministers have been remarkably successful in manipulating public opinion to their advantage; the second is that public opinion on Europe tends to fluctuate with the popularity of the Prime Minister of the day. Anne Deighton notes that both trends were evident in Harold Wilson's conduct of the second application in the 1960s.[56] In the 1975 referendum, Wilson managed to persuade over 67 per cent of the population to vote for Britain's remaining in the Community. It is problematic to draw the simple conclusion that a Prime Minister such as Blair, with a huge majority in the House of Commons and advanced techniques for managing the media, would easily be able to sway a referendum on the euro in the present climate; but such an outcome cannot be discounted. New Labour has a clear manifesto commitment to taking Britain closer to the EU, and joining the euro is part of that strategy. Surely if the public felt so strongly about this issue they would not have given such a ringing endorsement to Blair at the last election, when the

---

55 Becher and Trowler, *Academic Tribes and Territories*, p. 162.
56 A. Deighton, 'The Labour Party, Public Opinion and "the Second Try"', in Daddow (ed.), *Harold Wilson and European Integration*, pp. 39–55.

Conservative Party under William Hague did its best to make it seem like the 'last chance to save the pound'.

Future research

'Models in historiography, as well as in science, provide more than a mere heuristic for investigation. They focus attention, exclude possibilities, and reveal hidden connections.'[57] Viewing history as an industry is not to downplay the intellectual contribution made by its architects. Rather, it is an effort to open up the discipline to rigorous analysis as a means of enhancing our understanding of what scholars do, the knowledge communities to which they belong and the potential academic history has to assume greater numbers of social and political functions. It is in this spirit that I end the book by identifying two areas for further research into critical historiography that will either provide evidence in support of, or challenge, what has been said in this book about the historiography of British European policy. (It goes without saying that discourse analysis of political rhetoric about European integration is a source of further research, but I will limit my agenda to the historiographical rather than the political science arena.) One of the reasons for writing this book, after all, was to prompt a period of interrogation into contemporary history and historiography, and its discursive nature naturally leaves gaps and questions open for further debate.

Looking vertically first, into the workings of the model of historiographical progression developed above, there is more to be done in terms of explaining the origins and development of the schools of writing on British European policy. Becher and Trowler have observed that research into the social relationships in academic life has largely been carried out in the domain of the natural sciences; the door is open for analysis of historical knowledge production.[58] While a start has been made, it will be important to analyse greater numbers of non-English histories of European integration. Analysis of a wider range of literature, particularly that by continental politicians and scholars, would considerably deepen our understanding of the belief systems that exist, and have existed, about British European policy, and how these have shaped perceptions of Britain's role in Europe and the wider world. Lack of time and linguistic skills have hampered this author from attempting an in-depth study of these works, but there will be a lot to learn from them.

In terms of how the schools operate as vehicles for generating, validating and expressing belief systems about the past, a good deal more work needs be done on the networks of power and influence that have guided the historiography

---

57 Richards, 'Theories of Scientific Change', p. 209.
58 Becher and Trowler, *Academic Tribes and Territories*, pp. 90–5.

down the routes it has taken. In the academic field, there is more to be done on the overlapping social circles and social networks through which historical knowledge is produced and valorised, demanding attention to the formal and informal 'organisational infrastructure through which historical understanding is advanced and disseminated'.[59] Research into the origins and development of the various formal networks such as UACES and the ICBH (the outward expressions of the steady disciplinisation of contemporary British and European history) will give a clearer picture of the political drivers behind the production of contemporary British history.

Important insights might also be extracted from analysis of the workings of the key bodies that fund historical research in Britain, most obviously the British Academy, the Arts and Humanities Research Board (AHRB), the Leverhulme Trust and other charitable foundations. 'The criteria on which such decisions [about which applications for funding to accept and which to reject] and the advice on which they are based are ... of the utmost importance and amount to another set of tramlines (possibly the most important of all) along which the direction of historiographical development has to run.'[60] One provisional argument about these bodies to be put to the test is that which says that they are innately conservative, prolonging accepted historiographical practice and/or interpretations at the expense of radical or innovative methodologies that might take historiography down critical self-reflective avenues. This unspoken policy determines what gets funded, and so, of course, what applications are made in the first place, a self-filtering mechanism that discourages innovation from the outset by deterring potential applicants with new or radical methodologies from applying.

For the orthodox school, more attention could be paid to the political and social networks which have been put in place to generate support for the missed opportunities interpretation of British European policy. For the revisionist and post-revisionist schools the culture of academia and the production of historiography by the academics are in need of further investigation. Even admitting that individual agents can dramatically affect the structures within which they operate cannot detract from the argument that the writing of history is regulated at all sorts of levels, with governments, academic departments, universities, funding bodies and charities all forming the infrastructure that determines who gets admitted to the discipline, what gets studied and the methods employed to recover the past. The study of the simultaneous processes of socialisation and enculturation that are all part of becoming a historian provides fertile ground on which to consider the nature of historical knowledge and its relationship to other forms of knowledge production.

---

59 Thompson, *What Happened to History?*, p. 92.
60 *Ibid.*, p. 92.

Looking horizontally, across critical historiography as a field of inquiry, there is much research to be undertaken into the evolution of historiography, not just in other areas of contemporary history, but within the wider discipline of history and, on a comparative basis, within neighbouring disciplines. Such a project would help provide an answer to the pressing question: is this a special case, or is it indicative of historiographical trends in other fields? Judging by other critical historiographic work being undertaken at the moment, such as that on the writing on appeasement in the build-up to the Second World War, it is strongly suspected that this is not unique in terms of how knowledge grows across time.[61] Such works will also furnish us with the intellectual equipment for discussing newly popular themes such as: what is 'philosophy of history' as opposed to 'theory of history'?[62] How can postmodern concerns about the narration of the past be included in the historiographical enterprise itself? And, finally, what methodological prescriptions fall out of the application of postmodern philosophy to historical texts? Such questions demand answers that will, hopefully, involve historians and philosophers working together in collaborative enterprises. This book, in the meantime, is a reminder that politics has a history, history has a history and historians too have a history. If indeed there is 'a definable world of historians',[63] it would be fruitful for historians to begin defining it, and in this exercise critical historiography will play an important role.

---

61 For instance Finney, 'What Historians Actually Do'.
62 Notably H. Jansen, *The Construction of an Urban Past: Narrative and System in Urban History*, trans. Feike de Jong (Oxford and New York, Berg, 2001), especially pp. 3–13.
63 The words of an anonymous historian recorded in Becher and Trowler, *Academic Tribes and Territories*, p. 44.

Bibliography

Books and articles

Adamthwaite, Anthony, 'Britain and the World, 1945–9: The View from the Foreign Office', *International Affairs*, 61:2 (1985), 223–35

Adamthwaite, Anthony, 'Introduction: The Foreign Office and Policy–Making', in Young (ed.), *The Foreign Policy of Churchill's Peacetime Administration*, pp. 1–28

Adamthwaite, Anthony, 'John Bull v. Marianne, Round Two: Anglo-French Relations and Britain's Second EEC Membership Bid', in Daddow (ed.), *Harold Wilson and European Integration*, pp. 151–71

Aldrich, Richard J. (ed.), *British Intelligence Strategy and the Cold War 1945–51* (London, Routledge, 1992)

Aldrich, Richard J., 'European Integration: An American Intelligence Connection', in Deighton (ed.), *Building Post-War Europe*, pp. 159–79

Aldrich, Richard J., *The Hidden Hand: Britain, America and Cold War Secret Intelligence* (London, John Murray, 2001)

Alexandre-Collier, Agnès, *La Grande-Bretagne Eurosceptique? L'enjeu Européen dans le Débat Politique Britannique* (Nantes, Editions du Temps, 2002)

Allen, David, 'Britain and Western Europe', in Smith, Smith and White (eds), *British Foreign Policy*, pp. 168–92

Ambrose, Stephen E., *Rise to Globalism: American Foreign Policy 1938–1970* (Harmondsworth, Penguin, 1973)

Anderson, Terry H., *The United States, Great Britain, and the Cold War 1944–1947* (Columbia, University of Missouri Press, 1981)

Ankersmit, Frank, 'Historiography and Postmodernism', *History and Theory*, 28:2 (1989), 137–53

Appleby, Joyce, Lynn Hunt and Margaret Jacob, *Telling the Truth about History* (London, W. W. Norton, 1994)

Aron, Raymond, 'The Historical Sketch of the Great Debate', in Lerner and Aron (eds), *France Defeats EDC*, pp. 2–21

A Sense of Permanence? Essays on the Art of Cartoon (Canterbury, The Centre for the Study of Cartoons and Caricature, 1997)

Baker, David and David Seawright, *Britain For and Against Europe: British Politics and the Question of European Integration* (Oxford, Clarendon Press, 1998)

Barber, James, *Who Makes British Foreign Policy?* (Milton Keynes, The Open University Press, 1976)

Barker, Elisabeth, *Britain in a Divided Europe 1945–1970* (London, Weidenfeld and Nicolson, 1971)

Barker, Elisabeth, *The British Between the Superpowers 1945–50* (London, Macmillan, 1983)

Barker, Elisabeth, *The Common Market* (London, Wayland Publishers, 1973)

Barnes, John, 'From Eden to Macmillan, 1955–59', in Hennessy and Seldon (eds), *Ruling Performance*, pp. 98–149

Barnett, Corelli, *The Audit of War: The Illusion and Reality of Britain as a Great Nation* (London, Papermac, 1987)

Barnett, Corelli, *The Lost Victory: British Dreams, British Realities 1945–1950* (Basingstoke, Macmillan, 1995)

Baylis, John, 'Britain and the Dunkirk Treaty: The Origins of NATO', *Journal of Strategic Studies*, 5:2 (1982), 236–47

Baylis, John, 'Britain, the Brussels Pact and the Continental Commitment', *International Affairs*, 60:4 (1984), 615–29

Baylis, John, *The Diplomacy of Pragmatism: Britain and the Formation of NATO, 1942–49* (Basingstoke, Macmillan, 1993)

Baylis, John (ed.), *Anglo-American Relations since 1939: The Enduring Alliance* (Manchester, Manchester University Press, 1997)

Baylis, John and Steve Smith (eds), *The Globalisation of World Politics: An Introduction to International Relations* (Oxford, Oxford University Press, 1997)

Bayly, C. A., 'The Second British Empire', in Winks (ed.), *Historiography*, pp. 54–72

Becher, Terry and Paul R. Trowler, *Academic Tribes and Territories*, 2nd edn (Buckingham, The Society for Research into Higher Education and Open University Press, 2001)

Beetham, Roger (ed.), *The Euro Debate: Persuading the People* (London, The Federal Trust for Education and Research, 2001)

Beloff, Lord, *Britain and European Union: Dialogue of the Deaf* (Basingstoke, Macmillan, 1996)

Beloff, Max, *An Historian in the Twentieth Century: Chapters in Intellectual Autobiography* (London, Yale University Press, 1992)

Beloff, Max, *New Dimensions in Foreign Policy: A Study in British Administrative Experience 1947–59* (London, George Allen and Unwin, 1961)

Beloff, Max, *The United States and the Unity of Europe* (London: Faber and Faber, 1963)

Beloff, Nora, *The General Says No: Britain's Exclusion from Europe* (Harmondsworth, Penguin, 1963)

Beloff, Nora, 'What Happened in Britain after the General said No', in Uri (ed.), *From Commonwealth to Common Market*, pp. 51–88

Bentley, Michael, *Modern Historiography: An Introduction* (London, Routledge, 1999)

Bernstein, Barton J. and Allen J. Matusow, *The Truman Administration: A Documentary History* (New York, Harper and Row, 1968)

Blair, Alasdair, *The Longman Companion to the European Union since 1945* (London, Pearson Education, 1999)

Blondel, Jean, *The Government of France*, 2nd edn (London, Methuen, 1974)

Böhmer, Katharina, 'Germany and the Second British Application', in Daddow (ed.), *Harold Wilson and European Integration*, pp. 211–26

Bond, Martyn, Julie Smith and William Wallace (eds), *Eminent Europeans: Personalities Who Shaped Contemporary Europe* (London, The Greycoat Press, 1996)

Brandt, Willy, 'The Division of Europe', in Rodgers (ed.), *Hugh Gaitskell*, pp. 133–9

Brinkley, Douglas (ed.), *Dean Acheson and the Making of U.S. Foreign Policy* (Basingstoke, Macmillan, 1993)

Brinkley, Douglas and Clifford Hackett (eds), *Jean Monnet: The Path to European Unity* (Basingstoke, Macmillan, 1991)

Brivati, Brian, 'Cd-Rom and the Historian: Information Technology and the Writing of History', in Brivati, Buxton and Seldon (eds), *The Contemporary History Handbook*, pp. 471–8

Brivati, Brian and Harriet Jones (eds), *From Reconstruction to Integration: Britain and Europe since 1945* (Leicester, Leicester University Press, 1993)

Brivati, Brian, Julia Buxton and Anthony Seldon (eds), *The Contemporary History Handbook* (Manchester, Manchester University Press, 1996)

Broad, Roger and Virginia Preston (eds), *Moored to the Continent? Britain and European Integration* (London, Institute of Historical Research, 2001)

Brooke, Stephen (ed.), *Reform and Reconstruction: Britain After the War, 1945–51* (Manchester, Manchester University Press, 1995)

Bullock, Alan and Oliver Stallybrass (eds), *The Fontana Dictionary of Modern Thought* (London, Collins, 1977)

Bulmer, Simon, Stephen George and Andrew Scott (eds), *The UK and EC Membership Evaluated* (London, Pinter, 1992)

Burgess, Michael, *Federalism and European Union: Political Ideas, Influences and Strategies in the European Community, 1972–1987* (London, Routledge, 1982)

Burgess, Simon and Geoffrey Edwards, 'The Six Plus One: British Policy–Making and the Question of European Economic Integration, 1955', *International Affairs*, 64:3 (1988), 393–413

Burke, Peter, (ed.), *New Perspectives on Historical Writing*, (Cambridge, Polity Press, 1991)

Burke, Peter, *History and Social Theory* (Cambridge, Polity Press, 2001)

Cable, Sir James, 'Foreign Policy Making: Planning or Reflex?', *Diplomacy and Statecraft*, 3:3 (1992), 357–81

Cairncross, Alec and Barry Eichengreen, *Sterling in Decline: The Devaluations of 1931, 1949 and 1967* (Oxford, Basil Blackwell, 1983)

Callinicos, Alex, *Theories and Narratives: Reflections on the Philosophy of History* (Cambridge, Polity Press, 1995)

Campbell, David, 'Contra Wight: The Errors of Premature Writing', *Review of International Studies*, 25:2 (1999), 317–21

Camps, Miriam, *Britain and the European Community 1955–1963* (London, Oxford University Press, 1964)

Camps, Miriam, *European Unification in the Sixties: From the Veto to the Crisis* (London, Oxford University Press, 1967)

Camps, Miriam, 'Missing the Boat at Messina and Other Times?', in Brivati and Jones (eds), *From Reconstruction to Integration*, pp. 133–43

Camps, Miriam, *What Kind of Europe? The Community since De Gaulle's Veto* (London, Oxford University Press, 1965)

Carr, E. H., *What is History?* (Harmondsworth, Penguin, 1990)

Catterall, Peter, 'Conclusion', in Daddow (ed.), *Harold Wilson and European Integration*, pp. 243–52

Challener, Richard D., 'The Moralist as Pragmatist: John Foster Dulles as Cold War Strategist', in Craig and Loewenheim (eds), *The Diplomats*, pp. 135–66

Charlton, Michael, 'How and Why Britain Lost the Leadership of Europe (1): "Messina! Messina!" or, the Parting of Ways', *Encounter*, 57:3 (August 1981), 8–22

Charlton, Michael, 'How (and Why) Britain Lost the Leadership of Europe (2): A Last Step Sideways', *Encounter*, 57:3 (September 1981), 22–35

Charlton, Michael, 'How (and Why) Britain Lost the Leadership of Europe (3): The Channel Crossing', *Encounter*, 57:3 (October 1981), 22–33

Charlton, Michael, *The Price of Victory* (London, British Broadcasting Corporation, 1983)

Charmley, John, *Churchill's Grand Alliance: The Anglo-American Special Relationship 1940–57* (London, Hodder and Stoughton, 1995)

Chatham House, *Britain in Western Europe: WEU and the Atlantic Alliance* (London and New York, Royal Institute of International Affairs, 1955)

Checkel, Jeffrey T., 'Social Construction and European Integration', in Christiansen, Jørgensen and Wiener (eds), *The Social Construction of Europe*, pp. 50–64

Christiansen, Thomas, Knud Erik Jørgensen and Antje Wiener (eds), *The Social Construction of Europe* (London, Sage, 2001)

Clarke, Michael, 'The Policy-Making Process', in Smith, Smith and White (eds), *British Foreign Policy*, pp. 71–95

Coles, John, *The Making of Foreign Policy: A Certain Idea of Britain* (London, John Murray, 2000)

Collingwood, R. G., *The Idea of History* (Oxford, Oxford University Press, 1961)

Collini, Stefan, *English Pasts: Essays in History and Culture* (Oxford, Oxford University Press, 1999)

Combs, Jerald A. 'Review Essay: Norman Graebner and the Realist View of American Diplomatic History', *Diplomatic History*, 11:3 (1987), 251–64

Cook, Chris, *A Dictionary of Historical Terms*, 3rd edn (Basingstoke, Macmillan, 1998)

Craig, Gordon A. and Frances L. Loewenheim (eds), *The Diplomats 1939–1979* (Princeton, NJ, Princeton University Press, 1994)

Croft, Pauline 'Political Biography: A Defence (1)', *Contemporary British History*, 10:4 (1996), 67–74

Croft, Stuart, 'British Policy Towards Western Europe: The Best of Possible Worlds?', *International Affairs*, 64:4 (1988), 617–29

Cromwell, William C., *The United States and the European Pillar* (Basingstoke, Macmillan, 1992)

Curry, W. B., *The Case for Federal Union* (Harmondsworth, Penguin, 1939)

Daddow, Oliver J., 'Britain, America and European Integration: Exposing the Cracks in the "Special Relationship"', in Alexandre-Collier (ed.), La 'Relation Spéciale' Royaume-Uni/États-Unis: Entre Mythe et Réalité (Nantes, Éditions du Temps, 2002), pp. 66–82

Daddow, Oliver J., 'Does a Change of Foreign Secretary Make a Difference?', British Foreign Policy Network newsletter, http://foreign-policy.dsd.kcl.ac.uk/daddow.htm

Daddow, Oliver J. (ed.), *Harold Wilson and European Integration: Britain's Second Application to Join the EEC* (London, Frank Cass, 2003)

Daddow, Oliver J., 'Introduction: The Historiography of Harold Wilson's Attempt to Take Britain into the EEC', in Daddow (ed.), *Harold Wilson and European Integration*, pp. 1–36

Dahrendorf, Ralf *On Britain* (London, British Broadcasting Corporation, 1982)

Danaher, Geoff, Tony Schirato and Jenn Webb, *Understanding Foucault* (London, Sage, 2000)

de Carmoy, Guy, 'Defence and Unity of Western Europe since 1958', in Waites (ed.), *Troubled Neighbours*, pp. 344–74

Dedman, Martin J., *The Origins and Development of the European Union 1945–95: A History of European Integration* (London, Routledge, 1996)

Deighton, Anne, 'British–West German Relations, 1945–1972', in Larres (ed.), *Uneasy Allies*, pp. 27–44

Deighton, Anne (ed.), *Building Post-War Europe: National Decision-Makers and European Institutions*, 1948–63 (Basingstoke, Macmillan, 1995)

Deighton, Anne, 'Missing the Boat: Britain and Europe 1945–61', *Contemporary Record*, 4:1 (1990), 15–17

Deighton, Anne, 'Say it with Documents: British Policy Overseas 1945–1952', *Review of International Studies*, 18:4 (1992), 393–4

Deighton, Anne, 'The Cold War in Europe, 1945–1947: Three Approaches', in Woods (ed.), *Explaining International Relations*, pp. 81–97

Deighton, Anne, 'The Labour Party, Public Opinion and "the Second Try"', in Daddow (ed.), *Harold Wilson and European Integration*, pp. 39–55

Dell, Edmund, *The Schuman Plan and the British Abdication of Leadership in Europe* (Oxford, Oxford University Press, 1995)

Denman, Roy, 'Joining the Euro', in Beetham (ed.), *The Euro Debate*, pp. 79–86

Denman, Roy, *Missed Chances: Britain and Europe in the Twentieth Century* (London, Cassell, 1996)

Diebold, William, 'Foreign Economic Policy in Acheson's Time and Ours', in Brinkley (ed.), *Dean Acheson*, pp. 233–55

Diez, Thomas, 'Speaking "Europe": The Politics of Integration Discourse', in Christiansen, Jørgensen and Wiener (eds), *The Social Construction of Europe*, pp. 85–100

Dockrill, Michael and John W. Young (eds), *British Foreign Policy, 1945–56* (Basingstoke, Macmillan, 1989)

Dockrill, Saki, *Britain's Retreat from East of Suez: The Choice between Europe and the Wider World?* (Basingstoke, PalgraveMacmillan, 2002)

Dougherty, James E. and Robert L. Pfaltzgraff, *Decision Making Theories: Contending Theories on International Relations* (New York, Harper and Row, 1990)

Duchêne, François, 'Jean Monnet – Pragmatic Visionary', in Bond, Smith and Wallace (eds), *Eminent Europeans: Personalities Who Shaped Contemporary Europe* (London, The Greycoat Press, 1996), pp. 45–61

Dulles, Allen, *The Craft of Intelligence* (London, Weidenfeld and Nicolson, 1964)

Dulles, Eleanor L., *American Foreign Policy in the Making* (New York, Harper and Row, 1968)

Dunne, Tim, *Inventing International Society: A History of the English School* (Basingstoke, Macmillan, 1998)

du Réau, Elisabeth (ed.), *Europe des Élites? Europe des Peuples? La Construction de L'éspace Européen 1945–1960* (Paris, Presses de la Sorbonne Nouvelle, 1999)

Dyson, Kenneth (ed.), *European States and the Euro: Europeanization, Variation and Convergence* (Oxford, Oxford University Press, 2002)

Edmonds, Robin, *Setting the Mould: The United States and Britain, 1945–1950* (Oxford, Oxford University Press, 1986)

Edwards, Ruth Dudley, *The Pursuit of Reason: The Economist 1843–1993* (London, Hamish Hamilton, 1993)

Ellison, James, 'Dealing with de Gaulle: Anglo-American Relations, NATO and the Second Application', in Daddow (ed.), *Harold Wilson and European Integration*, pp. 172–87

Ellison, James R. V., 'Perfidious Albion?: Britain, Plan G and European Integration, 1955–1956', *Contemporary British History*, 10:4 (1996), 1–34

Ellison, James, *Threatening Europe: Britain and the Creation of the European Community 1955–58* (Basingstoke, Macmillan, 2000)

Elman, Colin and Miriam Fendius Elman, 'Diplomatic History and International Relations Theory: Respecting Differences and Crossing Boundaries', *International Security*, 22:1 (1997), 5–21

Elms, Alan S., *Uncovering Lives: The Uneasy Alliance of Biography and Psychology* (Oxford, Oxford University Press, 1994)

Elton, Geoffrey, *Return to Essentials* (Cambridge, Cambridge University Press, 1991)

Elton, Geoffrey, *The Practice of History* (London, Methuen, 1967)

Epp, Roger, 'The English School on the Frontiers of International Relations', *Review of International Studies*, 24:1 (1998), 47–63

Epstein, Leon D., *Britain: Uneasy Ally* (Chicago, The University of Chicago Press, 1954)

Evans, Richard J., *In Defence of History* (London, Granta, 1997)

Evans, Richard J., *Telling Lies About Hitler: The Holocaust, Hitler and the David Irving Trial* (London, Verso, 2002)

Finney, Patrick, 'International History, Theory and the Origins of the Second World War', *Rethinking History*, 1:3 (1997), 357–79

Finney, Patrick, 'Still "Marking Time"? Text, Discourse and Truth in International History', *Review of International Studies*, 27:2 (2001), 291–308

Fontaine, Pascal *A New Idea for Europe: The Schuman Declaration – 1950–2000* (Luxembourg, Office for Official Publications of the European Communities, 2000)

Foot, Michael, 'Introduction', in *Vicky's Supermac*, pp. 11–18

Forster, Anthony, *Euroscepticism in British Politics: Opposition to Europe in the Conservative and Labour Parties since 1945* (London, Routledge, 2002)

Forster, Anthony, 'No Entry: Britain and the EEC in the 1960s', *Contemporary British History*, 12:2 (1998), 139–46

Forster, Anthony and Alasdair Blair, *The Making of Britain's European Foreign Policy* (London, Pearson, 2002)

Foster, Stephen, 'British North America in the Seventeenth and Eighteenth Centuries', in Winks (ed.), *Historiography*, pp. 73–92

Frankel, Joseph, *British Foreign Policy 1945–1973* (London, Oxford University Press, 1975)

Frankel, Joseph, *The Making of Foreign Policy: An Analysis of Decision Making* (Oxford, Oxford University Press, 1968)

Frazier, Robert, 'Did Britain Start the Cold War?: Bevin and the Truman Doctrine', *Historical Journal*, 27:3 (1984), 715–27

Friedlander, Saul, *History and Psychoanalysis: An Inquiry into the Possibilities and Limits of Psychohistory*, trans. S. Suleiman (New York, Holmes and Meier, 1975)

Fursdon, Edward, *The European Defence Community: A History* (London, Macmillan, 1980)

Gaddis, John Lewis, 'Corporatism: A Skeptical View', *Diplomatic History*, 10:4 (1986), 356–62

Gaddis, John Lewis, *Now We Know: Rethinking Cold War History* (Oxford, Oxford University Press, 1998)

Gaddis, John Lewis, 'The Emerging Post-Revisionist Synthesis on the Origins of the Cold War', *Diplomatic History*, 7:3 (1983), 171–90

Gaddis, John Lewis, 'The United States and the Question of a Sphere of Influence in Europe, 1945–1949', in Riste (ed.), *Western Security*, pp. 60–91

Gamble, Andrew and Gavin Kelly, 'Britain and EMU', in Dyson (ed.), *European States and the Euro*, pp. 97–119

Gardner, Lawrence C., Lawrence S. Kaplan, Warren F. Kimball, and Bruce R. Kuniholm, 'Responses to John Lewis Gaddis', *Diplomatic History*, 7:3 (1983), 191–204

George, Stephen, *Politics and Policy in the European Community*, 2nd edn (Oxford, Oxford University Press, 1991)

George, Stephen, *An Awkward Partner: Britain in the European Community*, 2nd edn (New York, Oxford University Press, 1994)

Gilmour, Ian and Mark Garnett, *Whatever Happened to the Tories: The Conservative Party since 1945* (London, Fourth Estate, 1997)

Ginsborg, Paul, *A History of Contemporary Italy: Society and Politics 1943–1988* (London, Penguin, 1990)

Gowing, Margaret, 'Nuclear Weapons and the "Special Relationship"', in Louis and Bull (eds.), *The Special Relationship*, pp. 117–28

Gowland, David and Arthur Turner, *Reluctant Europeans: Britain and European Integration, 1945–1998* (London, Pearson, 2000)

Gramer, Regina U., 'On Poststructuralisms, Revisionisms, and Cold Wars', *Diplomatic History*, 19:3 (1995), 515–24

Greenwood, Sean, *Britain and European Cooperation since 1945* (Oxford, Blackwell, 1992)

Greenwood Sean (ed.), *Britain and European Integration since the Second World War* (Manchester, Manchester University Press, 1996)

Griffiths, Richard T. and Stuart Ward (eds), *Courting the Common Market: The First Attempt to Enlarge the European Community 1961–1963* (London, Lothian Foundation Press, 1996)

Griffiths, Richard T. and Stuart Ward, '"The End of a Thousand Years of History": The Origins of Britain's Decision to Join the European Community, 1955–61', in Griffiths and Ward (eds), *Courting the Common Market*, pp. 7–37

Grigg, John, 'Policies of Impotence', *International Affairs*, 48:1 (1972), 72–6

Haas, Ernst B., 'Does Constructivism Subsume Neo-Functionalism?', in Christiansen, Jørgensen and Wiener (eds), *The Social Construction of Europe*, pp. 22–31

Haines, Gerald K. and J. Samuel Walker (eds), *American Foreign Relations: A Historiographical Review* (London, Francis Pinter, 1981)

Hamilton, Ian, *Keepers of the Flame: Literary Estates and the Rise of Biography* (London, Pimlico, 1992)

Hamilton, Nigel, 'The Role of Biography', in Seldon (ed.), *Contemporary History*, pp. 165–9

Hamilton, Nigel, 'In Defence of the Practice of Biography', *Contemporary British History*, 10:4 (1996), 81–6

Harper, John L., 'In Their Own Image – The Americans and the Question of European Unity, 1943–54', in Bond, Smith and Wallace (eds), *Eminent Europeans*, pp. 62–84

Hathaway, Robert M., *Ambiguous Partnership: Britain and America, 1944–1947* (New York, Columbia University Press, 1981

Hennessy, Peter, 'The Attlee Governments, 1945–1951', in Hennessy and Seldon (eds), *Ruling Performance*, pp. 28–62

Hennessy, Peter, 'The Press and Broadcasting', in Seldon (ed.), *Contemporary History*, pp. 17–29

Hennessy, Peter, 'Witness Seminar: 1949 Devaluation', *Contemporary Record*, 5:3 (1991), 483–506

Hennessy, Peter and Anthony Seldon (eds), Ruling Performance: British Governments from Attlee to Thatcher (Oxford, Basil Blackwell, 1987)

Heuser, Beatrice and Robert O'Neill (eds), *Securing Peace in Europe, 1945–62: Thoughts for the Post Cold War Era* (Basingstoke, Macmillan, 1989)

Hill, Christopher, Academic International Relations: The Siren Song of Policy Relevance', in Hill and Beshoff (eds), *Two Worlds of International Relations*, pp. 3–25

Hill, Christopher, 'The Historical Background: Past and Present in British Foreign Policy', in Smith, Smith and White (eds), *British Foreign Policy*, pp. 24–49

Hill, Christopher and Pamela Beshoff (eds), *Two Worlds of International Relations: Academics, Practitioners and the Trade in Ideas* (London, Routledge, 1994)

Hine, David, Governing Italy: *The Politics of Bargained Pluralism* (Oxford, Oxford University Press, 1993)

'History and Theory', editorial, *History Workshop*, 6 (1978), 1–6

Hitchcock, William I., 'France, the Western Alliance and the Origins of the Schuman Plan, 1948–1950', Diplomatic History, 21:4 (1997), 603–30

Hoffman, Elizabeth Cobbs, 'Diplomatic History and the Meaning of Life: Towards a Global American History', *Diplomatic History*, 21:4 (1997), 499–518

Hogan, Michael J., *A Cross of Iron: Harry S. Truman and the Origins of the National Security State, 1945–1954* (Cambridge, Cambridge University Press, 1998)

Hogan, Michael J., 'Corporatism: A Positive Appraisal', *Diplomatic History*, 10:4 (1986), 363–72

Hogan, Michael J., *The Marshall Plan: America, Britain and the Reconstruction of Western Europe, 1947–1952* (Cambridge, Cambridge University Press, 1987)

Hogan, Michael J., 'The Rise and Fall of Economic Diplomacy: Dean Acheson and the Marshall Plan', in Brinkley (ed.), *Dean Acheson*, pp. 1–27

Holland, Robert, *The Pursuit of Greatness: Britain and the World Role, 1900–1970* (London, Fontana, 1991),

Hollis, Martin and Steve Smith, *Explaining and Understanding International Relations* (Oxford, Clarendon Press, 1991)

Holmes, Martin (ed.), *The Eurosceptical Reader* (Basingstoke, Macmillan, 1996)

Holub, Robert, *Reception Theory: A Critical Introduction* (London, Methuen, 1984)

Howard, Anthony, 'Introduction', in *Twenty Years of Cartoons by Garland*

Howard, Michael, 'Introduction', in Riste (ed.), *Western Security*, pp. 11–12

Howarth, David, 'Discourse Theory', in Marsh and Stoker (eds), *Theory and Methods in Political Science* (Basingstoke, Macmillan, 1995), pp. 115–33

Huntington, Samuel P., *The Soldier and the State: The Theory and Politics of Civil-Military Relations* (London, The Belknap Press of Harvard University Press, 1998)

Iggers, Georg G., *Historiography in the Twentieth Century: From Scientific Objectivity to the Postmodern Challenge* (Hanover, NH, Wesleyan University Press, 1997)

Immerman, Richard H., 'In Search of History–and Relevancy: Breaking Through the Encrustations of "Interpretation"', *Diplomatic History*, 12:2 (1988), 341–56

Isaacson, Walter and Evan Thomas, *The Wise Men: Six Friends and the World They Made* (New York, Touchstone, 1988)

Izenberg, Gerald N., 'Text, Context, and Psychology in Intellectual History', in Kozicki (ed.), *Developments in Modern Historiography*, pp. 40–62

Jansen, Harry, *The Construction of an Urban Past: Narrative and System in Urban History*, trans. Feike de Jong (Oxford and New York, Berg, 2001)

Jenkins, Keith, 'Introduction: On Being Open About Our Closures', in Jenkins (ed.), *The Postmodern History Reader*, pp. 1–30

Jenkins, Keith, On *'What is History?' From Carr and Elton to Rorty and White* (London, Routledge, 1995)

Jenkins, Keith (ed.), *The Postmodern History Reader* (London, Routledge, 1997)

Jenkins, Keith, *Why History? Ethics and Postmodernity* (London, Routledge, 1999)

Jenkins, Roy, 'Foreword', in Mayne and Pinder, *Federal Union*, p. 8

Jensen, John, 'The End of the Line? The Future of British Cartooning', in *A Sense of Permanence?*, pp. 11–22

Jones, Harriet, 'The Post-War Consensus in Britain: Thesis, Antithesis, Synthesis?', in Brivati, Buxton and Seldon (eds), *The Contemporary History Handbook*, pp. 41–9

Jones, Roy E., *The Changing Structure of British Foreign Policy* (London, Longman, 1974)

Jordanova, Ludmilla, *History in Practice* (London, Arnold, 2000)

Jørgensen, Knud Erik, 'European Integration as a Field of Study in Denmark', *Journal of Common Market Studies*, 33:1 (1995), 157–62

Kaiser, Wolfram, 'To Join or not to Join? The "Appeasement" Policy of Britain's First EEC Application', in Brivati and Jones (eds), *From Reconstruction to Integration*, pp. 144–56

Kaiser, Wolfram, *Using Europe, Abusing the Europeans: Britain and European Integration 1945–63* (Basingstoke, Macmillan, 1996)

Kane, Liz, 'European or Atlantic Community? The Foreign Office and "Europe", 1955–1957', *Journal of European Integration History*, 3:2 (1997), 7–33

Kane, Elisabeth, 'The Myth of Sabotage: British Policy Towards European Integration, 1955–6', in du Réau (ed.), *Europe des Élites?*, pp. 291–301

Kaplan, Lawrence S., 'Dean Acheson and the Atlantic Community', in Brinkley (ed.), *Dean Acheson*, pp. 1–27

Kaplan, Lawrence S., 'An Unequal Triad: The United States, Western Union, and NATO', in Riste (ed.), *Western Security*, pp. 107–27

Kaplan, Morton A., *On Historical and Political Knowing* (London, The University of Chicago Press, 1971)

Kavanagh, Dennis, 'Why Political Science Needs History', *Political Studies*, 39 (1991), 479–95

Kavanagh, Dennis and Peter Morris, *Consensus Politics From Attlee to Major*, 2nd edn (Oxford, Blackwell, 1994)

Keegan, John, *The Battle for History: Re-fighting World War Two* (London, Pimlico, 1997)

Kennedy, Paul, *The Realities Behind Diplomacy: Background Influences on British External Policy 1865–1980* (London, Fontana, 1985)

Kent, John, 'Bevin's Imperialism and the Idea of Euro-Africa, 1945–49', in Dockrill and Young (eds), *British Foreign Policy*, pp. 47–76

Kent, John, 'The "Western Union" Concept and British Defence Policy, 1947–8', in Aldrich (ed.), *British Intelligence*, pp. 166–92

Kent, John and John W. Young, 'British Policy Overseas, The "Third Force" and the Origins of NATO – In Search of a New Perspective', in Heuser and O'Neill (eds), *Securing Peace in Europe*, pp. 41–61

Killick, John, *The United States and European Reconstruction 1945–1960* (Edinburgh, Keele University Press, 1997)

Kitzinger, Uwe, *Diplomacy and Persuasion: How Britain Joined the Common Market* (London, Thames and Hudson, 1973)

Knight, Wayne, 'Labourite Britain: America's "Sure Friend"? The Anglo-Soviet Treaty Issue, 1947', *Diplomatic History*, 7:4 (1983), 267–82

Koslowski, Rey, 'Understanding the European Union as a Federal Polity', in Christiansen, Jørgensen and Wiener (eds), *The Social Construction of Europe*, pp. 32–49

Kozicki, Henry (ed.), *Developments in Modern Historiography* (Basingstoke, Palgrave, 1998)

Kuhn, Thomas S., *The Structure of Scientific Revolutions* (London, The University of Chicago Press, 1970)

Kuhn, Thomas S., 'The Road since *Structure*', in Tauber (ed.), *Science and the Quest for Reality*, pp. 231–45

Kuklick, Bruce, *American Policy and the Division of Germany: The Clash with Russia over Reparations* (London, Cornell University Press, 1972)

LaFeber, Walter, *America, Russia, and the Cold War 1945–1992*, 7th dn (New York, McGraw–Hill, 1993)

Larres, Klaus (ed.), *Uneasy Allies: British–German Relations and European Integration since 1945* (Oxford, Oxford University Press, 2000)

Laurent, Pierre-Henri, 'Reappraising the Origins of European Integration', in Michelmann and Soldatos (eds), *European Integration*, pp. 99–112

Lee, Sabine, 'German Decision-Making Elites and European Integration: German "Europolitik" during the Years of the EEC and Free Trade Area Negotiations', in Deighton (ed.), *Building Post-War Europe*, pp. 39–54

Lee, Sabine, *Victory in Europe? Britain and Germany since 1945* (Harlow, Pearson Education, 2001)

Leonard, Dick, 'Eye on the EU', *Europe*, 357 (June 1996), 3

Leonard, Dick, *The Economist Guide to the European Union: The Original and Definitive Guide to all Aspects of the European Union* (London, Hamish Hamilton, 1994)

Lerner, Daniel and Raymond Aron (eds), *France Defeats EDC* (London, Thames and Hudson, 1957)

Levy, Jack S., 'Too Important to Leave to the Other: History and Political Science in the Study of International Relations', *International Security*, 22:1 (1997), 22–33

Little, Richard, 'The Study of British Foreign Policy', in Smith, Smith and White (eds), *British Foreign Policy*, pp. 245–59

Lord, Christopher, *British Entry to the European Community Under the Heath Government of 1970–4* (Aldershot, Gower, 1985)

Lord, Christopher, 'Sovereign or Confused? The "Great Debate" About British Entry to the European Community 20 Years On', *Journal of Common Market Studies*, 30:4 (1992), 419–36

Louis, W. Roger, 'Foreword', in Winks (ed.), *Historiography*, pp. 7–11

Louis, W. Roger and Hedley Bull (eds), *The Special Relationship: Anglo-American Relations since 1945* (Oxford, Clarendon Press, 1989)

Ludlam, Steve, 'The Cauldron, Conservative Parliamentarians and European Integration', in Baker and Seawright, *Britain For and Against Europe*, pp. 31– 56

Ludlow, N. Piers, 'A Short-Term Defeat: The Community Institutions and the Second British Application to Join the EEC', in Daddow (ed.), *Harold Wilson and European Integration*, pp. 133–50

Ludlow, N. Piers, *Dealing With Britain: The Six and the First UK Application to the EEC* (Cambridge, Cambridge University Press, 1997)

Lustick, Ian, 'History, Historiography, and Political Science: Multiple Historical Records and the Problem of Selection Bias', *American Political Science Review*, 90:3 (1996), pp. 605–18

Maclean, Donald, *British Foreign Policy since Suez, 1956–68* (London, Hodder and Stoughton, 1970)

Marcussen, Martin, Thomas Risse, Daniela Engelman-Martin, Hans Joachim Knopf and Klaus Roshcer, 'Constructing Europe? The Evolution of Nation-State Identities', in Christiansen, Jørgensen and Wiener (eds), *The Social Construction of Europe*, pp. 101–20

Marsh, David and Gerry Stoker (eds), *Theory and Methods in Political Science* (Basingstoke, Macmillan, 1995)

Marshall, P. J., 'The First British Empire', in Winks (ed.), *Historiography*, pp. 43–53

Marwick, Arthur, *The New Nature of History: Knowledge, Evidence, Language* (Basingstoke, Palgrave, 2001)

May, Alex (ed.), *Britain, the Commonwealth and Europe: The Commonwealth and Britain's Applications to Join the European Communities* (Basingstoke, Palgrave, 2001)

May, Ernest R. 'The News Media and Diplomacy', in Craig and Loewenheim (eds), *The Diplomats 1939–1979*, pp. 665–93

Mayne, Richard, *Postwar: The Dawn of Today's Europe* (London, Thames and Hudson, 1983)

Mayne, Richard, 'Schuman, De Gasperi, Spaak – The European Frontiersmen', in Bond, Smith and Wallace (eds), *Eminent Europeans*, pp. 22–44

Mayne, Richard, *The Community of Europe* (London, Victor Gollancz, 1962)

Mayne, Richard, *The Recovery of Europe: From Devastation to Unity* (London, Weidenfeld and Nicolson, 1970)

Mayne, Richard and John Pinder, *Federal Union: The Pioneers* (Basingstoke, Macmillan, 1990)

McBride, Ian, *History and Memory in Modern Ireland* (Cambridge, Cambridge University Press, 2001)

McKercher, Brian, 'Reaching for the Brass Ring: The Recent Historiography of Interwar American Foreign Relations', *Diplomatic History*, 15:4 (1991), 565–98

McGrew, Tony, 'Security and Order: The Military Dimension', in Smith, Smith and White (eds), *British Foreign Policy*, pp. 99–123

McLean, Ian, *The Oxford Concise Dictionary of Politics* (Oxford, Oxford University Press, 1996)

Mearsheimer, John J., 'Back to the Future: Instability in Europe after the Cold War', *International Security*, 15:1 (1990), 5–56

Meehan, Eugene J., *The British Left Wing and Foreign Policy: A Study of the Influence of Ideology* (New Brunswick, NJ, Rutgers University Press, 1960)

Melanson, Richard A., *Writing History and Making Policy: The Cold War, Vietnam and Revisionism, Volume 6* (London, Lanham, 1983)

Melissen, Jan and Bert Zeeman, 'Britain and Western Europe, 1945–51: Opportunities Lost?', *International Affairs*, 63:1 (1987), 81–95

Michelmann, Hans J. and Panos Soldatos (eds), *European Integration: Theories and Approaches* (Lanham, MD, University Press of America, 1994)

Milward, Alan S., *The European Rescue of the Nation-State* (London, Routledge, 1992)

Milward, Alan S., *The Reconstruction of Western Europe, 1945–51*, (London, Methuen, 1984)

Monas, Sidney 'Introduction: Contemporary Historiography', in Kozicki (ed.), *Developments in Modern Historiography*, pp. 1–16

Moon, Jeremy, *European Integration in British Politics 1950–1963: A Study of Issue Change* (Aldershot, Gower, 1985)

Morgan, Kenneth O., *Labour People: Leaders and Lieutenants: Hardie to Kinnock* (Oxford, Oxford University Press, 1989)

Morgan, Kenneth O., *The People's Peace: British History 1945–1990* (Oxford, Oxford University Press, 1990)

Morrow, Raymond A. and David D. Brown, *Critical Theory and Methodology* (London, Sage, 1994)

Munslow, Alun, *Deconstructing History* (London, Routledge, 1997)

Neustadt, Richard E. and Ernest R. May, *Thinking in Time: The Uses of History for Decision-Makers* (New York, The Free Press, 1986)

Newton, C. C. S., 'The Sterling Crisis of 1947 and the British Response to the Marshall Plan', *Economic History Review*, 37:3 (1984), 391–408

Newton, Scott, 'Britain, the Sterling Area and European Integration, 1945–50', *Journal of Imperial and Commonwealth History*, 13:3 (1985), 163–82

Newton, Scott, 'The 1949 Sterling Crisis and British Policy Towards European Integration', *Review of International Studies*, 11:1 (1985), 169–82

Nicholls, Anthony J., 'Britain and the EC: The Historical Background', in Bulmer, George and Scott (eds), *The UK and EC Membership Evaluated*, pp. 3–9

Northedge, F. S., *British Foreign Policy: The Process of Readjustment 1945–1961* (London, George Allen and Unwin, 1961)

Northedge, F. S., *Descent from Power: British Foreign Policy 1945–73* (London, George Allen and Unwin, 1974)

Nutting, Anthony, *Europe Will Not Wait: A Warning and a Way Out* (London, Hollis and Carter, 1960)

O'Brien, Patrick, 'Is Political Biography a Good Thing?', *Contemporary British History*, 10:4 (1996), 60–6

Onuf, Nicholas, *World of our Making* (Columbia, University of South Carolina Press, 1989)

Ovendale, Ritchie, 'Britain, the U.S.A. and the European Cold War, 1945–8' *History*, 67 (1982), 217–35

Ovendale, Ritchie, 'Introduction', in Ovendale (ed.), *The Foreign Policy of the British Labour Governments*, pp. 1–17

Ovendale, Ritchie, *The English-Speaking Alliance: Britain, the United States, the Dominions and the Cold War* (London, George Allen and Unwin, 1985)

Ovendale, Ritchie (ed.), *The Foreign Policy of the British Labour Governments, 1945–1951* (Leicester, Leicester University Press, 1984)

Pagedas, Constantine A., *Anglo-American Strategic Relations and the French Problem 1960–1963: A Troubled Partnership* (London, Frank Cass, 2000)

Painter, David S., *Private Power and Public Policy: Multinational Oil Corporations and US Foreign Policy 1941–1954* (London, I. B. Tauris, 1986)

Palme Dutt, R., *Problems of Contemporary History* (London, Lawrence and Wishart, 1963)

Paxman, Jeremy, *Friends in High Places: Who Runs Britain?* (London, Penguin, 1991)

Peden, George C., *British Rearmament and the Treasury: 1932–1939* (Edinburgh, Scottish Academic Press, 1979)

Peden, George C., *British Economic and Social Policy: Lloyd George to Margaret Thatcher*, 2nd edn (London, Phillip Allen, 1985)

Perkins, Bradford, 'Unequal Partners: The Truman Administration and Great Britain', in Louis and Bull (eds), *The Special Relationship*, pp. 43–64

Pfaltzgraff Jr., Robert L., *Britain Faces Europe* (Pennsylvania, University of Pennsylvania Press, 1969)

Pilkington, Colin, *Britain in the European Union Today*, 2nd edn (Manchester, Manchester University Press, 2001)

Pimlott, Ben, *Frustrate Their Knavish Tricks: Writings on Biography, History and Politics* (London, HarperCollins, 1994)

Pinder, John (ed.), *Altiero Spinelli and the British Federalists: Writings by Beveridge, Robbins and Spinelli 1937–43* (London, Federal Trust, 1998)

Pinder, John, *Britain and the Common Market* (London, The Cresset Press, 1961),

Pinder, John, *Europe Against de Gaulle* (London, Pall Mall Press for Federal Trust, 1963)

Pinder, John, 'Introduction', in Pinder (ed.), *Altiero Spinelli*, pp. 1–18

Pinder, John, 'Prewar Ideas of Union – The British Prophets', in Bond, Smith and Wallace (eds), *Eminent Europeans*, pp. 1–21

Pinto-Duschinsky, Michael, 'From Macmillan to Home, 1959–64', in Hennessy and Seldon (eds), *Ruling Performance*, pp. 150–85

Popper, Karl R., *Objective Knowledge: An Evolutionary Approach* (Oxford, Oxford University Press, 1972)

Prins, Gwyn, 'Oral History', in Burke (ed.), *New Perspectives*, pp. 114–39

Pritt, D. N., *The Labour Government, 1945–1951* (London, Lawrence and Wishart, 1963)

Pryce, Roy, *The Dynamics of European Union* (London, Routledge, 1990)

Pryce, Roy, *The Political Future of the European Community* (London, John Marshbank, 1962)

Rabinow, Paul, *The Foucault Reader: An Introduction to Foucault's Thought* (London, Penguin, 1991)

Reiter, Dan, 'Learning, Realism and Alliances: The Weight of the Shadow of the Past', *World Politics*, 46:4 (1994), 490–526

Reynolds, David, *Britannia Overruled: British Policy and World Power in the Twentieth Century* (London, Longman, 1991)

Reynolds, David, 'The Origins of the Cold War: The European Dimension, 1944–1951', *Historical Journal*, 28:2 (1985), 497–515

Richards, Robert, 'Theories of Scientific Change', in Tauber (ed.), *Science and the Quest for Reality*, pp. 203–30

Riste, Olav (ed.), *Western Security: The Formative Years* (Oslo, Norwegian University Press, 1985)

Roberts, Frank, 'Ernest Bevin as Foreign Secretary', in Ovendale, (ed.), *The Foreign Policy of the British Labour Governments*, pp. 21–42

Rothwell, Victor, *Britain and the Cold War 1941–1947* (London, Jonathan Cape, 1982)

Ruane, Kevin, *The Rise and Fall of the European Defence Community: Anglo-American Relations and the Crisis of European Defence, 1950–55* (Basingstoke, Macmillan, 2000)

Sainsbury, K., 'Selwyn Lloyd', in Shlaim, Jones and Sainsbury (eds), *British Foreign Secretaries*, pp. 117–43

Sainsbury, K., 'Harold Macmillan', in Shlaim, Jones and Sainsbury (eds), *British Foreign Secretaries*, pp. 110–16

Sampson, Anthony, *Anatomy of Britain* (London, Hodder and Stoughton, 1962)

Sanders, David, *Losing an Empire, Finding a Role: British Foreign Policy since 1945* (Basingstoke, Macmillan, 1990)

Saville, John, *The Politics of Continuity: British Foreign Policy and the Labour Government 1945–46* (London, Verso, 1993)

Schneer, Jonathan, *Labour's Conscience: The Labour Left 1945–51* (London, Unwin Hyman, 1988)

Schaad, Martin, 'Plan G – A "Counterblast"? British Policy Towards the Messina Countries, 1956', *Contemporary European History*, 7:1 (1998), 39–60

Seldon, Anthony, *Churchill's Indian Summer: The Conservative Government, 1951–55* (London, Hodder and Stoughton, 1981)

Seldon, Anthony (ed.), *Contemporary History: Practice and Method* (Oxford, Basil Blackwell, 1988)

Seldon, Anthony, 'Interviews', in Seldon (ed.), *Contemporary History*, pp. 3–16

Seldon, Anthony, 'Preface' in Brivati, Buxton and Seldon (eds), *The Contemporary History Handbook*, pp. 11–14

Seldon, Anthony, 'The Churchill Administration, 1951–55', in Hennessy and Seldon (eds), *Ruling Performance*, pp. 63–97

Seymour-Ure, Colin, 'The Centre for the Study of Cartoons and Caricature and the University of Kent', in A *Sense of Permanence?*, pp. 9–10

Seymour-Ure, Colin 'What Future for the British Political Cartoon?', *Journalism Studies*, 2:3 (2001), 333–55

Shlaim, Avi, *Britain and the Origins of European Unity 1940–1951* (Reading, The Graduate School of Contemporary European Studies, 1978)

Shlaim, Avi, 'The Foreign Secretary and the Making of Foreign Policy', in Shlaim, Jones and Sainsbury (eds), *British Foreign Secretaries since 1945*, pp. 13–26

Shlaim, Avi, Peter Jones and Keith Sainsbury (eds), *British Foreign Secretaries since 1945* (London, David & Charles, 1977)

Sked, Alan and Chris Cook, *Post-War Britain: A Political History*, 4th edn (London, Penguin, 1993)

Smith, Geoffrey, '"Harry, We Hardly Know You": Revisionism, Politics and Diplomacy, 1945–54', *American Political Science Review*, 70 (1976), 560–82

Smith, Michael, Steve Smith and Brian White (eds), *British Foreign Policy: Tradition, Change and Transformation* (London, Hyman, 1988)

Smith, Steve, 'New Approaches to International Theory', in Baylis and Smith (eds), *The Globalisation of World Politics*, pp. 165–90

Smith, Steve and Michael Smith, 'The Analytical Background: Approaches to the Study of Foreign Policy', in Smith, Smith and White (eds), *British Foreign Policy*, pp. 3–23

Southgate, Beverley, *History: What and Why? Ancient, Modern, and Postmodern Perspectives* (London, Routledge, 1996)

Steele, N. "Method is More than the Sum of its Parts', *The Times Higher Education Supplement*, 17 March 2000, p. 38

Steiner, Zara, 'The Historian and the Foreign Office', in Hill and Beshoff (eds), *Two Worlds of International Relations*, pp. 45–9

Steinnes, Kristian, 'The European Challenge: Britain's EEC Application in 1961', *Contemporary European History*, 7:1 (1998), 61–79

Stevens, Anne, *The Government and Politics of France* (Basingstoke, Macmillan, 1992)

Stoker, Gerry, 'Introduction', in Marsh and Stoker (eds), *Theory and Methods*, pp. 1–18

Tauber, Alfred I. (ed.), *Science and the Quest for Reality* (Basingstoke, Macmillan, 1997)

Theakston, Kevin (ed.), *British Foreign Secretaries since 1974* (London, Frank Cass, forthcoming)

Theakston, Kevin, 'The Changing Role of the Foreign Secretary', in Theakston (ed.), *British Foreign Secretaries*

Thompson, Willie, *What Happened to History?* (London, Pluto, 2000)

Thucydides, *History of the Peloponnesian War*, 2nd edn (London, Guild, 1993)

Tivey, Leonard, *Interpretations of British Politics: The Image and the System* (Hemel Hempstead, Harvester-Wheatsheaf, 1988)

Tolstoy, Leo, *War and Peace* (Ware, Wordsworth Editions, 1993)

Toomey, Jane, 'Ireland and Britain's Second Application to Join the EEC', in Daddow (ed.), *Harold Wilson and European Integration*, pp. 227–42

Tooze, Roger, 'Security and Order: The Economic Dimension', in Smith, Smith and White (eds), *British Foreign Policy*, pp. 124–45

Tosh, John, *The Pursuit of History*, 3rd edn (London, Longman, 2000)

Tratt, Jacqueline, *The Macmillan Government and Europe: A Study in the Process of Policy Development* (Basingstoke, Macmillan, 1996)

Trevelyan, G. M., *An Autobiography and Other Essays* (London, Longman, Green and Co., 1949)

Twenty Years of Cartoons by Garland (Edinburgh, The Salamander Press, 1984)

Ullman, Richard H., 'America, Britain, and the Soviet Threat in Historical and Present Perspective', in Louis and Bull (eds), The Special Relationship, pp. 103–14

Uri, Pierre (ed.), *From Commonwealth to Common Market* (Harmondsworth, Penguin, 1968)

Vicky's Supermac: Harold Macmillan in Cartoons by Victor Weisz of the Evening Standard (London, Park McDonald, 1996)

Vital, David, *The Making of British Foreign Policy* (London, George Allen and Unwin, 1971)

Waites, Neville (ed.), *Troubled Neighbours: Franco-British Relations in the Twentieth Century* (London, Weidenfeld and Nicolson, 1971)

Walker, J. Samuel, 'Historians and Cold War Origins: The New Consensus', in Haines and Walker (eds), *American Foreign Relations*, pp. 207–36

Wallace, William, *The Foreign Policy Process in Britain*, 2nd edn (London, Royal Institute of International Affairs, 1977)

Warner, Geoffrey, 'Ernest Bevin and British Foreign Policy, 1945–1951', in Craig and Loewenheim (eds), *The Diplomats*, pp. 103–34

Warner, Geoffrey, 'The British Labour Government and the Atlantic Alliance, 1949–1951', in Riste (ed.), *Western Security*, pp. 247–65

Warner, Geoffrey, 'The Labour Governments and the Unity of Western Europe, 1945–51', in Ovendale (ed.), *The Foreign Policy of the British Labour Governments*, pp. 61–82

Warner, Geoffrey, 'The Reconstruction and Defence of Western Europe after 1945', in Waites (ed.), *Troubled Neighbours*, pp. 259–92

Watt, Donald C., 'Demythologising the Eisenhower Era', in Louis and Bull (eds), *The Special Relationship*, pp. 65–85

Watt, David, 'Introduction: Anglo-American Relations', in Louis and Bull (eds), *The Special Relationship*, pp. 1–14

Watt, Donald Cameron, *Succeeding John Bull: America in Britain's Place 1900–1975* (Cambridge, Cambridge University Press, 1984)

Wendt, Alexander, 'Anarchy is What States Make of It: The Social Construction of Power Politics', *International Organization*, 46:2 (1992), 391–425

White, Hayden, *The Content of the Form: Narrative Discourse and Historical Representation* (London, The Johns Hopkins University Press, 1992)

White, Hayden, *Metahistory: The Historical Imagination in Nineteenth-Century Europe* (London, The Johns Hopkins University Press, 1975)

Wight, Colin, 'Meta Campbell: The Epistemological Problematics of Perspectivism', *Review of International Studies*, 25:2 (1999), 311–16

Wilford, Hugh, 'The Information Research Department: Britain's Secret Cold War Weapon Revealed', *Review of International Studies*, 24:3 (1998), 353–69

Wilford, Hugh, '"Unwitting Assets?" British Intellectuals and the Congress for Cultural Freedom', *Twentieth Century British History*, 11:1 (2000), 42–60

Wilkes, George (ed.), *Britain's Failure to Enter the European Community 1961–63: The Enlargement Negotiations and Crises in European, Atlantic and Commonwealth Relations* (London, Frank Cass, 1997)

Wilkes, George, 'The First Failure to Steer Britain into the European Communities: An Introduction', in Wilkes (ed.), *Britain's Failure*, pp. 1–32

Williams of Crosby, Baroness, 'Foreword', in Daddow (ed.), *Harold Wilson and European Integration*, pp. 10–13

Winand, Pascaline, *Eisenhower, Kennedy, and the United States of Europe* (Basingstoke, Macmillan, 1993)

Winks, Robin W. (ed.), *The Oxford History of the British Empire, Volume 5: Historiography* (Oxford, Oxford University Press, 2001)

Winks, R. W., 'Preface', in Winks (ed.), *Historiography*, pp. 13–15

Woods, Ngaire, (ed.), *Explaining International Relations since 1945* (Oxford, Oxford University Press, 1997)

Young, Hugo, *This Blessed Plot: Britain and Europe from Churchill to Blair* (Basingstoke, Macmillan, 1998)

Young, John W., *Britain and European Unity 1945–1992* (Basingstoke, MacMillan, 1992)

Young, John W., *Britain and European Unity 1945–1999*, 2nd edn (Basingstoke, Macmillan, 2000)

Young, John W., 'Britain and "Europe": The Shape of the Historiographical Debate', in Brivati, Buxton, and Seldon (eds), *The Contemporary History Handbook*, pp. 207–14

Young, John W., *Britain, France and the Unity of Europe 1945–1951* (Leicester, Leicester University Press, 1984)

Young, John W. (ed.), *The Foreign Policy of Churchill's Peacetime Administration 1951–1955* (Leicester, Leicester University Press, 1988)

Young, John W., 'The Schuman Plan and British Association', in Young (ed.), *The Foreign Policy of Churchill's Peacetime Administration*, pp. 109–34

Young, John W., '"The Parting of Ways"? Britain, the Messina Conference and the Spaak Committee, June–December 1955', in Dockrill and Young (eds), *British Foreign Policy*, 1945–56, pp. 197–224

Diaries, memoirs, autobiographies and biographies

Acheson, Dean, *Present at the Creation: My Years in the State Department* (London, Hamish Hamilton, 1969)

Aster, Sidney, *Anthony Eden* (London, Weidenfeld and Nicolson, 1976)

Attlee, Clement, *As It Happened* (London, William Heinemann, 1954)

Ball, George W., *The Discipline of Power: Essentials of a Modern World Structure* (London, The Bodley Head, 1968)

Ball, George W., *The Past Has Another Pattern: Memoirs* (London, W. W. Norton and Co., 1982)

Benn, Tony, *Out of the Wilderness: Diaries, 1963–7* (London, Hutchinson, 1987)

Benn, Tony, *Office Without Power: Diaries, 1968–72* (London, Hutchinson, 1988)

Bird, Alexander, *Thomas Kuhn* (Chesham, Acumen, 2000)

Boothby, Lord , *My Yesterday, Your Tomorrow* (London, Hutchinson, 1962)

Boothby, Lord, *Recollections of a Rebel* (London, Hutchinson, 1978)

Brinkley, Douglas, *Dean Acheson: The Cold War Years, 1953–71* (London, Yale University Press, 1992)

Brinkley, Douglas and Clifford Hackett (eds), *Jean Monnet: The Path to European Unity* (Basingstoke, Macmillan, 1991)

Brittan, Leon, *A Diet of Brussels: The Changing Face of Europe* (London, Little, Brown and Company, 2000)

Brivati, Brian, *Hugh Gaitskell* (London, Richard Cohen, 1997)

Brown, George, *In My Way: The Political Memoirs of Lord George-Brown* (London, Victor Gollancz, 1971)

Browne, Anthony Montague, *Long Sunset: Memoirs of Winston Churchill's Last Private Secretary* (London, Indigo, 1996)

Bryant, Christopher, *Stafford Cripps: The First Modern Chancellor* (London, Hodder and Stoughton, 1997)

Bullock, Alan, *Ernest Bevin: Foreign Secretary* (London, Heinemann, 1983)

Cairncross, Alec (ed.), *The Robert Hall Diaries 1947–53* (London, Unwin Hyman, 1989)

Callaghan, James, *Time and Chance*, (London, Collins, 1987)

Campbell, John, *Edward Heath: A Biography* (London, Pimlico, 1994)

Carlton, David, *Anthony Eden: A Biography* (London, Allen Lane, 1981)

Castle, Barbara, *The Castle Diaries, 1964–70* (London, Weidenfeld and Nicolson, 1984)

Crossman, Richard, *The Diaries of a Cabinet Minister: Vol. 1, Minister of Housing, 1964–66* (London, Hamish Hamilton and Jonathan Cape, 1977)

Crossman, Richard, *The Diaries of a Cabinet Minister: Vol. 2, Lord President of the Council and Leader of the House of Commons, 1966–68* (London, Hamish Hamilton and Jonathan Cape, 1976)

de Gaulle, Charles, *Memoirs of Hope: Renewal 1958–62*, trans. Terence Kilmartin (London, Weidenfeld and Nicolson, 1971)

Donoghue, Bernard and G. W. Jones, *Herbert Morrison: Portrait of a Politician* (London, Weidenfeld and Nicolson, 1973)

Drummond, Roscoe and Gaston Coblentz, *Duel at the Brink: John Foster Dulles' Command of American Power* (London, Weidenfeld and Nicolson, 1961)

Duchêne, François, *Jean Monnet: The First Statesman of Interdependence*, trans. Richard Mayne (London, W. W. Norton and Co., 1994)

Dutton, David, *Anthony Eden: A Life and Reputation* (London, Edward Arnold, 1997)

Eden, Anthony, *Full Circle: The Memoirs of Sir Anthony Eden* (London, Cassell, 1960)

Fisher, Nigel, *Harold Macmillan* (London, Weidenfeld and Nicolson, 1972)

Foot, Michael, *Aneurin Bevan: A Biography, Volume 2, 1945–1960* (London, Davis-Poynter, 1973)

Foot, Paul, *The Politics of Harold Wilson* (Harmondsworth, Penguin, 1968)

Gladwyn, Lord, *The Memoirs of Lord Gladwyn* (London, Weidenfeld and Nicolson, 1972)

Goold-Adams, Richard, *The Time of Power: A Reappraisal of John Foster Dulles* (London, Weidenfeld and Nicolson, 1962)

Guhin, Michael A., *John Foster Dulles: A Statesman and His Times* (New York, Columbia University Press, 1972)

Harris, Kenneth, *Attlee*, 2nd edn (London, Weidenfeld and Nicolson, 1995)

Healey, Denis, *The Time of My Life* (London, W. W. Norton, 1990)

Heath, Edward, *The Course of My Life: My Autobiography* (London, Hodder and Stoughton, 1998)

Heseltine, Michael, *Where There's a Will* (London, Hutchinson, 1987)

Home, Lord, *The Way the Wind Blows: An Autobiography* (London, Collins, 1976)

Hoopes, Townsend, *The Devil and John Foster Dulles* (London, Andre Deutsch, 1974)

Horne, Alistair, *Macmillan, 1894–1956: Volume 1 of the Official Biography* (London, Macmillan, 1988)

Horne, Alistair, *Macmillan 1957–1986: Volume 2 of the Official Biography* (London, Papermac, 1991)

Hutchinson, George, *Edward Heath: A Personal and Political Biography* (London, Longman, 1970)

Immerman, Richard H., *John Foster Dulles: Piety, Pragmatism, and Power in U.S Foreign Policy* (Wilmington, Scholarly Resources Inc., 1999)

James, Robert Rhodes, *Anthony Eden* (London, Weidenfeld and Nicolson, 1986)

James, Robert Rhodes (ed.), *Chips: The Diaries of Sir Henry Channon* (London, Penguin, 1970)

Jay, Douglas, *Change and Fortune: A Political Record* (London, Hutchinson, 1980)

Jenkins, Roy, *A Life at the Centre* (New York, Random House, 1991)

Jenkins, Roy, 'Leader of the Opposition', in Rodgers (ed.), *Hugh Gaitskell*, pp. 115–31

Jenkins, Roy, *Mr Attlee: An Interim Biography* (London, William Heinemann, 1948)

Jenkins, Roy, *Churchill* (London, Macmillan, 2001)

Kay, Earnest, *Pragmatic Premier: An Intimate Portrait of Harold Wilson* (London, Leslie Frewin, 1967)

Kilmuir, Earl of, *Political Adventure: The Memoirs of the Earl of Kilmuir* (London, Weidenfeld and Nicolson, 1964)

Kirkpatrick, Ivone, *The Inner Circle: Memoirs of Ivone Kirkpatrick* (London, Macmillan, 1959)

Krug, Mark M., *Aneurin Bevan: Cautious Rebel* (London, Thomas Yoseloff, 1961)

Laing, Margaret, *Edward Heath: Prime Minister* (London, Sidgwick and Jackson, 1972)

Lamb, Richard, *The Failure of the Eden Government* (London, Sidgwick and Jackson, 1987)

Lamb, Richard, *The Macmillan Years 1957–1963: The Emerging Truth* (London, John Murray, 1995)

Lankford, Nelson D. (ed.), *OSS Against the Reich: The World War Two Diaries of Colonel David K. E. Bruce* (London, The Kent State University Press, 1991)

Lankford, Nelson D., *The Last American Aristocrat: The Biography of David K. E. Bruce, 1898–1977* (London, Little, Brown and Company, 1996)

Lewis, Russell, *Tony Benn: A Critical Biography* London, Associated Business Press, 1978)

Macmillan, Harold, *Tides of Fortune, 1945–1955* (London, Macmillan, 1969)

Macmillan, Harold, *Riding the Storm, 1956–1959* (London, Macmillan, 1971)

Macmillan, Harold, *Pointing the Way, 1959–61* (London, Macmillan, 1972)

Macmillan, Harold, *At the End of the Day, 1961–1963* (London, Macmillan, 1973)

Marjolin, Robert, *Architect of European Unity* (London, Weidenfeld and Nicolson, 1989)

Maudling, Reginald, *Memoirs* (London, Sidgwick and Jackson, 1978)

McDermott, Geoffrey, *Leader Lost: A Biography of Hugh Gaitskell* (London, Leslie Frewin, 1972)

Monnet, Jean, *Memoirs*, trans. Richard Mayne (London, Collins, 1978)

Montgomery of Alamein, *Memoirs* (London, Collins, 1958)

Moran, Lord, *Winston Churchill: The Struggle for Survival* (London, Constable, 1966)

Morgan, Austen, *Harold Wilson* (London, Pluto, 1992)

Morgan, Kenneth O., *Callaghan: A Life* (Oxford, Oxford University Press, 1997)

Mosley, Leonard, *Dulles: A Biography of Eleanor, Allen, and John Foster Dulles and Their Family Network* (London, Hodder and Stoughton, 1978)

Owen, David, *Time to Declare* (London, Michael Joseph, 1991)

Pimlott, Ben (ed.), *The Political Diary of Hugh Dalton, 1918–40, 1945–60* (London, Jonathan Cape, 1987)

Rees-Mogg, William, *Sir Anthony Eden* (London, Rockliff, 1956)

Rodgers, W. T. (ed.), *Hugh Gaitskell 1906–1963* (London, Thames and Hudson, 1964)

Rothwell, Victor, *Anthony Eden: A Political Biography, 1931–1957* (Manchester, Manchester University Press, 1992)

Sampson, Anthony, *Macmillan: A Study in Ambiguity* (London, Allen Lane and Penguin, 1967)

Schuman, Robert, *Pour l'Europe*, 2nd edn (Paris, Les Éditions Nagel, 1964)

Smith, Dudley, *Harold Wilson: A Critical Biography* (London, Robert Hale, 1964)

Spaak, Paul-Henri, *The Continuing Battle: Memoirs of a European 1936–1966*, trans. Henry Fox (London, Weidenfeld and Nicolson, 1971)

Stephens, Mark, *Ernest Bevin: Unskilled Labourer and World Statesman 1881–1951* (Stevenage, SPA Books, 1985)

Stewart, Michael, *Life and Labour: An Autobiography* (London, Sidgwick and Jackson, 1980)

Stuart, Mark, *Douglas Hurd, The Public Servant: An Authorised Biography* (Edinburgh, Mainstream, 1998)

Thatcher, Margaret, *The Downing Street Years 1979–1990* (London, HarperCollins, 1996)

Thorpe, D. R., *Alec Douglas-Home* (London, Sinclair-Stevenson, 1996)

Turner, John, *Macmillan* (London, Longman, 1994)

Weiler, Peter, *Ernest Bevin* (Manchester, Manchester University Press, 1993)

Who's Who 2000 (London, A and C Black, 2000)

Williams, Francis, *Ernest Bevin: Portrait of a Great Englishman* (London, Hutchinson, 1952)

Williams, Philip M., *Hugh Gaitskell: A Political Biography* (London, Jonathan Cape, 1969)

Wilson, Harold, *The Labour Government, 1964–70: A Personal Record* (London, Weidenfeld and Nicolson and Michael Joseph, 1971)

Wilson, Harold, *Memoirs: The Making of a Prime Minister 1916–64* (London, Weidenfeld and Nicolson and Michael Joseph, 1986)

Young, Kenneth, *Sir Alec Douglas-Home* (London, J. M. Dent and Sons, 1970)

Ziegler, Philip, *Wilson: The Authorised Life of Lord Wilson of Rievaulx* (London, Weidenfeld and Nicolson, 1993)

Official histories and other official publications

Ambitions for Britain: Labour's Manifesto 2001

'A Note for Friends About the Federal Trust' (London: The Federal Trust, October 1999)

Bullen, Roger and M. E. Pelly (eds), *Documents on British Policy Overseas*, 1,2, 1945 (London, HMSO, 1985)

Bullen, Roger and M. E. Pelly (eds), *Documents on British Policy Overseas*, 1,3, 1945 (London, HMSO, 1986)

Bullen, Roger and M. E. Pelly (eds), *Documents on British Policy Overseas*, 1,4, 1945 (London, HMSO, 1987)

Butler, Rohan and M. E. Pelly (eds), *Documents on British Policy Overseas*, 1,1, 1945 (London, HMSO, 1984)

Pelly, M. E. and Heather J. Yasamee (eds), *Documents on British Policy Overseas*, 1,5, 1945 (London, HMSO, 1990)

Pelly, M. E. and Heather J. Yasamee (eds), *Documents on British Policy Overseas*, 1,6, 1945–1946 (London, HMSO, 1991)

Yasamee, Heather J. and Keith A. Hamilton, *Documents on British Policy Overseas*, 1,7, 1946–1947 (London, HMSO, 1995)

Unpublished Papers, theses and dissertations

Condon, Christopher, 'A Semiotic Approach to the Use of Metaphor in Human–Computer Interfaces' (Brunel University Ph.D., 2000)

Daddow, Oliver J., 'Rhetoric and Reality: The Historiography of British European Policy, 1945–73' (University of Nottingham Ph.D., 2000)

Deavin, Mark, 'Harold Macmillan and the Origins of the 1961 British Application to Join the EEC' (London School of Economics Ph.D., 1996).

de Brabant, Charles P. A., 'Anglo-French Colonial Co-operation Principally in West African Affairs, 1943–1954' (Oxford University M Litt, 1989)

Finney, Patrick, 'What Historians Actually Do: Politics, Historiography and Writing the Road to War in 1939/41', European Social Science History Conference, The Hague, 2 March 2002

Francis, Martin, 'Labour Policies and Socialist Ideals: The Example of the Attlee Government, 1945–51' (Oxford University Ph.D., 1992)

McInnes, Colin, 'So Who Needs Doctrine Anyway?', paper presented to the British International Studies Association Annual Conference, December 2001, draft 4, version 2

Schulte, Markus, 'Industry Politics and Trade Discrimination in West Germany's European Policy 1957–1963' (London School of Economics Ph.D., 1996)

Newspapers

Daily Mail
Daily Telegraph
Guardian
Observer
Sunday Telegraph
Economist

The Times
The Times Higher Education Supplement
The Times Literary Supplement

Book reviews

Anand, P., review, 'A Manual of Model Behaviour: Models as Mediators: Perspectives on Natural and Social Science. Edited by Mary S. Morgan and Margaret Morrison', *The Times Higher Education Supplement*, 17 March 2000, p. 26

Ashford, N., review, 'Eisenhower, Kennedy and the United States of Europe. By Pascaline Winand', *Journal of Common Market Studies*, 33:2 (1995), 309–10

Bosco, A., review, 'European Unity and World Order: Federal Trust 1945–1995. By John Pinder', *Journal of Common Market Studies*, 35:2 (1997), 325

Brewin, C., review, 'Maastricht and Beyond: Building the European Union. By Andrew Duff, John Pinder and Roy Price', *Journal of Common Market Studies*, 34:1 (1996), 134

Bullen, Roger, review, 'Britain, France and the Unity of Europe 1945–1951. By John W. Young; The Foreign Policy of the British Labour Government 1945–1951. Edited by Ritchie Ovendale', *Journal of Common Market Studies*, 24:1 (1985), 77–8

Cesarani, D., review, 'When Hens and Hitler Do Not Mix', *The Times Higher Education Supplement: Textbook Guide*, 25 February 2000, p. 6

Crowson, N. J., review, 'Backbench Debate within the Conservative Party and its Influence on British Foreign Policy, 1947–58. By Sue Onslow', *Contemporary British History*, 11:4 (1997), 133–4

Deighton, Anne, review, 'Europe in Our Time: A History, 1945–1992. By Walter Laqueur', *International Affairs*, 69:1 (1993), 149

Edgerton, D., review, 'Declinism, Lost Victory, British Dreams, British Realities, 1945–50. By Corelli Barnett', *London Review of Books*, 18:5 (1996), 14–15

Forsyth, M., review, 'The Recovery of Europe: From devastation to Unity. By Richard Mayne', *International Affairs*, 48:1 (1972), 100–1

Gehler, M., review, 'Interdependence Versus Integration, Denmark, Scandinavia, and Western Europe, 1945–1960. By Thorsten B. Olesen', *Journal of European Integration History*, 3:2 (1997), pp. 100–2

George, S., review, 'Britain and European Co-operation Since 1945. By Sean Greenwood', *Journal of Common Market Studies*, 31:1 (1993), 128

George, S., review, 'Britain and European Unity, 1945–1992. By John W. Young', *Journal of Common Market Studies*, 33:2 (1995), 306–7

Ghosh, Peter, review, 'How We Got Where We Are: Hope and Glory, Britain 1900–1990. By Peter Clarke', *London Review of Books*, 18:23 (November 1996), 18–19

Greenwood, Sean, review, "Britain For and Against Europe: British Politics and European Integration. Edited by D. Baker and D. Seawright', *Journal of Common Market Studies*, 36:4 (1998), 603–4

Gunn, S., review, 'Short on Pope-Burning', *The Times Higher Education Supplement: Textbook Guide*, 25 February 2000, p. 6

Harrison, B., review, 'R. Coopey, S. Fielding and N. Tiratsoo (eds), 'The Wilson Governments 1964–1970', *Contemporary Record*, 7:2 (1993), 490–1

Hollowell, J., review, 'Callaghan: A Life. By Kenneth O. Morgan', *Contemporary British History*, 11:4 (1997), 129–33

Hopkins, M., review, 'Britain and European Unity 1945–1992. By John Young', *International Affairs*, 70:4 (1994), 811

Jefferys, K., review, 'Harold Wilson. By Austen Morgan; Harold Wilson. By Ben Pimlott', *Contemporary Record*, 7:1 (1993), 198–200

Jefferys, K., review, 'The Myth of Consensus: New Views on British History 1945–64. Edited by Harriet Jones and Michael David Kandiah', *Contemporary British History*, 11:1 (1997), 157–8

Jones, Harriet, review, 'Bob Boothby: A Portrait. By Robert Rhodes James', *Contemporary Record*, 6:2 (1992), 403–4

Kane, E., review, 'Using Europe, Abusing the Europeans: Britain and European Integration, 1945–63. By Wolfram Kaiser', *Contemporary British History*, 11:4 (1997), 134–64

Keitch, R., review, 'Britain and Europe since 1945. By A. May', *Journal of Common Market Studies*, 38:1 (2000), 183

Kent, John, review, 'The End of Superpower: British Foreign Office Conception its of a Changing World. By Stuart Croft', *Contemporary Record*, 9:2 (1995), 477–9

Lee, S., review, 'Bullying Bonn: Anglo-German Diplomacy on European Integration, 1955–1961. By Martin P. C. Schaad', *Cold War History*, 3:1 (2002), 168–9

Leslie, S. C., review, 'Britain and the European Community 1955–1963. By Miriam Camps', *International Affairs*, 41:1 (1965), 121–2

Lowe, R., review, 'The Macmillan Years, 1957–1963: The Emerging Truth. By Richard Lamb', *Contemporary British History*, 10:2 (1996), 239–41

Lucas, W. S., review, 'Britain and the World in the Twentieth Century. By John W. Young', *Contemporary British History*, 11:3 (1997), 125–6

Mayne, Richard, review, 'The Price of Victory. By Michael Charlton', *International Affairs*, 60:2 (1984), 326–7

Middlemas, R. K., review, 'Tides of Fortune, 1945–1955. By Harold Macmillan', *International Affairs*, 46:3 (1970), 568–9

Milward, Alan S., review, 'Robert Schuman: Homme d'État. By Raymond Poitevin', *Journal of Common Market Studies*, 26:2 (1987), 344–5

Morgan, Kenneth O., review, 'Ernest Bevin. By Alan Bullock; The Diary of Hugh Gaitskell 1945–1960. Edited by Philip Williams; Breach of Promise. By John Vaizey', *The Times Literary Supplement*, 11 (November 1983), pp. 1243–4

Ovendale, Ritchie, review, 'British Foreign Policy 1945–1973. By Joseph Frankel', *International Affairs*, 51:4 (1975), 574–5

Paterson, W. E., review, 'Eminent Europeans: Personalities Who Shaped Contemporary Europe. Edited by Michael Bond, Julie Smith and William Wallace', *Journal of Common Market Studies*, 35:3 (1997), 488–9

Phipps, C., review, 'The Nature of the Book: Print and Knowledge in the Making. By Adrian Johns', *The Times Higher Educational Supplement*, 3 March 2000, p. 32

Ramsden, J., review, 'N. Lankford, Aristocrat: The Biography of Ambassador David K. E. Bruce', *Contemporary British History*, 11:2 (1997), 166–8

Rees, Nicholas, review, 'Britain and European Co-operation Since 1945. By Sean Greenwood', *International Affairs*, 69:4 (1993), 792–3

Reynolds, D., review, 'J. W. Young (ed.), The Foreign Policy of Churchill's Peacetime Administration, 1951–55', *International Affairs*, 65:1 (1989), 144

Seymour-Ure, Colin, review, 'Cabinet Decisions on Foreign Policy: The British Experience October 1938–June 1941. By Christopher Hill', *International Affairs*, 51:4 (1975), 574–5

Steyn, M., review 'Is Hillary Hurting? Hillary's Choice. By Gail Sheehy', *Sunday Telegraph*, 19 December 1999, p. 18

Urwin, D., review, 'The European Rescue of the Nation-State. By Alan S. Milward', *Journal of Common Market Studies*, 32:1 (1994), 112–13

Urwin, D., review, 'The Origins and Development of the European Union 1945–95: A History of European Integration. By M. J. Dedman', *Journal of Common Market Studies*, 35:1 (1997), 170

Wagner, J., review, 'The Diplomacy of Pragmatism: Britain and the Formation of NATO, 1942–49. By John Baylis', *International Affairs*, 69:4 (1993), 781–2

Wallace, William, review, "Inside the Foreign Office. By John Dickie; The European Rescue of the Nation-State. By Alan S. Milward', *The Times Literary Supplement*, 30 April 1993, p. 25

Internet sources

http://europa.eu.int/eur-lex/en/treaties/dat/ec_cons_treaty_en.pdf (accessed 31 January 2002)

http://foreign-policy.dsd.kcl.ac.uk/daddow.htm (accessed 4 June 2001)

http://library.ukc. ac.uk/cartoons/cartoonhub.html (accessed 10 May 2002)

http://library.ukc.ac.uk/cartoons/main.html

http://politics.guardian.co.uk/eu /story/0,9061,669387,00.html (accessed 1 May 2002)

http://politics.guardian.co.uk/politicsobituaries/story/0,1441,563453,00.html (accessed 13 February 2002)

www.cix.co.uk/~fedtrust/aboutus_home.htm (accessed 5 February 2002)

www.conservatives.com/conference/2002news.cfm?obj_id=41258&class_id=Speeches (accessed 11 October 2002)

www.democracy-movement.org.uk (accessed 2 May 2002)

www.eiu.com (accessed 12 February 2002)

www.euromove.org.uk/00_navigation%20frame.html (accessed 5 February 202)

www.europa.eu.int/scadplus/leg/en/lvb/e4001.htm (accessed 13 April 2002)

www.europa-web.de/europa/011vkvjf/113ebw/monnet.htm (accessed 31 January 2002)

www.europarl.eu.int/ppe/tree/schuman/en/biography.htm (accessed 4 February 2002)

www.eurplace.org/federal/monnet.html#greatness (accessed 14 November 2001)

www.fco.gov.uk/new/newstext.asp?6225

www.federalunion.uklinux.net/about.htm (accessed 4 January 2002)

www.federalunion.uklinux.net/news/chairmansmessage.htm (accessed 8 February 2002)

www.fordfoundation.org/about/mission.cfm (accessed 11 January 2002)

www.guardian.co.uk/Archive/Article/0,4723,4268838,00.html (accessed 15 March 2002)

www.hesa.ac.uk/holisdocs/pubinfo/student/subject78.htm (accessed 20 April 2002)

www.labour.org.uk/gbconfspeech/ (accessed 1 October 2002)

www.labour.org.uk/tbconfspeech/ (accessed 2 October 2002)

www.mtholyoke.edu/offices/library/arch/col/ms0627r.htm (accessed 10 November 2000)
www.observer.co.uk/worldcup2002/story/0,11031,718176,00.html (accessed 24 May 2002)
www.phoenix-tv.net/ubirmingham/eriscript.htm (accessed 24 November 2001)
www.pro.gov.uk/ (accessed 28 March 2000)
www.pro.gov.uk/about/access/access.htm (accessed 10 January 2002)
www.redwines.btinternet.co.uk/chris/phd.html (accessed 15 December 2001)
www.standards.dfes.gov.uk/schemes2/ks4citizenship/cit11/ (accessed 25 April 2002)
www.sussex.ac.uk/Units/SEI/oern/index.html
www.telegraph.co.uk/news/main.jhtml?xml=/news/2002/05/13/neur13.xml (accessed 14 May 2002)
www.time.com/time/special/moy/1954.html (accessed 7 February 2002)
www.trumanlibrary.org/oralhist/acheson.htm (accessed 6 November 2001)
www.uaces.org
www.sbs.ox.ac.uk/html/news_article.asp?ID=80 (accessed 1 May 2002)

Interviews

Lord Beloff, 15 April 1998
Peter Hennessy, by telephone, 12 May 2002
Michael Kandiah, by telephone, 7 May 2002
John Kent, 16 April 2002
Anthony Seldon, by telephone, 23 April 2002
Geoffrey Warner, 30 April 2002
John Young, by telephone, 16 May 2002

Primary sources

Ford Foundation Archives
Minutes of the Annual General Meeting of UACES, 24 January 1969

Index